THE LONG SONATA OF THE DEAD

A STUDY OF SAMUEL BECKETT

by Michael Robinson

RUPERT HART-DAVIS LONDON 1969

First published 1969

Rupert Hart-Davis Limited
3 Upper James Street
Golden Square London W1

Printed in Great Britain by
C. Tinling & Co. Ltd
London and Prescot

SBN 246 97441 9

THE LONG SONATA OF THE DEAD

A Study of Samuel Beckett

For Jan

AUTHOR'S NOTE

Detailed references are given for quotations in the first two, general chapters of this work. Thereafter, for reasons of space their use is limited to only those quotations, either from Bechett's other books or from writers other than Beckett, which lie outside the particular work under discussion.

The author wishes to acknowledge that permission for extracts from *Malone Dies*, *Unnamable*, *Watt*, *Molloy*, *Proust*, and *Murphy* has been given by Calder & Boyars Ltd, who publish these works in Great Britain. Extracts from *Waiting for Godot*, *Krapp's Last Tape*, *Embers*, and *Happy Days* are reprinted by permission of Faber & Faber Ltd.

B.—The only thing disturbed by the revolutionaries Matisse and Tal Coat is a certain order on the plane of the feasible.

D.—What other plane can there be for the maker?

B.—Logically none. Yet I speak of an art turning from it in disgust, weary of puny exploits, weary of pretending to be able, of being able, of doing a little better the same old thing, of going a little further along a dreary road.

D.—And preferring what?

B.—The expression that there is nothing to express, nothing with which to express, nothing from which to express, no power to express, no desire to express, together with the obligation to express.

And yet it sometimes seems to me I did get born and had a long life and met Jackson and wandered in the towns, the woods and wildernesses and tarried by the seas in tears before the islands and peninsulas where night lit the little brief yellow lights of man and all night the great white and coloured beams shining in the caves where I was happy, crouched on the sand in the lee of the rocks with the smell of the sea-weed and the wet rock and the howling of the wind the waves whipping me with foam or sighing on the beach softly clawing the shingle, no, not happy, I was never that, but wishing night would never end and morning never come when men wake and say, Come on, we'll soon be dead, let's make the most of it. But what matter whether I was born or not, have lived or not, am dead or merely dying, I shall go on doing as I have always done, not knowing what it is I do, nor who I am, nor where I am, nor if I am.

MALONE DIES

All I know is what the words know, and the dead things, and that makes a handsome little sum, with a beginning, a middle and an end as in the well-built phrase and the long sonata of the dead.

MOLLOY

CONTENTS

PART ONE

ONE: AN INTRODUCTION

I

A MAN ALONE in a room covers paper with words. As he does so, time passes. It is the most elementary description of an activity, the writer's. Concerned, as always, with the fundamentals of the form he is using Beckett makes this situation the basis of his central work, the trilogy of novels *Molloy*, *Malone Dies* and *The Unnamable*. Unlike Beckett's earlier English fiction where the author enjoys the relatively omniscient position of the third person narrative the hero now tells his own story in the first person, writing his monologue in a notebook which, supposedly, is identical in content to the volume we are reading. Even when, in the struggle to remove everything extraneous to the Self for which he is searching, pencil and paper are discarded or lost, the hero still continues with his story, speaking it aloud for, he suggests, an unknown and probably non-existent scribe to copy down.

In the ambiguous relationship which he has with his characters it is Beckett who undertakes this role. Like his characters his life has been spent, with a remarkable purity and tenacity of purpose, creating what he regards as an arduous pensum. In the attempt to discover the fixed nature of the Self, the constant search within all his work, he has made use of these seemingly autonomous characters, Malone and the Unnamable, as they in their turn claim to have invented others, Macmann, Mahood or Worm, in the endeavour they share with him to escape from the prison of time and words into the timeless and changeless condition of Selfhood they believe was lost at birth. 'Yes I have a pensum to discharge, before I can be free. I was given a pensum, at birth perhaps, as a punishment for having been born perhaps. . .'[1] says the Unnamable. This task, as we shall see, Beckett considers both necessary and futile, an unending labour in which, he writes in the dialogues with Duthuit, 'the obligation to express' earns him (the artist) the right 'to fail, as no other dare fail'.[2]

With the exception of *Murphy*, the greater part of which takes place in London, and certain of the later novels and plays where all trace of any known terrestrial landscape has finally been erased, the background against which this pensum is discharged is almost exclusively that of Dublin and the surrounding countryside. It is the remembered landscape of Beckett's youth, the suburb of Foxrock, Leopardstown racecourse, and the station nearby where Watt alights on his way to Mr Knott's house. Two miles away is the mental institution of the Hospitaller Brothers of St John of God where Macmann (*Malone Dies*) comes to end his life, and close at hand is the strand where Henry sits in *Embers* and Molloy goes to replenish his stock of sucking stones. Bally, the county town of *Molloy*, is Baille atha Cliath (the Irish name for Dublin; also Ballyclee, Town of Ford of Hurdles) and somewhere nearby is the suburban villa with the chickens at the back from which Moran departs on his search for Molloy; while leading up to a village station, perhaps the one already mentioned, is the dusty road that Mrs Rooney treads to meet her Dan in *All That Fall*. It is a landscape which, for all the author's hatred of the life it upholds, is regarded with affection, most notably when Beckett and Malone, author and character, enjoy a moment of Proustian remembrance and in some of Beckett's most beautiful writing recall:

> ...the hearing of my boyhood. Then in my bed, in the dark, on stormy nights, I could tell from one another, in the outcry without, the leaves, the boughs, the groaning trunks, even the grasses and the house that sheltered me. Each tree had its own cry, just as no two whispered alike, when the air was still. I heard afar the iron gates clashing and dragging at their posts and the wind rushing between their bars. There was nothing, not even the sand, on the sand, that did not utter its cry. The still nights too, still as the grave as the saying is, were nights of storm for me, clamorous with countless pantings. These I amused myself with identifying, as I lay there...The sound I liked best had nothing noble about it. It was the barking of the dogs, at night, in the hovels up in the hills, where the stone-cutters lived, like generations of stone-cutters before them. It came down to me where I lay, in the house in the plain,

> wild and soft, at the limit of earshot, soon weary. The dogs of the valley replied with their gross bay all fangs and jaws and foam.[3]

Such moments of tenderness, however, are rare.

On to this landscape comes the archetypal Beckett figure, to be identified later as the intellectual clown. He brings with him the appurtenances of the clown, the battered bowler hat, the misfitting boots, the tattered overcoat, a pocket full of turnips and with a bit of luck a carrot too, stones to suck, a stick and best of all, a bicycle, though of doubtful worth. However, although his exterior may at first elicit mirth or provoke disgust he is, within himself, tormented and despairing, and unable for long to hide his resemblance, not to the traditional figure of popular fancy but to the scarred and anguished Christ-clowns of Rouault or, in literature, to Lear's Fool.

The pain and suffering which enter with him, however, are not caused by the social and moral dilemmas of the traditional novel. This man, as far as is possible, avoids all contact with the other human beings in his vicinity. He builds no city, erects no memorial for himself and above all propagates no dynasty. The earth will show little trace of his passing save perhaps the transient scar of a bicycle wheel or the faint impression of a crutch by which he manoeuvres when his body no longer permits him to negotiate the perils of his beloved machine. Within the well-ordered confines of Mansfield Park, Howards End or Washington Square he has no place. He is not concerned with either the well-being or the machinations of society, and he does not appear to be even a marginal participant in the preoccupations that have absorbed fiction over the last three centuries. Nevertheless, if his appearance as a representative of homo sapiens would outrage the inhabitants of Washington Square, it will be seen later that the work of fiction as an artefact, as a phenomenon in a world of mentally seen phenomena, a bound book allegedly holding the mirror up to man in society, is most relevant to the way in which his fictional nature has evolved. Whereas this figure in person seems entirely unreconcilable to our conception of fiction when placed in the firmly rooted context of the bourgeois novel, it will emerge that in form and essence he is probably the last mould of the fictional character and the most fundamental, and that the book he inhabits is both the successor of, and commentary on, the whole library of apparently secure volumes that have gone before.

The hero regards himself as having been forcibly ejected into the world and usually speaks of his birth as an 'expulsion'. He remembers it as a time of agony though it is his own pain at leaving the womb which he recalls rather than the physical agony of the mother. In his birth pangs he discerns the harsh origins of the suffering with which he has since lived and they continue to remind him of that moment of deprivation when, to his knowledge, the Self which is truly his outside time and the world was lost and the search to recover it became a necessity. Without his own consent he was forced out into the grey indifference of day, 'through the hole in her arse if my memory is correct. First taste of the shit.'[4] Birth is the first integer in an arbitrary series of cause and effect whose last point may or may not be death, and though, intellectually, he admits this, he spends much of his life hopelessly longing to return to the womb ('the only endurable, just endurable period, of my enormous history')[5], which is apparent in his habitual assumption of the foetal position (Estragon, Belacqua and the Unnamable) and the pleasure he finds in living in a single small room—a garret or the padded cells of a lunatic asylum for preference.

Once he has been 'expelled' or 'whelped' the hero finds himself in a world where those around him are either hostile or a nuisance, and he tries to disregard their attitude even when they show their feelings in a physical manner. Estragon is beaten every night but does not seem surprised or troubled, while Malone describes how other people would not allow him to follow his own interests in solitude: 'The grown-ups pursued me, the just caught me, beat me, hounded me, back into the game, the round, the jollity'.[6] It is their determined attempt to get him back into the life from which he has, with a purpose, deliberately excluded himself that hurts him more than their blows. Similarly Murphy cannot understand, and seeks to escape, the persistent attentions of his acquaintances, and Belacqua prefers a low pub 'where the porter was well up, first; and the solitary shawly like a cloud of latter rain in a waste of poets and publicans, second; and he neither knew nor was known, third',[7] for, in their search for identity, any interference from without reminds them where they are and sets them right back at the beginning. Moreover they have learnt the lesson of their birth and expect nothing but suffering from life; they were 'born grave as others syphilitic'. As with Sophocles, not to be born is the best for man though 'some people are lucky, born of a wet dream and dead before morning'.[8] At one level of their existence Beckett's characters are filled with outrage and compassion for humanity, compelled as it is to exist in this arbitrary condition not of its own making, and subject only to decay. When the hero can forget his personal search for identity he speaks eloquently and movingly about the transience of life, but his compassion is for humanity in general: humanity as an individual is too often the interrupter of his meditation.

The actual existence of the hero in the world of his fellow men is only of secondary importance, however; it is the life in the mind which is his major concern. In the trilogy the hero has almost entirely left the world behind. All that remains of his life there are a few memories and certain reflections on the past which are written into the stories he occupies himself with telling. Instead of the erstwhile distractions of fiction—marriages, travels, crimes—we have the mind, the discursive intellect, an intelligence encased in layers of ignorance about its own nature, continually shifting about among its particles of knowledge. The words which the hero writes or utters—ultimately they are the same—mirror closely the working of our own minds intent upon discovering, in the useless complexity of possible detail within the skull, some certainty about our being-here, and repeatedly failing. We are witnessing the final incarnation of European rationalism; the Cartesian labour reduced from a debate on first causes to the notation of an old man dying in bed and meditating as he does so on how to distribute sixteen sucking stones in only four pockets and at the same time ensure that he does not suck the same one twice until all the rest have received the same treatment in strict rotation. If this man also dwells on the mysterious workings of Christian grace or the problematical interaction of mind and body there is, given the meaningless world that he conceives, little to choose between the respective preoccupations.

The need to rely on the intellect, on the painful industry of reason within the isolation of the mind, is the ordeal of this man whose epistemology is heavily indebted to the *Discours de la Méthode* and the *Meditations* of Descartes.[9] Lacking the means to grasp at any form of transcendence, either heavenly or terrestrial, with which to oppose the contingency of his condition, it is only with his mind that he can approach his situation in the world. But if this characteristic is his distinction it is also a burden. Where the famous cogito of Descartes carried the proud resilience of a boast, the febrile and hesitant cogito of Beckett's hero is an attribute he would gladly renounce for an intimation of his own identity. When to think is to be he cannot achieve the ultimate realization of the Self outside this world until thinking has ceased.

It is within what Molloy describes as 'all that inner space one never sees, the brain and heart and other caverns where thought and feeling dance their sabbath'[10] that the search for the Self, the overriding concern of the hero's interminable monologue, takes place. His condition is not only one of exile from the life around him but also from himself, from that part of him which by definition should be timeless, dimensionless and motionless. This Self is spoken of as a 'speck in the void... a little bit of grit in the middle of the steppe',[11] so small that it would be 'lost in the eye of a needle'. If it could be reached the hero would escape this world with its sentence of decay and the obligation to think, to speak and to wait. But the task is impossible because he is seeking to contain the infinite with finite weapons. To define the Self as he tries to, involves the use of words from a place in time, and even if he did succeed he would merely have translated what is eternal into the perishable terms of this life. This, as we shall see more clearly when we come to examine the individual works in detail, is part of Beckett's own life-long struggle with time and words, a struggle in which he knows he will never succeed.

Time—'that double-headed monster' as it is called in *Proust*—does not allow man a moment in which to capture even an illusion of the Self for, under its influence, he is only acquainted with a multitude of continually changing selves. 'We are not merely more weary because of yesterday, we are other, no longer what we were before the calamity of yesterday,'[12] Beckett writes, again in *Proust*. What was known and may have been certain yesterday is of no significance today because, immersed in passing time, we are no longer the same self but another with a totally new significance. This countless succession of daily—even hourly—selves creates an unending series of misrepresentations of the real Self which is only to be discovered in the desired stasis of timelessness.

Moreover, beneath the pressure of time the searcher 'wastes and pines';[13] body and senses crumble away as he waits, not for death which is most probably only a minor alteration to his present condition, but for the true end when the arbitrary series of cause and effect begun at birth will be closed in reunion with his own identity. Ironically, however, one sees in *Endgame* that the nearer one comes to this end the farther it seems to recede. Time appears to 'slow down' because, like a series of figures after the decimal point which with every succeeding figure comes closer to zero yet never reaches it, the moment when the finite being is able to enter the essential reality of the infinite is also logically impossible. 'Finished,' says Clov without much hope at the beginning of *Endgame*:

> it's finished, nearly finished, it must be nearly finished. Grain upon grain, one by one, and one day, suddenly, there's a heap, a little heap, the impossible heap.[14]

But when the curtain falls at the end of the evening the moments are still mounting 'to a life',[15] the heap of days remains incomplete, and the following night Clov will open the performance with exactly the same words. By a typical inversion of the usual attitude which regards man as having only a temporary existence in time, Beckett has postulated the hero as an individual being imprisoned in time apparently for eternity. There is no way (no absolute death) by which he can escape and become one with the Void surrounding life. It is also ironic that the motive behind his search for identity, the attempt to discover a dimension of life which supplies a solution to the immediate sense of transience and mortality, and therefore a purpose beneath the arbitrary conditions of existence, has provided man with an immortality precisely the opposite of the one he seeks. He has, in fact, an 'immortality' in time, not beyond it. The Unnamable is left to continue his existence even after death; death, the original final integer, has become insignificant, but the final transcendence, the leap into the timelessness of the ultimate Self still eludes him, precisely because he is a being in time:

> ...the question may be asked, off the record, why time doesn't pass, doesn't pass from you, why it piles up all about you, instant on instant, on all sides, deeper and deeper, thicker and thicker, your time, other's time, the time of the ancient dead and the dead yet unborn, why it buries you grain by grain neither dead nor alive, with no memory of anything, no hope of anything, no knowledge of anything, no history and no prospects, buried under the seconds, saying any old thing, your mouth full of sand, oh I know it's immaterial, time is one thing, I another, but the question may be asked, why time doesn't pass...[16]

Time and the impossibility of an escape from time passing into the supposed infinity of the Self is one dimension of Beckett's art: the other is language. Words are the foundation of Beckett's self-confessed art of failure for they form the impenetrable barrier that prevents us from knowing who we are and what we are. Watt's endless verbal analysis may encompass the total of data and experience arising out of his stay at Mr Knott's curious establishment, but the sum of that data is not equal to the whole. Not one of the combinations of words he assembles with such pedantic thoroughness succeeds in positing the definitive statement on his experience. The negative Mr Knott and his effect on Watt cannot be reduced to the rationally satisfying security of language; something of their nature remains, undiscernible but disturbing, between, behind or beyond the words so that Watt, despairing of language as a method of knowledge, finally becomes incapable of any rational discourse at all. Nevertheless, as the characters have been left to fend for themselves with only the doubtful worth of their reason to carry their search to a satisfactory conclusion, language is necessary. The stream of words which is the form of their thoughts is the language of their exile in time even after death. The words, like time, will only cease once the Self has been reached.

Words, of course, are the materials of the stories which the characters tell themselves and it is here that the link with life in time is most ironically apparent. For the stories they tell help to pass the interminable time (for example Malone: 'that passed the time, I was time').[17] The irony exists, however, not in the illusion that Malone gives himself, of 'becoming time', but in the fact that these stories are yet another attempt to define the nature of the teller's identity. Through the stories the narrator creates a series of vice-existers (fictional characters who relive parts of the hero's life and through whom he can explore his obsession with guilt, suffering, time and language) in the hope that one day he will accidently describe *the* vice-exister, a version of himself that will be his true Self. What he forgets—or tries to ignore—is that to define this Self in words would be to place it in the world and therefore to destroy it. It is not difficult to see from this the further irony; that of Beckett writing about one vice-exister who in turn writes of a third. The shifting layers of identity within a single novel will be examined in the chapters on the trilogy.

These stories, at first distinct from the narration proper, have, by the end of the trilogy become indistinguishable, the one from another. The final novel is a continuous woof of words in which the vice-existers and the narrator merge and flow onwards almost as one voice. Sitting in the grey gloom of after-death he has become barely distinguishable as anything other than a voice 'murmuring my old stories'.[18] In accordance with the task he has envisaged for himself, he is trapped into defining the silence in his head and the silence that surrounds him, seeking a way that will allow him never to speak again, but he is unable, in being forced to define the lesser silence through words, to attain the freedom of the greater silence of the Self:

Yes, in my life, since we must call it so, there were three things, the

> inability to speak, the inability to be silent, and solitude, that's what I've had to make the best of.[19]

This is at the heart of the art of the impossible. The Unnamable describes his condition as one where he himself, the walls, the floor, the whole intelligible world, are made of words tumbling over one another in an incoherent, unformed storm of particles through which his own voice must stubbornly persevere '...you must go on, I can't go on, I'll go on.'[20] This way to the Self, like the struggle with time, leads straight into an impasse.

The location of the Self is like the location of Irrational numbers or the centre of a circle. The rational mind knows it is there, either through intimation or understanding, but is incapable of actually arriving at it. One may, as in *Watt*, attempt the construction of a series of cause and effect which will take all known phenomena into account, but in this series man himself will always appear as an Irrational number, unstatable except in particulars because his essential nature is unknowable even to himself. One can no more define the centre of a circle which with each definition gains a new centre, than define the essential quality of an individual being. This failure, and the impasse at which the trilogy closes, leads to two further attempts in the pursuit of the Self which must also be examined later. If this Self is so elusive the hitherto isolated individual becomes aware of a need for a companion, an Other whose presence will remove the newly arisen doubt, that perhaps after all he IS nothing. This leads to the series of couples in the plays, Estragon and Vladimir, Lucky and Pozzo, Hamm and Clov, etc. and to the bizarre pair Bom and Pim in the later novel *How it is*. By beating on another's backside or being beaten on his own Bom is able to sense his own condition in the mud and attempt to speak of it. The complications which this introduction of an Other add to the search must remain unelucidated in this present summary of Beckett's world but needless to say the impasse is not removed. Even in the most obvious sense, being seen by another does not deepen one's own insight into the area in which the Self may be found. Furthermore, each encroachment upon the individual's selfhood is both painful and resented. To the Beckett hero a platitude like 'there you are' is agonizing. For example in *Waiting for Godot* Vladimir returns to the stage and sees Estragon:

> VLAD: So there you are again.
> EST: Am I?[21]

The crucial question can elicit no firmer response than that.

II

This search, for a dimension of the Self outside both time and words, is the main preoccupation of the Beckett hero. It is, however, by no means his only affliction and although it becomes the most urgent, this urgency is only the result of a variety of underlying influences which are the human and concrete motives from which the search begins.

A fundamental cause of his *angoisse* is the knowledge that he is living in an age from which God is absent. Beckett is writing in what Heidegger has called a time of need:

> It is the time of the gods that have fled and of the god that is coming. It is the time of need because it lies under a double Not: the No-more of the gods that have fled and the Not-yet of the god that is coming.[22]

This much discussed and crucial situation has, not unnaturally, deeply influenced the nature of Beckett's works, but one sees there that the absence of God has ceased to enliven the sense of shock and bewilderment that it aroused in writers of an earlier generation; there remains instead, only the anger, the outrage, the desolation and the real need to discover on what affirmative terms life can exist where God does not. The journey of Beckett's mind during the course of this search is, in its own way, strangely religious and the despair that ensues is aggravated by the thirst of the forsaken man for a new transcendence as well as by the more immediate sense of his spiritual impotence. The discovery of the Self therefore, of the irreducible element that exists somewhere in man and which is opposed to the nothingness in the void about him, is more crucial now than in the past precisely because of this awareness of an 'empty hole' in the sky. It springs from a demand that his own unrepeatable being shall always *be*. Like Unamuno, Beckett cannot reconcile himself to the notion that the thinking and feeling being which is each individual man should be compelled to cease, and the timelessness of the Self is a way for him to remain immortal in spite of God's demise. Like Nietzsche's doctrine of eternal recurrence which is another attempt to resolve the same problem, it calls for an increase in the spiritual possibilities of man.

It is the absence of God which brings his characters face to face with the void. Estragon and Malone both call on God, not because they believe he will answer but because it is still a prominent reflex action. In *Endgame* Hamm orders his parents and Clov to pray to God and although the image of a group of derelicts pantomiming a spiritual action is both ludicrous and amusing, Hamm's cry 'The bastard! He doesn't exist!'[23] contains more agony than pathos. Although the prayer is made without any expectation of a reply the pain of His absence is still very real for it is followed by a greater silence, loneliness and despair. The questions of Ivan Karamazov still echo faintly behind all the writings, the silences and the waitings: can I forgive God for not existing, and if He did exist, could I forgive Him for all the suffering He has caused?

Man therefore is left in the meaningless context of infinity: Pascal's intimations have become a reality. Here time and space, let alone man, his thinking and his actions, are rendered meaningless. Around us in time and space lies the incomprehensible void which science has succeeded in making more real for us but no less frightening. In this void the actions of man appear absurd and his substitutes for God—humanism, love or social purpose—are all alike the imaginings of men who have blinded themselves to reality. Communication between individuals in Beckett is at best a vulgarity, and love, that dream of terrestrial transcendence, a patent folly. Only the love of Celia for Murphy or the inactive affection of Belacqua for the Alba in *More Pricks Than Kicks* resemble literature's customary treatment of the tender passion. The succeeding relationships between the sexes are all grotesque, painful, repellent and cruel. The love affair of Macmann and Moll in *Malone Dies*, for example, is more bitter and more disgusting than even Swift, in his most violent moments, cared to imagine. Whatever may be the hero's pity for the world at large, and this pity is very deep, hatred and violence are the traffic of his dealings with the individual. Both Molloy and Moran murder a man in the course of their journey. Molloy detests his mother and normally communicates with her by blows upon the head, while the Unnamable describes with great relish the way in which he trod down the entrails of his dead—or dying—family with the ends of his crutches.

This hatred of human kind, however, is not gratuitous or deliberately perverse. If it were there would be no cause to read Beckett for the pathos and compassion which is so evidently in his works. This hatred rather, arises from the heros' despair over the meaninglessness of their existence. The world, both in itself and in its human dimension, revolts and disgusts not from a deliberate effort of will on their part but precisely because their compassion for man's helpless situation within it is so deep. The hatred which the hero feels is similar to the turning from the world in anger and disgust of the Old Testament prophets or the early Fathers of the Church, a renunciation which originates in the conviction that 'whatsoever is not God is nothing'.[24] If the heroes cannot communicate effectively they will do it in the most crude and painful way possible; if there is no God of grace and mercy they will not assume the responsibility for dispensing any of those qualities that have been rendered meaningless by His absence. This inversion of traditional attitudes is apparent in the relationship between Molloy and his mother. The hallowed mother figure is hated not less but more than any other creature. Molloy finds her as odious and pernicious as ever the King of Brobdingnag found the human race in general. He describes the way in which he always added the letter 'g' to her name:

> I called her Mag, when I had to call her something. And I called her Mag because for me, without my knowing why, the letter g abolished the syllable Ma, and as it were spat on it better than any other letter would have done ...[25]

She is hated not for herself but because she was a cause of his birth and hence all the consequent suffering. Other human beings may interfere with the course of the hero's life but their presence is negligible beside that of his mother. She reminds him of the terrible severance that placed him where he is and the thought of her recalls him to the contingency of his being here. Again, in *Endgame*, the three generations portrayed on the stage all attempt to make one another suffer as deeply as possible because each is filled with a nauseous sense of an opportunity missed, that had things been otherwise they might not have been born. 'Why did you engender me,'[26] Hamm shouts at Nagg, 'Accursed progenitor.'[27] The suffering within finds its only release in the infliction of pain on the cause of that suffering. Thus Molloy's attitude to his mother reveals an additional dimension in the hero's distrust of love. Beckett's heroes not only believe love to be all too inadequate a substitute for the totality lost with God but are aware that love also leads to copulation and the birth of more suffering. Love therefore is the most revolting and sinful of all human activities. 'Like dogs,'[28] comments Malone, when he sees two people making love in a window across the way.

Birth, however, is not merely the result of 'sin', it is also *the* tragic act. Man's life is the working out 'of the original and eternal sin...the sin of having been born.'[29] In the trilogy the consciousness that in being born man has somehow committed a grave sin for which he must always live to expiate is built by the hero into a cosmology of guilt and suffering. He believes that if he suffers deeply enough, consciousness as he knows it will perhaps cease: 'I'm not suffering enough,'[30] say both Clov and the Unnamable. Although he knows in his more truthful moments that his cosmology is only his own invention (in *How it is* we see the hero destroy, in the final lines of the book, a system which he has spent 130 pages laboriously erecting), and that the whole 'college of tyrants'[31] which he has postulated in order to give a meaning to his suffering is all an illusion, this cosmology is necessary to him if he is going to orientate himself in the void and grasp any insight into his condition. Ultimately, however, the only demonstration of his existence is that if he is living he will be crying. All the heroes shed gratuitous tears on behalf of mankind, from Belacqua at the Frica's party[32] to the Unnamable, seated in his pot with the tears coursing down his face. When Hamm asks Clov if Nagg is dead yet he gets the following reply:

> CLOV: Doesn't look like it.
> (He closes the lid and straightens up).
> HAMM: (letting go his toque) What's he doing?
> (Clov raises the lid of Nagg's bin, stoops, looks into it)
> Pause.
> CLOV: He's crying.
> HAMM: Then he's living.[33]

There remains one further observation on the effect which the flight of the Gods has had on Beckett. This rejection of the world and of human kind is not only not perverse, as we have seen, but the result of what would seem to be a still more fundamental compulsion. As has been said, for the Beckett hero all that is not God is nothing. The force at work beneath the words is recognizable as the spiritual compulsion of the mystic in all its austerity; a compulsion that is written out as if it were a penance and which rejects all that is not God's as negative and indifferent. As Horace Gregory has written in his essay *Beckett's Dying Gladiators:*

> In his prose Beckett has sustained the ancient, sometimes parallel association of religion with poetry; and if at times they seem to vanish, they are just around the corner. Scratch an Irish poet, and if the scratch is deep enough to draw blood, the result, however heretical it may be, will be a religious poem.[34]

Beckett has rejected the power of reason and all claim to intellectual eminence and searched with a spiritual intensity for the presence that ought to be at the centre of the universe. Not finding that presence he cannot escape the conviction that such a world is worthless. In a world without the divine presence at its core the whole expanse is a valley of bones and everything in it equally valuable and equally valueless. One can make no distinction between the affirmative qualities such as love or friendship and the opposites of hate or hypocrisy. In this world a rose is not a rose is a rose, a rose is no better than dung and dung no worse than love. As Molloy murmurs, on finding himself in a new dwelling:

> it's a change of muck. And if all muck is the same muck that doesn't matter. It's good to have a change of muck.[35]

Similarly the hero of *How it is* crawls through a landscape made entirely of mud, but the fact that it is mud in which he lives does not revolt him unduly. Whatever the place the absence of a divine presence to make meaningful that which is meaningless would make it one with the mud.

Where Beckett differs from the early mystics, however, is that even before he commences to search he knows that what he is looking for does not exist. He is without a centre of conviction to which he can return in times of emergency and must suffer the torture of an unquenchable thirst (a recurrent symbol) in a world where water not only appears unobtainable but, which is more likely, is non-existent. Deprived of any certainty the hero disgusts even himself and, as he describes, even rats refuse to live beside him. Repeating over and over, from place to place, the eternal, tortuous, burdensome questions in his brain he despairs of ever finding peace.

He suffers many illusions of arrival and has created, in the contemplation of numbers ('not count! one of the few pleasures in life')[36] in the riding of bicycles (for example Belacqua 'who could on no account resist a bicycle')[37] or in the sucking of stones picked up on the sea-shore, harbours of relative quiet in the course of his journey. But he tires of these harbours very quickly. The second time Murphy attempts to capture the pneumatic bliss of sitting in a chair in a Lyon's Corner House is not so rapturous as the first, and Pozzo observes that the second pipe full one smokes cannot compare with its predecessor. Man's ultimate freedom, says Beckett, taking his image from the Cartesian Geulincx, is similar to the freedom of the galley slave who lays down his oar to crawl eastward under the whip while the boat is sailing West, and the nearest one can approach to peace or happiness is of a similar nature. As Arsène describes it in *Watt:*

> The glutton castaway, the drunkard in the desert, the lecher in prison, they are the happy ones. To hunger, thirst, lust, every day afresh and every day in vain, after the old prog, the old booze, the old whores, that's the nearest we'll ever get to felicity.[38]

The hero, born into 'a veritable calvary with no limits to its stations and no hope of crucifixion,'[39] is neither able to accept the place he has arrived at, out of fear that further on he might discover a more harmonious place of rest; nor see the advantage of going on to a haven which in all probability does not exist. For example Molloy:

> For in me there have always been two fools, among others, one asking nothing better than to stay where he is and the other imagining that life might be slightly less horrible a little further on.[40]

The hero therefore moves forward perpetually but with an extremely hesitant motion, frantically desiring to cease yet determined to arrive at this problematic and elusive destination. His dilemma is heightened by the existence, at moments when he almost believes he has reached the end, of a voice bidding him to continue. This voice he christens the 'hypothetical imperative'. He hears it as a murmur, 'something gone wrong with the silence',[41] but never discovers where it comes from. Is it perhaps a message from the place he desires to reach, giving him hope? Is it something in his own brain playing tricks on him? Or is it the taunting command of some malevolent task-master determined to screw the last ounce of suffering out of him? For it is an addition to his suffering. Desiring nothing more than to enter the final and eternal oblivion of his true Self this voice calls him back, whispering insidiously into his head ('you hear it with your head not your ears') the compulsion to continue:

> But I could not, stay in the forest I mean, I was not free to. That is to say I could have, physically nothing could have been easier, but I was not purely physical, I lacked something, and I would have had the feeling, if I had stayed in the forest, of going against an imperative.[42]

The voice calls him back from the expiatory task that is his from birth, and demands that he should face the image of his condition which he prefers to forget. Thus the hero batters upon the limits of his being, attempting the impossible end, and, like the figure in *Act Without Words* who continually tries to leave the stage but always fails, he is repeatedly repulsed, sent sprawling back into the excrutiating tension of a life where to stay where one is and to attempt to move a little further along the way creates a need which in the given circumstances of this world can never be resolved.

Finally, and fundamental to all Beckett's works, there is his compassion; an intense and moving regard for man's condition in this world from which meaning is withheld and mortality—'a long day's dying'—the one certainty. In *Waiting for Godot* the tree flowers between the acts but Godot still does not come. Pozzo goes blind, Lucky dumb, things human decay and Lucky's famous speech of the first act is realized. This speech is a lament for:

> man in short for man in brief (who) wastes and pines...abandoned... and...for reasons unknown (continues) to shrink and dwindle (into) the great cold the great dark the air and the earth abode of stones in the great cold alas alas...[43]

It is in this that the universality of Beckett's writing lies, and the haunting, poetically resonant language of such passages is the flowering of his futile yet continual revolt against the whole idea of mortality, that fact that we 'breathe, we change! We lose our hair, our teeth! Our bloom! Our ideals!'[44] His writing in this dimension does not make any ultimate pretensions for our existence or attempt to provide a final answer. Instead he speaks of the heroic absurdity of human endeavour in the face of death, a subject which always leads to his most sustained passages of poetic prose filled with a basic imagery and emotion yet all the more powerful for their constraint within a form that is classical in its precision. This revolt, which begins in *Watt*, is against the intolerable imprisonment of man within the determination of cause and effect, of beginning and ending, of being obliged to end because something else is beginning or begin because something else is ending in the transient course of life. At its most basic it is a revolt against the meaningless limitations and compulsions of birth and death, and the universe which imposes such conditions on man can never be accepted even if the earth is neutral. As Beckett writes in *Proust*: 'The mortal microcosm cannot forgive the relative immortality of the macrocosm,'[45] and then adds, in what might be taken as an epigraph for all his work, the superb and enigmatic comment:

> The whisky bears a grudge against the decanter.[46]

TWO: THE POETICS OF FAILURE

I

SO LONG AS he remains concerned with the use of language the Beckett hero knows he has failed to discover the Self which exists beyond the temporal world of words. The word 'failure' also lies at the core of Beckett's own poetics. To write, for Beckett, is necessarily to fail, and literature in the traditional sense, with its promise to enlarge man's experience and to explore or resolve his relationship with the world about him, is rejected as an illusion. His books, if they concern themselves with these earlier purposes, do so in order to mock them, and to emphasize the impotence of an art that seeks to discover some ultimate deep where the particulars are reconciled in a universal and meaningful whole: 'it's for the whole there seems to be no name'. This strange position of creative futility is not only expressed by his characters; it is also at the heart of Beckett's own brief but important attempts to define the nature of his task.

The dissatisfaction with literature which Beckett's characters experience is similar to the actual dissatisfaction of Antonin Artaud—the Artaud who, in violent reaction against the French nineteenth century tradition of *poètes maudits* and their attempt to use the 'alchemy of the word' by which poetry was given the extra-literary task of attaining the 'unknown', the 'elsewhere or 'the great mystery', acknowledged the futility of the literary endeavour and wrote:

> All writing is pigshit.
> People who leave the obscure and try to define whatever it is that goes on in their heads, are pigs ...
> ...all those for whom words have a meaning; all those for whom there exist sublimities in the soul and currents of thought...are pigs.[1]

In consequence, when Jaques Rivière, the editor of the *Nouvelle Revue Française* and the critic who had described 'all the literature of the nineteenth century' as 'a vast incantation toward the miracle,'[2] suggested to Artaud that their correspondence should be written up and published in a fictional form, Artaud replied: 'why give an appearance of fiction to what is made up of the ineradicable substance of the soul, to what is a wail of reality?'[3] It is not fiction that Artaud writes: like the monologues of the trilogy it is 'the very cry of life'.[4] His statement to Rivière, 'Literature, in the strict sense of the word, interests me rather a little,'[5] is of a kind with Moran's less dogmatic 'but it is not at this late stage...that I intend to give way to literature.'[6] If one of Beckett's characters does start to invent, to give a fictional meaning to the universe he is in, he becomes aware that it is an illusion and is forced to destroy what he has made. It is the 'ineradicable substance of the soul' that they are writing, and if Bom, in *How it is*, attempts to explain himself away by erecting a complex system of mud-bound pairs, each member alternately tormented and tormenting in a long line that stretches to infinity, watched over by a hierarchy of scribes who sit and record their murmurs, he knows it is an affront to his condition, 'an appearance of fiction', and so he is forced to destroy it in a frenzy of iconoclasm.

Much of what Beckett thinks about his own activity is contained in the works themselves. His writings have the additional dimension of being, in the act of their writing, a critical examination of the form in which they are cast. The trilogy, whatever else it may be, is an observation on the residual nature of a work of fiction, on a creation of the imagination that tells of human beings, the events and feelings that make up their lives, and all the incidental means writers have used, from Defoe to Joyce, to keep the reader contented and credulous. Likewise the plays reveal and comment on the nature of a dramatic presentation, demonstrating through their structure and dialogue, exactly what is taking place when one group of people spend two hours observing the posturings of another group upon an elevated platform. Beckett works with the basic resources of his form. His fiction is limited to the activity of a man in a room writing words in a notebook, the simulacrum of all novelists. His plays expose to the auditorium simply a naked stage with one tree (scenery) and two men who *are there*, again the simplest dimension of what we know as theatre. This aspect of his writing is an example of the modern flight from Literature; from the convention of plot and character in the novel, and from the illusion of the fourth wall in the theatre. Exactly what the implications of this tendency are is best discussed in the later examination of the individual works, but the technique of this method can be recognized in his venture into the convention of the cinema, known simply as *Film*.

Film starts with the dictum of Bishop Berkeley, *Esse est percipi*, to be is to be perceived. Berkeley's words define exactly the nature of cinematic convention and its possibilities. In the novels, what is not written down by Malone will remain forever unknown (thus it is a great event when he mislays his pencil); in the radio plays everything that is not established in terms of sound might as well not exist. So in *Film* all that is relevant must fall within the vision of the camera. Beckett goes further, however, and turns what is only a formal limitation into a metaphysical truth, for Berkeley's words do not apply only to the cinema screen.[7] The film tells of a man who, like most of Beckett's later heroes, is seeking not to exist. He therefore conceives the idea that if he can hide from all human, animal and divine vision he will achieve his end. He rushes to his room and destroys all watching eyes: he screens the window, covers a mirror, hides a fish in a bowl, shuts out a cat and a dog and tears up an image of God which is hanging on the wall. Finally he takes a packet of photographs of himself from when he was a baby to when he was about thirty and after looking through them a last time he tears them up as well (thus destroying the film within the film, a life in miniature. Significantly the earliest portrait, taken when he was only six months old, is the most difficult to tear: in Beckett the distant past is always more tenacious than recent events). Believing that he has now done all he need he sits down and awaits death. But as always his attempt is futile, for slowly, in the silence, he comes face to face with himself. He is unavoidably self-perceived.

In 1949 Beckett published three dialogues between himself and Georges Duthuit, editor of *transition*. The dialogues take for their subject three painters, Tal Coat, Masson and Bram Van Velde. What emerges from Beckett's side of the discussion is, with the exception of the monograph on Proust, the only *ex cathedra* indication of his own creative intentions. During the conversations Beckett wears the clown's mask. He allows himself to be stunned into silence by Duthuit and at one point gives himself the stage direction 'B:—(Exit weeping).[8] The tone he uses is one of flippant anguish at his incapacity to express what he wants to express for he knows that this last is ultimately impossible. What he is seeking to define is the essence of the indefinable art he is engaged in, the art of the impossible.

In the first dialogue he deals with Tal Coat. He sees him as a man who is still engrossed in the toils of previous painting. The tendency and accomplishment of this painting, says Beckett, are fundamentally those we have seen before; it is a mere 'straining to enlarge the statement of a compromise.'[9] This traditional compromise between art and the world is precisely what Beckett rejects. He dismisses the art which remains 'on the plane of the feasible'[10] as now irrelevant. This art, which has always taken possession of what it depicts, that has made its vision into a thing ('Art has always been bourgeois'),[11] has now become an anachronism, for the 'bourgeois' order of values from which it arises and which it reflects, has been rendered meaningless by the discovery of the Void. In the passage quoted as his credo at the beginning of this book, Beckett expresses his desire for an art that will abandon the feasible and attempt to deal only with the nothing of the individual encompassed by the greater nothing of the Void.

In the second dialogue Duthuit confronts Beckett with a painter who has apparently assigned himself this Void as a subject. But Beckett is not easily appeased. Although Masson concerns himself with the 'inner emptiness' which, according to Chinese aesthetics, is the prime condition of the art of painting, Beckett detects behind Masson's search, the presence of two familiar maladies: 'the malady of wanting to know what to do and the malady of wanting to be able to do it.'[12] To the follower of the old tradition of the feasible even nothingness has become something to be possessed, and Beckett will have no truck with such a desire. For he has 'no desire to express,'[13] his art is merely a painful, unavoidable obligation which, he is aware, must end in failure. The man who still wants to be able to succeed has not yet admitted his own essential impotence.

The third painter is Bram Van Velde. Beckett has been an admirer of Van Velde, a Dutch artist, since he first came to Paris, and in this dialogue it becomes clear that he regards him as his counterpart in the field of painting.[14] What Beckett sees as Van Velde's intentions, therefore, are pretty much his own, and if 'write' is substituted for 'paint' the following passage is a clear indication, by Beckett, of his own situation:

B: The situation is that of him who is helpless, cannot act, in the event cannot paint, since he is obliged to paint. The act is of him who, helpless, unable to act, acts, in the event paints, since he is obliged to paint.

D: Why is he obliged to paint?

B: I don't know.[15]

Van Velde is seen as the first painter to abandon the plane of the feasible and 'admit that to be an artist is to fail, as no other dare fail, that failure is his world and the shrink from it desertion.'[16] But as neither Beckett nor Van Velde are trying to express anything definable (for to define Nothing is to make it be), the exposition ends in failure. Enough has been said, however, to see that it is not separate from Beckett's other attempts, cast in the guise of fiction or drama, to articulate from the surroundings of the Void. As Beckett begins his summing up:

> There are many ways in which the thing I am trying in vain to say may be tried in vain to be said. I have experimented as you know, both in public and in private, under duress, through faintness of heart, through weakness of mind, with two or three hundred.[17]

Beckett acknowledges the obsessive nature of his task. He has written about man in book after book, portraying him in such decay that he appears to be almost nothing. But precisely because he is nothing, all the attempts to return him to a meaningful plane of the feasible are simply acts of bad faith. These attempts place around him a semblance of a metaphysical order that is not there; the whole agony of his absurd situation is that he is trapped into defining a meaning where one no longer exists. As Beckett explains it in *Watt*:

> For the only way one can speak of nothing is to speak of it as though it were something, just as the only way one can speak of God is to speak of him as though he were a man, which to be sure he was, in a sense, for a time, and as the only way one can speak of man, even our anthropologists have realized that, is to speak of him as though he were a termite.[18]

This is the way Beckett takes, the only way that is open to him though one fraught with danger. For as a user of words he is liable to give a meaning to, and so start believing in, something rather than nothing. Words threaten to build up systems ('We're not beginning to mean something!'[19] cries Hamm) and Beckett's abiding distrust of them springs precisely from that. The monologue once started always founders on the determination of the words to begin stories, build up possibilities, frame meanings, that come between the speaker and his search for nothing, the Void of the Self.

II

The exponent of this impossible art, steering his precarious path along the tightrope of futility, is a familiar figure among the images of our century. He is the well known amalgamation of clown and tramp; an alliance of the comically-absurd with the pathos of rejection. Beckett's art draws deeply on the anti-literary tradition of the clown as he has appeared in the circus, the vaudeville and on the silent screen. In this figure he has detected both a companion traveller into the realm of failure and a fellow sufferer on the cross of the Cartesians.

Expelled into the world (the first, irrevocable pratfall), the clown is left to turn his own evident incapacity in the art of living into a mechanical parody of that art performed well. To those who watch him he shows only his mask-like face on which is enscribed the obsessive nature of his endeavour, and the fixed intent of appearing capable where it is known he is destined to fail. But beneath this unchanging exterior is a recurrent pain which may, in unguarded moments, split the mask into an expression of deepest suffering. Hence Malone describes the continual demands that existence makes on him:

> Live and invent. I have tried. I must have tried. Invent. It is not the word. Neither is live. No matter. I have tried. While within me the wild beast of earnestness padded up and down, roaring, ravening, rending. I have done that. And all alone, well hidden, played the clown, all alone, hour after hour, motionless, often standing, spell-bound, groaning.[20]

The clown is a suitable exponent of the art of failure because he too is concerned with virtuosity to no end. However finely wrought and aptly phrased the words of the Beckett hero may be they will never succeed in encompassing the great end he demands of them. Similarly, however brilliantly and intently the circus clown may imitate the acrobat or the juggler, he is fated to miss the rope, drop the balls or lose his trousers (like Estragon). Kenner has seen 'Emmet Kelly's solemn determination to sweep a circle of light into a dustpan'[21] as the source of the plays, and the comparison is apt for what Kelly is presenting is an image of impotence. It is this area of man's striving, ignored by artists hitherto concerned with the plane of the feasible, that interests Beckett. As he has said: 'I'm working with impotence, ignorance. I don't think impotence has been exploited in the past.'[22] Nevertheless, despite his evident incapacity Kelly's justification is that he has stubbornly persisted in his task. It is both his glory and his absurdity. The same applies to Vladimir and Estragon. Whatever else occurs during the two hours of *Waiting for Godot* their achievement can also be seen as both absurd and positive:

> We are waiting for Godot to come...Or for night to fall. We have kept our appointment and that's an end to that. We are not saints, but we have kept our appointment. How many people can boast as much?[23]

Although Estragon immediately deflates this statement by replying 'Billions', he does not absolutely detract from Vladimir's boast. Even if this achievement is the only pittance which all humanity can produce for its daily labour, it is still the ludicrous failure with which it mocks the inhospitable circumstance of the universe. Vladimir and Estragon, as essential representatives of humanity, reveal the onerous demands that existence makes on man, and their pathetic failure cannot detract from their endurance. Neither can their waiting, like Kelly's dustpan, avoid making a direct comment upon the manner in which the audience pass their own lives. It is a particular faculty of the clown to question the assumptions of his audience, and when the audience is travelling the same limited series of cause and effect from birth to death, its own day-to-day tasks are diminished to the same level of significance as the tramps' waiting or Kelly's concern with a circle of light. And the clown's endeavour shows what prodigies of skill and infinite labour are required of man merely to fail, let alone to succeed.

Beckett's constant obsession with the philosophy of Descartes also finds expression in the figure of the clown. Exactly what importance Descartes has for Beckett is best discussed in connection with *Murphy* where the hero is the first in a succession of suffering Cartesians tormented by the legacy of the French philosopher. Murphy's desire to 'come alive in his mind' and to abandon the alleged superfluity of the body is understandable only in terms of Cartesian thought. The apparently insoluble problem of the disparity between mind and matter, which follows from Descartes' initial discovery of himself as a 'thinking thing', fascinates and disturbs each of the heroes in turn. For them the mind is 'body-tight' and the body insulated against the mind, just as for Descartes the 'thinking thing' which is his fundamental certainty ('I think therefore I am') is confined to the brain and the body is regarded as an independent machine which he compares to a clock. Both Descartes and the hero can witness the functioning of the body—as they can observe the corporality of any particular thing—but neither achieves a satisfactory explanation of the assumed interaction that exists between body and mind.

The Cartesian position introduces a further approach to the comic as it affects both the clown and Beckett's hero. In his essay on *Laughter* Henri Bergson demonstrated that rigidity is a prerequisite of comedy —in action and movement, in appearance and character, and in language and plot. The more rigid, repetitive and fixed a movement becomes, the likelier it is of being comic. In Bergson's definition: 'The attitudes, gestures and movements of the human body are laughable in exact proportion as that body reminds us of a mere machine.'[24] He demonstrates that, in the comic, limbs become fixed in stilted gestures and patterns, and that often a repeated movement assumes an ascendancy over all others. Likewise the humour of an expression is created by an underlying trait or disfiguration being exaggerated and fixed so as to exclude the normal rapid interchange of emotion underneath.

Nowhere is this tendency better illustrated than in the clown with his mask face and automaton of a body. His demeanour has become so mechanical that even physical mishap often fails to affect the set position of his facial muscles. There is a moment in *Watt* when the hero is struck on the head by a stone, flung at him by Lady McCann. Although he is in no doubt about the nature of this assault he reveals no discomfiture. He accepts the outrage as a matter of course and 'Beyond stopping, and laying down his bags, and picking up his hat, and setting it on his head, and picking up his bags, and setting himself, after one or two false starts, again in motion, Watt, faithful to his rule, took no more notice of this aggression than if it had been an accident.'[25] Moreover, Bergson, in company with the clown, reveals the comic to be an apt expression of the Cartesian mind-matter dualism. The clown, with his machine-like body, is the perfect illustration of a regulated body operating apparently devoid of mind or spirit. When Watt strides away from his encounter with Lady McCann his limbs are set in motion and perform the function of walking quite independently of the mind which they bear along:

> Watt's way of advancing due east, for example, was to turn his bust as far as possible towards the north and at the same time to fling out his right leg as far as possible towards the south, and then to turn his bust as far as possible towards the south and at the same time to fling out his left leg as far as possible towards the north, and then again to turn his bust as far as possible towards the north and to

> fling out his right leg as far as possible towards the south, and then again to turn his bust as far as possible towards the south and fling out his left leg as far as possible towards the north, and so on, over and over again, many many times, until he reached his destination and could sit down. So, standing at first on one leg, and then on the other, he moved forward, a headlong tardigrade, in a straight line.[26]

In describing the mechanical in the body Beckett chooses to reflect the repetitive details in the language he uses. By the standards of certain of his descriptions the one above is short. Molloy's mathematical tussle with the sixteen sucking-stones covers over six pages of unparagraphed prose and, again in *Watt*, several hundred words are expended on describing the logical possibilities of Mr Knott's movement in a room which contains a door, a window, a fire and a bed. The most stringent exercise in repetitive explicitness, however, is perhaps the meeting of the five-man grant committee to hear Louit's dissertation, *The Mathematical Intuitions of the Visicelts*. Before even the farcical and extensive dissertation can begin Beckett employs many hundreds of words describing how easy it is for five men who set out to look at each other, to take not the twenty looks which are in theory necessary for their enterprise, but many more besides. What with impatience, cramp in the neck and body odours, the venture is not easily completed and Beckett is thorough enough to chart each misplaced glance. In his hands language, the tool of thought, is as obdurate and mechanical as the body and conceals the flow of vital thought behind it.

The body, however, though a machine, still retains a possibility of graceful movement. The clown, as Beckett describes him, guards against this in his choice of dress. With his battered bowler hat, attached by string to the button-hole of his torn, capacious overcoat, which in turn reaches down to the ground where his feet are encased in all but useless shoes or boots, his clothes have the appearance of a uniform. Such ancient properties are near the heart of the clown's humour. Boots and hats appear frequently in both novels and plays. Watt departs from Mr Knott's in an oversized boot and an undersized shoe; in *Waiting for Godot* Estragon is recurrently concerned with his boots; and in the second act the stage directions give thirty-three permutations for an exchange of three identical bowler hats. At his most extreme the clown ceases to even be mechanical and takes on the appearance of an object. Bergson also noted this tendency and stated that 'We laugh every time a person gives us the impression of being a thing.'[27] Here the Cartesian machine ceases to be active and becomes a mere object. It is in this situation that Watt first appears:

> Tetty was not sure whether it was a man or a woman. Mr Hackett was not sure that it was not a parcel, a carpet for example, or a roll of tarpaulin, wrapped up in dark paper and tied about the middle with a cord.[28]

Not for some minutes do they discover it to be Watt.

III

Throughout his long tradition the clown has always been inept in the restricting logic of the everyday where two and two always equal four. His anarchic excursions into the ordered, rational society that he finds about him threaten the accepted norms of that world. His own illogic, which he employs logically, is disruptive, and at its extreme point the laugh becomes a scream and the laughing are possessed by it. The wisdom of the satyr Silenus which Nietzsche saw at the root of the tragic experience also finds expression in the frequently grotesque and cruel world of the comic. Of this world the clown is the priest, even the seer. With his wit, his insight and also his despair, he attempts to recall society to an awareness as clear-sighted as his own. As such he is both feared and respected, and the temptation of the artist to cast himself in this role is strong; the ironic Pierrot of Laforgue or the destructive (and self-destructive) buffoon of Jarry are only two of his modern disguises. As the Polish critic and philosopher Kolakowski has written:

> The Clown is he who, although moving in high society, is not part of it, and tells unpleasant things to everybody in it; he, who disputes everything regarded as evident. He would not be able to do this, if he were part of that society himself; then he could at most be a drawing-room scandal-monger. The Clown must stand aside and observe good society from the outside,...in order to get to know its sacred cows, and have occasion to tell unpleasant things...The philosophy of Clowns is the philosophy that in every epoch shows up as doubtful what has been regarded as most certain; it reveals contradictions inherent in...what seems obvious common sense, and discovers truth in the absurd.[29]

Although the clown may invert logical reasoning, reveal an inability to understand the simplest rules of rational relationship, become entangled in endless semantic speculations and misunderstandings and even enter an hallucinatory world where everything appears immersed in a flood of real or feigned madness, his irrational insight only emphasizes the tenuous hold which the mind places upon the world. Like an irrational number he lurks in the interstices of the known and shows men the precariousness of their unstable order. And because these insights threaten both the rational order of the mind and the social order of the state, he is hounded like Malone or arrested like Molloy. The clown calls into question what the other members of his society would rather not tamper with, and so they try to ignore him or else divert him into sentimentality in the circus where his red nose becomes a children's sugar plum.

What occurs when a life built on rationalism encounters this dark and irrational side of being is the disaster that befalls Moran in his search for Molloy. Moran, who lives in a neat little cottage surrounded by a well-tended garden, goes about his business according to a series of well-worn axioms. He scrupulously performs his religious duties, expects his meals to be served on the stroke and characteristically takes a nap after eating. But when his mysterious master orders him to find Molloy he meets with catastrophe. The timeless rough-hewn figure of Molloy asserts itself into Moran's timebound, ordered world, and both Moran and his surroundings disintegrate until he is compelled to acknowledge the terrible wisdom of that side of life which he has so long denied. Moran's experience, which will be discussed in detail later, is an example of the comic at an extreme point of anguish.

Although Moran is an exception, he and his kind have generally shown themselves incapable of learning from the clown in the way Lear steeled himself to patience and listened to the barbed words of his fool. In *King Lear* Shakespeare departed from the convention of the court fool and created a character who, though speaking in the accustomed inverted syllogisms of his predecessors, was sufficiently human to overcome the barrier of his role and reveal the inner nature of the clown. The mask is withdrawn in *Lear* and the man beneath the motley revealed, as frightened and tormented as the princes who employ him but also more knowledgeable. Blinded by pomp and living in the illusions of the 'robes and furr'd gowns' which 'hide all', Lear comes to see into the heart of things partly through the intercession of the Fool who all along knows the nature of 'unaccommodated man'. Lear's own purgatorial journey across the heath moves through 'sovereign shame' and regeneration to the momentary bliss of being reunited with Cordelia, and then inexorably on to death. It is the path of the tragic hero. The path of the Fool is less magnificent but equally instructive. Out of his fear and his knowledge he discovers the language of the absurd where metaphysical truths lurk in the poetry of the irrational. The Fool is not tragic like Lear. The tragedian incautiously walks the brink which others can see, and his ignorant tempting of the abyss fills us with awe; but the Fool sees too clearly and is never, like Gloucester, blind when he saw. The lesson that Gloucester and Lear learn through suffering is also learnt by that debased relic of the tragic stage, Pozzo, who likewise goes blind and discovers that how he has lived has been mere illusion. His great speech which ends: 'They give birth astride of a grave, the light gleams an instant, then it's night once more',[30] is of the same order as Lear's great stage of fools and 'ripeness is all.' It is a lesson, magnificent in itself, but not one that the clown has to learn; Clov, Malone, Molloy etc. are all born knowing it.

It is the tragi-comedy of the Fool that finds expression in the Absurd and in particular in Beckett's work. There, the greatest tension is the divide between what man is and what he desires, between the actual facts of his characters' lives, the sealed series that bind them, and their longing to escape, to return to nothingness. For Beckett, as for Unamuno, 'consciousness is a disease'. In Beckett's case this applies both to the immediate condition of being forced to think here and now, and also to the dilemma of living under an awareness that it would be better for him to be nothing. Like Camus, who analysed the fundamental conditions of this outlook in *The Myth of Sisyphus*, Beckett is aware of the dreadful absurdity of modern existence. In one of his essays, written at the time when he first felt the impact of the absurd, Camus described the *angoisse* which lies near the centre of this standpoint: 'What is absurd is the confrontation of the irrational and the wild longing for clarity whose call echoes in the human heart.'[31] It is the conflict of men made aware of the limitations of their being, the dilemma that arises when reason is forced to recognize its frontiers. The inescapable knowledge of his finite condition recalls man to an awareness of his limitations yet he still desires the certainty and omnipotence he believes is his due. The annunciation of the absurd is a sudden unbidden questioning of existence and the meaning of the lives we lead, deadened as they are by the routine of modern industrial life. A man is in contact with the absurd when he senses his isolation both from other men and from the neutral earth. He suddenly sees himself a stranger here, and is awakened to a knowledge of decay and death which, because it is inescapable, renders the existence he has taken on trust, apparently valueless and futile. In a moment, perhaps when a man is tired and pauses for rest, the chain of mechanical responses that form his life are broken, the slumber of habit is disturbed and consciousness in its most acute form is awakened.

In *Proust* Beckett also describes what happens when habit is suddenly punctured. The 'compromise effected between the individual and his environment,' is supplanted by 'the perilous zones in the life of the individual...when for a moment the boredom of living is replaced by the suffering of being.'[32] Such a moment reveals the tension between the microcosm and the macrocosm, the absurdity of the finite striving under the shadow of the infinite. In the novels and plays his characters are continually recalled from the boredom of living in which they try to tell stories or occupy each other with badinage, to a suffering of being in which the futility and isolation of their lives is thrust upon them. The longing for clarity which lent an impetus to the centuries of rationalist confidence have similarly been replaced by a sobering recognition of things as they really are. Placed in a time of misery therefore, this 'suffering of being' has become more prevalent. It is the suspension of habit that makes the silence apparent and painful to the tramps in *Godot*. The fabric of diversions, games and stories which they attempt to build over the silence of their waiting is no longer powerful enough to sustain the illusion that the passing of time can be made pleasant. The 'suffering of being' asserts itself into their world in the silence out of which their words come and it is now inherent in the words themselves:

> EST: In the meantime let's try and converse calmly, since we're incapable of keeping silent.
> VLAD: You're right, we're inexhaustible.
> EST: It's so we won't think.
> VLAD: We have that excuse.
> EST: It's so we won't hear.
> VLAD: We have our reasons.
> EST: All the dead voices.
> VLAD: They make a noise like wings.
> EST: Like leaves.
> VLAD: Like sand.
> EST: Like leaves.
> .... Silence
>
> VLAD: What do they say?
> EST: They talk about their lives.
> VLAD: To have lived is not enough for them.
> EST: They have to talk about it.
> VLAD: To be dead is not enough for them.
> EST: It is not sufficient.
> Silence

VLAD: They make a noise like feathers.
EST: Like leaves.
VLAD: Like ashes.
EST: Like leaves.

Long silence

VLAD: Say something!
EST: I'm trying!

Long silence

VLAD (*in anguish*): Say anything at all![33]

The absurd situation is at root a tension between the temporal and the infinite and centres around the grudge which the whisky bears the decanter. It is, moreover, a dilemma not only confined to those writers for whom God is dead. Kierkegaard, many years before the meaning of his words became evident, declared: 'In truth no age has so fallen victim to the comic than this,' and explained that for the writer to be true to this time any serious description of it must use a fusion of comedy and pathos:

> Pathos that is not reinforced by the comic is illusion; the comic that is not reinforced by pathos is immaturity...Existence itself, the act of existing, is a striving as pathetic as it is comic; pathetic because the striving is infinite, i.e. directed towards infinity, an act of making itself infinite which is the summit of the pathetic; comic because such striving is self-contradictory. Seen pathetically a second has infinite value; seen comically, ten thousand years are a mere flash of foolery like yesterday; and yet time, in which the existing individual finds himself, is made up of such parts...[34]

This passage, from Kierkegaard's *Concluding Unscientific Postscript*, is of significance not only in regard to his own pseudonymous books. It helps to define the conditions under which many contemporary writers whose experience is essentially tragic, have expressed themselves in terms of the comic. The dilemma of the critic who attempts to find a place in traditional literary categories for the novels of Kafka or the plays of Pirandello, is without end. These works, and comparable masterpieces such as Dostoevsky's *The Possessed* or Faulkner's *As I Lay Dying*, clearly reveal the imprint of tragic experience. But this experience has found a new means of utterance, one that often appears comic but also testifies to an experience so bleak that tragedy, in the sense of being able to uplift and transfigure both the audience and the hero, becomes almost mild in the comparison.[35] This new tone is close to the heartbreak of the clown whose art is the exemplum of the comic and pathetic. As we have seen, both the clown and the Beckett hero are expressions of impotence, and repeated failure is essentially comic. When what is involved in this failure assumes metaphysical proportions, it is also deeply pathetic.

The laughter which the Absurd occasions is often closer to a cry of anguish than to an expression of genial good humour. Schopenhauer defined the nature of this bitter laugh as 'the sudden perception of incongruity' between our ideals and the reality about us. This notion of incongruity lies at the heart of the absurd with its dichotomy of the pathetic and the comic, and it is also the knowledge that leads Molloy to characterize all that is not God as muck. This disgust of the mystic without a centre, where the certainty of the past is no more and the certainty he seeks is not yet, is the most absurd of all positions and again emphasizes the pathetic nature of man's striving and the comic terms of its expression. The incongruity of the ideal beside the real is seen by Beckett's gallery of moribunds to be man's natural condition. Thirsting after certainty, eager to reach the Self or some other haven of arrival, he is conscious instead only of the decay of his body, the need to eat and excrete '(What matters is to eat and excrete,' says Malone, 'Dish and pot, dish and pot, these are the poles'.)[36] and the acute discomfort he receives from his ill-fitting boots.

IV

An incongruity between the ideal and the real lies at the root of Beckett's own definition of the laugh. In the first section of *Watt* Arsène, who reveals a deep concern with the arbitrary nature of cause and effect, concludes a moving description of the inescapable cycle of the seasons and of the transitory nature of all things living, with a laugh. This laugh, as one might expect from the context, is in no way humorous. Because Watt, who is listening, remains silent during this outburst Arsène proceeds to instruct him on the application of the three laughs. The passage sets out Beckett's conception of the comic as the vehicle of modern absurdity and succinctly describes the technique which supports the later novels and plays:

> Of all the laughs that strictly speaking are not laughs, but modes of ululation, only three I think need detain us, I mean the bitter, the hollow and the mirthless...the passage from the one to the other

> is the passage from the lesser to the greater, from the lower to the higher, from the outer to the inner, from the gross to the fine, from the matter to the form. The laugh that now is mirthless once was hollow, the laugh that once was hollow once was bitter. And the laugh that once was bitter? Eyewater, Mr Watt, eyewater...The bitter laugh laughs at that which is not good, it is the ethical laugh. The hollow laugh laughs at that which is not true, it is the intellectual laugh. Not good! Not true! Well well. But the mirthless laugh is the dianoetic laugh, down the snout—haw!—so. It is the laugh of laughs, the *risus purus,* the laugh laughing at the laugh, the beholding, the saluting of the highest joke, in a word the laugh that laughs—silence please—at that which is unhappy.[37]

Arsène—or Beckett—is here quite explicit about the application of each mode, and the ascent involved from one to another. The bitter and the hollow laughs point to the incongruity between an ideal good and an ideal true, and the reality of man's moral and intellectual pretensions. The bitter laugh, for example, is goaded into action during the final anarchic scene of *Malone Dies* when Lady Pedal, that biennual philanthropist, organizes an outing for the inmates of the lunatic asylum of St John of God. Lady Pedal who 'was all right in her head' and 'lived for doing good'[38] sets off with the warder, Lemuel, and five lunatics, among them Macmann, on a country outing. Hearing an insane roar from one of 'the little flock'[39] Lady Pedal assumes it is a sign of joy and appreciation, and encourages them by breaking into song herself. They go by boat to an island where Lady Pedal takes pity on her party. 'The poor creatures...let them loose.'[40] At this point Lemuel also goes insane and, cheered on by the patients, kills Lady Pedal's two servants with a hatchet. The good lady sees the bodies and falls, 'holding in her hand a tiny sandwich. She must have broken something in her fall, her hip perhaps, old ladies often break their hips, for no sooner had she recovered her senses than she began to moan and groan, as if she were the only being on the face of the earth deserving pity.'[41] Leaving her in agony on the beach Lemuel and the lunatics return to the boat and row out into the bay, at which point Malone, who is telling the story, brings it to a close by dying. The passage is narrated with characteristic brevity and its speed precludes any intrusion of pity. The result is the bitter laugh at its most acid. However, one is aware, and it is this which keeps the violence and outrage within bounds, that the satire is not gratuitous but springs from a hatred that things should be so. Beckett's characters shed tears over humanity in general but can spare none for individuals like the misguided Lady Pedal. Her disaster is negligible in a universal context and is brought on by her own philanthropic stupidity. What sympathy the hero has is reserved for all the nameless beings on earth whose suffering is the suffering of being alive.

The hollow laugh, aptly named to describe the emptiness of intellectual pretensions, is a step above the bitter. It laughs at that which is not true, and is especially potent against the rationalist presumption of believing that the world can be explained in intellectually satisfying terms. Thus Molloy describes how he dons the tramps' traditional insulation against the cold:

> The Times Literary Supplement was admirably adapted to this purpose, of a never failing toughness and impermeability. Even farts made no impression on it. I can't help it, gas escapes from my fundament on the least pretext, it's hard not to mention it now and then, however great my distaste. One day I counted them. Three hundred and fifteen farts in nineteen hours, or an average of over sixteen farts an hour. After all it's not excessive...Not even one fart every four minutes. It's unbelievable. Damn it, I hardly fart at all, I should never have mentioned it. Extraordinary how mathematics helps you to know yourself.[42]

This passage is an implicit condemnation of that well-known literary weekly whose impenetrable denseness, Molloy claims, is admirably suited to this unexpected purpose. More radical, however, is the condemnation of mathematics. Self-knowledge is the desire of every Beckett hero, but the ability of mathematics to further this search is splendidly debunked. The abstract science of the mind may analyse the regularity with which a man farts, but that is as close as it will come to a definition of the Self.

But it is the mirthless laugh which dies into silence that is the *risus purus* of Beckett's world. This is the laugh which laughs at the funniest of all jokes, the horror of life and human unhappiness. 'You're on earth, there's no cure for that,'[43] says Hamm; so much misery, so deep a knowledge of suffering denies the expressive grandeur of the tragic. It can only be apprehended through the laughter of the impotent clown which, as will emerge in the following discussion of the novels and plays, prevails over all other modes of expression. In a Godless world, this laughter directs itself against the deformed, decaying body of man; exposes the brutal source of his existence in the cycle of eating and excreting, and denigrates the emotion of love and the pathetic urge to procreate. The 'bitter' and the 'hollow' laughs mock man's own presumption and failure, the 'mirthless' goes deeper and sees him as the decrepit victim of mortality.

The Irish imagination has often tended to view the human animal in such debased terms. Beckett's exploration of the so-called sordid functioning of the body, although perhaps pursued in greater detail than elsewhere, is familiar when viewed in the same context as the writing of Synge and Swift. The bitter humour of *The Playboy of the Western World* and *The Tinker's Wedding* is close to the tragi-comedy of *All That Fall* or *Godot*. The Irish imagination habitually cuts through the tissue of rationalist illusion down to the intrinsic nature of the creature on two legs, man. Beckett's tramps are occupied with the same necessities as Synge's tinkers, and the dilemma of the man who seeks to stay where he is yet is not sure that it might not be better a little further along the road, is common to all of them. To examine existence at its lowest denominator is a peculiarly Irish characteristic.

It is the acid tongue and vehement condemnation of Swift, however, that is closest to Beckett. John Fletcher has already pointed to the stylistic similarities between the two writers, and behind Beckett's mirthless laugh one hears an echo of the Dean's own paeans of hatred. Beckett's alienated hero shuns the opposite sex with feelings as violent as Gulliver's on his return from the country of the Houyhnhnms:

> And when I began to consider, that by copulating with one of the Yahoo species I had become a parent of more, it struck me with the utmost shame, confusion and horror.
>
> As soon as I entered the house, my wife took me in her arms, and kissed me; at which, not having been used to the touch of that odious animal for so many years, I fell into a swoon for almost an hour...I could not endure my wife or children in my presence, the very smell of them was intolerable; much less could I suffer them to eat in the same room.[44]

It is irresistibly funny but also horrible. Gulliver's dread of copulation is comparable to Molloy's discomfort when he is made a captive by the enchanting Lousse. But what might otherwise be of only grotesque interest in Beckett and in Swift, becomes of consequence by the way in which both authors make their writing reflect a challenge on to the reader's complacent assumptions. Thus Gulliver's apparently amusing account of the structure of English society becomes radically changed in its passage from his lips to the incredulous ears of the king of Brobdingnag. The habits of the English outrage the monarch, and Swift intends Gulliver's innocent narrative to cause similar consternation in the mind of his reader. A comparable effect is created by

Molloy's account of his affair with Edith (or Ruth, he cannot quite remember) in a rubbish dump. As he describes it:

> She had a hole between her legs, oh not the bunghole I had always imagined, but a slit, and in this I put, or rather she put, my so-called virile member, not without difficulty, and I toiled and moiled until I discharged or gave up trying or was begged by her to stop. A mug's game in my opinion and tiring on top of that, in the long run.[45]

The experience affects him deeply because Edith, who always takes the initiative, tells him that what he has just done is 'love'. This assertion places the reader in a vulnerable position. Like Molloy, he is called upon to compare this grotesque débâcle, which Molloy describes, with his own, usually favourable, notions on the subject. Molloy dubiously asks, 'Have I ever known true love after all?' and wonders if Edith might not have been a man, holding his testicles in his hand to keep them out of the way. It is important to Molloy, as it should be to everyone, to know if he has experienced 'love' or not ('I would have made love with a goat just to know what true love was'[46]), especially when the reality belies the hoped-for expectation of joy. Molloy eventually concludes that though this method is inferior, on pleasurable grounds, to 'the so-called joys of self abuse,' it is yet the closest he has been to the real thing: 'Our commerce was not without tenderness, with trembling hands she cut my toe nails and I rubbed her rump with winter cream.'[47] Enough has been said, however, to undermine Molloy's conclusion. Both the hero and the reader have been placed in a very unsure position, just as Swift manouvered Gulliver into a world where all previous certainties were questionable. The reader has been forced to reconsider his previous assumptions, as the reader of Swift must resolve whether or not man is truly the 'odious animal' that he appears to some of Gulliver's interlocutors.

The debt to Swift, however, may lie even deeper than devices of style and technique. In *More Pricks Than Kicks* Beckett calls a particularly aged and weak character a Struldbrug. The Struldbrugs were perhaps the oddest, and certainly the most pathetic, race that Gulliver met with in the course of his travels. Their uniqueness consisted in their being immortal. Gulliver, in his innocence, envies them their fate, and imagines the wisdom and security which immortality must bestow on a man. He conceives a state in which the elders are free of the fear of death, and pass their time instructing others in the way of virtue. But his guide is quick to dissuade him. The immortality of the Struldbrugs is not a liberation; it creates only a longing for extinction. For, in addition to the average course of physical decline, the infinity of years after four score bring, not peace, but a still more horrible succession of deformities. Their state is a perpetual agony of disintegration, not the eternal youth Gulliver imagines:

> He said they commonly acted like mortals, till about thirty years old, after which by degrees they grow melancholy and dejected, increasing in both till they came to fourscore. This he learned from their own confession: for otherwise there not being above two or three of that species born in an age, they were too few to form a general observation by. When they came to fourscore years, which is reckoned the extremity of living in this country, they had not only all the follies and infirmities of other old men, but many more which arose from the dreadful prospect of never dying. They were not only opinionative, peevish, covetous, morose, vain, talkative, but incapable of friendship, and dead to all natural affection, which never descended below their grandchildren. Envy and impotent desires are their prevailing passions ...They have no remembrance of anything but what they learned and observed in their youth and middle age, and even that is very imperfect...At ninety they lose their teeth and hair, they have at that age no distinction of taste, but eat and drink whatever they can get, without relish of appetite. The diseases they were subject to continue without increasing or diminishing. In talking they forget the common appellation of things, and the names of persons, even of those who are their nearest friends and relations. For the same reason, they can never amuse themselves with reading, because their memory will not serve to carry them from the beginning of a sentence to the end; and by this defect they are deprived of the only entertainment whereof they might otherwise be capable.[48]

What with his diseased body, his failed memory and numbed senses. the Struldbrug is a distinct antecedent of the later Beckett hero. The early desire of Belacqua and Murphy, who see happiness as a life spent dreaming over the life just lived, becomes, in the trilogy, a longing to cease, a thirst for extinction. Consciousness that cannot conceive of itself as non-existing becomes pathetic and absurd. It is this condition, explored briefly by Swift in his fable of the Struldbrugs, that Beckett explores in ever more desperate terms. Malone in bed or the Unnamable in his pot have no memory of events that have occurred after their youth or middle age, but live in an instantaneous decay where the body dissolves and the words struggle towards an end as impossible as the elusive term of the figures after a decimal point. The Unnamable's longing to be nothing and the direction of the digits after, for example, 4·9999, both reach out to the same impossible consummation. It is the 'calvary with no limits to its stations and no hope of crucifixion,'[49] the purgatory of the Struldbrugs. Beckett transforms Swift's fable into a tragic portrait of the terms of being where, beneath the impotent exterior, and the dereliction and the struggle of the mind for a place of rest, lies the agony of 'those who are condemned without any fault of their own to a perpetual continuance in the world'.[50]

V

The impotence that concerns Beckett is mental as well as physical. The fallibility of the body soon ceases to be of paramount importance, and the tenacious, recurrent problems of the mind come to the fore. Beckett has renounced his own claim to erudition and uses the large body of knowledge at his disposal only as an incidental means of expression. His attitude is reminiscent of the wandering scholar. The depth and extent of his knowledge is undeniable: it is apparent in his early academic achievements, in the various translations he has made from several languages, and, most evidently, in the texture of his works themselves. But Beckett prefers the role of academic clown in which he can use his erudition, not as Joyce did to cram everything he knew into his works, but to laugh at it and reveal its inherent impotence. Thus he has transferred the area of the clown's activity from the circus ring to the arena of the mind. He makes the scenario of *Endgame* represent this skull, a huge grey dome of emptiness with two windows looking out on to the greater emptiness of the world outside like eyes; or actually describes it in *The Unnamable*:...'which is perhaps merely the inside of my distant skull where once I wandered, now am fixed, lost for tininess...and ever murmuring my old stories, my old story, as if it were the first time.'[51]

All his characters are erstwhile scholars, but they remember that time, if at all, as one which was in general ill spent. None of them, except perhaps Belacqua in his desultory study of Dante, expect anything of their knowledge; it is one more layer of illusion between them and their Selves. Molloy gives a fairly standard resumé of their main intellectual pursuits:

> Yes, I once took an interest in astronomy, I don't deny it. Then it was geology that killed a few years for me. The next pain in the balls was anthropology and the other disciplines, such as psychiatry, that are

> connected with it, disconnected, then connected again, according to the latest discoveries. What I liked in anthropology was its inexhaustible faculty of negation, its relentless definition of man, as though he were no better than God, in terms of what he is not...Oh I've tried everything. In the end it was magic that had the honour of my ruins, and still today, when I walk there, I find its vestiges.[52]

At the time of *Murphy* Beckett's hero still has an interest in astronomy and astrology. Celia first sees Murphy gazing at the sky, and the whole of his chequered search for employment is based upon a series of astrological prognostications made up for him by a swami in Berwick market. By the time of *The Unnamable* or *How it is*, however, knowledge is only a murmur of 'old words' that appears unsummoned ('the humanities I had my God and with what flashes of geography'),[53] and surprises the hero by its tenacity and stubborn refusal to remain forgotten.

Beckett's own personal erudition cannot be easily denied either. His works contained repeated references to the thinkers and writers who concern him most, but their presence (apart from in the early stories) is always subordinate to the purpose of the text. Often they are only introduced to reveal their total inadequacy as solutions to the general dilemma of living. Occasionally a passing reference catches at a thread of old knowledge, as when Molloy alludes to Balzac's *Le Peau de Chagrin* or Malone describes 'this window that sometimes looks as if it were painted on the wall, like Tiepolo's ceiling at Wurzburg' (also reminding one that in their day the tramps were great travellers). The most repeated allusions, however, are to Dante, the Cartesians and the Bible, but in these cases the original has become so integrated into Beckett's own imaginative creation, that it appears as proper in the new mould as it was in the old.[54]

The attention of the scholar is also discernible in Beckett's technique. The very idea of his task, that of a necessary pensum set for him at birth, is reminiscent of the scribe's detailed labour. The task is then complicated by the translation of the original either from French into English or from English into French. The interminable succession of words appears, moreover, to have been set down in order to be judged; the testament of a lifetime recorded for examination, though by whom remains obscure. This intimation is borne out by the particulars. The disquisition of Louit in *Watt*, already mentioned, has the aridity of a paper drawn up for learned perusal. Lucky's famous speech with its references to the authorities 'Puncher and Wattmann' has also been likened to a parody of a Master's Oral. *More Pricks*

Than Kicks is cross-referenced like a learned text, and the poem *Whoroscope*, which has almost as many footnotes as it has lines, is impenetrable without the aid of Adrien Baillet's 1691 *Life of Descartes* from which it arose. Beckett has turned pedantry into art. The texture of the writing not only testifies to an obsession with the ordering of minute details, it also reflects the cast of his character's minds. Watt's painful analysis of all the logical possibilities suggested by a particular problem has already been noted, as has the way in which the writing precisely reflects these obsessive researches. The other heroes rarely carry out their examination of experience in such rigid, mechanical terms, but on several occasions they draw up a list of questions connected with a dilemma that particularly concerns them. Moran, near the close of his disastrous journey, poses sixteen questions of a theological nature that have preoccupied him strangely. Among them are: 'Did Mary conceive through the ear, as Augustine and Adobard assert? Does nature observe the sabbath? What was God doing with himself before the creation?' and 'Is it true that Judas' torments are suspended on Saturdays?'[55] This collection of questions, agitated by superstition, Biblical inconsistency and dogma, is followed by a further seventeen (Beckett lists them in full) relating to Moran's own immediate experience. Each question is impossible to answer in rational terms, and the passage is yet another example of the hero's determination to use the disabled means of analysis for an explanation of extra-rational certainties. The hero, however, is at heart aware of his mental impotence and variously acknowledges the inherent futility of his labours. 'But deep down I didn't give a fiddler's curse,' says Molloy as he ends the monumental intellectual epic of the sucking stones.

Before he entirely buried his own learning within the distrustful pages of his novels, Beckett turned aside and wrote the short monograph on Proust. This book, first published in 1931, seems to have been a study he needed to write. Written under no duress from any established body, at a time when the author's name was not sufficiently known to ensure its success, the style reveals a highly individual approach, and in many of the asides with which the book is littered Beckett is already experimenting with the devastating effects of the clown's mask. In *Proust* one discovers many of the ideas and themes that appear in the mature novels and plays: like Gide's *Dostoevsky* it tells us as much about the author as about the subject. That is not to declare it valueless as a study of Proust; its insights are many and illuminating, but the force of the writing and an obvious commitment to some of the questions involved show that Beckett's interest is personal as well as exegetical. He is not interested in the Proust of legend nor the chronicler of French high society. What concerns him is the perpetual conflict between time, habit and memory, and the individual's attempt to surmount it towards an immediate awareness of the Self. In addition, what appeals to him is Proust's 'Impressionism,' by which he means the technique of escaping from causality and the examination of experience in depth, not extension.

Proust's creatures, says Beckett, are the victims of time: 'There is no escape from the hours and the days.'[56] Their aspirations are condemned to disappointment because attainment ('The identification of the subject with the object of his desire') is betrayed by the passing of time in which 'The subject has died—and perhaps many times—on the way.'[57] The Self, where it impinges on time, is in a constant state of flux, and the individual holds within himself many selves, each changing under the influence of time:

> The individual is the seat of a constant process of decantation, decantation from the vessel containing the fluid of future time, sluggish, pale and monochrome, to the vessel containing the fluid of past time, agitated and multicoloured by the phenomena of its hours.[58]

The attempt to reach the absolute reality outside time and space where Proust believed the human essence would be found, involves at least a suspension of the action of time. As long as the individual remains in time he is denied a full awareness of his own Self in as much as that Self has been lost in the unreal distortion of the past. In addition, the individual as he stands, is not his true Self but a variety of changing selves mutating according to the circumstances of any given moment in time. Both Beckett and Proust attempt to reach this final, real Self, whose essence would be reached in an instantaneous moment, in a leap beyond the immediate fetters of time. But whereas Proust felt he had reached a solution through his idea of 'involuntary memory' Beckett cannot entirely concur.

Proust's solution creates the dialogue between Memory and Habit—both 'attributes of the time cancer'. Habit is the compromise between man and reality in the name of dullness and for the creation of boredom. Man capitulates to habit and distorts his view of reality. However, there are interstices between man's successive compromises, moments when he is especially vulnerable and susceptible to reality. These are the moments when 'the boredom of living is replaced by the suffering of being...Suffering...opens a window on the real and is the main condition of the artistic experience.'[59] It is also during these moments that man is most open to the action of 'involuntary memory'.

Proust and Beckett distinguish between two types of memory, voluntary and involuntary. The conscious life is only in contact with the practical world, with the uninspired artefacts of existence such as bicycle bells, boots and bowler hats. This paraphenalia of existence is the surface domain of time-bound voluntary memory: it is the area in which the 'uniform memory of intelligence...can be relied on to produce for our gratified inspection those impressions of the past that were consciously and intelligently formed.'[60] Voluntary memory is only an extension of habit, and its consoling images can be called upon almost at will. However, beneath this level of consciousness there lies 'the ultimate and inaccessible dungeon' where time cannot enter. Here 'is stored the essence of ourselves, the best of our many selves... the best because accumulated shyly and painfully under the nose of our vulgarity.'[61] This part of the Self, which lies deeper than the habitual experience of eating, working and sleeping, is only unlocked by the intercession of involuntary memory. Yet because we are not conscious of this underlying dimension and were not alert to its formation we cannot call on it at will. We can only wait—as for Godot—for the Proustian moment of revelation when 'by some miracle of analogy the central impression of a past sensation recurs an immediate stimulus.' At such a moment, for example, when Marcel eats the madeleine dipped in tea and rediscovers the lost paradise of his Combray childhood, time is suspended and for Proust at least, one is given a glimpse of the pure Self. As Beckett describes this process:

> The most trivial experience...is imprisoned in a vase filled with a certain perfume and a certain colour and raised to a certain temperature. These vases are suspended along the height of our years, and, not being accessible to our intelligent memory, are in a sense immune, the purity of their climatic content is guaranteed by forgetfulness, each one is kept at its distance, at its date. So that when the imprisoned microcosm is besieged in the manner described, we are flooded by a new air and a new perfume (new precisely because already experienced) and we breathe the true air of Paradise, of the only Paradise that is not the dream of a madman, the Paradise that has been lost.[62]

Beckett, although he may have looked to involuntary memory for a solution to the problem of the Self at that time, cannot accept the Proustian synthesis in its entirety. It does appear in his later works—as in the passage on his early childhood already quoted, or in Nell's memory of Lake Como ('It was deep, deep. And you could see to the bottom. So white. So clean');[63] and Krapp has attempted to crystallize the past into an eternal present on his tape-recorder—but in general Beckett comes to find Proust's methods inconclusive. Involuntary memory may recreate the past Self, momentarily liberated from time, but by now the Self has become other than it then was. The irony of Krapp lies in the discrepancy between the hopeful voice imprisoned on the tape, and the degenerate figure who listens, mesmerized by the memory of a promise he has now lost. A succession of timeless moments may reveal the purity of these hidden memories, but the final release of the Self is still not attained except by proxy; the dark of habit soon reforms across the illuminating suffering of being. *Proust* acknowledges the efforts of an honoured forbear: the novels and plays search for an alternative solution to the great division between the finite and the infinite.

Other of Beckett's preoccupations make their appearance in this study of Proust. The most evident is 'that desert of loneliness and recrimination that men call love,'[64] which brings with it the attendant concerns of isolation, non-communication and the discontinuity of the personality. He examines Marcel's love for Albertine and discovers the tragic impossibility of fulfilment. The individual who loves is, through his immersion in time, in a constant state of flux. Proust, in his honest analysis, discovered that our emotions are composed of an infinity of successive loves, each of which is transient, although by their uninterrupted multitude they give us the impression of continuity and the illusion of unity. It follows that if the continuity and unity of emotion is an illusion, the unity of the person who suffers those emotions must be an illusion too. Furthermore, the beloved is seen as only a figment of the imagination, an externalization of our own personal needs and desires. Our subjective needs demand an object which we choose from an anonymous crowd (as Marcel picked Albertine among all the girls at Balbec), and invest it with our own conflicting emotions of desire and jealousy. Fulfilment is denied the lover, because neither he nor the beloved can achieve constancy in the face of flux. Beckett sees in Proust the seed of his own later hatred of love. Love gives an appearance of unity, holds out a hope of joy and represents a demand for the whole, but its end is always disaster. The lover makes the sudden discovery that behind the innumerable illusions of love lies the nothingness of the void. At the heart of both Beckett and Proust is the knowledge that in the act of physical possession, the possessor actually possesses nothing.

Love emphasizes the 'irremediable solitude to which every human being is condemned.'[65] It throws the fragmented 'I' back from its hope of unity into the knowledge of its inconstant isolation. Nevertheless it is a more respectable mode of communication than friendship. Love, says Beckett after Proust, is a function of man's sadness, and the failure to possess may have the nobility of the tragic. Friendship, on the other hand, is 'the attempt to communicate where no communication is possible.' It 'is merely a simian vulgarity, or horribly comic.'[66] These attitudes of personal relationships, first stated in *Proust*, help to explain the feelings which Beckett's heroes have for the rest of mankind. The determination of the hero to maintain his isolation, in the novels, and the ambivalent love-hate relationship of the series of pairs, in the plays, are illuminated by this discussion of love and friendship in *Proust*.

Finally one notes that Beckett applauds Proust for his 'Impressionism'. In his discussion of time, memory and habit Beckett discovers an aesthetic that makes for a greater understanding of his own work. In *Waiting for Godot* Vladimir reminds himself 'But habit is a great deadener.'[67] Habit is used by man to distort reality; it is an expression of his cowardice. Man uses habit to see the new, not as it is but as he would like it to be. However, in those transitory moments between the boredom of living and the suffering of being man is also open to the intrusion of beauty and spiritual enlargement. Beckett considers Proust fortunate in having both a defective habit and a poor memory. His disposition to the workings of involuntary memory have brought him into contact with the intermittences of being that transcend the norm of the voluntary. Beckett sees here the crux of the creative experience. The world is not the rational construction of causality which habit has attempted to create and because of this Beckett opposes the realist authors for he considers them the prisoners of habit and voluntary memory. They seek to create a world of cause and effect and therefore describe only the surface: he has nothing but contempt for 'the literature that "describes", for the realists and the naturalists worshipping the offal of experience, prostrate before the epidermis and swift epilepsy, and content to transcribe the surface, the façade, behind which the Idea is prisoner.'[68] The world of the realist creates a false sense of security. It shows the novelist finding harmony with rationalism, in the determination to make the world intelligible through the erroneous technique of causality. Rather, the artist discovers the world in the moments of suffering when, for a moment, the compromise of habit is broken. For Beckett-Proust 'the only possible spiritual development is in the sense of depth...the work of art...(is) neither created nor chosen, but discovered, uncovered, excavated, pre-existing in the artist, a law of his nature.[69]

Beckett admires both Proust and Dostoevsky for the way in which they have gone behind the surface after the Idea and yet avoided the opposite extreme of arid abstraction. The impurity of the will does not enter into their aesthetics—'The Proustian stasis is contemplative, a pure act of understanding, will-less'—for the will is a subject of the intelligence and habit and as such gravitates towards causality. The ideal of the artist is he who sees what he does see and not what he feels he ought to see (i.e. to bring it into accordance with his habit), he who acknowledges the irrational flux of being and restrains the temptation to apply causality to all experience. The 'impressionist' is intuitive, not afraid of being misunderstood and entirely faithful to his experience:

> By his (Proust's) impressionism I mean his non-logical statement of phenomena in the order and exactitude of their perception, before they have been distorted into intelligibility in order to be forced into a chain of cause and effect. The painter Elstir is the type of the impressionist, stating what he sees and not what he knows he ought to see: for example, applying urban terms to the sea and marine terms to the town, so as to transmit his intuition of their homogeneity. And we are reminded of Schopenhauer's definition of the artistic procedure as 'the contemplation of the world independently of the principle of reason'. In this connection Proust can be related to Dostoyevski, who states his characters without explaining them. It may be objected that Proust does little else but explain his characters. But his explanations are experimental and not demonstrative. He explains them in order that they may appear as they are—inexplicable. He explains them away.[70]

Beckett's description of Proust's aesthetic now appears to stand as an introduction to his own creative work. At a time when his own plays and novels were still unwritten he explored the process which he was to follow faithfully for over thirty years. If the reader of *Proust* takes nothing else from the study but the knowledge that Beckett is a writer who states what he sees and not what he thinks he ought to see, he will have started to understand the body of work before him. Beckett has stated at the outset of his career that the only possible spiritual development is in depth, and that 'The artistic tendency is not expansive but a contraction.'[71] This belief supports his recurrent endeavour in an apparently limited area of experience. His novels and plays form a closed circuit, each one an attempt to descend to a slightly deeper level than the one before. His works can be seen as a series of which each is a continuation and a growth from its predecessor. There is a beginning and then each successive book is another integer in a line whose end and release is unknown. They represent an urge to pare away all the extraneous offal that lies both outside and within the words, and aspire to a purity whose reticence is not unexpected. From the bustle and sterility of *More Pricks Than Kicks* they descend to the mathematical conclusion of the recently published *Imagination Dead Imagine*. They revolve round certain given objects—bicycles, boots, stub-ends of pencils—and a limited group of memories. Just as the hero himself decays from a reluctantly active young Dubliner to a legless and anonymous figure confined to a pot, so the memories become briefer and the bicycles disappear, leaving behind only a rusted bell to be viewed with nostalgia. A character from an earlier book may reappear in one of the later volumes, and each individual 'I', whether he be Watt, Molloy or the Unnamable, can call upon the experiences of his predecessors. Malone, as he lies waiting for death, is aware of this kinship. He even wonders if he may not be the last: 'Then it will be all over with the Murphys, Merciers, Molloys, Morans and Malones, unless it goes on beyond the grave.'[72] They form a 'gallery of moribunds' involved in the writing of stories, torrents of words that may, in the end, add up to *the story*.

The narrative which they successively tell is that of a rootless, detached and ineffectual young man at Trinity College who, after failing miserably in human intercourse (the stories), turns his back on his place of birth (*Echo's Bones*). He wanders for some time on the Continent and in London (*Murphy*), and, looking back on Ireland, discovers within himself a series of mental preoccupations which are to concern him for the rest of his days (*Watt*). He travels for a while with a friend (the jettisoned *Mercier et Camier*) but leaves him to go in search of his mother (*Molloy*). He does not find her but makes his way, in a condition of ever increasing decay, to a room where he settles down to die (*Malone Dies*). Shortly after arriving at the impasse of a death which his consciousness survives (*The Unnamable*) he discovers a need for companionship, and there is a slight shift in the direction of the writing towards the plays and *How it is*. It is to a study of this journey in contraction that we must now turn, making the descent, book by book, into the centre of Beckett's world.

PART TWO

THREE: BELACQUA

'Brother,' said he, 'what use to go up yet?'

DANTE

I

IN 1934 Beckett published a group of ten short stories under the general (and suggestive) title, *More Pricks Than Kicks*. The stories originally formed part of an unfinished and unpublished first novel, *Dream of Fair to Middling Women*, an apprentice work which was begun and abandoned during his post-Dublin *wanderjahre*. The *Dream* furnished Beckett with the hero and several episodes in the stories, and a passage from it was also published in *transition* under the title *Sedendo et Quiescendo*.[1] In their present form the stories are uneven in quality and evidently the work of a young man intent on exploring the possibilities of his learning and early impressions. Nevertheless *More Pricks Than Kicks* is remarkable for the way in which it already suggests the majority of Beckett's later preoccupations, and at least two of the stories reveal the presence of an individual and disturbing sensibility. They trace the career of Belacqua Shuah—student, philanderer, failure and anti-hero—through a series of grotesque situations that end with his accidental and needless death upon an operating table. The various stories unite to create the total personality of Belacqua, the initial guise of the Beckett hero, whose origins and nature are important to one's understanding of his later evolution. Indeed, much that seems obscure in Beckett's mature writing is illuminated by the name which his first hero inherits.

The opening lines of the first story, *Dante and the Lobster*, read: 'It was morning and Belacqua was stuck in the first of the canti of the moon. He was so bogged that he could neither move backward or forward.' Here, on his first appearance, the Beckett hero is discovered in his now familiar condition of stasis. He is, moreover, reading Dante, and his own Christian name has been taken from the fourth canto of the *Purgatorio*. The original Belacqua was in real life a lute maker of Florence whom Dante had known as notorious for his indolence and apathy. In the poem he has been placed on the second terrace of Ante-Purgatory, the dwelling of the late-repentant who have postponed their reconciliation with God until the last moment—*in articulo mortis*. As a punishment they are obliged to wait at the foot of the mountain through a time as long as their lives on earth, enduring the indolence in which they used to indulge, before making the ascent that will prepare them for Paradise. In the relevant lines Virgil has just warned Dante not to rest before his journey's end when the poets are arrested by a voice:

> He'd hardly spoken when, from somewhere fast
>   Beside us, came a voice which said: 'Maybe
>   Thou'lt need to sit ere all that road is passed.'
>
> At this we both glanced round inquiringly,
>   And on our left observed a massive boulder,
>   Which up till then we had not chanced to see.
>
> This, when explored, revealed to the beholder
>   A group of persons lounging in the shade,
>   As lazy people lounge, behind its shoulder.
>
> And one of them, whose attitude displayed
>   Extreme fatigue, sat there and clasped his knees,
>   Drooping between them his exhausted head.
>
> 'Oh good my lord,' said I, 'pray look at this
>   Bone-lazy lad, content to sit and settle
>   Like sloth's own brother taking of his ease!'
>
> Then he gave heed, and turning just a little
>   Only his face upon his thigh, he grunted:
>   'Go up then, thou, thou mighty man of mettle.'
>
> I knew him then; and proved that, though I panted
>   Still from the climb, I was not so bereft
>   Of breath, I could not reach him if I wanted.

When I drew near him he would scarcely shift
His head to say: 'Nay, hast thou, really though,
Grasped why the sun's car drives upon thy left?'

My lips twitched at the grudging speech, and slow
Gestures. 'Belacqua,' I began, 'I see
I need not grieve for thee henceforward; no.

But tell me: why dost thou resignedly
Sit here? Is it for escort thou must wait?
Or have old habits overtaken thee?'

'Brother,' said he, 'what use to go up yet?
He'd not admit me to the cleansing pain,
That bird of God who perches at the gate.

My lifetime long the heavens must wheel again
Round me, that to my parting hour put off
My healing sighs; and I meanwhile remain

Outside, unless prayer hasten my remove—
Prayer from a heart in grace; for who sets store
By other kinds, which are not heard above?'[2]

This passage evidently made a deep impression on Beckett during his own reading of Dante for its influence is discernible throughout his works. Dante's Belacqua, who does not appear unduly distressed by his penance, becomes the prototype for all Beckett's heroes and the persistence of his image, from the first stories to the plays some twenty years later, suggests that his significance exceeds the youthful plagiarism of his name. In fact the true importance of Belacqua in Beckett's work is not yet apparent in *More Pricks Than Kicks* where he appears as a character: only in the trilogy does Beckett begin to explore the real implications of his waiting and remembering at the foot of Mt Purgatory.

Belacqua's favoured position, described in the fourth verse above, is adopted by his namesake in the story *A Wet Night.* Returning home after a miserable and intemperate evening he is afflicted with severe stomach pains and 'disposed himself in the knee-and-elbow position on the pavement.' Beckett's Belacqua is by nature 'sinfully ignorant, bogged in indolence, asking nothing better than to stay put', and if he does not lie under the shadow of a rock he finds an agreeable substitute in a low public house where he is not known. It is in such a place that he makes his apathetic and reluctant attempt at salvation with its overtones of the theology on which Dante based his fourth canto. In the story *Ding-Dong* he is approached by a hatless woman who offers him two seats in heaven: ' "Seats in heaven," she said in a white voice, "tuppence a piece, four for a tanner." ' Belacqua is struck by her face, 'it was so full of light...it bore no trace of suffering and in this alone it might be said to be a notable face.' The woman persists and, mortified by the stares of the other drinkers, Belacqua overcomes his indolence. He buys four, a needless extravagance, and asks: 'have you got them on you?' In reply the woman tells him that heaven goes round and round: ' "Rowan," she said, dropping the d's and getting more of a swing into the slogan, "rowan an' rowan an' rowan." ' Her words recall Belacqua's explanation to Dante: that the heavens must revolve about him his lifetime long before St Peter will admit him to 'the cleansing pain.'

Although Belacqua, as a character, disappears with the stories, his name is evoked as that of a respected antecedent in several of the later novels. *Molloy* opens with the hero in the shadow of a rock under which 'I crouched like Belacqua, or Sordello, I forget,'[3] and Murphy has what he terms his 'Belacqua fantasy' in which he dreams of being released by death into the inaction of Ante-Purgatory. There he will sit in 'embryanal repose, looking down at dawn across the reeds to the trembling of the austral sea.'[4] The 'knee-and-elbow position,' or state of 'embryanal repose,' approximates to the foetal image of the unborn. (Peggy Guggenheim records that Beckett himself 'retained a terrible memory of life in his mother's womb.')[5] The security and apparent peace of this position attract almost all the heroes in moments of especial suffering or at the height of their longing for nothingness. To be in the womb is, of all the attitudes they have experienced, the nearest terrestrial analogy to the timeless and spaceless ideal of being a speck in the Void. Belacqua declares, 'I want very much to be back in the caul, on my back in the dark forever;' Watt is so overcome by weariness that he 'settled himself at the edge of the path, with his hat pushed back and his bags beside him, and his knees drawn up, and his arms on his knees, and his head on his arms;'[6] and in *The Unnamable* the most extreme incarnation of the hero, Worm, is literally in embryo, enclosed in the womb. He is motionless and perhaps timeless but not ideally so: as Beckett ironically observes, 'it would be to sign his life-warrant to stir from where he is.'[7] Once again the Dante prototype is recalled—'Brother,' said he, 'what use to go up yet?'

The significance of Beckett's debt to Dante, however, transcends the particulars of Belacqua's position in the shadow of the rock. His heroes are suspended between time and timelessness, fragment and whole, actual and ideal. They have an impression of that final, glorious release towards which they struggle, but are halted at an impasse which forever denies them entrance. They have been expelled into life and so committed 'the original and eternal sin ... the sin of having been born.'[8] At first their condition appears reminiscent of Milton's fallen angels, scouring hell in search of relief only to discover everything inhospitable, monstrous and perverse. The angels find their progress barred in every direction and the Miltonic 'mournful gloom' seems to foreshadow the perpetual greyness of the Beckett landscape. Satan's followers, like Beckett's hero, search for a dimension of life (or death) that will give purpose and meaning to their exile from Paradise. Some entertain themselves with feats of arms, some by celebrating their heroic deeds in song, while:

> Others apart sat on a hill retir'd,
> In thoughts more elevate, and reason'd high
> Of Providence, Foreknowledge, Will and Fate,
> Fixt Fate, Free Will, Foreknowledge absolute,
> And found no end, in wan'dring mazes lost.[9]

They turn in despair to the succour of reason and find that without the grace of God reason not only does not remove their problems but complicates them still further. All Hells have one quality in common. Whether the punishment is in the mind or the body nature is irrevocably a meaningless round, and endless marking-time. In hell the sinners symbolize their sin throughout eternity, perpetually relive the past or else stay fixed—grotesquely mounted specimens—in horrible parody of their guilt, tormented by a memory of 'the only Paradise that is not the dream of a madman, the Paradise that has been lost.'[10]

Such a place seems at first to compare with the futile, distorted activity or sterile inactivity of Beckett's world. In Dante, the grovelling of the Gluttonous and the aimless fisticuffs of the Wrathful in the Marsh of the Styx, the ceaseless change and interchange of forms among the Thieves, and the Violent against God, Nature and Art stretched on a desert of burning sand, appear to stand behind the geography of *How it is*, the flux in identity of the hero of *The Unnamable*, and the plight of Winnie in *Happy Days* respectively. But the transference of the Belacqua episode into Beckett's thought belies this apparently feasible and frequently made identification as to the location of his world. Beckett's heroes are not in Hell but Purgatory: a Purgatory of waiting on the verge of timelessness. It is a grimmer place than that imagined by Dante and at times—in *Endgame* or *How it is*—almost indistinguishable from Hell. In Dante's *Purgatorio* eventual ascent, the toil uphill, was certain for even the most indolent of its inhabitants, but in Beckett there is no certitude; only the confusion and doubt of a limbo with no known end and no discernible path. What perhaps misleads is the appearance of Belacqua, a character from the *Purgatorio*, as one of Beckett's central images, against a landscape which often relies heavily upon the imagery of the *Inferno*. Yet in Hell one pursues one's monotonous activities without reason through all eternity, while in Beckett's cosmology a shred of hope remains. Paolo and Francesca, tossed and flailed upon a howling wind, are for ever hopeless; the hero of the trilogy, aware that one of the thieves was saved even upon the cross, and prompted by the mysterious intervention of the Hypothetical Imperative, still anticipates an ultimate relief.

The Beckett hero progresses to the edge of timelessness where he is compelled to wait, like Hamm, for 'the moments to mount up to a life.'[11] Again Dante's Belacqua provides the image, Belacqua who is also trapped at an impasse by his late repentance and unable to ascend. Belacqua's dilemma, that of a man whose life is over but not yet ended, reliving his existence on his foothold at the base of Mt Purgatory, becomes the dilemma of the hero in the trilogy. For example Molloy who puzzles over the contradiction of his life as something over and yet continuing—'My life, now I speak of it as something over, now as a joke which still goes on, and it is neither, for at the same time it is over and it goes on, and is there any tense for that?'[12] and Malone who, on the brink of departure, goes over his life yet again.

In the end Beckett's heroes are left waiting, like the figures in Dante's Ante-Purgatory, for the gate to be unlocked and the angel to guide them on their way to Paradise, but with the important difference that waiting remains the limit of their progress. The stasis is unrevoked; the angel, like Godot, does not come.

VLAD: Well? Shall we go?
EST: Yes, let's go.

They do not move

CURTAIN[13]

Yet neither does their life in time regress; earth is the purgatorial now between before and after, the contingent present encircled by the void. Out of Belacqua's inactive position overlooking what Beckett calls 'the austral sea,' emerges the tremor of an archetypal association which extends this image of Purgatory. For the sea, which stretches away from the earth into the unknown and against which man is as nothing, has repeatedly aroused overtones of the eternal. On earth man is finite—three score years and ten—but in the sea he finds an image for the eternity from which he has come and to which he will soon return. From the Epic of Gilgamesh to Baudelaire's *Le Voyage* the earth-confining sea has been viewed with awe, and poetry has often given to it a significance that outweighs even its natural, implacable force. The hero of the Gilgamesh epic crosses the ocean to find Utnapishtim the Faraway who alone knows the secret of everlasting life, and Baudelaire enlists the aid of Death himself to weigh anchor and captain the ship that will take him 'Into the unknown in search of the new!' The rock where Belacqua and Beckett's heroes shelter also appears to be on the verge of this eternal ocean of release. Several of the heroes make their way to the sea-shore where they experience moments of unusual peace. Beckett himself stands there in the four, short Dieppe poems;[14] Henry in *Embers*, attempts to contact the dead from his past while the waves claw at the shingle on which he sits; and Malone ends the story of Macmann with the boatful of lunatics drifting out into the immensity of the ocean, significantly at the moment when he himself crosses over from life into death.[15]

But the most trenchant of these examples is Molloy's journey to the seaside in search of sucking stones. He recalls that 'Much of my life has ebbed away before this shivering expanse,'[16] and describes some of the advantages of life on the sea-shore: the excitement of digging holes in the sand, how one's sight improves with the uninterrupted view, and the pleasure of living in caves. Then briefly he remembers an instance when he journeyed on the sea itself:

> And I too once went forth on it, in a sort of oarless skiff, but I paddled with an old bit of driftwood. And I sometimes wonder if I ever came back, from the voyage. For if I see myself putting to sea, and the long hours without landfall, I do not see the return, the tossing on the breakers, and I do not hear the frail keel grating on the shore.[17]

This disappearance into the unseen distance of the ocean is as close as Molloy comes to being a speck in the void, at one with nothingness. It raises one of the frequent imponderables in Beckett's work, and creates the poetry of uncertainty which gives to his writing those moments of intimation with their suggestion of a half-forgotten, preconceptual and non-rational truth.

Thus Dante, in the person of Belacqua, gave Beckett an image for the condition which he has explored with obsessive honesty throughout his work. Belacqua with his certainty of eternity and Beckett's hero with his dubious hope, both cling tenaciously to the rock overlooking the infinite sea where they dream again the events of their past and suffer the Purgatory of waiting for the final voyage into bliss. In Beckett's beginning is his end for, true to the dictum he applauded in *Proust*, his later writing is a descent into the area originally suggested by the character and fate of a one-time lute maker of thirteenth-century Florence.

II

The ten stories of *More Pricks Than Kicks* are arranged chronologically but there is no explicit link between them. The transition from one story to another is abrupt and each is readable as an entity in itself yet the book has been carefully constructed. The various sections combine to give an overall impression of Belacqua's life and Beckett already employs his technique of making the reader conscious that what he is busied with is a book and not life by footnotes and cross-references from story to story. Although the hero alone appears in all ten episodes certain of the other characters appear in more than one. This composition of fragments is one aspect of Beckett's early academic iconoclasm (John Fletcher quotes a declaration from the *Dream*: 'the only unity in this story is please God, an involuntary unity.'),[18] but the final effect is more close-knit and integrated than one expects.

In *Dante and the Lobster* Belacqua is first seen troubled by the intricacies of Dante's theology and science. His progress is slow and at noon 'Three large obligations presented themselves. First lunch, then the lobster, then the Italian lesson.' He lunches off two rounds of black, peppered toast and gorgonzola cheese, a characteristically eccentric meal which he takes with him to a public house. From there he calls at a fishmonger to collect the lobster which his aunt has ordered, and then goes to his Italian lesson with the Signorina Adriana Ottolenghi. Finally he watches his aunt cook the lobster and learns to his impotent horror that it is put live into the cooking pot.

In the second story, *Fingal*, Belacqua takes his girl friend, Winnie, up the Hill of Wolves outside Dublin. 'They had not been very long on the top,' remarks Beckett, remembering Galen's *omne animal post coitum triste est*, 'before he began to feel a very sad animal indeed.' From there they look down on Portrane Lunatic Asylum. Belacqua expresses an affinity for the asylum and Winnie is friendly with a doctor there so, for once united, they walk down to it. Belacqua, however, having found a bicycle, leaves Winnie with Dr Sholto and rides away into the evening. He prefers a bicycle to a woman in the true Beckett evaluation of priorities and, once mounted, his 'sadness fell from him like a shift.' Winnie and the doctor search for him but without success: he is already in Mr Taylor's public house 'laughing and drinking in a way that Mr Taylor did not like.'

In *Ding-Dong* the scene is again Dublin. Beckett intrudes personally into the narrative to speak of the stories with which his 'sometime friend...enlivened the last phase of his solipsism.' Motion, Belacqua has found, calms his furies. On one of these 'boomerangs out and back' he sees a little girl knocked down by a bus in Pearse Street. The girl was carrying a bottle of milk and a loaf of bread and as a result, 'The good milk was all over the road and the loaf, which had sustained no injury, was sitting up against the curb, for all the world as though a pair of hands had taken it up and set it down there.' Belacqua is not disturbed by the fate of the girl and shows more interest in the effect of the accident on a cinema queue who are torn between the conflicting desires of taking a look or losing their places. He moves on to a public house where he wonders if such a haven of peace might not be the answer to the disastrous effects of his forays into motion upon his naturally indolent disposition. It is there that he buys the seats in heaven already mentioned.

In the fourth story, *A Wet Night,* Belacqua is invited to a Christmas gathering of intellectuals at the home of Miss Caleken Frica. Knowing that the party offers only soft drinks, Belacqua first gets drunk in a low public house. He arrives only after urinating over a policeman who knocks him into his own filth, and rolling up his shirt to feel the icy rain and sleet beating upon his naked stomach. At the party he meets the Alba ('Belacqua's current one and only') who alone is exempt from the artificiality and vulgarity of the pretentious aesthetes. In anguish Belacqua breaks into the first gratuitous tears shed by a Beckett hero ('At it again,' says the Alba). The Alba takes pity on him, gets him into a taxi, and he returns home across the grey, rain-drenched streets of Dublin.

Love and Lethe which follows is a bizarre description of a suicide pact between Belacqua and the spinster, Ruby Tough. 'The revolver, and balls, the veronal, the bottle and glasses, and the notice,' all prove superfluous when the revolver goes off by accident, harming no one. As a result 'a great turmoil of life blood sprang up in the breasts of our two young felons, so that they came together in the inevitable nuptial.' Unusually, in the situation, Beckett's concluding comment solicits compassion for his protégé: 'May their nights be full of music at all events.'

In the next story, *Walking Out*, Belacqua is now betrothed to Lucy and experiencing stubborn opposition: 'Time and again he had urged her to establish their married life on this solid basis of cuckoldry.' But Lucy will not consent to take the cicisbeo that this request entails. Belacqua, it appears, is a peeping Tom who prefers the passive observation of the sexual indulgences of others to his own active participation. If Lucy would oblige him he could satisfy himself in his own home and not have to spend uncomfortable evenings hiding in bushes with the likelihood of a severe drubbing on discovery. However, all is changed shortly afterwards when Lucy is knocked from her horse by a Daimler and 'crippled for life and her beauty dreadfully marred.' They marry and are happy; the problem of a cicisbeo is permanently solved.

The seventh story, *What a Misfortune*, describes Belacqua's marriage (Lucy has since died) to Thelma bboggs who 'brought neither the old men running nor the young men to a standstill.' It is the most consistently amusing of the stories, the satire is less esoteric than usual and broadened by a rich vein of farce. Mr bboggs, who made his fortune in toilet requisites, now collects antique furniture, while Mrs bboggs ('neutral to the point of idiocy') has a lover, Walter Draffin, who claims he is an author. Ironically Beckett attributes to his hand the writing of ' "Dream of Fair to Middling Women", held up in the limae labor stage for the past ten or fifteen years.' Beckett already reveals that tendency for internal allusion between his different works which is to become prominent in his mature writing. The wedding reception is a fiasco. Belacqua arrives late, his speech is a failure, the valuable antique furniture is broken up, and he and Thelma have to make an anonymous escape in which they are followed by Walter Draffin who has now attached himself to the Alba, and two aged relatives who attempt to kindle the last element of senile desire for each other in their wrinkled and grotesque old bodies.

Smeraldina's Billet Doux which follows is an incoherent and mis-spelt letter from one of Belacqua's old lovers in Vienna: a parody of the foreigner's use and misuse of English. In the next story, *Yellow*, Belacqua is in hospital waiting for an operation on a tumour the size of a brick on his neck. His life ends in a whimper as a result of an accident while he is under the anaesthetic.

The final story, *Draff*, relates his burial by the Smeraldina (who, we learn, became his third wife on the death of 'Thelma née bboggs perished of sunset and honeymoon') and Capper 'Hairy' Quin. Hairy seems to have taken over many of Belacqua's personal qualities now that he is dead, particularily his idiosyncratic and perverse use of language. On their return from the cemetery he and the Smeraldina discover that the gardener has ravished the servant girl and set the house on fire. It is an ending of convenience for author and characters. Hairy invites the Smeraldina to live with him. ' "Perhaps after all," murmured the Smeraldina, "this is what darling Bel. would wish." '— 'So it goes with the world,' adds Beckett and closes the book.

With the possible exception of Murphy, Belacqua is the only Beckett hero to retain at least a partial liaison with the world about him. The Dublin background of *More Pricks Than Kicks* is carefully documented after the manner of *Ulysses*: the street names, the Liffey, Trinity College and the statue of Thomas Moore, combine to present the busy city landscape against which Belacqua is drawn. But already there is a distance between the hero and his fellow men. Intimacy is rare even in the thrice-married Belacqua and he avoids, when he can, the demands that passion makes on his indolence. Only the Alba is thought of with respect, for her detached serenity compliments the hero's self-centred introspection. His friend, Hairy, is close only by comparison, and Belacqua prefers the company of the anonymous public house with its 'rough but kindly habitués,...recruited for the most part from dockers, railwaymen and vague joxers on the dole.' When he walks out to take his dinner in *Dante and the Lobster* he chooses to be an alien: 'Now the great thing was to avoid being accosted. To be stopped at this stage and have conversational nuisance committed all over him would be a disaster.' If he is accosted by friend or stranger he responds with rudeness and even direct belligerence.

This voluntary exile from society is a movement in the direction which Murphy is to follow more thoroughly. As yet the implications of Cartesianism and the urge to subjugate one's desires and needs so as to enter into the freedom of the mind do not have the importance they effect in the later novel. Belacqua only touches upon the distinction between mind and body. Though the author observes that 'his hunger' is 'more of the mind, I need hardly add, than of the body,' the incongruous interaction of mind and matter does not trouble him. Belacqua is not sufficiently advanced in Cartesianism to attempt Murphy's experiments in reaching the will-less, passive dark of the mind: he is only, says Beckett, a 'mystique raté'. Thus, though he is aware that the body has no significance and is divorced of all contact with the mind—'Belacqua scoffed at the idea of a sequitur from his body to his mind'—he neither feels the need, nor is able to achieve, the liberation from his decaying shell of matter that plays so important a part in the lives of all his successors.

Belacqua's vaguely motivated alienation from the 'poets and Politicians' of Dublin is ultimately unsuccessful. Like Murphy the desires of his body often overcome the ideal in his mind. In spite of his grotesque, clown-like appearance Belacqua is forced to perform an active, if marginal, social function. The sight of Belacqua entering the Frica's drawing-room prompts the Alba to think 'she had never seen anybody look quite such a sovereign booby,' and he frequently provokes 'comment and laughter.' Belacqua is small, fat and balding. He wears spectacles which he delights in polishing and dresses shabbily with a slovenly unconcern. He 'always looked ill and dejected' and his feet are in ruins. He moves with a 'spavined gait' and his general physical decay anticipates the hero's future disintegration, particularly his difficulty in movement which anticipates Molloy's attempts to progress with the aid of bicycle and crutch.

The natural apathy of Belacqua's temperament is supported by a conviction that inaction is the only possible and positive attitude towards existence. Where Dante censures him for his indolence and hurries past him up the mountain, Beckett treats him with indulgence and supplies the reasoning by which a man believes in the virtue of being idle. Beckett enters the narrative as he does in *Watt*—' "Behold Mr Beckett," said Belacqua whitely'—and describes their relationship: 'We were Pylades and Orestes for a period.' Belacqua explains to him the motives by which he is inspired. He does not attempt to conquer the pinnacles of success, fame or reality, and if he moves unceasingly from place to place (as in *Ding-Dong*) 'he was at pains to make it clear...that it was in no way cognate with the popular act of brute labour, digging and the such like, exploited to disperse the dumps... and for which he expressed the greatest contempt.' Belacqua lives between the heights of endeavour in what he terms 'A Beethoven pause,' though he is unable to explain what he means by that. He aspires, if it is possible, to nothingness, the nothingness which makes all rewards such as fame or success futile, and all endeavour a failure. 'What I am on the lookout for,' said Belacqua, 'is nowhere, as far as I can see.' Indolence is the only response he can imagine in the face of this 'nowhere'.

Beckett wonders if the mental asylum where Belacqua says his heart is, might not be the best place for him, for in the world outside he is consistently miserable. His only moment of real happiness comes when he mounts the bicycle he has found in a field and rides off into the evening. Otherwise 'he was in his element in dingy tears,' and we are told 'Belacqua could not resist a lachrymose philosopher and still less when, as was the case with Heraclitus, he was obscure at the same time.' Typically that which makes him suffer most deeply is the passing of time. Dante's Belacqua sits well back in the shadow of a rock where the heavenly bodies, revolving about him his lifetime long, are out of sight. Thus he remains ignorant of the moment in which their cycle will be completed and the time to ascend arrives. Belacqua Shuah 'would not tolerate a chronometer of any kind in the house,' since for him the 'local publication of the hours was six of the best on the brain every hour, and even the sun's shadow a torment.' (It was the sun's shadow, we remember, that tormented his predecessor on Mt Purgatory.) When Thelma gives him a clock he almost breaks off their engagement. Time is a reminder that even indifference is finite. It removes Belacqua from the self-sufficiency on which he prides himself, back into the activity of the world around him. The 'nowhere' will remain unknown until the human microcosm has lulled itself into a passivity analogous to non-being.

Beckett recognizes Belacqua's failings, his vanity, incompetence and self-centred separation from others about him, but in general treats him with indulgence. (Beckett comments: 'I gave him up in the end because he was not serious.') He has a sympathy for his 'shabby hero' which he withholds from the other characters. Belacqua may be mistaken in his indolence and an 'impossible person', but the unceasing activity of the secondary characters is still more ludicrous and futile. What is of greater importance, they delude themselves into believing that their purposes and aspirations have significance, a mistake which Belacqua neither intends nor makes. Therefore Beckett is able to deflate their conceit with the social and moral satire so prominent in his first two works of fiction. As Belacqua remains untouched by the most destructive shafts of Beckett's disdain he emerges as a broader and more appealing character.

Beckett's satirical style is exuberant and lively. At its most acute it pinions a character in a single deft phase. For example Ruby Tough of the suicide pact who 'saw her life as a succession of backstairs jests;' Walter Draffin, that 'presumptive cuckoo'; or the student who arrives at the Christmas Party 'looking Della Robbia babies at the Frica.' His ear for conversational and spiritual emptiness catches the exact tones of society gossip, and in the artificial but amusing inventory of Miss Caleken Frica's guests one sees the banal background against which Belacqua moves:

> Two banned novelists, a bibliomaniac and his mistress, a palaeographer, a violinist d'amore with his instrument in a bag, a popular parodist with his sister and six daughters, a still more popular professor of Bullscrit and Comparative Ovoidology, the Saprophile the better for drink, a Communist painter and decorator fresh back from Moscow reserves, a merchant prince, two grave Jews, a rising strumpet, three more poets with Lauras to match, a disaffected cicisbeo, a chorus of playwrights, the inevitable envoy of the fourth estate, a phalanx of Grafton Street sturmers and Jemmy Higgins now arrived in a body.

This passage indicates Beckett's youthful assault on the proprieties of language. Words are forced to yield before his disdainful intellectual wit. The pun and the misinterpreted or coined word are prominent features, often, as in the title of the book itself or in the phrase 'violinist d'amore with his instrument', bearing suggestive overtones. But the effect, though at first invigorating, soon becomes facile; used to excess only the occasional phrase makes an impact. At its worst the satire is mannered and Beckett's style pedantic and obscure. The secondary characters are all two-dimensional, and their bewildering number becomes repetitive. There is a certain perverse tendency at work in *More Pricks Than Kicks* which allows Beckett to imagine so many ineffectual and shallow creations, simply for the pleasure of demolishing them with the apt, unanswerable phrase.

The style is also obscured by a youthful, almost arrogant, display of learning. It is esoteric in manner, weighted with allusions and often self-consciously clever. Sometimes the erudition, the mis-quoted or parodied phrase included to emphasize a contrast between its new context and original form, is admissible. But this technique, made fashionable at the time by the publication of *The Waste Land*, too often gives an unwarranted importance to the passage in question or obscures an idea which could otherwise have been developed with clarity and meaning. In *What a Misfortune* Walter Draffin and Hairy meet in a Dublin street:

> 'This is where I stand,' said the little creature, with a sigh that made Hairy look nervously round for prisons and palaces, 'and watch the Liffey swim.'

The association of the words 'stand' and 'sigh' remind Beckett of Byron's famous description of Venice in *Childe Harold's Pilgrimage* but, while his intention is to collapse Walter Draffin's pose, the allusion not only will not bear scrutiny but also dissipates the intended effect. Hairy's response is unlikely even among the suburban pseudo-scholars of Beckett's Dublin (and why 'nervously'? The word is selected arbitrarily), and the narrative is slowed down while the reader absorbs an aside which may be comprehensible but which, on reflection, cheapens the original and weakens the force of the adaptation.

The use of allusion is most effective when the knowledge has been integrated into the text, not as an intellectual conundrum but as the spontaneous reappearance of learning from the subconscious. In *More Pricks Than Kicks* the erudition has too often been grafted on to the page in pursuit of a facile effect; in the trilogy these fragments are welded unconsciously into the whole as the natural remnants of an intellect that has abjured knowledge but is recalling its past in an introspective monologue. Molloy's reference to *Le Peau de Chagrin* is no more consciously sought than, for example, the evocatory passage of childhood memory in *Malone Dies*.

There are, however, occasions on which the writing suggests the qualities of precision, restraint and poetry as they appear in Beckett's later books. In *Draff* there is a sense of the incomprehension of the living when confronted with the finality of death. The drunken groundsman of the cemetery in which Belacqua is buried, cannot make the effort to encounter the ultimate mystery and 'rose and made his water agin' a cypress.' The gulf between the silence of the tombs and the cloacal necessity of the groundsman under the funereal tree, gives way to an impression of the absolute nothingness surrounding them all. Similarily, the incident in the public house when Belacqua is sold two seats in heaven conveys, by its rapid transitions and significant omissions of rational meaning, an intimation of hope. The old woman's face, 'brimful of light and serene...luminous, impassive and secure, petrified in radiance,' is the face of a heavenly messenger, the Dantean angel at last. Like the young boy who comes to the tramps in *Waiting for Godot*, it holds out a faint hope of salvation which Belacqua only grasps at in time. But the outstanding achievement in this collection is *Dante and the Lobster*. Here Beckett reveals an ability to control events that is lacking in the other stories, and its underlying theme of bewilderment in the face of suffering, coupled with its certainty of execution, looks forward to his mature creations.

On his way to his Italian lesson with the Signorina Adriana Ottolenghi, Belacqua collects a lobster for his aunt which, he is told, is 'lepping fresh'. He does not query the phrase and 'supposed the man to mean that the lobster had very recently been killed.' When he arrives at the lesson he expects his teacher to elucidate the intricacies of the *Paradiso* which have been perplexing him all morning. But his question 'Where were we?' arouses the Otto to a characteristic Beckettian outburst:

> . . Neapolitan patience has its limits.
> 'Where are we ever?' cried the Otto.
> 'Where we were, as we were.'

Her words are reminiscent of the opening line of *The Unnamable* and reappear in the tramps' dialogue in *Godot*. It is the constant enquiry of the later heroes which Belacqua appears to be learning for the first time.

Instead of studying the *Paradiso* she advises him to pay attention to Dante's 'rare movements of compassion in Hell.' This turns Belacqua's mind to the fate of 'poor McCabe', a murderer from Malahide, whose petition for mercy has, according to that morning's paper, been rejected and who 'would get it in the neck at dawn.' From there he moves on to the first murderer, 'Cain with his truss of thorns, dispossessed, cursed from the earth, fugitive and vagabond,' and of all the damned which Dante saw in Hell. A crown of thorns was not worn by Christ alone and Belacqua cannot justify God's ways to man, just as all Beckett's heroes wonder about the strange decree which saved one of the thieves but not the other. 'Why not,' he wonders, 'mercy and Godliness together?' What is one to make of the God of love's treatment of Jonah, 'and the pity of a jealous God on Nineveh.' In his own minor way Belacqua is questioning the apparently arbitrary dispensation of suffering which lead Ivan Karamazov to return his ticket to heaven; a ticket which Belacqua apparently accepts. Although his conclusions on the problem of pain, the fundamental question of Christian dissent, are not set forth in this story, Belacqua moves into the same area of values with its inversion of pity and cruelty, as the heroes of the trilogy. When the little girl is knocked down in *Ding-Dong* he remains detached, more interested in the fate of her loaf of bread than the extent of her injuries. Again, on Lucy's death, he outrages his acquaintances by wearing 'none of the proper appurtenances of grief.' In describing Belacqua's attitude Beckett is already revealing an aspect of the trilogy's cosmology of guilt and suffering. As he says, Belacqua cannot shed any tears over an individual like Lucy:

> his small stock of pity being devoted to the living by which is not meant this or that particular unfortunate, but the nameless multitude of the current quick, life, we dare almost say, in the abstract.

In *Dante and the Lobster* his compassion is for both the quick and the dead, and it is during his evening meal that his thoughts of McCabe, Cain and Dante's damned reach their climax. He hands the lobster to his aunt who puts it into a pot of boiling water:

> 'They assured me it was fresh,' said Belacqua.
> Suddenly he saw the creature move, this neuter creature.
> Definitely it changed its position. His hand flew to his mouth.
> 'Christ!' he said, 'it's alive.'

Belacqua, in his indolence, has subdued his normal existence to the boredom of Proustian habit. But today the meditations prompted by his Italian teacher's advice and now this sudden revelation in his aunt's kitchen make him aware of the 'suffering of being'. His aunt replies brusquely, and in the passage which follows, Belacqua attempts to heal the wound with yet another of the 'countless treaties' by which habit deadens suffering:

> 'Have sense,' she said sharply, 'Lobsters are always boiled alive. They must be.' She caught up the lobster and laid it on its back. It trembled. 'They feel nothing,' she said.
>
> In the depths of the sea it had crept into the cruel pot. For hours, in the midst of its enemies, it had breathed secretly. It had survived the Frenchwoman's cat and his witless clutch. Now it was going alive into the scalding water. It had to. Take into the air my quiet breath.
>
> Belacqua looked at the old parchment of her face, grey in the dim kitchen.
>
> 'You make a fuss,' she said angrily, 'and upset me and then lash into it for your dinner.'
>
> She lifted the lobster clear of the table. It had about thirty seconds to live.
>
> Well, thought Belacqua, it's a quick death, God help us all.
>
> It is not.

The disembodied voice which intrudes to utter those last three words over the domestic quibbling of Belacqua and his aunt is a unique and frightening invention. It continues to disturb long after the other stories have been read and returns in the agonized hesitations of the trilogy. It undermines both the babbling activity of the Dublin aesthetes and Belacqua's own apathetic self-sufficiency, and is perhaps the sum of all Molloy's, Malone's and the Unnamable's knowledge—that dismissed with a flippant 'oh well, it's a quick death, whatever else life may be', the Beckett truth replies,

It is not.

FOUR: MURPHY

'There is a mind and there is a body—'
'Shame,' cried Neary. 'Kick her arse! Throw her out!...
'Everywhere I find defiled,' continued Miss Counihan, 'in the crass and unharmonious unison, the mind at the cart-tail of the body, the body at the chariot wheels of the mind. I name no names.'

MURPHY

I

'MURPHY', Beckett's first full-length novel, published in 1938 with the help of Herbert Read, is a natural development from *More Pricks Than Kicks*. It is more accessible than the later novels but its apparent lightness of texture should not be mistaken for a lack of substance. Although Beckett himself has tended to dismiss the early English novels as of lesser importance than his works in French, as one critic has observed *Murphy* 'is that rarity in modern fiction, a completely successful novel of ideas'.[1]

Who is Murphy? His lover, Celia, attempts the answer:

> ...Celia replied that Murphy was Murphy. Continuing then in an orderly manner she revealed that he belonged to no profession or trade; came from Dublin—'My God' said Mr Kelly—knew of one uncle, a Mr Quigley, a well-to-do ne'er-do-well, resident in Holland, with whom he strove to correspond; did nothing that she could discern; sometimes had the price of a concert; believed that the future held great things in store for him; and never ripped up old stories. He was Murphy. He had Celia.

Murphy is a youngish man not in the best of health. He suffers from heart attacks and like Belacqua has pains in his neck and feet. He never wears a hat (it reminds him of the caul) and dresses in an unkempt suit that through long wear is shaped like a tube and stained the colour of verdigris. He is a defunct scholar (of theology), and has recently come to London as the intended of a Miss Counihan. Described as a 'seedy solipsist', he is supposedly set on amassing a comfortable fortune and setting up a home where she will join him. But Murphy is not disposed to an active life; apart from an interest in astrology and chess he is content to live in idolence on the pittance which he fraudulently extracts from his rich uncle in Holland. However, his indolence is not purposeless. Murphy bases his life on the belief that his mind is 'a large hollow sphere hermetically closed to the universe without.' He retreats from the world because its aimless bustle distracts him from the attempt to enter this place of rest where, he is certain, the total freedom of the Self is to be found. Murphy wants to be 'a mote in the dark of absolute freedom,' and in his search for the timeless void of absolute existence his only aid is the impersonal assistance of his rocking chair. Our first glimpse of him is in this chair, sitting out of the sun, 'as though he were free, in a mew in West Brompton.' By strapping himself into his 'rocking-chair of undressed teak, guaranteed not to crack, warp, shrink, corrode, or creak at night,' and beginning to rock and rock and rock, he seeks to 'come alive in his mind.'

Murphy's experience in the rocking-chair is perhaps the closest any of Beckett's characters ever come to happiness. The release achieved in a trance-like abandonment to the chair's motion is so great that Murphy has created what he calls his 'Belacqua fantasy', in anticipation of which the rocking-chair is only a dubious substitute. Murphy believes that the ephemeral pleasure of his chair—a pleasure, after all, at which he has to work—will in the moment of death be transformed into a total freedom where his Self, redeemed at last from both past and future, will relive in an instantaneous present which is timeless, the whole of his past life. In his expectation of Antepurgatory he sees himself in the embryanal position of his Dante prototype, sheltering under the lea of a rock and:

> looking down at dawn across the reeds to the trembling of the austral sea and the sun obliquing to the north as it rose, immune from expiation till he should have dreamed it all through again, with the downright dreaming of an infant, from the spermarium to the crematorium. He thought so highly of this post-mortem situation, its advantages were present in such detail to his mind, that he actually hoped he might live to be old. Then he would have a long time lying there, watching the dayspring run through the zodiac, before the toil up hill to Paradise. The gradient was outrageous, one in less than one. God grant no godly chandler would shorten his time with a good prayer.[2]

The desire for a long life is exceptional in Beckett: it arises from

Murphy's expectation of untroubled timelessness. In the *Purgatorio* of Dante the inference is that Belacqua is happy to rest undisturbed before the gateway to the mountain; the way up is steep and to a man who has already spent one lifetime in indolence a second holds no horrors. The transference to Murphy's situation is a happy one; neither he nor Belacqua would be pleased by the unbidden prayers of a 'godly chandler'.

Murphy, it is evident, needs no one. He is complete within himself, the closed circle of the microcosm opposed to the 'big blooming buzzing confusion' of the world outside. But other people who lack his Belacqua fantasy need Murphy, and his destiny is complicated by a variety of aliens, notably Neary and Celia.

Neary, once a tutor of Murphy, meets Miss Counihan during the hero's absence. He conceives a great passion for her but is rejected until he is able to provide evidence of Murphy's death, infidelity or economic failure. It therefore becomes imperative for Neary to contact Murphy again and so he sends his servant, Cooper, a dull-witted, intemperate creature, to London. But while Neary is discovering a need for Murphy, Murphy is picked up by Celia, an Irish prostitute working in Chelsea, who accosts him one night as he is standing motionless 'considering alternatively the sky and a sheet of paper'. She falls in love with him (strangely, the love is returned) and before long Murphy proposes to her. However, his income is too small and his reluctance for work too great to support them both, and Celia is forced to leave him and return to the streets. Murphy is unable to live without her for long and he finally agrees to seek work if she will first obtain his horoscope from a swami in Berwick market. His faith in astrology is such that if his search for employment accords with the prognostications of the Thema Coeli compiled by Ramaswami Krishnaswami Narayanswami Suk, he will undertake to work.

Meanwhile in Dublin Neary has given way to despair. Cooper has found and then, through an excess of alcohol, lost Murphy, and Neary is only restrained from knocking his skull in against the statue of Cuchulain in the G.P.O. by Wylie (another of his students) who advises him to go to London himself. With Neary out of the way Wylie becomes Miss Counihan's lover and Cooper, now dismissed from Neary's service, works for them instead. Eventually they too leave for London: the peace-seeking Murphy is in great demand.

While these machinations threaten to enclose him, Murphy has taken care to avoid all chance of employment. But one day over lunch in a Lyon's Corner House he is seen by Austin Ticklepenny, 'Pot Poet From the County of Dublin'. Ticklepenny is employed as a male nurse in the Magdalen Mental Mercyseat. However, he fears that the work there is undermining his own sanity and suggests to Murphy that he might like to replace him. Murphy is struck by the offer for it contains two of Suk's motifs, 'that of lunatic in paragraph two and that of custodian in paragraph seven'. As a result he leaves Celia for his duties in the wards of the Mercyseat, where he seems blissfully happy having discovered in the psychotics 'the race of people he had long since despaired of finding'.

Meanwhile beyond the asylum walls, Cooper has found Celia and assuming that 'where a man's woman is, there it is only a question of time before the man is also', he informs Neary, Wylie and Miss Counihan that Murphy has been found. After a wildly funny scene where their differences are settled in Neary's bedroom they all descend on Celia. Murphy, of course, is not there and so they take up residence with the uncomplaining girl. But Murphy forestalls them. His first spell of night duty reveals the limitations of his intimacy with the patients and in a state of undress he returns to his room intending to go back to Celia in the morning. However his room is heated by a make-shift gas-fire which is switched on by a tap in the lavatory downstairs. That night, while Murphy is sleeping, someone pulls the tap instead of the chain and—exit Murphy. Suddenly the futility of Murphy's life, snuffed out by a confusion between chain and tap, becomes apparent.

There follows the identification of the charred body (Celia alone recognizes him—by a birthmark on his buttocks) and the reading of Murphy's will which runs as follows:

> With regard to the disposal of these my body, mind and soul, I desire that they be burnt and placed in a paper bag and brought to the Abbey Theatre, Lr. Abbey Street, Dublin, and without pause into what the great and good Lord Chesterfield calls the necessary house, where their happiest hours have been spent, on the right as one goes down into the pit, and I desire that the chain be there pulled upon them, if possible during the performance of a piece, the whole to be executed without ceremony or show of grief.

This document is typical of the grotesque humour of Beckett's hero. His whole being turned firmly away from humanity, he attempts to invert the normal order of things even in death. Without his uniting presence the gaggle of humanity now go their separate ways; Wylie and Miss Counihan to be married, Neary back to Ireland, Celia sadly back to the streets and Cooper, to whom Murphy's remains have been entrusted, to the nearest pub. But Murphy's desires are thwarted even on his last journey; incompetence still stalks him beyond death. Later that evening:

> Cooper took the packet of ash from his pocket, where earlier in the evening he had put it for greater security, and threw it angrily at a man who had given him great offence. It bounced, burst, off the wall onto the floor, where it at once became the object of much dribbling, passing, trapping, shooting, punching, heading and even some recognition from the gentleman's code. By closing time the body, mind and soul of Murphy were freely distributed over the floor of the saloon; and before another dayspring greyened the earth had been swept away with the sand, the bear, the butts, the glass, the matches, the spits, the vomit.

The 'dayspring' of sordid reality described here is contrasted with the radiant 'dayspring' which Murphy had hoped to see 'run through the zodiac' in his Belacqua fantasy. The irony between the reality and the dream is implicit when these two passages are read together. However, although Beckett obliquely points to the illusory hope of his late hero, one feels that he extends the same tolerance towards the ashes of Murphy's tragi-comic existence as he brought to the series of failures which made up his life.

II

All Beckett's novels revolve around the central character. Although the eventful progression of the story is often farcically displayed, the posturing of Neary and his friends would be nothing without the reflective quality of Murphy's mind. This 'mind' is the centre of the novel, and it is necessary to understand the various considerations with which it is beset before one passes on to the more traditional aspects of the story.

Murphy is actively compelled into his turn away from external reality by a series of insistent philosophical convictions. At intervals throughout the narrative the reader is referred to 'section six' where Beckett has inserted a description of Murphy's mind. Here we are introduced to Beckett's recurrent preoccupation—Descartes—and in the discourse which follows, Murphy emerges as the first of what is to be a succession of suffering Cartesians. At the heart of Murphy's outlook lies an understanding of the mental process in Cartesian terms, and his dilemma arises from the insoluble problem which such an understanding introduces.

Beckett's characters are rationalists. They examine all problems in rational terms, often arriving at the brink of the irrational in the course of their researches. But where Descartes was confident in his rationalism Beckett is hesitant and often crushed under the many irreconcilables which his mind discovers. Rationalism has not succeeded in its undeclared aim, the elucidation by reason of 'this' world, and the irrational continues to make alarming intrusions into the closed world of the mental microcosm. Beckett is finally driven to hope that if only the words in the skull can be silenced, peace might come and with peace some measure of self-knowledge. The philosophy of Descartes, which stands at the beginning of the Western rational tradition, makes the whole of intelligible reality depend upon the mental processes of solitary man, and it is easy to see how Beckett, aware of his position at the end of this tradition, might be drawn to examine the discrepancy between our present condition and the assertive confidence of its beginnings. As Hugh Kenner has pointed out, the burden of a man conscious that he is conscious is a peculiarly Western burden. It forms the Cartesian cross that oppresses all Beckett's characters and Murphy is their first representative. However, though Murphy understands the Cartesian position, he is not able to make the complete withdrawal from external reality which he sees as a necessary adjunct to his beliefs. Not until Malone, who like Descartes prefers to think in bed, does the Beckett hero come alive only in his mind.

Murphy's mind pictures itself as a microcosm closed to the world without. He distinguishes between the 'actual' and the 'virtual' of his mind, the former being that of which he has both mental and physical experience, and the latter that of which he has mental experience only. For Murphy a kick was actual knowledge and a caress virtual. In addition his mind is divided into three zones, light, half-light and dark. Each of these zones affords him a certain type of pleasure and, like the three laughs of Watt, the descent from light to dark is the passage from the lesser to the greater. In the zone of light, that of the actual, he takes pleasure in reorganizing physical experience to his own ends: 'Here the kick that the physical Murphy received, the mental Murphy gave... here the whole physical fiasco became a howling success.' In the second zone, that of the virtual, the pleasure is contemplative, and it is here that Murphy indulges in his Belacqua fantasy. But in the third zone all is 'a flux of forms, a perpetual coming together and falling assunder of forms'. Here, in the dark, Murphy is not even as active as he is in contemplation, he is no longer an actor but acted upon. In this zone he surrenders himself to the bliss of being a passive mind in a motionless body, will-less, free and quiet:

> Thus as his body set him free more and more in his mind, he took to spending less and less time in the light, spitting at the breakers of the world; and less in the half light, where the choice of bliss introduced an element of effort; and more and more and more in the dark, in the will-lessness, a mote in its absolute freedom.

The desire to achieve this most treasured of all conditions is created by the discovery of the incongruity between mind and body. The problem of Cartesian dualism leads to the need for an escape into the zone of will-less dark but, at the same time, forms an obstacle to its attainment. The peace of Murphy's mind is disturbed by Celia and the demands she arouses in his body: 'the part of him that he hated craved for Celia, the part that he loved shrivelled up at the thought of her'. To escape from her Murphy has to enter into his mind, but her body calls to his body and distracts him from his purpose. The two 'parts' appear to be counter-principles, and the action of the mind on the body and vice-versa is a complication which both Murphy and Descartes find impossible to explain. If the mind is body-tight and the body mind-tight how can mental concept and physical experience be related? As it is stated:

> Thus Murphy felt himself split in two, a body and a mind. They had intercourse apparently, otherwise he could not have known that they had anything in common. But he felt his mind to be bodytight and did not understand through what channel the intercourse was effected nor how the two experiences came to overlap. He was satisfied that neither followed from the other. He neither thought a kick because he felt one nor felt a kick because he thought one. Perhaps the knowledge was related to the fact of the kick as two magnitudes to a third. Perhaps there was, outside space and time, a non-mental non-physical Kick from all eternity, dimly revealed to Murphy in its correlated modes of consciousness and extension, the kick *in intellectu* and the kick *in re*. But where then was the supreme caress?

In attempting to extract himself from this problem Murphy reveals a sympathy for the group of seventeenth-century philosophers known as the Occasionalists. The figures of Malebranche and Geulincx attend Descartes in the background of Beckett's works, their presence revealing the deep impression which their theories have made on his mind. in *How it is* Bom refers to 'Malebranche less the rosy hue,'[3] and the hero of the stories receives a copy of Geulincx' *Ethics*. As developers of Cartesianism their ideas reappear among the movements of the hero's thought (we have already noted the image of the slave on the ship) and

Geulincx, certainly, is responsible for the direction of many of their intellectual excursions.

The Occasionalists attempted to solve the problematic legacy of Descartes by attributing all reciprocity between mind and body to the miraculous intervention of the deity. For Malebranche the interaction of mind and matter is inconceivable since they are two different substances; what appears to be interaction (the thinking and feeling of a kick) is the coincidental conjunction of what are really two separate actions determined by the will of God. Malebranche even went so far as to claim that the action of mind on itself is also divine coincidence.

Geulincx' view was less extreme and finds greater favour in the eyes of Murphy and the other heroes. He expounds a doctrine of a body-tight mental world around which the body performs a series of actions which the mind not only does not understand, but also need not. Before he came to write, the law of the conservation of momentum had been discovered, according to which the total quantity of motion in the world in any given direction is constant. Geulincx, therefore, considers that the action of matter on matter and mind on mind may both be exempted from miraculous intervention, the incongruity of mind and body alone needs an extra-rational explanation. Geulincx states that, from the fact that I do not know how I lift my hand, I did not do it, and explains interaction by an image of two clocks both keeping perfect time. The clock of the mind points to the hour; the clock of the body strikes. Although the two appear to be linked causally it is only an illusion of circumstance. Once this divine coincidence is appreciated a character can only view the workings of his body with incredulity. The mind watches the body and does not describe but reports what takes place in the other sphere. Thus the Beckett hero narrates physical occurrences in terms of a series of unrelated actions which spring from no known intention of the mind. Movement is mechanical and the novels contain a series of geometrical, precise descriptions of the apparently fluid movements of the human body.

Murphy shows less amazement than his successors over the discrepancy between mind and matter. He is content to accept that the world of his mind and the world of his body are no more than 'partly congruent', and will be satisfied with any theory which does not oppose his conviction that the mind is a closed system. Murphy can never be a complete Occasionalist because he is aware of the lack of God, that fundamental property of the seventeenth-century thinker; but this absence does not cause him pain (as it will the later heroes) and he is content with the ruminative, sceptical inquiry 'But where then was the

Supreme Caress?' However, in his desire for the will-less zone of dark he is a true follower of Geulincx. If the mind is not dependent on divine intervention it is, in its interior life, absolutely free. The mind, where perhaps the Self is concealed, is incapable of influencing the outside world, but within itself is discovered the only freedom open to man, the freedom of the intellect apprehending itself.

Geulincx advocates a withdrawal into the inner freedom of the mind and the cultivation of indifference towards the confusion of the macrocosm. This is the motive behind Murphy's apparently senseless behaviour. Murphy is always turned in upon himself and the description of his mind has as an epigraph 'Amor intellectualis quo Murphy se ipsum amat'. He abandons himself to the rocking-chair induced state of euphoria where he experiences the introspective freedom of Geulincx, and becomes 'a mote in the dark of absolute freedom;' free because he has rid himself of all desire and need, those inferior impulses of the world outside, and replaced them by:

> the freedom of indifference, the indifference of freedom, the will dust in the dust of its object the act a handful of dust let fall.

Murphy's approach to the ideal existence of the mind leads to a conclusion which, not unnaturally, is ironically different to the final position of Geulincx. Although Murphy dismisses this discourse as of no interest Beckett follows it to a logical end. As Richard N. Coe has shown,[4] if the mind in relation to the world outside is valueless, within itself it can only have a value in relation to God. But if God is now non-existent (and Murphy infers that He is) then Murphy's mind must be—Nothing. This irony is intensified by the elevation of astrology to the place of God. Every event in *Murphy* is exactly dated and each location carefully particularized. In part a Joycean parodic comment on the nature of fiction, this obsession with exactitude is also an extension of Murphy's way of forging his destiny out of the questionable materials of astrology. We are invited to see the supreme rationalism of Descartes come to rest in a 'Swami in Berwick Market who cast excellent nativities for sixpence.'

Murphy's stay in the Magdalen Mental Mercyseat is introduced by a quotation from André Malraux: '*Il est difficile à celui qui vit hors du monde de ne pas rechercher les siens*' ('It is difficult for him who lives outside the world not to seek his own kind'). Murphy has turned in upon himself even before he is offered a post at the Mercyseat, and what he sees in the confined environment of the asylum appears to support his decision. As he discovers, his 'experience as a physical and rational being obliged him to call sanctuary what the psychiatrists called exile and to think of the patients not as banished from a system of benefits but as escaped from a colossal fiasco.' The chance encounter with Ticklepenny leads him to the one place where he finds a race of people with an outlook similar to his own, and where he is best able to immerse himself in the absolute freedom of Geulincx.

He has not been there very long before he distinguishes between two radically opposed modes of being, the 'psychiatric' and the 'psychotic'. To Murphy the head nurse, Bim, and his associates, Bom and Bum (a foretaste of *How it is*), are far more grotesque than the lunatics with whom he has to deal. Indeed, so deep is the sympathy between Murphy and the patients that he can make them behave without using physical violence, a fact which astounds Bim. In their turn the patients give Murphy the impression of having reached the degree of 'self-immersed indifference to the contingencies of the contingent world which he had chosen for himself as the only felicity and achieved so seldom.'

In describing Murphy's reaction to the world of the Mercyseat Beckett inverts familiar attitudes and by a searching use of irony undermines natural confidence in the science of the psychiatrist who equates well-being with a grasp of outer reality. The psychiatrist, like the future tormentors of Malone, believes in a rational norm from which he considers the psychotic has been cut off and to which he endeavours to return him. He seeks to:

> translate the sufferer from his own pernicious little dungheap to the glorious world of discrete particles where it would be his inestimable prerogative once again to wonder, love, hate, desire, rejoice and howl in a reasonable balanced manner, and comfort himself with the society of others in the same predicament.

The psychiatrist would return one to the great world where one suffers the unquenchable torments of the body divorced from the mind, seeks in vain for a place to hide and where the opportunity to escape into the silence of the mind is withheld from one: it does not take long for Murphy to dissociate himself from such an aim. If a patient is sad Murphy attributes it to the inability of the psychiatrist to leave him in peace. He compares the intrusion of the psychiatrist into the inner world of the psychotic with Christ's raising of Lazarus which 'seemed to Murphy perhaps the one occasion on which the Messiah had overstepped the mark'.

Three factors encourage Murphy in the belief that he has found his kindred at last. Firstly, he is impressed by the impassiveness of the higher schizoids in the face of rigorous treatment; secondly, he is overwhelmed by the padded cells; and thirdly, he is aware of his success with the patients. The microcosm seeks its equivalent in the macrocosm and the padded cells seem to Murphy the physical counterparts of his hollow mind. They approximate both to the womb and to the self-enclosed inner spaces of the skull:

> The pads surpassed by far all he had ever been able to imagine in the way of indoor bowers of bliss. The three dimensions, slightly concave, were so exquisitely proportioned that the absence of the fourth was scarcely felt...The compartment was windowless, like a monad,... Within the narrow limits of domestic architecture he had never been able to imagine a more creditable representation of what he kept on calling, indefatigably, the little world.

Murphy's joy over such a residence raises an important question in our approach to Beckett. Murphy is not the only hero who is in sympathy with the psychotics. Belacqua looks down on Portrane Lunatic Asylum and says 'My heart's right there'; Watt ends his days in one and Malone, who may or may not be an inmate himself, tells the story of Macmann who definitely is. All Beckett's heroes would agree with Murphy and identify themselves with the psychotics. Therefore the reader, who almost certainly comes to the book with the causal, rational attitude of the psychiatrist, has often to make, not merely a suspension of disbelief, but a complete reversal of understanding.

Murphy's happiness in the asylum is short-lived, however. The limit of his expectation is revealed during his first spell of night duty when the inner world he has built up crashes around him and the unfortunate accident of his death is interpreted by Bim as an incidence of a warder going insane in the course of his work.

Murphy's favourite patient is a Mr Endon 'a schizophrenic of the most amiable variety,' who 'drifted about the wards in a fine dressing-gown of scarlet byssus faced with black braid, black silk pyjamas and neo-merovingian poulaines of deepest purple.' Mr Endon is Murphy's 'tab' (an inmate for whom he held individual responsibility) and has expressed a desire to commit suicide by apnoea. But with Murphy he is never violent and the two spend all their time playing chess. On this particular night they play a game (Beckett lists all 86 moves in full), Murphy calling in on Mr Endon's cell at regular intervals during his round of the wards, to make his move.

However, Mr Endon plays in such a way that Murphy is forced to realize that the patients are neither as happy as he thinks nor, although they do separate him from the other warders, willing to accept him as one of them. Mr Endon moves his pieces in a series of movements which are aesthetically satisfying to himself but which prove that he is entirely unaware of his partner's existence. While Murphy sits in despair at this discovery Mr Endon escapes and rushes round the cells, pressing the indicator which records the times of the warders' visits in as personal a pattern as he made his moves in chess. Murphy at length recaptures him and returns him to his cell where he tucks him into bed and bends over him in concern. In Mr Endon's staring eyes, as in a mirror, Murphy sees himself: 'in the cornea, horribly reduced, obscured and distorted, his own image.' He feels compelled to speak and in halting phrases attempts to encompass what for him is the moment of truth:

> 'the last at last seen of him
> himself unseen by him
> and of himself'
>
> A rest.
>
> 'The last Mr Murphy saw of Mr Endon was Mr Murphy unseen by Mr Endon. This was also the last Murphy saw of Murphy.'
>
> A rest.
>
> 'The relation between Mr Murphy and Mr Endon could not have been better summed up than by the former's sorrow at seeing himself in the latter's immunity from seeing anything but himself.'
>
> A long rest.
>
> 'Mr Murphy is a speck in Mr Endon's unseen.'

In *Proust* Beckett described attainment as 'the identification of the subject with the object of his desire'.[5] Murphy had sought to identify himself with the psychotics and believed himself favoured with their attention, but here, in the last words he is ever to speak, he learns his mistake. In the formal simplicity of his grief Murphy sees himself repulsed from Mr Endon's unseeing eye back upon himself—inescapable self-perception and isolation is the knowledge he carries, distraught and naked, back to his lonely garret and the banality of his death.

III

Murphy's undertaking is threatened by the group of grotesques headed by Neary. Their way of life is an absolute antithesis to Murphy's mode of existence, and it is from the juxtaposition of these two modes that much of the comedy in the novel derives. The book is a dialogue between the Cartesian immobility of the hero and the peripatetic Newtonians, Neary, Wylie, Miss Counihan and Cooper. Murphy needs, or believes he needs, no one, but outside himself he is needed by five people:

> By Celia, because she loves him. By Neary, because he thinks of him as The Friend at last. By Miss Counihan, because she wants a surgeon. By Cooper, because he is being employed to that end. By Wylie, because he is reconciled to doing Miss Counihan the honour, in the not too distant future, of becoming her husband.

While Murphy goes in search of the will-less dark, Neary and his friends are constantly in motion, careering from Dublin to Holyhead, from Holyhead to London and back again. They are of the confusion, their motives and desires changing from moment to moment in the painful series of cause and effect from which Murphy has almost escaped.

Murphy prefers any position of rest to the perpendicular with its threat of motion. His mind, we are told again, 'functioned not as an instrument but as a place, from whose unique delights precisely these current facts withheld him'. The 'current facts' which threaten the solitude of his inner spaces are the offal of everyday experience, the concerns of a mind orientated towards external reality. A mind which is constructed 'on the correct cash-register lines, an indefatigable apparatus for doing sums with petty cash of current facts,' is Beckett's description of Neary's mental process, the scientific concordance of the worldly Newtonian.

In the section on his mind Murphy implicitly disavows the Newtonians. He cherishes the pleasure of being 'a missile without provenance or target, caught up in a tumult of non-Newtonian motion.' We have already noted that during the interval between Descartes and Geulincx the physicists discovered the law of the conservation of momentum, according to which the total quantity of motion in the world in any given direction is constant. To emphasize the contrast between Neary and Murphy who is searching for a liberation from desire and need, Beckett adapts this law and attributes a closed system of desire to his journeying Newtonians. 'For every symptom that is eased,' says Wylie, 'another is made worse. The horse leech's daughter is a closed system. Her quantum of wantum cannot vary.' The theory of the 'quantum of wantum' (the macrocosm *too* is a closed circuit) is the affliction of the group pursuing Murphy for their mobility is aroused by some unquenchable need. The 'horse leech's daughter' is an allusion to Proverbs XXX:15 where the torments of insatiable desire are described. To those such as Neary, who live in the mindtight macrocosm of the great world one desire only arouses another. Murphy is supported by the conviction that he can achieve a desire-free peace of mind which gives him 'such pleasure that pleasure was not the word.' But the Newtonians are condemned to a circle of futility where the total quantity of desire is constant even though individual desires may vary: 'Of such was Neary's love for Miss Dwyer who loved a Flight-Lieutenant Elliman, who loved a Miss Farren of Ringskaddy, who loved a Father Fitt of Ballinclashet, who in all sincerity was bound to acknowledge a certain vocation for a Mrs West of Passage, who loved Neary.'

Beckett builds the structure of *Murphy* on the contrast between the Cartesian and Newtonian attitudes. The chapters alternate between the extended introspection of those which feature Murphy himself, and the rapid, staccato interchanges in speech and place of Neary and his acquaintances. Their inconclusive conversations remain on the surface of experience and Beckett intends us to appreciate the irony in Wylie's conclusion: 'Once a certain degree of insight has been reached...all men talk when talk they must, the same tripe.' Murphy, with whom Beckett's sympathies lie, is explored in detail, but the Newtonians, being mindtight, have no interior life at all. As Beckett intrudes to say: 'All the puppets in this book whinge sooner or later, except Murphy who is not a puppet.' In general the secondary characters are the butts of Beckett's satire and strictly two dimensional, like Cooper who is unable to either take off his hat or sit down. 'It was indifferent to him whether he stood or lay, but sit he could not.' This affliction, from which Clov too is to suffer, disappears on Murphy's death and he celebrates by taking off his hat for the first time and sitting on it—hard.

What makes *Murphy* a successful novel of ideas is not the profundity of its philosophy but the brilliance of its execution. The novel of ideas as a form, often fails under the inappropriate weight of thought which it is made to convey, but in *Murphy* the impressive metaphysical exposition is buried underneath a tale of pubs, seduction, bawdry and Irish humour. On this level it is a forerunner of a succession of contemporary novels which have created the image of the intelligent but misguided and accident-prone anti-hero, moving through a world which he is not fitted to understand. Beckett's achievement is to have written a book which is effective on both these levels.

Beckett's style has increased in range from the stories of *More Pricks Than Kicks*. It is more economical, capable of a refinement that leads to a certain muted, poetical quality, and in places foreshadows the aridity of *Watt*. It is also satirical and flexible enough to include parodies of other spoken and written mannerisms, as when Miss Counihan cries: ' "Oh, if you have . . . if you have news of my love, speak, speak, I adjure you." She was an omnivorous reader.' Although allusion and quotation are still prominent features of this style they are used with greater effect and tact. The obscure misquotation of the stories has been replaced by a conscious play upon a well-known phrase, usually with a satirical intention. These adaptations of learning divide into two groups, the secular and the biblical. Beckett's technique is to contrast the debased version with the original which is in the reader's mind, making the discrepancy reflect back on to the character in question, usually to his detriment. For example: 'You may sneer,' said Neary, 'and you may scoff, but the fact remains that all is dross, for the moment at any rate, which is not Miss Dwyer.' By comparing Neary's feelings for Miss Dwyer with the awe of Faustus on seeing Helen of Troy, Beckett intends the reader to make the obvious comparison himself and so achieves a double effect. Firstly he punctures Neary's pretensions, and secondly he uses a minimum of words to render his satire effective. Even more stringent is his treatment of the foul-smelling Miss Carridge. This prying, detestable, suburban landlady sits down 'with the conviction of having left undone none of those things that paid and done none of those things that did not pay.' The pointed overtones of this reference are sufficient for Beckett not to have to elaborate further: the trait has been noted and the impression made.

As a feature of style this technique is an extension of the pun. Beckett shares the Irish penchant for verbal humour, double-meanings and advised misuse of language. Joyce's influence was still strong when he wrote *Murphy* and his admiration for *Ulysses* and *Work in Progress* as it then was, perhaps encouraged in him a cavalier but learned use of language. Beckett declares, 'In the beginning was the pun,' and as a device it is conspicuous in *Murphy*. Sometimes its use is straightforward: 'Why did the barmaid champagne? . . . Because the stout-porter bitter,' but at others it is subjected to a much more far-reaching treatment. The logical incongruity of the clown is carried into the medium of language, and the punning of *Murphy* is the beginning of Beckett's assault on the residual meaning of words. Under this assault words disintegrate into sounds—as in *Watt*—or into the suggestive tones of his titles—*Krapp's Last Tape*, *Endgame*—and the obsession with the syllables Ma-Ma/lone, Ma/hood—or Mol—Moll, Mol/loy. The pun suggests a certain freedom within language, a possibility of another significance beneath the overt definition. It is also anti-rational: the reference meaning is by-passed for another with an entirely separate significance. (It is instructive to remember that Swift's name for his floating Isle of Reason, Laputa, contains a pun on the French La puta.) But if the pun is a beginning it is also an end. The freedom it suggests is an illusion and its limits are emphasized in 'the sad pun' which Mr Kelly finds impossible to expand: 'Celia, s'il y a, Celia, s'il y a.'

There is an exception among the grotesque secondary characters, one who is neither satirized nor passed over lightly. Celia, friend to Mr Kelly and lover of Murphy, is treated throughout with a muted tenderness that makes a profound contrast with the ridicule in which the other characters move. Celia is attractive (Beckett tabulates her physical features) and inviting—'She stormed away from the call-box, accompanied delightedly by her hips etc.' But stranger still she loves Murphy and for the only time Beckett allows himself to write without disgust of a relationship which is not entirely rational, and based on a genuine depth of feeling. When she is with Murphy she is the 'music' beyond the words; she is 'Celia—serenade, nocturne, albada' and when they are separated she becomes a down-trodden Penelope who awaits the return of her beloved from the realm of thought.

Celia remains unobtrusively in the background. She rarely speaks yet her presence influences both the reader and those around her. Wylie and Neary feel something approaching awe in her presence and the book is pervaded by her grace and fundamental purity. She is an additional cause of Murphy's failure, for his desire for her intrudes into his search for the will-less dark, but her own life too ends in sadness. She alone has the influence to send Murphy out into the great world only to discover too late 'how her efforts to make a man of him had made him more than ever Murphy, and how by insisting on trying to change him she had lost him, as he had warned her she would. "You, my body, my mind...one must go".' She senses, as he leaves for the Mercyseat, that she is about to lose him for ever. From the moment she watches him walk away, multiplied in the burlesque of a group of derisive schoolboys 'long after her own eyes could see

D

him no more,'[6] Celia is written about with respect and a poignant restraint. When she returns from a walk to find that Murphy has been to collect his rocking-chair, a sure sign that he has left for good, her grief is portrayed obliquely:

> 'Mr Murphy came while you were out,' said Miss Carridge. 'You can't have been gone five minutes.'
>
> For a full second Celia mistook this to mean that Murphy had come back.
>
> 'He took his bag and the chair,' said Miss Carridge, 'but couldn't wait.'
>
> There was the usual silence, Miss Carridge missing nothing of Celia's expression, Celia appearing to scrutinize her hand on the banister.
>
> 'Any message,' said Celia, at last.
>
> 'I can't hear you,' said Miss Carridge.
>
> 'Did Mr Murphy leave any message?' said Celia, turning away and taking another step upward.
>
> 'Wait now till I see,' said Miss Carridge.
>
> Celia waited.
>
> 'Yes,' said Miss Carridge, 'now that you ask me, he did say to tell you that he was all right and would be writing.' A lie. Miss Carridge's pity knew no bounds but alms.
>
> When it was quite clear that this was the whole extent of the message Celia went on slowly up the stairs. Miss Carridge stood with a finger on the switch, watching. The turn of the stair took the body out of sight, but Miss Carridge could still see the hand on the banister, gripping, then sliding a little, gripping again, then sliding a little more. When the hand also disappeared Miss Carridge switched off the light and stood in the dark that was so much less extravagant, not to mention richer in acoustic properties, listening.

The writing turns away from Celia's suffering; it concentrates on the physical facts, on the movement of her hand on the banister, as if the actual experience is too painful for direct expression. Yet much is contained in this unpretentious passage. The words 'usual silence' indicate how common such a scene is, and the omission of a question mark after 'Any message' is sufficient to convey Celia's knowledge and despair. It is reminiscent of the early Hemingway: inner sentiment is illuminated by silence and gesture. The writing at these moments seems wholly pure, the 'big 'words, the magniloquent expressions of emotion, are forgotten and it is what is not said that is important. When Celia does attempt to express her feelings for Murphy her words are few and hesitant. It is perhaps the most human and tender moment in the novels:

> I was a piece out of him that he could not get on without,
> no matter what I did...I was the last exile.

Alone in Beckett's works their love endures, and until the ambivalent love-hate partnerships of the plays such a note remains unique.

Murphy ends with the resigned and sorrowful figure of Celia, pursuing once more her disagreeable profession, alone in the park across which sounds the haunting call of the ranger's 'All Out', and 'looking at the sky...simply to have that unction of soft sunless light on her eyes that was all she remembered of Ireland.' It is a pathetic rather than a tragic ending to a book in which the humour remains this side of despair. The absurdity of the plot does not as yet bring forth the mirthless laugh. *Murphy* is Beckett's last venture into the traditional novel, well-written and rich in style and character. But his true note, the extended cry of anguish and despair, is absent. Hugh Kenner has remarked: 'To write it he simply evaded the madness in himself. To write the later books he confronted this madness.'[7] With *Murphy* Beckett leaves the grotesque confusion of incapacity that is the real world for the fearful, tragic inner-world of his mature works: most particularly for *Watt* where he uncovers the dilemmas he is to explore in depth in the French novels and plays.

FIVE: WATT

'When I use a word,' said Humpty Dumpty, in rather a scornful tone, 'it means just what I choose it to mean—neither more nor less.'

'The question is,' said Alice, 'whether you can make words mean so many different things.'

'The question is,' said Humpty Dumpty, 'which is the master—that's all.'

LEWIS CARROLL

I

A MAN SETS OUT from a city and makes his way to a large house in the country where he becomes a domestic servant. On his arrival an outgoing servant meets him in the kitchen and, on the evidence of his own experience, describes the probable course of the man's stay there. The man works for an undetermined length of time on the ground floor, rarely coming close to his employer, until a replacement arrives for the servant in charge of the first floor. The man is then automatically promoted to the first floor where he lives beside his master. The real nature of the master, however, continues to elude him. When yet another servant arrives the man departs, passing a newcomer in the kitchen as he leaves. He walks to the station at which he also arrived when he was outward bound and takes a train to the further end of the line. Some time afterwards the man is discovered in a lunatic asylum attempting to describe his experiences at the large house to a fellow patient who records them in a book which, though it makes few pretensions to literature and is demonstrably inaccurate in its veracity, is later published as a novel.

Watt was written during the years (1942-44) when Beckett was in hiding from the gestapo in the Vaucluze. It is the product of a deepening awareness and of a uniformly bleaker vision of man's condition than *Murphy*. After the opening twenty pages, as richly humorous as anything in its predecessor, the tone changes and for the first time pain and despair strike a dominant note. *Watt* appears now as Beckett's first attempt to face the implications inseparable from his preoccupation with time and words. It is the opening encounter with the disturbing meaning of the imponderables that have occupied him ever since; an encounter which extends his technical virtuosity to its limit.

Watt is also the last novel in English and the style, which anticipates the French precision of his maturity, has dismissed the youthful exuberance and Joycean mannerisms of *Murphy* and the Belacqua stories. But the Ireland of his boyhood which provides the setting for the story of Watt's journey and sojourn at the mysterious establishment of Mr Knott has none of the imprecision attendant on the memories of the unquenchable 'I' in the French novels. Whatever Watt's personal vagaries and indistinctness, the background of decaying country houses, local trains, trams and verdurous ditches is as unmistakably Irish as the railwaymen and other citizens with whom he comes into contact. The outward events of the novel are, however, negligible; it is Watt's attempt to define the world about him in satisfactory, rational terms that provides the essence. The action itself barely exceeds the skeleton of journey, servitude and return journey, yet from this Beckett creates a novel that exposes Watt's 'soul-landscape' with alarming effects on both reader and hero.

The novel is in four parts with an addenda of omissions which could, had they been included, have prolonged the novel indefinitely. As Beckett remarks of this section: 'The following precious and illuminating material should be carefully studied. Only fatigue and disgust prevented its incorporation.' Watt's experiences at Mr Knott's are presented in strict chronological sequence but the book as a whole is not. At first it appears to be a straightforward third person narrative in the style of *Murphy*. It opens with Watt's seemingly unmotivated departure from Dublin, witnessed by Mr Hackett and Mr and Mrs Nixon as they take their evening stroll; and carries the narrative as far as his inexplicable entrance into Mr Knott's house and his conversation with the outgoing servant, Arsene. The second section then describes Watt's service on the ground floor; the mysterious visit of the Galls, father and son, to 'choon the piano,' and the beginning of Watt's mental collapse as the peculiar circumstances of the house obstinately remain outside all his attempts at rational explanation. The incident of the Galls, everyday objects, the meaning of a geometrically composed picture in Erskine's (the other servant's) room, and the ringing of a bell which proves on inspection to be broken, all defy his mental efforts to reach a consoling explanation, right or wrong. His only success is in the discovery of the outrageously complex arrangements for the preparation of Mr Knott's food and the disposal of the left-overs to a dog which is not kept on the premises. To ensure the infallibility of these arrangements Watt is forced to accept not one but a whole family of dogs looked after by the twenty-eight ailing and eccentric members of the Lynch family. This calculation which 'gave very little trouble' covers slightly more than thirty-one pages of involved, mathematical prose. The section closes with the arrival of Arthur to replace Erskine and Watt's admission that of Mr Knott, his master, he has learnt—nothing.

In the third part, however, we are introduced to a fellow-inmate of Watt's in a mental asylum. How or when Watt arrived at the asylum is not disclosed but he has formed, with Sam, one of Beckett's curious 'friendships' which thrive on a fusion of remoteness and sympathy. Watt endeavours to describe his experiences to Sam who enters them in a notebook, the one, in fact, we are now reading, in order of occurrence. But in this particular section the third-person convention is abandoned so that Sam may explain the difficulty Watt now experiences in speaking and he, Sam, in hearing, about the period of Watt's service on the first floor. Watt's mind becomes increasingly deranged and as his thought collapses so language, the vehicle of thought, is also affected. The only coherent reminiscence is the story which Arthur told to Mr Graves, the gardener, who has the misfortune to be impotent. It describes the adventures of Ernest Louit, a managing director of the House of Bando. A capsule of Bando before and after meals in a little warm milk will, says Arthur, cure Mr Graves of his affliction—hence the tenuous connection. But the account of Louit's momentous dissertation, *The Mathematical Intuitions of the Visicelts* is left incomplete, and Watt, defeated by the imponderables of Mr Knott's house, lapses into silence.

The fourth section tells of the arrival of Micks and therefore the necessary departure of Watt. He is unable to speak 'the few simple words at parting, that mean so much, to him who stays, to him who goes,' as Arsene had predicted in part one. Watt goes to the station and spends the night in the waiting room. The next morning he is concussed when the door is suddenly flung open by a porter and further injured when the bucket of slops which they bring to revive him falls on his head. Watt remains unperturbed, gets up, retrieves his hat and buys a ticket to 'the nearer end of the line'. As the train carries him brokenly away the railwaymen enthuse over the joys of life:

All the same, said Mr Gorman, life isn't such a bad old bugger. He raised high his hands and spread them out...When all is said and done, he said.

And they say there is no God, said Mr Case.

All three laughed heartily at this extravagance.

The ending is ferociously ironic, for these platitudes have already been undermined by the contrary experience of Watt which, by the time shift, we know is taking him towards the asylum. The glib certainty of the railwaymen helps to explain the anathema with which Beckett's heroes regard the society around them. After Belacqua's mistaken 'Well...it's a quick death' his successors do not fall into the same error.

The shift in time thus adds force to the ironic ending. It also supports the illusion of a third-person narrative. The peculiar content of Watt's experience is given credibility by its subsequent narration in the grounds of a mental asylum. The comments by Sam and the not infrequent discrepancies of the manuscript, acknowledged by the author, enforce the illogical aspects of the story. Moreover the use of an ordering, commentating intelligence within the text is one of the most successful ways in which fictional material presented in the third person can attain the illusion of fact rather than imagination.

In addition this arrangement aids the formal conception of the book. The four parts of *Watt* are almost as finely interwoven as the two circular acts of *Waiting for Godot*. Beckett, especially in the plays, reveals a classical control of form which is inseparable from content. For example in *Play* the musical, *da capo* like repetition of the text in which the three voices speak as in counterpart, emphasizes the closed circuit of their unending recriminations. So in *Watt* the two outside parts describing Watt's arrival and departure create a satisfying unit, satisfying because it is complete in itself. Excepting the change in Watt himself, the novel ends almost as it began. It was summer when he set out; it is summer again as he leaves. The intervening sections likewise complement each other (the one devoted to his stay on the ground floor, the other to the second period of his service on the first), in a way that would have been impossible had Beckett ended the novel with his entry into the asylum. Thus the last appearance of the perplexed and incoherent anti-hero is not getting into a train near Leopardstown racecourse but his poignant withdrawal 'over the deep threshing shadows backwards stumbling, towards his habitation' at the end of part three.

The use of an internal narrator works in sympathy with Beckett's distrust of literature and ultimately interferes less with the actual narrative than the intrusive comments of the omniscient author in *Murphy*. It is still a stage removed from the form of the trilogy in which the actual process of the novel itself dictates the situation. There, a man in a room writing word upon word in his own person out of the store of memories in his head—which is the residual nature of the fictional process—is itself the almost unbounded limit of his creation. Here, in *Watt*, the hero's friend Sam, becomes the 'mouthpiece' and tells the story which he himself is in no condition to write down meaningfully.

Sam anxiously insists that he has 'scant aptitude' for his task. It took him 'some years' to assemble all the information, not least because he and Watt only met on the days when the weather was right for them both. As Sam liked the sun and Watt the wind the days are few when there is a satisfactory combination of the two. Then again Sam acknowledges the possibility of inaccuracies:

> I may...have left out some of the things that Watt told me, though I was most careful to note down all the time, in my little notebook. It is so difficult, with a long story like the story that Watt told, even when one is most careful to note down all the time in one's little notebook, not to leave out some of the things that were told and not to foist in other things that were never told, never never told at all.

Frequently the narrative is interrupted by a question mark in place of a word or phrase which Sam either did not hear, cannot recognize from his notes, or can't be troubled to insert. Towards the end of the fourth section his stamina is evidently decreasing: 'hiatus in MS' he remarks at one point, 'MS illegible' at another. Like the addenda such insertions emphasize that this is only a printed book and its contents open to alternative treatment, omissions or whatever else the author feels suitable to the occasion. The reader only receives what the author is able to give. It is one response of the modern distrust of language, the reaction to the 'incantation toward the miracle' of the nineteenth-century French tradition. Against Baudelaire's endeavour to discover the forest of unifying symbols in *Les Correspondences* or Rimbaud's determined 'derangement of the senses', Beckett places a fallible artefact which is not the vision of the priest or the seer but the failure of a man too tired and disgusted to complete his work. At intervals Sam intrudes to mock the craft he is engaged in: 'how hideous is the semicolon,' he observes, and then gives an example in the following sentence. He digresses at length to satisfy his own mania for mathematical repetition as in the story of Louit, for example, which is not attributable to the untiring logic machine of Watt's mind; and deliberately compels attention to the illogical nature of his story, as in the footnote 'haemophilia is, like the enlargement of the prostrate, an exclusively male disorder. But not in this work.' But this tendency, as Hugh Kenner has suggested, is also an Irish peculiarity. Swift in *A Tale of a Tub* treated a book as a typographical artefact rather than a human document, and Joyce, in *Ulysses,* enforced his effects with changes of type, footnotes, variety in the spacing and the frequent use of mid-chapter titling. However, the most persuasive influence seems to be Sterne. The flouting of logical propriety, a dependence on visual rather than linguistic effects, and the introduction of extraneous matter all recall *Tristram Shandy* and hence the original 'anti-novels' of Rabelais and Cervantes. Like Sterne Beckett is happy to digress, to include snatches of song and even, at one point, all four parts of a mixed choir singing a threne that Watt heard while resting in a ditch. Reminiscent too are the exhaustive lists, the marginalia and the almost entire absence of plot. Beckett, it would seem, is more in sympathy with the originators of the novel than with the modern practitioners of the *nouveau roman.*

Apart from these violent dismissals of the act of literary creation Sam tells his story in a very much less embellished and ornate style than *Murphy*. After the first few pages in which the familiar rapid transitions predominate, the style achieves a new austerity. It is still capable of humour and sufficiently flexible to admit the apt ironic phrase or the passing witticism but what is new is the way every action and each thought over which Watt labours is exhaustively and precisely described. *Watt* turns the cataloguing process of *Ulysses* into a nightmare of pedantry. In part, as we shall see, this is a reflection of the philosophical basis on which the book is formed. As a rationalist faced with the inexplicable Watt resorts to the enumeration of every logical possibility implicit in a given situation, hoping to find in the sum of all the data a permutation of the facts that will include the correct assumption and so set his mind at rest. Nevertheless pedantry is embedded in the style. It appears in the formal shape of the sentences, in the frequent archaic or emphatically colloquial phrases and in the insistent repetition of individual words, as for example:

> ...there were times when he felt a feeling closely resembling the feeling of satisfaction, at his being so abandoned, by the last rats. For after these there would be no more rats, not a rat left, and there were times

> when Watt almost welcomed this prospect, of being rid of his last rats, at last. It would be lonely, to be sure, at first, and silent, after the gnawing, the scurrying, the little cries.

The obsessive comma after each short phrase accentuates the precision of a prose that is scientific in its exhaustive accuracy.

At the asylum Sam and Watt live in what Beckett calls either 'mansions' or 'pavilions'. From there, 'when exceptionally the desired degrees of ventilation and radiance were united,' they meet in the garden where the pointed absence of natural beauty alone, recalls the contrary image of the Garden of Eden—or perhaps The Field of the Cloth of Gold:

> In it great pale aspens grew, and yews ever dark, with tropical luxuriance, and other trees, in lesser numbers.
>
> They rose from the wild pathless grass, so that we walked much in shade, heavy, trembling, fierce, tempestuous.
>
> In winter there were the thin shadows writhing, under our feet, in the wild withered grass.
>
> Of flowers there was no trace, save of the flowers that plant themselves, or never die, or die only after many seasons, strangled by the rank grass. The chief of these was the pissabed.

The consciously imagined ugliness of this garden, in particular in the final paragraph, creates a dissentient image. There is an intentional disparity between this description and a previously formed image that reinforces the echo of the absent scene with which it is suggestively compared. The contrast emphasizes the forsaken aspect of Watt's garden: after the Fall grace has withdrawn and luxuriance become barren. The implication is continued when Sam describes, in a parody of Milton's treatment of Adam, himself walking in the garden while, confusingly, the use of the archaic 'pavilion' suggests that Sam and Watt could be seen as debased descendants of medieval chivalry. But this description of the garden is written up only that it may finally be deflated with greater effect. Beckett's concluding sentence violates the leisurely description: a linguistic counterpart to the physical collapse of the clown's pratfall.

Sam and Watt are united when the bridge connecting their respective walks collapses and Sam saves Watt from the stream below. Lying on their stomachs, face to face across the stream, they repair the damaged bridge. Suddenly their eyes meet, an 'exceptional smile' crosses their faces, and they begin 'to draw ourselves forward, and upward, and persisted in this course until our heads, our noble bulging brows, met, and touched.' The embrace which follows is a unique moment of mutal human sympathy.

Their usual pastimes, however, are less idyllic. In the garden:

> Birds of every kind abounded, and these it was our delight to pursue, with stones and clods of earth. Robins, in particular, thanks to their confidingness, we destroyed in great numbers. And larks' nests, laden with eggs still warm from the mother's breast, we ground into fragments, under our feet, with peculiar satisfaction, at the appropriate season, of the year.
>
> But our particular friends were the rats, that dwelt by the stream. They were long and black. We brought them such tit-bits from our ordinary as rinds of cheese, and morsels of gristle, and we brought them also birds' eggs, and frogs, and fledglings. Sensible of these attentions, they would come flocking round us at our approach, with every sign of confidence and affection, and glide up our trouser legs, and hang upon our breasts. And then we would sit down in the midst of them, and give them to eat, out of our hands, of a nice fat frog, or a baby thrush. Or seizing suddenly a plump young rat, resting in our bosom after its repast, we would feed it to its mother, or its father, or its brother or its sister, or to some less fortunate relative.
>
> It was on these occasions, we agreed, after an exchange of views, that we came nearest to God.

Allusion and mis-quotation are no longer prominent features of Beckett's style but parody is common in *Watt*. Louit's dissertation is couched in academic language, *Paradise Lost* and *Robinson Crusoe* are echoed more than once and the Bible, as in the genealogy of Mr Knott's servants or here, in the sitting down in the midst and the feeding of the rats, frequently affects the direction of Beckett's prose. In his mature writing a recollection of Biblical material, even the total re-writing of a parable as in the Unnamable's modern version of the wise and foolish virgins, is ordinary. It suggests the hesitant non-faith of contemporary uncertainty and disseminates a resonant undertone to the poetic movements of his character's thoughts.

In this passage, however, parody is only an incidental feature. The savagery of Sam's description, tempered with cruel irony, is an expression of the human situation in terms of the aesthetic which Beckett adopts as the only feasible approach for the writer who is surrounded by the immensity of nothingness. For the writer such as Beckett, compelled to attempt the definition of meaning in a world where meaning no longer exists, the only way 'one can speak of God is to speak of him as though he were a man...and the only way one can speak of man...is to speak of him as though he were a termite.' This is the method Sam advocates when he describes the breakdown of Watt's mind before the nothingness of Mr Knott's house, and Beckett, through the medium of Sam, uses it to describe his own reaction to the human condition in this passage. Watt and Sam are given the God-like power of grace or destruction over the birds in their garden, and the rats—if not termites—assume the position of humankind. It is, however, very much more than a metaphorical disguise. The situation is not real: rats do not nestle in men's bosoms nor do men habitually feed young rats to their parents. But in *Proust* Beckett disavows the methods of the realists in favour of what he terms, 'The Idea'. What he achieves here is precisely the Proustian imaginative descent to the Idea behind appearances. This extremity of horror reveals man as the devourer of his own and God as malignant, capricious and cruel:

> As flies to wanton boys are we to the gods;
> They kill us for their sport.[1]

Gloucester's words, unredeemed by the love of Cordelia, remain apposite in this response to the 'Idea' which Beckett sees beneath the external conditions of being. For if man (and the designation rat in itself is a sufficiently complete condemnation) is vile, the portrait of God is still more terrible. The ironic conclusion implies that it is God's nature to betray and destroy the helpless. The rats, one supposes, 'know not what they do', but He in whom absolute power is invested consciously favours some at the expense of others. Again Beckett returns to the arbitrary nature of grace and suffering. Yet the real implications of the passage have still not been mentioned. The irony does not reside in Watt's consideration that his treatment of the birds is god-like but that though he destroys he is, from the rats (or man's) point of view, being benevolent, apparently as God is supposed to be. The rats who are not preyed upon themselves flourish. The passage works on a tension between the 'aspiration' to divinity and the 'actual' events in the garden. In its combination of these two elements it is the apotheosis of the 'mirthless laugh'.

Sam himself is thinly characterized. He remains an interpreter for the incoherent Watt and a functional mouthpiece for Beckett's own 'ex cathedra' comments on the narrative. Watt himself is a reincarnation of Murphy; he still remembers the stars 'he had once known familiarly by name, when dying in London.' But he has not got Murphy's distinct personality. He remains throughout the questioning enigma, the uncertain cypher which is implicit in his name. He is, of course, 'a university man' and 'a very fair linguist' though he speaks rarely ('Mute on top of blind, said the porter') and when he does pays more attention to the rules of grammar than to content. His past contains 'two well-defined romances' though in his fumbling affair with Mrs Gorman, the fishwoman, who 'called every Thursday, except when she was indisposed,' he shows no desire to know fulfilment. This is perhaps as well, 'for Watt had not the strength, and Mrs Gorman had not the time, indispensable to even the most perfunctory coalescence.' Desire and opportunity are fortunately equated in this instance of Beckett's mathematical description of emotions. The affair remains on the humorous side of the 'mirthless laugh' unlike his later treatment of Molloy and Edith. Mrs Gorman is drawn to Watt by the bottle of stout he reserves for her visit, and he is attracted by the aroma of fish about her person. Thus they content themselves with sitting on one another's knees, turn and turn about, 'kissing, resting, kissing again, and resting again' until it is time for Mrs Gorman to continue with her rounds.

Watt extends this lack of passion into his other associations with mankind. He is passive, detached and introverted. He is happy sleeping in a ditch where he is barely distinguishable from the surrounding vegetation, and in spite of his eventual collapse the proximity of Mr Knott is a matter of indifference to him:

> Watt suffered neither from the presence of Mr Knott, nor from his absence. When he was with him, he was content to be with him, and when he was away from him, he was content to be away from him. Never with relief, never with regret, did he leave him in the night or come to him in the morning again.

Nor does his own appearance attract others. Watt's habitual expression is 'that of Judge Jeffreys presiding the Ecclesiastical Commission' and the vacancy in his eyes terrifies his successor, Micks, who 'raising in amaze an astonished hand to a thunderstruck mouth, recoiled to the wall, and there stood, in a crouching posture.' Watt has difficulty in smiling but from observing the efforts of other people he 'thought he understood how it was done.' The result, however, is not encouraging and 'to many it seemed a simple sucking of the teeth.' He prefers, with none of Murphy's conscious intent, to be by himself, either talking to himself in a long dribble of words or listening to the voices he hears in his head:

> Now these voices, sometimes they sang only, and sometimes they cried only, and sometimes they stated only, and sometimes they

> murmured only...and sometimes they sang and cried and stated and murmured all together, at the same time, as now, to mention only these four kinds of voices, for there were others. And sometimes Watt understood all, and sometimes he understood much, and sometimes he understood little, and sometimes he understood nothing, as now.

These voices occasionally give Watt information but more often exist as 'the soundless tumult of an inner lamentation.' They anticipate the voices of all the dead things in *Waiting for Godot* or recall the whispering of the sand to the prophet which in the trilogy assumes the terrifying aspect of the hypothetical imperative.

Watt walks strangely, drinks only milk and is a curiosity in Beckett's world as 'a man of some bodily cleanliness.' He is most obviously distinct, however, in his appearance. In dress he is closer to Molloy than Murphy. He is rarely without his 'black hat, of a pepper colour' which was picked up on a racecourse by his grandfather who bequeathed it to his successors. When he leaves Mr Knott's Watt wears a greatcoat, some seventy years old, voluminous and unwashed 'except imperfectly by the rain, and the snow, and the sleet;' baggy trousers, no collar or tie; and on his feet a boot and a shoe both 'happily of a brownish colour.' For this, of course, there is a logical explanation:

> This boot Watt had bought, for eightpence, from a one-legged man who, having lost his leg, and a fortiori his foot, in an accident, was happy to realize, on his discharge from hospital, for such a sum, his unique remaining marketable asset. He little suspected that he owed this good fortune to Watt's having found, some days before, on the seashore, the shoe, stiff with brine, but otherwise shipshape.

His other clothes are not described, being hidden from sight, but in either hand he carries a small grousebag, three-quarters empty, containing his toilet necessities and a change of body linen.

Watt's apparel presents, for the first time, the completed image of the hobo-clown. The long overcoat and immovable hat foreshadow the trilogy, and the problem of foot-wear, *Waiting for Godot*. Watt's feet, like Estragon's, are a continual cause of pain for though he takes a size eleven, the boot is a twelve and the shoe a ten. Typically the figures just avoid the harmony which would bring Watt bliss.

Watt's affinity with the clown, however, is more fundamental than an external similarity in dress. His rigid uniform is only an outward indication of the essentially comic-pathetic nature within. It is Watt's assumption of the metaphysical and archetypal qualities of the clown that emphasizes his alienation from the surrounding society and, disconcertingly, questions the norms on which it relies. Whenever Watt appears questions predominate: the real trembles on the margin of the unreal, meaning is inverted and becomes un-meaning and certainty is replaced by doubt.

When Watt is first seen, alighting from a tram, by Mr Hackett and Mrs Nixon, he is mistaken for an inanimate object 'a parcel, a carpet for example, or a roll of tarpaulin.' Only Mr Nixon, to whom Watt owes six and ninepence, knows otherwise. Watt, at Mr Nixon's request, is unable to meet the debt but offers to pay four and fourpence, all that he has about him. As he is setting out on a journey, however, payment is charitably not enforced: fate does not intervene to obstruct his progress and he continues on his way to the station leaving Mr Hackett perplexed at Mr Nixon's inability to speak of his debtor: 'he does not invite mention, he said, there are people like that.' But that Watt is an experienced traveller with no fixed address, red-nosed, mild and inoffensive, and 'a little strange at times' Mr Nixon can tell him nothing. Of Watt's 'Nationality, family, birthplace, confession, occupation, means of existence, distinctive signs' Mr Nixon is in 'utter ignorance.' Watt's existence in the world remains an enigma. Why he went to Mr Knott's, where he had come from and where he went to on the conclusion of his service are questions which Watt answers only in the most circumspect manner. This introductory scene anticipates the uncertainty of the events that follow and draws attention to the aura of vagueness in which Watt moves.

Mr Nixon's incomplete description is endorsed by Arsene. Mr Knott's servants, he explains, are either 'big bony shabby seedy haggard knock-kneed men, with rotten teeth and big noses' or 'little fat shabby seedy juicy or oily bandy-legged men, with a little fat bottom sticking out in front and a little fat belly sticking out behind.' Watt is of the former group, Arsene the latter. Again the familiar appearance of the clown is envoked and side by side two such men recall the double act of the music-hall, the circus and, more immediately, Vladimir and Estragon. Once more, however, the description is general rather than explicit: as in the disparaging observation of the railwayman, Mr Nolan, at the end of the novel to whom Watt is 'the long wet dream with the hat and the bags,' little that is distinguishing or individual in his appearance is recorded.

Watt encourages insult. On the tram he is shouted at by the conductor; Lady McCann shies a stone at him and knocks his hat off and the railwaymen are undismayed by the injuries they inflict on him. On each occasion his assailant is unprovoked and Watt's progress is a succession of ignoble and obvious pratfalls. When he arrives at the station, outwardbound, he accidentally bumps into a porter envolved in a Sisyphean labour—wheeling milk cans from one end of the platform to the other. The porter and his can emerge undamaged from the collision. Watt, however, is knocked to the ground. Yet it is the porter who is vociferous in complaint. He shouts, harangues and insults Watt who merely gets to his feet, retrieves his hat and bags, and remains mute and smiling before the onslaught.

This passivity before violence adds to the impression of detachment. Even before the actively hostile Lady McCann Watt is not moved to retaliate: 'there was no more room in his mind for resentment at a spit in the eye, to take a simple example, than if his braces had burst, or a bomb fallen on his bum.' Frequent repetition has led Watt to outward indifference: he regards these assaults as accidents and doesn't question the cause. But the cause too is part of his inheritance from the clown. Without premeditation Watt makes an anarchic excursion into the arena of traditional values. His is a journey in search of meaning that ends in the discovery of non-meaning. At Mr Knott's all that is usually assumed true disintegrates into an ill-defined series of phenomena unknowable by the formal exercise of rational examination. To this experience Watt is not indifferent as is shown by his breakdown and ensuing incarceration in a mental hospital. This journey, moreover, is a reflection of the clown's inward endeavour to oppose his own incapacity to the mystery of the irrational and in which, as always, his insights disturb the sleep of habit of those about him. Watt discovers the irreconcilable disparity between rational meaning and the immensity of nothingness and this discovery—or at least the threat of it in Watt's appearance—is the cause of the hostility with which he is everywhere received. Watt is set apart, immediately recognized and feared by the effect of his inward experience on his outward mien. He is marked, as the clown is marked, by an aura that disturbs and antagonizes: something that is not explicit but unignorable. It is this impression which Micks recoils from as he passes Watt in Mr Knott's kitchen:

> Or was it not perhaps something that was not Watt, nor of Watt, but behind Watt, or beside Watt, or before Watt, or beneath Watt, above Watt, or about Watt, a shade uncast, a light unshed, or the grey air aswirl with vain entelechies?

Thus Watt receives the traditional reward for his alarming discoveries, the clown's irrevocable pratfall. Because of his insight into concerns usually hidden by *mauvais foi* or habit Watt is treated as the scapegoat, the victim, as he-who-gets-slapped.

This dimension of Watt's character introduces a more general consideration.

The most extreme aspect of the victim, at least for the western imagination, appears at the heart of the christian mythology. There Christ himself, the son-of-God or God-on-earth, is crucified on man's behalf by those he 'disturbed'. Christ's presence as a man amongst mankind, as Dostoevsky's *Legend of the Grand Inquisitor* explains, is intolerable. The demands in Christ's teaching cannot be absorbed into the actualities of living which need habit and *mauvais foi* to continue, and his death is a necessity in the cause of general happiness. The figure of Christ, the last promise of eternal salvation for the finite self, has, over the last century become humanized. The suffering figure on the cross who carries the burden of man's sins, appears as a scapegoat and sacrifice but one from which divinity has steadily receded.

In *The Idiot* Dostoevsky gives fictional expression to the effect which was made on him by Holbein's *Descent from the Cross* in the Basle Museum. The incident is recorded by his second wife Anna Snikin:

> He stood for twenty minutes before the picture without moving. On his agitated face there was the frightened expression I often noticed on it during the first moments of his epileptic fits. He had no fit at the time, but he could never forget the sensation he had experienced in the Basle museum in 1867: the figure of Christ taken from the cross, whose body already showed signs of decomposition, haunted him like a horrible nightmare.[2]

Dostoevsky, in his novels, places the figure of Christ above both truth and reason. Christ's image, credible or not, is the centre of affirmation in all his writings. Yet Dostoevsky inclined to distinguish the human from the divine in Christ, and it was for this reason that Holbein's painting made so deep an impression. Dostoevsky sought to glorify Christ the man, but the picture which shows God in a state of human decay, raised the problem of whether there could be any redemption out of such an event. Christ appeared *merely* human. As Dostoevsky's spokesman, Prince Myshkin, exclaims: 'Why, some people may lose their faith by looking at such a picture!'[3]

Dostoevsky himself, after a period of spiritual despair, overcame his doubts, but to his successors Christ becomes more and more a companion-victim, a fellow self who has also endured the agony of mortality. Dostoevsky had marked Christ's image in the idiot prince beloved by children, in the convicts of Siberia and the holy beggars who wandered across Russia, and this entirely human dimension has been explored either implicitly in Kafka or directly in Joe Casy in Steinbeck's *Grapes of Wrath* and Faulkner's victim of prejudice, Joe Christmas, in *Light in August.*

In these instances the portrayal is directly human but in the images of modern painting Christ has been seen as the quintessential victim, the clown. In the sad-eyed, red-nosed crucifixions of Rouault or the clowns of Kocoshka and the salimbatiques of Picasso, the distinction between the two images is often negligible. The crucified saviour appears as the clown and the clown as the humanized son-of-god. It is this fusion which appears in both the composition of Beckett's characters and the religious imagery of their meditations. Beckett's hero is far closer to the archetypal nature of the clown than the fumbling little-man imposed on by a ruthless society as portrayed by Wells or Svevo. His dilemma goes beyond the external concerns of the metropolitan clerk and re-examines the problems which confronted Dostoevsky in the painting by Holbein. Indeed, the combination of comedy and pathos in such moments as Myshkin's breaking of Mrs Ypanchin's treasured vase are the antecedents of the acute discomfort caused by the absurd and the three laughs of *Watt.*

To humanize Christ is to diminish his promise of salvation. Christ as a man is associated with the hero in almost all of Beckett's writing. Murphy is found by Celia lying 'fully prostrate in the crucified position;'[4] Molloy talks of his life as an endless crucifixion and sees his meaningless circling 'progress' as a cycle of 'flight and bivouac, in an Egypt without bounds, without infant, without mother;'[5] while Moll has two earrings in the form of ivory crucifixes to represent the two thieves, and Christ himself in her mouth 'a long yellow canine bored to the roots and carved, with the drill probably, to represent the celebrated sacrifice.'[6] But the most extended association between the hero and Christ occurs in *Watt.* Sam sees Watt coming towards him in the garden, walking backwards, striking against trees and falling over the undergrowth into clumps of brambles:

> But still without murmur he came on, until he lay against the fence, with his hands at arm's length grasping the wires. Then he turned, with the intention very likely of going back the way he had come, and I saw his face, and the rest of his front. His face was bloody, his hand also, and thorns were in his scalp. (His resemblance, at that

> moment, to the Christ believed by Bosch, then hanging in Trafalgar Square, was so striking, that I remarked it.) And at the same instant suddenly I felt as though I were standing before a great mirror, in which my garden was reflected, and my fence.

This tentative but implicit association acquired by Watt after his experiences at Mr Knott's is not a suggestion of hope in the revelation of Christ's sacrifice. Like Molloy's reference to the flight into Egypt the inference is that the redemption of the self is precisely what is lacking: Molloy is trapped in the Egypt from which Christ eventually escaped (but only to end looking as Watt now does). The most obvious implication of this passage is that once Christ is treated as an ordinary man he is merely a victim like Watt. The meaningless speech of the backward-walking Watt is as important as the words of Christ. Thus the danger foreseen by Dostoevsky has become a reality. The clown remembers Christ and discovers a similarity in their lives and treatment: Watt is stoned as Christ was crucified. In *Godot* Estragon announces his intention of leaving his ill-fitting boots behind:

> VLAD: But you can't go barefoot!
> EST: Christ did.
> VLAD: Christ! What's Christ got to do with it? You're not going to compare yourself to Christ!
> EST: All my life I've compared myself to him.[7]

Estragon's statement has the simplicity of a declaration of faith, one of the few in Beckett which is not rescinded in the next line. But his faith is not in Christ the saviour, it is in Christ the fellow man. Christ is the norm against which Beckett's characters examine themselves, one who suffered like them, lived like them and ostensibly died for them. But it is with bitterness that Estragon recalls that where Christ lived 'they crucified quick.' Christ become man has lost his power to save—if ever he had it—life is long and dying longer; those who look at his human image have, as Myshkin feared, lost their faith.

II

The kernel of the novel is Watt's encounter with Mr Knott and the mysterious shifts of meaning and experience which occur under his roof. Once again the hero appears as the suffering Cartesian condemned to define the universe in rational terms. However, Watt's only aid in the task of rendering phenomena acceptable to the mind is language:

Watt is the opening of Beckett's struggle to subdue language into revealing both the instantaneous and the verifiably true.

Words are names for things. A thing may or may not exist but so long as it has been pinned down by a word it apparently does exist. In the beginning was the word, the word which broke up the formless continuum of existence. The word was power and man's magical support: a thing named was a thing subdued and the incantations of early man were designed, like the more famous cave drawings, to give him control over the world about him. Even in the void and the silence with which Beckett is concerned, words still appear as man's contact with reality and an object is incomplete until it has received the sacrament of a name. A man is nothing but an abstraction until he has been named and this naming renders him at once less mysterious and apparently harmless. On the journey to Mr Knott's Watt meets a man: ' "My name is Spiro," said the gentleman. Here then was a sensible man at last. He began with the essential.' The essential is the word by which the mind can classify the phenomena, and in this the man is no different from the dog, Cis, who is so called 'because the dog had to be called something, to distinguish it, for itself, and for others, from all other dogs, and that Cis was as good a name as any other, and indeed prettier than many'. Watt is not concerned with the real nature of Spiro. For him, at least before he arrives at Mr Knott's, meaning equals language and no other implication need be considered. Once a statement has been formed in words the event can therefore be dismissed. If all remained as simple as this encounter Watt would have little to concern him.

Immediately on Watt's arrival the imponderables arise. His entrance is inexplicable:

> ...Watt never knew how he got into Mr Knott's house. He knew he got in by the back door, but he was never to know, never, never to know, how the back door came to be opened. And if the back door had never opened, but remained shut, then who knows Watt had never got into Mr Knott's house at all, but turned away, and returned to the station, and caught the first train back to town. Unless he got in through a window.

The insistent repetition of 'not' and 'never' introduces the negative value of the experience Watt undergoes during the remainder of the book. Almost everything that he sees or does at Mr Knott's remains as uncertain as this entrance: Watt (or What?) is answered by Not or Naught, the negation of the void behind appearances, behind the words.

Neither does Watt notice the exact moment of Arsène's entrance. But the look of 'weary watchful vacancy' on Watt's face encourages Arsène to attempt a survey of his own experiences. He arrived, he remembers, bleeding like Christ 'in his head, in his side, in his hands and feet'. Again the extreme position of the victim is recalled. He describes Mr Knott's as the place to which all the old ways led. It is the peace of nothingness, apparently marked by an absence of 'will' and 'need' beyond all Murphy's fantasies. One has come to stay in the quiet house where:

> there are no roads, no streets any more, you lie down by a window opening on refuge, the little sounds come that demand nothing, ordain nothing, explain nothing (one has come to)...sites of a stirring beyond coming and going, of a being so light and free that it is as the being of nothing.

The pleasure of this arrival is increased by a sense of being 'the right man' in the 'right place' at last. Murphy at the Mercyseat had given himself the illusion that the stars he saw through his skylight were *his* stars, that he was the '*prior system*'.[8] At Mr Knott's the 'premonitions of harmony are irrefragable;' there the hero feels certain of having concluded his endless crucifixion. For a moment the dichotomy between the need to go on and the urge to stay where one is, journey and stasis, appears to be over. The hero seems to have arrived at a point:

> when all outside him will be he, the flowers the flowers that he is among them, the sky the sky that he is above him...when in a word he will be in his midst at last, after so many tedious years spent clinging to the perimeter.

At this instance the eternal questioning of 'Where now, who now, when now?' has ceased; he believes 'he may abide, as he is, where he is, and that where he is may abide about him, as it is.' Yet this sense of wholeness, this harmony, is again an illusion. A change takes place: Mr Knott's is only one more haven of particulars, not the ultimate release into the longed-for euphoria of timeless bliss.

Arsène finds it difficult to speak of this change. In his case he was sitting in the sun, smoking his pipe, when 'something slipped.' It was as though two or three million grains of sand had been fractionally, almost imperceptibly, displaced 'out of their old place, into a new one nearby;' immediately the sunlight on the wall at which he gazed seemed different and the pipe in his mouth felt unfamiliar, like a 'thermometer, or an epileptic's dental wedge'. In what the change consisted he is unsure, but slipping into a Welsh accent he attempts a description with the help of a very old joke, the one about the ladder: 'What was changed was existence off the ladder. Do not come down the ladder, Ifor, I haf taken it away.' Exactly what the implications of this ladder image are must necessarily remain unclear. Arsene is attempting to put his experience of Nothing into words. Nothing, however, cannot be defined except in terms which mean something, but something which describes nothing cannot be something. The cryptic phraseology of the ladder therefore, attempts to convey the impossible, the meaning of un-meaning. Perhaps the most explicit conclusion is to see it as the ladder of logic which is both superfluous and dangerous in the infinite, impregnable silences of Mr Knott's house. (Jacqueline Hoeffer's comparison with Wittgenstein's ladder in the *Tractatus* by which one ascends to his meanings only to cast it away as superfluous once those meanings are understood, is too fortunate if attractive. Beckett admits to not having read the *Tractatus* until after *Watt* was written.)[9] Arsene is warning Watt that logic and the void are incompatibles and that the former will not elucidate the latter. He describes the discovery as 'the reversed metamorphosis, the Laurel into Daphne, the old thing where it always was, back again.' Thus the servant of Mr Knott can expect to be repelled from his first illusion of harmony by this moment when he encounters the 'presence of what did not exist'. Arsene informs Watt that he too will experience the same feeling; that at Mr Knott's the unknown, the void, nothingness or 'what did not exist', will assert itself and destroy his premonition of having reached the centre, of being 'in the midst', at rest, for ever.

At the heart of 'what did not exist', if, for a moment, the void can be imagined to have a heart, is Mr Knott. Negative in name and nature he is the improbable end of all Watt's enquiries. Unlike the everchanging servants he 'is one who neither comes nor goes,...but seems to abide in his place, for the time being at any rate, like an oak.' He appears as a tree in whose branches the passing servants rest a while or around which 'in tireless assiduity turning' they carry out their necessary tasks. Yet despite his permanence and his proximity to Watt whose stay is not short, Mr Knott too remains an inscrutable mystery: he is the fount of nothingness which ever so slightly displaces intelligible reality.

While he is on the ground floor Watt catches, in the vestibule or in the garden, only brief glimpses of his elusive master. At no time does he confront Mr Knott face to face; his principal activity, carried out at a distance, is to supervise the regularity of Mr Knott's meals. 'On

Saturday night a sufficient quantity of food was prepared and cooked to carry Mr Knott through the week' and this concoction is served to him 'cold, in a bowl, at twelve o'clock noon sharp and at seven p.m. exactly, all the year round.' If all the food is eaten that is an end, if part or all is left Watt's duty is to give it to the dog. Within this routine he experiences little deviation and when the time comes for him to replace Erskine on the first floor he can truthfully say 'What did he know of Mr Knott? Nothing.'

During the second stage of his servitude this ignorance is prolonged. Watt discovers some of the particulars under which Mr Knott exists but the actual nature of his master becomes still more confused. Mr Knott's clothes are various—'now heavy, now light; now smart, now dowdy; now sober, now gaudy; now decent, now daring;' he moves about his house and grounds 'as one unfamiliar with the premises' and in his room he subjects his 'solid and tasteful furniture' to a multiplicity of positional changes, as often as not standing it on its side, its back or even upside down. Watt notices several other idiosyncracies which amplify the portrait of this strange Irish householder. At times Mr Knott sings, using all the male registers from bass to tenor or talks to himself but so softly that it sounds 'a wild dim chatter, meaningless to Watt's ailing ears'. He is also 'addicted to solitary dactylic ejaculations of extraordinary vigour, accompanied by spasms of the members. The chief of these were: Exelmans! Cavendish! Habbakuk! Echymose!' but not once do master and servant actually exchange conversation. However, perhaps Mr Knott's most disturbing feature is his continually changing appearance. Like the redoubtable Klamm in Kafka's *The Castle* he is never the same from day to day:

> For one day Mr Knott would be tall, fat, pale and dark, and the next thin, small flushed and fair, and the next sturdy, middle-sized, yellow and ginger, and the next small, fat, pale and fair...

So Watt is precluded from understanding in every way. His senses, he remarks, are in decay and neither visually nor aurally, to name but the most obvious methods of sensory divination of another, is he able to know his master. In all he reaches only two conclusions which are uttered 'halting' and 'faint with dubiety'. First, that Mr Knott needs nothing, and second, that he needs to be witnessed by someone 'that he might not cease'. His servant's perception of him seems essential to his existence.

This is not Watt's final, contradictory observation on his stay at Mr Knott's. In conversation with Sam at the asylum he reveals that his own need was fundamentally religious. His journey was a quest in which he came and dwelt by the side of the ultimate, offering himself naked and alone, to the 'source':

> Abandoned my little to find him. My little to learn him forgot. My little rejected to have. To love him my little reviled. This body homeless. This mind ignoring. These emptied hands. This emptied heart. To him I brought. To the temple. To the teacher. To the source. Of nought.

This uncharacteristic utterance, comparable in form and language to a religious incantation, is almost the only occasion on which Watt admits the extra-rational aspect of his quest. It belies his frequent assertion that he has lost all desire to understand his surroundings, that he passively accepts the irreconcilables of his servitude. He reaches the asylum not in resignation but in despair and anguish, knowing that what he sought, what he offered his whole self to, is 'nought'.

Mr Knott, in fulfilment of Beckett's aesthetic, is spoken of as if he were a man, but the enigma of his religious dimension is also acknowledged within the imagery. He is on several occasions compared to the sun. Meditating on the length of his service on the ground floor Watt considers that should he be there for less than one year some time, a month, a week or a day, must elapse 'on which the light of Mr Knott's service had not shone'. Again when speaking of Mr Knott's habits of 'rising' and 'retiring' the same implication is suggested: he is glimpsed through 'an eastern window at morning, a western window at evening,' and in bed 'Mr Knott's head, Mr Knott's feet, in nightly displacements of almost one minute, completed in twelve months their circuit of this solitary couch.' Moreover the 'empty hush' of Mr Knott's establishment gives Watt the impression that nothing can be added to it or taken away. His description is significant. In language that is resonant with a religious intimation of the ineffable nature of the world he has entered, Watt believes 'that as it was now, so it had been in the beginning, and so it would remain to the end.'

The nature of Mr Knott is perhaps illuminated by a comparison with the thought of Heidegger. Watt's failure and its causes would have been easily understood by the German philosopher. In the *Introduction to Metaphysics* Heidegger continues with his endeavour to explain and define the nature of Being. He contends that the meaning of this word, so self-evident to the Pre-Socratics, has been obscured by the Western rational tradition. In breaking up the totality of existence which is Being into a multitude of individual concepts, or 'essents', man's original instinctive understanding of wholeness has been lost. Man has separated himself from nature and accorded reason an importance which is unwarranted, with the result that Being as a meaningful term universally understood has become a 'haze'. In part III of the *Introduction* Heidegger sees an abundance of 'essents': 'Essent is the swarming crowd of people in the busy street. Essent are we ourselves. Essent are the Japanese. Essent are Bach's fugues. Essent is the Strassburg cathedral.'[10] Each of these phenomena can be seen and examined in itself but the power of Being that lies behind them and in which they were once immersed and united has become a cloudy vapour. We cannot see, Heidegger maintains, *The* tree for the trees.

Heidegger's search for Being is in its own way a religious search. Like Watt's quest it would seem to fail because for too long we have been nurtured in a rational tradition. Heidegger encounters almost as much difficulty defining Being as Watt does Mr Knott. The meaning of Being is as elusive as the 'meaning' of Mr Knott and perhaps it is not over heretical to wonder if Heidegger's quest too has not foundered on a nothingness similar to the one in which Watt becomes enmeshed. Watt is repulsed by the individual pots and dogs at Mr Knott's house which lose their certainty of definition in the presence of their master. Similarly Heidegger has difficulty getting beyond the phalanx of 'essents' to the residual meaning of Being, and the 'essents' themselves threaten to become meaningless during the discussion. One of Mr. Knott's pots is as indefinable to Watt's ultimate satisfaction as are the individual 'essents' to Heidegger. The quality of one of Mr Knott's pots is to be there; it has an 'isness' quite as definite as any of the 'essents' posited by Heidegger, yet in both cases their 'isness' is accompanied by an absence: by the undefinable haze that is Being, in the case of Heidegger, and by the non-understood nature of Mr Knott in the case of Watt. To attempt any strict parallel between these two works is an evidently misguided and irrelevant task, if only because Beckett himself in the addenda, implies that Mr Knott too is not permanent but a member of yet another series like that of his servants. This suggests an area of enquiry which Watt overlooked. Yet the fundamentally religious endeavour of both writers and the similarity in problems if not result, makes this digression worth while. Certainly Heidegger would understand the inherent incapacity of Watt to satisfactorily conclude his quest.

For Watt, of course, is a rationalist: he approaches the world with logic and empiricism. Watt's mind, which makes no essential distinction between words and objects, resembles that of a logical positivist to whom thinking is the process of using language, the formation of logically satisfying combinations from words. He professes an unconcern for absolute values and when faced with new phenomena 'the least plausible' (explanation) 'would have satisfied Watt, who had not seen a symbol, nor executed an interpretation, since the age of fourteen.' He comes to Mr Knott's having lived his adult life among face values and cannot remember a time when he wasn't able to dismiss an event with the conviction that 'that is what happened then.' Even when his 'dead father appeared to him in a wood, with his trousers rolled up over his knees and his shoes and socks in his hand', he had been able to explain away the troubling aspect of the experience by thinking of his father as 'dressed for wading'. Watt's concern, until he arrives at the forbidding and inexplicable silence of Mr Knott's, has been to derive comfort from words. For Watt the meaning of an event is in the language by which it is described and if an event, such as the appearance of his dead father, is disturbing it ceases to be so once he has found the right combination of words with which to encompass it. Thus he contrives to turn 'little by little, a disturbance into words;' he is not concerned with what events 'really meant', he merely wants to make 'a pillow of old words, for a head'.

The basis of this attitude is expressed in the linguistic theories of Fritz Mauthner (whose *Beitrage zu einer Kritik der Sprache* Beckett used to read aloud to Joyce)[11] and the *Tractatus logico-philosophicus* of Ludwig Wittgenstein. The main stages of Wittgenstein's theory are first that man identifies the artefacts of the universe which the mind has distinguished. To do this successfully he uses language, separating each thing from another in the cataloguing beloved of the rational mind. For Wittgenstein therefore language equals thought; the one is meaningless (and impossible) without the other. Where there is no thought and therefore no rational conception of the universe, there is only the formless continuum of phenomena. Thus there is either this totality distinguished by means of a language which is inseparable from thought, or there is nothing, the formless void. Wittgenstein's conclusion is that there are words or silence. As he writes, in the philosophic counterpart to the linguistic collapse of the nineteenth-century literary tradition: *Wovon man nicht sprechen kann darüber muss man schweigen.*[12] Man is thus confined once again, as he must be under rationalism, to the limitations of his skull.

The outcome of this attitude which he reflects is that Watt knows nothing about the phenomena for which words stand as symbols, only what the words are in themselves. As the words come only from the mind which has broken up the universe into conceptual units, they must be arbitrary. Watt is not concerned with what an event *does* mean; he only tries, by assembling all known data, to see what 'it can be induced to mean'. The world, therefore, is a series of possibilities which Watt examines for their logical motivation. This accounts for the continual lists, sequences and exhaustive permutations of words which, by the power of logic, explain away such problems as, how it can be made certain that Mr Knott's dinner is eaten by a dog. Watt does not ask *why* the scraps are given to a dog, he only wonders 'by what means then were the dog and the food to be brought together.' If meaning and language are identical then this event must, if it is surrounded in Watt's mind by every possible combination of words that could be used to describe it, somewhere be given its correct description. Watt is content to construct a series of possible relationships between the dog and his food. Assuming that his fabrication of words is exhaustive he has imprisoned the solution to his original question within it. To look for other meanings outside this web of words is absurd for beyond the word lies...Nothing.

This approach to experience may have satisfied Watt in the past but at Mr Knott's he is faced with the silence of which, Wittgenstein says, one cannot speak. There he is faced with the Void against which his logic is useless and he can no longer be comforted by the sedative of language because the Void will not admit of classification as an object. Foolishly Watt ignores Arsène's warming; that any attempt to speak of 'the unutterble or ineffable...is doomed to fail'. His predictable end, 'This body homeless...dum, num and blin' is the tragic exit of disinherited modern man for whom the pre-conceptual correspondence between his cognitative faculties and the nature of the world has broken down. This faith has been lost; all that remains is language which no longer expresses the reality of the world in which it is used.

Soon after his arrival the inadequacy of Watt's logic becomes apparent. Two men, 'the Galls, father and son' make a 'fugitive penetration' into the house to tune the piano. Watt watches them and is suprised to see that it is the younger man, rather than the aged, blind father who actually does the work. As they pack up to leave they exchange the following conversation:

> The mice have returned, he said.
> The elder said nothing. Watt wondered if he had heard.
> Nine dampers remain, said the younger, and an equal number of hammers.
> Not corresponding, I hope, said the elder.
> In one case, said the younger.

> The elder had nothing to say to this.
> The strings are in flitters, said the younger.
> The elder had nothing to say to this either.
> The piano is doomed, in my opinion, said the younger.
> The piano-tuner also, said the elder.
> The pianist also, said the younger.

There is a strange anti-poetry here but it is not this which disturbs Watt. The scene continues 'to unfold, in Watt's head... over and over again' until it is emptied of its rational meaning. It soon ceases to signify the event that Watt witnessed and takes on a form: it 'became a mere example of light commenting bodies, and stillness motion, and silence sound, and comment comment.' The scene arrogates to itself its own meaning; it becomes symbolic of itself and owes its significance to nothing in the world outside. For the first time, therefore, Watt is made to look for a meaning beyond the external event. But what distresses him is not that he did not know what happened, but that in incidents like this (and it is offered as one example among many)

> ...a thing that was nothing had happened, with the utmost formal distinctness, and that it continued to happen, in his mind...Watt could not accept...that nothing had happened, with all the clarity and solidity of something...

No words can explain this event because words, to the positivist, have only arbitrary value. Here the meaning is not relative but is something that exists as an absolute value and is therefore only definable in terms of itself.

From this point Watt's condition deteriorates rapidly. He finds himself in the midst of things which only consent to be named 'with reluctance'. Even one of Mr Knott's pots exists outside the logic of Watt's mind:

> Looking at a pot, for example, or thinking of a pot, at one of Mr Knott's pots, of one of Mr Knott's pots, it was in vain that Watt said, Pot, pot. Well, perhaps not quite in vain, but very nearly. For it was not a pot, the more he looked, the more he reflected, the more he felt sure of that, that it was not a pot at all. It resembled a pot, but it was not a pot of which one could say, Pot, pot, and be comforted.

Watt is no longer seeing what he is supposed to see and when the name will not settle on the object he experiences actual physical discomfort. Here it is just too much of a pot for him to say that it is not a pot, and not quite enough of one for him to say that it is a pot. He feels sure that for everyone else it remains a pot but in his case reality has been disturbed and reality's mirror, language, reflects a distorted image. There is an element here, one supposes, of the dismissal of realism and the advocacy of the Idea as set forth in *Proust* but still more an anticipation of the anger and impotence before existence in *The Unnamable*. In the later novel the position of the hero who is 'in' words, who does not exist outside of language (or thought) is the end towards which Watt is moving. Watt finds that he can no longer apply the term 'man' to himself 'as he used to do, with the intuition that he was perhaps not talking nonsense.' Language and identity have begun to diverge, each following its own path to a position where reconciliation becomes impossible. This tragic gulf is a dominant preoccupation of the plays as well as the later novels.

The refusal of things to assume their time-honoured names is a modern dilemma which has occupied writers since it was first acknowledged by Hofmannsthal, Rilke and Proust to be part of the more general crisis in language apparent at the turn of the century. Watt's *angoisse* and the failure of his finite weapons to encompass the infinite is an experience which Sarte has examined, with greater renown. In the now famous passage from *La Nausée* which describes Roquentin's walk in Bouville Park, Sartre's hero also finds the meaning of words slipping away from him and, interestingly, describes the situation in words very similar to those used by Watt.

In the past, Sam tells us, 'to explain had always been to exercise, for Watt;' and after his disturbing encounter with the pot 'Watt's need of semantic succour was at times so great that he would set to trying names on things, and on himself, almost as a woman does hats.' In *La Nausée* Roquentin, suffering one of his acute attacks of nausea, puts his hand on a park bench but pulls it away hurriedly, disturbed again by the sensation of the object he touches. He tries to steady himself: 'I murmur: "It's a seat," rather like an exorcism. But the word remains on my lips, it refuses to settle on the thing.'[13] As for Watt, language and reality have come separate. Roquentin knows that it *is* a seat just as Watt admits that for everyone apart from himself the pot is still a pot, but it is in vain that he murmurs 'It's a seat': he too cannot be 'comforted'.

The experience reveals to Roquentin the tenuous hold with which rationalism actually orders the world. Later that evening he writes in his diary: 'Words had disappeared, and with them the meaning of things, the methods of using them, the feeble landmarks which men have traced on their surface.'[14] Roquentin has discovered that the world is contingent, not intuitive: he has fallen out of the realm of being into the realm of existence and his nausea always strikes him at the moment in which he becomes aware of the existence of things in the world. In the case of the seat the uncomfortable sensation of the framework beneath his hand is accompanied with a shocked exclamation 'the thing exists'.[15] His great discovery is that what does exist, everywhere, is brute and nameless, it escapes from the logical relations in which we imagine we have enclosed it. Existence is more than language, it is indefinable because it is greater than any dispassionate description of it. Roquentin has yearned for logical necessity, for an ordered world, but he realizes that:

> Things have broken free from their names. They are there, grotesque, stubborn, gigantic, and it seems ridiculous to call them seats or say anything at all about them: I am in the midst of Things, which cannot be given names.[16]

Although he is more coherent Roquentin is in a very similar position to Watt. In the midst of the nameless he too sets to trying names on things. Why not centipede instead of tongue? he wonders, just as Watt called his pot a 'shield' or, growing bolder, a 'raven'. Moreover both Sartre and Beckett use the word 'exorcise' in connection with their hero's attempts to gain comfort from language. This mutual disposition for a word with religious connotations perhaps returns us to the conjectured significance of Heidegger, an obvious presence in Sartre if not in Beckett.

Roquentin learns that all these existences are simply there. To attempt to create a series of causal relationships, as he has been doing, is a mistake: 'everything is gratuitous.'[17] This is the lesson which, with tragic results, Watt proves incapable of learning. On his journey away from Mr Knott's he sees a figure following him along the road. In his concern he halts and waits for it to come closer so that he may determine 'what the figure was, in reality'. In spite of all that he has suffered and all that he has professed to the contrary he is 'for ever falling into this old error,' the error of rational curiosity. Rational curiosity, the determination to catalogue and explain, is the weight under which Watt stumbles. Thus it is that Beckett ironically describes his appearance in the asylum. Watt is for ever stumbling over the obvious, over what is in front of his face, and this irony is deepened by his failure to speak with rational coordination. The man who spent his time at Mr Knott's laboriously compiling and editing all known data on each particular event or object collapses into incoherence. First he talks as he walks, back to front. Then he begins to invert, no longer the order of the words in the sentence, but that of the letters in the word. The next stage is to invert instead, the order of the sentences in the period which he follows by altering the order of the sentences in the period and the inversion of the letters. The fifth stage introduces alterations in the words in the sentences together with that of the sentences in the period while the sixth deletes the disorganization of the words in the sentence in favour of inverting the letters in the word. In the seventh phase he inverts the letters in the word together with that of the words in the sentence together with that of the sentences in the period. So we get:

> Dis yb dis, nem owt. Yad la, tin fo trap. Skin, skin, skin. Od su did ned taw? On. Taw ot klat tonk? On. Tonk ot klat taw? On. Tonk ta kool taw? On. Taw to kool tonk? Nilb, mun, mud. Tin fo trap, yad la. Nem owt, dis yb dis.

or to translate:

> Sid by sid, two men. Al day, part of nit. Dum, num, blin. Knot look at Wat? No. Wat look at Knot? No. Wat talk to Knot? No. Knot talk to Wat? No. Wat den did us do. Niks, niks, niks. Part of nit, al day. Two men, sid by sid.

This is the end of his utterly hopeless quest. Watt is left a derelict, without speech, without his senses, 'dum, num, blin.' Aptly the anguish and the tragedy is conveyed in absurd nonsense, but even nonsense is inadequate when describing the great 'niks'. It is, moreover, the nonsense of a rational mind. It is not pure irrationality but the inversion of words or letters according to an inflexible logic that adopts its own consistent form of expression rather than the equally arbitrary common form. This patois of the asylum is another extension of Beckett's pedantry: the words assume a peculiar cadence of their own, no less curious, if more personal, than the flow of normal speech, and the passage is carefully organized to 'develop' (both in the original and when translated) in a circular form. Yet Watt's failure is comic only on the surface. The account of his journey is disturbing material to read and the stumbling figure of the close is as terrifying as he is amusing. Any encounter with the 'niks', even at second hand, is an alarming experience.

III

Arsène's monologue, an unbroken paragraph covering twenty-two pages, anticipates the novel-length monologues of the trilogy. It forms Beckett's finest sustained passage of writing to that date and introduces the theme of revolt against the irreconcilables of the human condition. Here the novel ceases to be a critique of the tragic failure of rationalism and becomes a lament for man in isolation, man arbitrarily condemned to the laws of beginning and ending, for man who may be the rational machine that Descartes described, but who is a machine subject to decay and death.

Watt, as a servant at Mr Knott's, is trapped in the inexorable wheels of cause and effect. Arsene explains that from the moment of his entrance Watt's eventual departure is certain. The inevitable beginning and end is a vice of necessity as tight as birth and death:

> And then another night fall and another man come and Watt go, Watt who is now come for the coming is in the shadow of the going and the going is in the shadow of the coming.

The light will die away from the sky, the door will open onto 'slush or storm or the warm still scents of summer' as on all previous days, but this day Watt will be compelled to depart just as once before he was compelled to enter the gate conscious that he had arrived at last at the right place. It is a superb image for mortality. Mr Knott's is only an unintelligible place of passage and though the macrocosm of nature (with which Mr Knott is vaguely associated) continues, the mortal microcosm that is Watt remains for only an indeterminate period of time.

At first the idea of a coming that is in the shadow of the going, the concept of a series, is comforting to Watt. Like Sartre's Roquentin he finds sense, and therefore satisfaction, in music and numbers. Roquentin rediscovers his purpose while listening to a scratched gramophone record of a hoarse-voiced American singing 'Some of These Days'. Watt is delighted by three frogs croaking 'Krak!', 'Krek!' and 'Krik!' at mathematically exact intervals, and by the threne he hears when resting in a ditch. In Watt's case it is the proximity of the sounds to a mathematical series which principally delights. According to the fixed order of their croaks, and assuming that they all start together, it will take the frogs a series of 360 individual Krak, Krek and Kriks before they all croak simultaneously once again. This vocal image of the circle gives Watt great pleasure.

To explain an event as part of a series is to explain it away. In *How it is* the hero postulates an entire hierarchy of mud-bound figures watched over by a multitude of scribes. The creation is so convincing that for a moment his invented world, created to give credence to the actual, seems entirely believable. So in *Watt* the terrifying and unknown aspects of phenomena are explained away by assuming that the present is a necessary result of the past. A phenomena which in itself is inexplicable appears meaningful when it is placed in a series and helps to support Watt's 'pillow of old words.' If the arbitrary event is placed in 'a chain stretching from the long dead to the far unborn, the notion of the arbitrary could only survive as the notion of a pre-established arbitrary.'

However, Watt soon penetrates to the uncomfortable implications of a causal series. He realizes that not only is the effect determined by the cause but the cause is equally limited by its effect. In the series 1-2-3, 2 is as constricted by 3 as it is by 1. Therefore within a series there is no freedom in either direction for beginning determines ending just as every ending determines a new beginning.

When this knowledge is applied to the problem of Mr Knott's servants Watt begins the preoccupation with Time that is still apparent in the heap of sand in *Happy Days*. Watt suggests three servants, Tom, Dick and Harry and in their case the law which governs their arrival and departure leads literally 'from the long dead to the far unborn'. Their coming is motivated not only by who went before but also by those who are at that moment still stretching forwards into an infinite future. The idea that the present is determined by what is not yet (which is inescapable once the series takes place in time) is, to Watt, 'too horrible to contemplate'. In this human series 'Tom's two years on the first floor are not *because of* Dick's two years on the ground floor:' that is one conclusion to be drawn from the time series. The other is that there must be something in Tom, as Tom, and Dick, as Dick, which allows their servitude to be predetermined and their selves to fit exactly into the allotted span of beginning and ending:

> For otherwise in Mr Knott's house, and at Mr Knott's door, and on the way to Mr Knott's door, and on the way from Mr Knott's door, there would be a languor and a fever, the languor of the task done but not ended, the fever of the task ended but not done, the languor and the fever of the going of the coming too late, the languor and the fever of the coming of the going too soon.

In Watt's experience this is not so: 'Mr Knott was haven, calmly entered, freely ridden, gladly left.' Therefore he is presented with the dilemma, firstly that a human being is one of a series ordained by a being past and a being to come, and secondly, that he is indivisibly himself. As himself he is not Tom because of Dick but Tom because he is Tom, and as such he must contain an element which is outside time. Under the conditions of servitude at Mr Knott's Watt discovers that the human is both in time as part of a series and outside it, like an irrational number lurking unknown between and behind the cognates of the series. This dilemma is, writes Beckett via Sam, 'the ancient labour'. It is a logical impossibility and therefore incomprehensible to Watt but its resolution is soon to become an ever more urgent need to the hero exiled from his Self.

Behind all the individual series which Watt postulates to explain particular phenomena moves the shadow of the great series, that of birth and death, the passage of the seasons, the passing of time. Although Watt insists that he is interested only in face values his quest, as we have seen, is fundamentally religious and his concern with particular series is meaningless without the background of universal values against which they are placed. *Watt* is not an allegory nor is it a pattern of symbols intelligible to those who possess the key ('no symbols where none intended' writes Beckett in the addenda): but the hero's journey carries a definite extra-rational resonance. To speak of Mr Knott is to be guilty of 'anthropomorphic insolence' and the terms of one's stay in his house clearly contain various possible reflections on existence in the actual world. Interpretation cannot, however, be specific: as in the works of Kafka the reader himself gives value and significance to the recorded experience. Indeed, to attempt a logical explanation of 'niks' is to fail as Watt failed.

Nevertheless in Arsène's monologue one is given a hint of the universal concerns which the arid discourse of Watt seemingly conceals. Here the writing is both rich and poetic and Arsène, who adjusted himself to Mr Knott's in a way that Watt could not, sets Watt's intellectual despair in a context of real human anguish. As they pass in Mr Knott's kitchen the out-going and in-coming servants know a brief moment of human contact, a moment made all the more poignant by their knowledge of its passing:

> Yes, these moments together have changed us, your moments and my moments, so that now we are no longer the same as when they began—ticktick, ticktick!—to elapse, but we know that we are no longer the same, and not only know that we are no longer the same, but know in what we are no longer the same, you wiser but not sadder, and I sadder but not wiser, for wiser I could hardly become without grave personal inconvenience, whereas sorrow is a thing you can keep on adding to all your life long, is it not, like a stamp or egg collection...

Character and author, aware of Proust, attempt to imprison the passing moments in words. It is a prominent motive in the trilogy and an impossible task. The word written, writer, time and space are no longer the same, and his sadness and isolation have increased. *Watt* marks the first appearance in Beckett of man's failure to pierce the barrier of language. Arsène is already open to the experience of Molloy, to the continual shedding of tears. 'And often I turn, tears blinding my eyes', he begins; the acute tears of more than loneliness, the ceaseless tears of existence that must end, of the mortal anguish which leads him to pray for any kind of immortality, even:

> longing to be turned into a stone pillar or a cromlech in the middle of a field or on the mountain-side for succeeding generations to admire and for cows and horses and sheep and goats to come and scratch themselves against and for men and dogs to make their water against and for learned men to speculate regarding and for disappointed men to inscribe with party slogans and indelicate graffiti and for lovers to scratch their names on, in a heart, with the date, and for now and then a lonely man like myself to sit down with his back against and fall asleep, in the sun, if the sun happen to be shining.

A similar moment of tenderness mingles with the revolt in what is one of Beckett's finest passages. Arsène's description of the seasons combines the sensual beauty of nature with an anger directed against the spectral movement of decay that lies behind it. The passage reveals the classical precision of Beckett's language, the balance of emotion and thought, with the considered use of every word, each one as necessary to its context as if it had been poetry, which indeed, it is. It contains also humanity, compassion and a gentle irony, and stands, with the closing paragraph of Joyce's *The Dead,* as an example of what twentieth-century prose can achieve:

> The crocuses and the larch turning green every year a week before the others and the pastures red with uneaten sheep's placentas and the long summer days and the new-mown hay and the wood pigeon in the morning and the cuckoo in the afternoon and the corncrake in the evening and the wasps in the jam and the smell of the gorse and the look of the gorse and the apples falling and the children walking in the dead leaves and the larch turning brown a week before the others and the chestnuts falling and the howling winds and the sea breaking over the pier and the first fires and the hooves on the road and the consumptive postman whistling 'The Roses are Blooming in Picardy' and the standard oil-lamp and of course the snow and to be sure the sleet and bless your heart the slush and every fourth year the February debacle and the endless April showers and the crocuses and then the whole bloody business starting all over again.

SIX: THE TRILOGY: I

This dreary huddle has no hope of death,
  Yet its blind life trails on so low and crass,
  That every other fate it envieth...

God they blaspheme, blaspheme their parents' bed,
  The human race, the place, the time, the blood,
  The seed that got them, and the womb that bred.[1]

DANTE

There is a certain thing above all human activity: it is
the example of this monotonous crucifixion, this crucifixion
wherein the soul is forever being lost.[2]

ARTAUD

I

TO WRITE in a foreign language, as Hugh Kenner has observed, not only entails a new discipline; it also creates a different tone. From 1945 to 1949 Beckett retired to his room in Paris and in a remarkable period of sustained creation wrote, in French, the series of books which form the core of his work. After the not wholly successful experiments of *Mercier et Camier*[3] and the three short stories, collectively known as the *Nouvelles,* he wrote *Molloy*, *Eleuthéria* (a first play which was also abandoned), *Malone Meurt*, *En attendant Godot*, *L'Innommable* and the *Textes pour rien* in that order. It was a massive achievement of concentration as well as of content. Whether Beckett was impelled to act by his experiences during the Occupation (which has been suggested) or had merely arrived at the sudden maturity of his powers (which is more likely) it is impossible to deduce. What is certain is that these works contain the most comprehensive expression of Beckett's art and thought. The terms of their creation suggests a comparison with the explosive force that characterizes the marvellous but short-lived fusion of substance and ability one associates with the 'great' year of the romantic poet rather than with the modern prose writer, though the impulse to an almost monastic seclusion is reminiscent of Proust's decision to abandon society and begin work on *À la recherche du temps perdu.* The English novels lead up to the trilogy and it is from the impasse at which *The Unnamable* ends that the plays continue, enacted under the dramatic conventions first explored in *Waiting for Godot.*

Beckett's choice of French as his medium is unique. Political or geographical necessities have often compelled writers, for example Kafka and Conrad, to abandon their native languages, and a desire to imitate the classics prompted many English poets to turn their classical education into a reality. Admiration is a spur to emulation as Milton and Crashaw in Latin or, more recently, Eliot in French, have revealed. Beckett's decision, however, differs in purpose from all the accepted reasons. It seems to have been both voluntary *and* a necessity: voluntary because the decision was made without impersonal pressure, a necessity because it was urged by one of the frequent impasses at which his art arrives. Moreover the transition from English to French was made feasible by Beckett's self-imposed exile in France. In this he deliberately chose the condition of his early exemplars, Joyce and Dante, and it is not likely that he was unaware of its effect on the artist. For exile forces writers to consolidate a vision of the world and to attempt to give the latter total expression in their works. It lead Joyce to *Ulysses*, Dante to the *Divine Comedy* and Conrad to discover, in the British Merchant Marine, a moral standard that forms the centre of all his major books; one that applies as much to the Costaguanans of *Nostromo* as to the supposed cowardice and rehabilitation of Lord Jim. In Beckett's case this comprehensive angle of vision existed in embryo from the first stories of *More Pricks Than Kicks*; exile gave him a new means of expression. His adopted language proved more tractable and assisted in the creation of this vision which became at once more complete and incisive than it had been in the English novels. In French his hero discovers his true accent and assumes a universal significance; he is instructed now, as Moran describes, by 'a voice telling me things' but it is a voice that 'did not use the words that Moran had been taught when he was little'. This achievement was doubly unique because it involves not only the use of French but also the arduous process of retranslation into the author's native tongue.

Regarding this task which is both voluntary and a necessity Beckett has said that he writes in French *parce qu'en français c'est plus facile d'écrire sans style.*[4] The remark is at first misleading for the trilogy is not the loosely-written, flat and devious creation it seems to imply. There is an austerity and a precision in the works originally conceived in French which is absent from *Murphy* and *Watt*. The ambiguity occurs in one's interpretation of the word style. For Beckett 'sans style' suggests a writing that has abandoned the matrices of fiction, one that is, in the words of the trilogy, 'not literature', and the discovery of such a style was a necessary concomitant of the Art of Failure.[5] To be a writing and not literature is not to be tediously unreadable but to demonstrate the hesitant aesthetic which Beckett evolved during this period and later expressed in the dialogues with Duthuit. Like Artaud, Beckett had become dissatisfied with the screen that literature places between reality and the artist's purpose. To Artaud and Beckett literature might almost seem yet another anaesthesia of Proustian habit: literature diverts from 'what is the wail of reality' and Beckett, like Artaud, had come to feel the need to abandon the appearance of fiction and re-contact 'the resonant reality of things'.[6]

His choice of French as a medium was the original departure in search of the way in which 'the thing I am trying in vain to say may be tried in vain to be said'.[7] In *Watt* Beckett had reached the verge of his impossible art. *Watt* marks the decisive encounter with Nothing: it is the book in which Beckett met and tried to express the unsayable for the first time, and where he found himself trapped into defining a meaning where a meaning no longer existed. This, which Beckett sees as the task of the writer, is impossible for while he wishes to describe the void behind the words, the words accrete their own meanings and, sustained by habit in the patterns they form, operate independently to confound even the most careful user. The words threaten to become master of the mind that manipulates them, for Beckett now wishes to say not what the words lead him to say but what the words conceal. As a language English is more prone than most to these diversions of meaning: its power of suggestion far exceeds the more explicit French. Moreover in the writer's native tongue assimilated, concealed meanings are more difficult to discern than in the rational process of using a learnt language. The use of French, therefore, helps Beckett to maintain the tension on which his writing depends and replaces the Baroque mannerisms of his early work. In French Beckett creates another literary personality (almost as the heroes of the trilogy invent their pseudo-selves), one who is able at times to separate himself from the tissue of implied meanings within the words. The tone now suggests fragments brought back from the edge of experience. The comparative certainty of the third-person narrative is replaced by the pained and worried first-person whose monologue is broken into breath pause and articulatory emphasis by the obsessive comma. This voice, with its precarious conjectures, is repetitious and concerned with verbal accuracy: the style supports the hero's impression that he is engaged in a laborious pensum which is his only birth-right. Yet the result is an achievement in both languages, a purity of 'style' that led one critic to remark of the French version: '*le son de sa voix dans nos oreilles, c'est notre propre voix, enfin trouvée.*'[8]

The three *Nouvelles* (a fourth, *Premier Amour*, has not been published) were Beckett's first ventures within this new personality. Though their limitations are evident their importance as exploratory works which clearly anticipate the trilogy ensures their position in Beckett's development. They are all narrated in the first-person and the same, nameless hero appears throughout. He lives in what is described as a walled town, in the middle of a plain, trapped between the mountains and the sea. But this landscape (evidently the countryside of Bally in which Molloy is shortly to appear) remains ill-defined as does the temporal framework of the stories. No dates are given and the passage of the seasons is rarely recognized; while within individual stories event flows into event, at times as in a dream. The linear extension of the hero's life in time and space is subjected to sudden transitions: memory invades the present, his location suddenly changes, the whole seems open on all sides to causal contradictions and only the word in one's mind, isolated from those which preceded it and those about to follow, can be accepted as real. What the hero chooses to write is one's sole evidence: it is as if the words in which the hero exists form a plain surrounded by a silent abyss and one is unable to complete the imponderables from without as one can with the traditional novel. In, for example, the nineteenth-century fictional universe of Balzac or Tolstoy one is able to surround the text and any apparent inconsistencies it contains with material one brings from other novels or from one's personal experience; in the *Nouvelles* this is impossible for the words the hero speaks are answerable only to themselves and in this have passed beyond literature.

L'Expulsé (*The Expelled*) opens as the hero, who is 'in the prime of life', is flung down the steps of his house into the street. As he rests a moment, elbow upon the kerb, the door is re-opened and his hat is flung after him. Unconcerned by the violence of this gesture he contents himself, for the hat is his, with the ironic remark 'They were most correct, according to their god.' Then he relates the hat's history in a now familiar virtuoso performance. Boots, pieces of string, bicycles, pebbles, all alike prompt a similar reaction. They form the major events in the life of the Beckett hero and he performs a *lazzo* on them in language just as the *commedia dell' arte* actor would embellish his performance with a bravura set-piece on a subject for which he was famous. One expects to find one or all of these items in the repertoire of a hero and his skill in language is judged, just as one compares the identical acts of two clowns. As John Fletcher writes: 'One therefore expects, with the same assured anticipation with which one greets the clown, the Beckett hero, in every tale, to execute certain ritual gestures, to submit to certain regular happenings.'[9]

The performance over, the hero sets off through the town, walking in the road as the 'widest sidewalk is never wide enough for me'. He complains of a stiffness in his legs and though he claims to have lived in this town all his life he is only slightly acquainted with his surroundings. His disposition is for a solitary room and his naïvety in social conduct is soon made apparent by the difficulties he encounters with the passers-by. He almost knocks over a child and is warned and threatened about his behaviour by two policemen. He finds it simpler to travel by horse-drawn cab and becomes friendly with his cabman. They lunch together and the cabby narrates his life story ('We did our best, both of us, to understand, to explain'); then, because the cabby believes that this is what the hero wants, they travel round a number of houses looking for furnished rooms. However, they are not successful and the cabman, after a few drinks, invites the hero home for the night. He sleeps in the stable with the horse and a family of rats. At dawn he climbs through a window, without paying either his fare or his lodging, and goes off 'to meet the sun'.

La Fin (*The End*), the most complete of the three stories, describes the hero's expulsion from an unspecified charitable institution. He is told that he is as well as he ever will be and is given a set of clothes belonging to an unknown deceased, together with a small sum of money to ease his first days in the world outside. But the hero doesn't want to leave: he has identified himself with the inanimate objects in his room and simulates a violent scene in the hope that they will permit him to stay. However, the clerk, Mr Weir, is adamant and he is forced out into a town he again does not recognize. After many failures he eventually discovers suitable lodgings in the basement of a house where he sinks into euphoria interrupted only by a few rats and his Greek (or Turkish) landlady who once a day brings him his food and empties his chamber pot. This idyll ends when the landlady extracts six months' rent from him in advance and hastily disappears. The new landlord expels him immediately, even though he offers to share the basement with the man's pig.

He wanders into the country where he sleeps in a dungheap and is consequently put off three buses. Some time later he meets an old acquaintance who lives in a cave on the sea-shore with his ass, on which he carries shells and seawrack into the town for people's gardens.

He asks the hero home to his cave and though the latter at first refuses:

> to my amazement I got up on the ass and off we went, in the shade of the red chestnuts springing from the sidewalk. I held the ass by the mane, one hand in front of the other. The little boys jeered and threw stones...

The hero is, however, unhappy at the sea-side and the donkeyman realizes it. In a scene of uncharacteristic tenderness he offers to prepare the hero another cave nearby and to bring him food each day. But the hero refuses ('He was kind. Unfortunately I did not need kindness') and the man lends him the use of a cabin in the mountains instead. After an abrupt transition the hero is discovered in the cabin almost dying of malnutrition. One day he finds himself too weak to rise and is only saved by a cow which he manages to milk. Somehow he returns to the town where he begs on a street corner, using a begging-board of his own invention, and sleeps in a boat in a shed by the river. Soon he ceases to go out and feels death approaching. He has visions and sees himself floating out to sea in the boat, paddling with a bit of plank until he opens a hole in the keel and, swallowing the sedative he has brought with him in a phial, lies back and watches the gorse burning on the mountains behind the town as it did when he was a child.

The remaining story, *Le Calmant* (*The Sedative*), clearly anticipates the post-mortem monologue of *The Unnamable*. The hero is dead when it opens and, too frightened by the sound of his rotting body to lie silently, he determines to tell a story from *outre-tomb* which will act on his mind like a sedative. In it he imagines himself returning to his town which is lit by an apocalyptic, bright light and which seems deserted. He feels a need for human companionship and goes to the docks, hoping to enter into conversation with a seaman, but the only person he meets is a boy with a goat who gives him a sweet. When he tries to speak to the boy he finds that his mouth will only make an inarticulate, rattling sound. As he returns to the centre of the town the narrative becomes still more dream-like. He climbs to the top of a deserted cathedral; meets a man who, in exchange for a kiss, gives him a phial (perhaps a memory of the one in *The End*); and suddenly, when an impenetrable darkness falls, finds himself surrounded by a throng of people. However, the bright light returns almost immediately and the hero is left to pursue his disconsolate way in solitude.

In outline the stories, which portray three phases of one existence, anticipate the trilogy. In the first the hero is still reasonably active; he expires at the close of the second as Malone dies in the central section of the work that follows, and in both cases the final part attempts a portrait of the hero's existence after death. However, in the stories the particulars are more instructive than the whole: several incidents are directly recalled in the trilogy and certain passages are even reworked and integrated into the text of the later novels. For example, Molloy remembers the voyage in a boat when he visits the sea in search of sucking stones; *Malone Dies* elaborates on the notion of a solitary existence disturbed only by a woman who brings the hero his food and empties his pot; and life in a cave by the sea is one of Malone's most pleasurable memories. In *The End* the hero dismisses that time in a few words:

> I lay in the cave and sometimes looked out at the horizon. I saw above me a vast trembling expanse without islands or promontories. At night a light shone in the cave at regular intervals.

He insists that he hated the sea and was eager to escape to the cabin in the mountains: the tone is neutral and the experience apparently unimpressive. But in *Malone Dies* Malone speaks with feeling about those days when, he says, he was almost happy (see the passage headed 'text' at the opening of this study). In the interval the language has become richer, the moment is at once more personal and more universal and the experience has gained in significance.

This comparison demonstrates the relationship of the stories to the trilogy in general. The nameless hero of the stories experiences the same problems as his successors, Molloy, Malone and the Unnamable, but his narrative lacks the despair and the anguish by which they are transfigured and made universal. He is conscious of his lack of identity ('I whose soul writhed from morning to night, in the mere quest of itself'); feels that his body is alien and in decay; and is continually rebuffed by society. 'They', as he collectively terms his fellow men in deliberate, personal disassociation, laugh at his appearance, throw him into the street and out of his lodgings. He is the victim that society expels, whom landladies rob, communist orators harangue as a 'living corpse' or 'crucified bastard', dogs piss on and the police keep under constant observation. Not surprisingly therefore he hates mankind, especially children, and longs for the peace and security of a small, womb-like room from which he need never stir. Yet when he seems to have attained this sanctuary it immediately becomes another discomfort and the nature of his longing is reversed: 'To contrive a little kingdom, in the midst of the universal muck, and then shit on it, that was me all over.' He is perpetually unsatisfied for once in his room he is made aware of his isolation in which even the casual words of a seaman would be something he could cherish long after they are spoken. He discovers a silence that he himself must people if he is to be certain that he exists in a recognizable world, and in his extremity he is the first of Beckett's heroes to evolve the expedient of story telling. In the general context of Beckett's later work the closing sentences of *The Expelled* are prophetic:

> I don't know why I told this story. I could just as well have told another. Perhaps some other time I'll be able to tell another. Living souls, you will see how alike they are.

The failure of the stories to convey the anguish evidently present behind the hero's leisured sentences is the result of a deliberately chosen literalness of style. He knows himself to be a victim both of society and of his condition as an existing being. He even notices his affinity with the sacrificial Jesus who is invoked almost as frequently as he is in *Godot*, but in his narrative he withholds emotion from the description of his condition. Beckett distances the action to achieve a purity which at times is close to indifference. In both the stories and the trilogy Beckett writes of the apparently abnormal and of the extreme concerns of existence. In the stories his central preoccupation is with isolation and exile; in the trilogy his range expands to include the other universal experiences, birth, death, love, time, old age, suffering and cruelty. In order to emphasize that these elemental events in life are accepted in a spirit of negligence and without question and yet are often horrible and always disturbing, he inverts the terms and treats extremes as normality. For example Moran clubs a man to death but is unable to describe what actually happened; the drama of a struggle and a lurid death which is what the reader expects of the novelist is beyond him. As he says: 'I am sorry I cannot indicate more clearly how this result [the dead body] was obtained, it would have been something worth reading.' In the pages immediately following, however, he is able to give a detailed description of how he looked for a bunch of keys, lost in the grass. The prominence of this last incident draws attention to the paucity of information offered about the first. The reader himself is thus compelled to redress the discrepancy.

This technique, used sparingly in the trilogy, encourages the neutral, unemotional tone of the stories. It might seem at first to be another legacy from Swift who also used (in, for example, *A Modest Proposal*) a bitter irony that relied on an inversion of the ordinary for its effect. Yet the subtle range of metaphysical and moral distinctions which Beckett attempts in these works—particularly in the trilogy—reminds one at least as strongly of the fragmented world of Kafka where things have fallen apart and values become compounded into an incongruous but dead normality. Kafka's parable of sickness and compassion, *Metamorphosis*, was conceived in a similar technique: the hero, Gregor Samsa, sees nothing surprising in his transformation into a beetle and the reader's own objections are undermined by the literalness of the narrative. The discrepancy between extreme unreality and extreme precision of style based on a scrupulous regard for detail awakens, not disbelief, but a feeling of acute and painful reality. Swift had a firm and commonly-understood series of values against which he measured his irony; Beckett and Kafka have lost such a centre and can no longer be certain. Nevertheless Beckett's use, in the stories, of this ordinariness limits his range. The stories lack the emotional, poetic involvement of the trilogy and emerge as explorations in a single key: a meticulous but restricted prelude to the monologues which follow.

II

The four monologues of the trilogy (*Molloy* consists of two separate sections) are all written down by men confined to a room or, in *The Unnamable*, to an airless world beyond the tomb. In the first two, the self-conscious narrators, Molloy and Moran, describe the last stages of the journey that brought them to the room; in the last two, physical decay is so complete that movement is at first strictly localized and then impossible as the hero passes over into the grey wastes of mind-bound Purgatory. Molloy can still jest bitterly about his condition; his laugh is a harsh rattle, closer to invective than humour, which he opposes to the encroaching despair. In *The Unnamable* this release is no longer possible. *Molloy* is still literature, a consciously written description of an extreme situation; *The Unnamable*, in its gasping, breathless anguish, has ceased to pretend.

The room is a complex arena. It is a womb-like retreat where the hero is concealed from his fellow men, almost secure against the interference of an antagonistic humanity. It is a shell-like reflection of his own skull in which the interminable monologue continues, the four walls constituting the framework of rationalism (2+2 =4) on which his mind depends and to which, so long as he is divided from his Self, he is bound. As such it mirrors the place, the 'hollow sphere, hermetically closed to the universe without' that Murphy desired, where the hero walks among the ruins of his past in 'a place with neither plan nor bounds and of which I understand nothing,'[10] or where he meditates fiercely upon his present condition. It is 'the same place as always...which is perhaps merely the inside of my distant skull where once I wandered, now am fixed, lost for tininess, or straining against the walls.'[11]

Fundamentally, however, it provides a scenic image for the novelist himself; for the man in a room who is covering pages with words and, as he writes, is drawing instant by instant nearer to death. The trilogy turns in upon itself, spiralling down from all externals to an examination of the internal silence that fills each individual being. Beckett abandons narrator, setting and plot as the empirical tradition of the novel has known them. The trilogy writes itself. It evolves from the simplicity of this situation wherein the writer who has abandoned literature yet who is compelled to write by a force he doesn't understand, sits in a room and writes three novels that are, in themselves, a commentary on the fictional imagination and the techniques which this author has forsaken. From his reservoir of memories and the urgings of his mind Malone, an invention of Beckett, fills up his notebook. Sometimes Malone writes about a character he himself has invented: 'And yet I write about myself with the same pencil and the same exercise book as about him.' Malone, determined to 'die quietly, without rushing things,' fills in the interval with the story of Macmann who in many ways corresponds to the early life of his creator. Beckett, himself in a room that death is approaching, writes about Malone and through him remembers the Ireland of his youth.[12]

At one level therefore the trilogy is about the writing of novels. *Molloy* opens with a comment on the practical difficulties of authorship:

> There's this man who comes every week. Perhaps I got here thanks to him. He says not. He gives me money and takes away the pages. So many pages, so much money. Yes, I work now, a little like I used to, except I don't know how to work anymore...When he comes for the fresh pages he brings back the previous week's. They are marked with signs I don't understand. Anyway I don't read them. When I've done nothing he gives me nothing, he scolds me. Yet I don't work for money. For what then? I don't know.

—in the collapse of organized, purposeful culture does any writer, ultimately, know more? Molloy, who as yet has not recognized the final distinction to be made about his task, writing as a pensum, repeats in a less dramatic way the question Holderlin asked more than a hundred years before: 'in such spiritless times, why be poet at all?'[13]

The author, like the characters he invents, is bound by words. Molloy thinks continually for if he ceased to think he would cease to be. As he is also a writer the arrangement consists in the transfer of his thoughts to paper. Malone and the Unnamable, in inventing other characters, progress a stage further. They have learnt (as did Murphy) from Geulincx, that one is free only in the mind. Since this is so, fiction, or invention, which is an expression of the mind, also reflects its greatest freedom. In addition fiction creates the nearest approximation to the ideal life, one spent dreaming over again the life already lived. This is possible only in the mind and Malone is able to resurrect his past in the story of Macmann. This world of the novelist which is limited to the mental processes of a man in a room is founded on Cartesianism and the trilogy illustrates that the development of the novel, and its own precarious existence, would have perhaps been impossible had Descartes not discovered his *cogito ergo sum* in that lonely room with a stove it took him nine years to reach. Hugh Kenner has written:

> The philosophy which has stood behind all subsequent philosophies, and which makes the whole of intelligible reality depend on the mental processes of a solitary man, came into being at about the same time as the curious literary form called the novel, which has since infected all other literary genres.[14]

The association is not forced. Like Descartes the novelist thinks a world into existence and the author-heroes of the trilogy demonstrate the internal nature of this mental struggle with ideas. Beckett establishes the trilogy on the essential simplicity of Descartes' first precept and adopts his scenario from the pages of the *Discourse on Method* in the fourth section of which is written:

> I concluded that I was a substance whose whole essence or nature consists in thinking, and whose existence depends neither on its location in space nor on any material thing. Thus the self, or rather the soul, by which I am what I am, is entirely distinct from the body, is indeed easier to know than the body, and would not cease to be what it is, even if there were no body.[15]

Apart from the assertion that the soul is easy to know this conclusion is the core of knowledge of the trilogy's hero. It includes his conviction that the soul is an infinite attribute distinct from the body; explains

Molloy's contempt for his decaying body and describes, in brief, the independent, mental limbo in which the Unnamable is confined. However, although the Unnamable knows that he thinks he is uncertain if he exists. Even Cartesianism has begun to doubt itself and it is here that the stories the hero tells are once more an assistance. For they not only give an illusion of freedom; they also keep the character aware of his continuing existence. 'I shall be obliged, in order not to peter out, to invent another fairy-tale, yet another...' sighs the Unnamable.

However, the heroes know that the craft they are engaged in is worth little and condemned to failure. Author and characters have read their Dante and know Oderisi's words to the poet on the Cornice of the Proud. Therefore they have unlimited contempt for the creative act and draw attention to their skill only to illustrate its imperfections. Malone insists that writing is physical and a painful substitute required by human incapacity:

> My little finger glides before my pencil across the page and gives warning, falling over the edge, that the end of the line is near. But in the other direction, I mean of course vertically, I have nothing to guide me. I did not want to write, but I had to resign myself to it in the end. It is in order to know where I have got to, where he has got to. At first I did not write, I just said the thing. Then I forgot what I had said. A minimum of memory is indispensable, if one is to live really.

The reluctant authors, Molloy, Moran and Malone are all conscious that words betray the intentions of the author. For the writer, the discovery of identity seems even more impossible because the method he has chosen creates additional complications. 'It is midnight. The rain is beating on the windows', writes Moran. But as he writes all is changed so that the next sentence must read: 'It was not midnight. It was not raining.'

To the modern writer who has learnt, like Nathalie Sarraute, that 'there was no ultimate deep',[16] writing becomes at best a game or a process. One plays with an increasing despair at the former or tries to find some consolation in the activity of the latter. Describing *Finnegan's Wake* in a letter to Harriet Weaver (1926), Joyce remarked:

> I know it is no more than a game, but it is a game that I have learned to play in my own way. Children may just as well play as not. The ogre will come in any case.[17]

Behind Joyce's recognition of the game is the conciliatory sadness in which Malone begins his tale or which leads Hamm to declare 'Me to play'.[18] Malone convinces himself that his last hours and last stories will be happy ones: 'Now it is a game, I am going to play...I shall never do anything from now on but play.' However, he is not successful—'how false all this is' he soon says in disgust, 'mortal tedium...And I call that playing'. Hamm plays with words in his story about the last days of the earth even though everything outside his room is a waste of extinction. Nothingness will come in any case, as Joyce knew; it has already arrived before the gates, there is nothing to do but play with the fragments of meaning.

Joyce did not admit that literature was a game until after he had written *Ulysses*. *Ulysses* was the consummation of the western fictional endeavour that believed in the laws of cause and effect, in the appropriateness of each incident, item and circumstance in a creation in which all the minutiae have a discernible place in the whole. *Ulysses* is the apotheosis of the novel which encases and answers its logical possibilities. Joyce did not seek a mere imitation of life, he made life subordinate to an art which was complete in itself. As Beckett himself wrote in his essay on Joyce: 'His writing is not *about* something; *it is that something itself*.'[19] *Ulysses* is given the solidity which life lacks and Bloom's day has an underlying coherence that is based on all the novelist's incidental means to keep the reader contented and credulous. Only in *Murphy* did Beckett show a similar concern for the reader's reasonable well-being and satisfy his desire for causal coherence. In the trilogy he creates a literature which is open on all sides to the irreconcilables of the void. Where Joyce attempted to put everything in, Beckett tries to keep it out, and the fictional devices of Joyce and his predecessors are ridiculed by each of the heroes in turn.

Thus Molloy makes it clear that one's beginning is only apparently important ('I began at the beginning like any old ballocks, can you imagine that?'); that quite probably he will make obvious factual errors ('I cannot stoop, neither can I kneel, because of my infirmity, and if ever I stoop, forgetting who I am, make no mistake, it will not be me but another'); and that he could, if he wished, write something quite different ('I weary of these inventions and others beckon to me'). He already possesses an obsessive approach to his activity, the need to say and the nothing to say. He sees his task as a matter of 'complying with the convention that demands you either lie or hold your peace' and arraigns language for its impotence and deceit. As he writes his 'vast frescoes dashed off with loathing' the words sometime collapses into silence, for example here where he is describing his legs:

For it was shortening, don't forget, whereas the other, though

> stiffening, was not yet shortening, or so far behind its fellow that to all intents and purposes, intents and purposes, I'm lost, no matter...

But the monologue never stops entirely because even the fact that he is lost or that he would like to stop writing become subjects to be written down and thought about. However, this inability at times to continue is not only the result of incapacity. It depends too on the nature of the inquiry he is following. In the dialogues with Duthuit Beckett speaks of his dilemma as that of the man unable yet compelled to write. In *Molloy* the hero speaks of a similar compulsion and aesthetic: it is the only statement he makes on his task which he does not afterwards ridicule and once more expresses the ambivalent elements that force him to continue despite the absence of anything to write or the desire to write it:

> ...not to want to say, not to know what you want to say, not to be able to say what you think you want to say, and never to stop saying... that is the thing to keep in mind, even in the heat of composition.

Nevertheless, although Beckett's heroes mock literature and apparently abandon all the conventions of fiction, these three novels provide a commentary on the nature of the formal tradition to which they belong. The trilogy stands in relation to the novel as *Film* does to the cinema, and it has encouraged Hugh Kenner to see in it 'a compendious abstract of all the novels ever written reduced to their most general terms'.[21] In its entirety the trilogy both comments on what has been previously written within its genre and carries fiction to a point beyond which it may be impossible to continue.

Kenner's words are suggested by the way in which the trilogy recalls individual styles and authors in the course of the narrative, from *Robinson Crusoe* to Proust and Joyce, and remarks on the devices of fiction—reflection, description, even a brilliant parody of the romantic novel—which it uses to keep the narrative moving. It is with precisely these aids that the novelist, from his room, has occupied the attention of the public over the years, and the trilogy performs an autopsy on them, in which the matrices of fiction are exposed to the long-deluded reader. The novel, reflecting the empirical materialist society in which it flourished is remarkable for the amount of factual information it offers the reader and the number of objects it employs to either develop the narrative or create scenic reality. The great novelists have chronicled society, described manners and examined human responses to love, death and breakfast against a background that frequently possesses a solidity absent in life. Conrad declared that he knew every stone in his imagined Sulacco, and from Crusoe's box of tools to the two chairs, one squat and stuffed, the other upright and polished, that tell of Molly Bloom's meeting with Blazes Boylan, the novelist has supported his universe on a multiplicity of ordinary objects. In its beginning the novel was founded upon an assured reality both in itself and in the society it reflected. In *Robinson Crusoe* each artefact possesses a definite purpose and has a place in Defoe's novel and in the society in which he lived. In the journey to Beckett's room, however, there has been a decline from the exhaustive fictional universes of Dickens, Tolstoy or Balzac. Beginning with Dostoevsky the novelist descended into the spiritual possibilities *within* himself: he lost faith in an objective order imposed from without, in a reality that has disintegrated outside the pages of his book, and attempted to discover, in the human spirit, an inwardly revealed reality. In *The Age of Suspicion* Nathalie Sarraute remarks on this change which culminates in the hero of the trilogy:

> At that time (the age of Balzac) he (the hero) was richly endowed with every asset, the recipient of every attention; he lacked for nothing, from the silver buckles on his breeches to the veined wart on the end of his nose. Since then he has lost everything: his ancestors, his carefully built house, filled from cellar to garret with a variety of objects down to the tiniest gee-gaw; his sources of income and his estates; his clothes, his body, his face. Particularly, however, has he lost that most precious of all possessions, his personality—which belonged to him alone—and frequently, even his name.[20]

This description presents us with many of the characteristics inherent in the Beckett hero, yet in spite of the losses he has suffered the fragment who remains, naked in bed and uncertain as to whether he is actually alive, still grapples with the problems and objects of fiction. In Beckett's French novels the eventual validity of the information which the mind seeks to elicit is certainly dubious but no less pertinent or crucial to the hero than the dilemmas which fill the traditional novel. In place of Anna's anguished thoughts about Vronsky or Jude's struggles with his conscience Beckett present us with a mind that is concerned by apparently less imposing but no less universal problems:– how does one count the steps leading up to one's front door, for example, or what one means by the phrase 'I said to myself'. The mind is seen in action upon itself and looks for reality only in the limited possibilities of its own cerebration.

Objects also proliferate. The novels abound with sticks, hats, pebbles and bicycles which appear exactly as the narrative requires them. Just as Crusoe discovered his box of tools at the moment they were needed, so Molloy is presented with a bicycle: 'I got up, adjusted my crutches and went down to the road where I found my bicycle (I didn't know I had one...)" In *The Unnamable* the hero begins a story of love and hardship, parting and sorrow, which within no more than twenty lines has introduced a catalogue of things—trains, platforms, doors and bolts—which are necessary to its feasible conclusion. 'Where there are people,' he remarks, 'there are things:' it is also an immutable law of fiction. As the repository of his past life, preserving the only tangible evidence of a reality lost in time, Malone is fascinated by his possessions. He has no bicycle but the cap of a bicycle bell is enough to bring back the old pleasures of riding. He roots among these relics with his stick, promises himself the pleasure of an inventory (again reminiscent of *Robinson Crusoe* and the enthusiastic naming of phenomena, the calling a spade a spade, in which the novel began) and even comes to feel pity for them:

> ..that foul feeling of pity I have so often felt in the presence of things, especially little portable things in wood and stone, and which made me wish to have them about me and keep them always..

—so ends the acquisitive tradition of the novel.

Thus the hero's comments on his task and the means he employs to conclude it, simultaneously criticize and create the technical and imaginative universe in which the novelist moves. More than any other work the trilogy is evidence of Professor Heller's recent dictum: that in contemporary literature:

> ..every act of creation is inseparable from the critique of its medium, and every work, intensely reflecting upon itself, looks like the embodied doubt of its own possibility.[21]

This 'doubt' and 'critique' which are organically present within the text are fundamental to the trilogy's existence and must be recognized before the issues within the individual novels will yield their true meaning. For they are a sign of a splintered reality against which the work of art can no longer, as in *Ulysses* or the nineteenth-century incantation to the miracle, attempt to preserve within its own enclosed bastion of self-sufficiency, the shape and idea of a comprehensive definition of man's estate. *Ulysses* was an art upon the defensive, intent to provide in its own burgeoning formal existence the meaning that had been lost in the real world: the trilogy, which doubts even its own veracity and *raison d'être*, is of an entirely more precarious and troubled order.

III

The first monologue is spoken by Molloy. At least that is what he later calls himself. He lives in his mother's room, though how he arrived there is a mystery. 'Perhaps in an ambulance, certainly a vehicle of some kind,' he reasons, for it is a year since he had the use of his legs. He has no idea where his mother is nor if she is still alive. It is more likely she is dead but when or where he doesn't know. Molloy is not writing from choice. He would rather 'say my good-byes, finish dying', but his orders are to write the story of his journey to the room. He would prefer to remain silent for silence would mean he had reunited himself with his own identity, but he is compelled to go on talking, ignorant of who he is, where he is, why he is, in the hope that one day the forgotten words will be spoken that will restore him to himself. However, each skein of words merely enlarges the darkness in which his mind is encased. He can only console himself with the idea that the end must be approaching: 'This time, then once more I think, then perhaps a last time, then I think it'll be over with that world too. Premonition of the last but one but one.' By the third attempt, with the Unnamable to be exact, all that ought to have been spoken will have been said, or so Molloy hopes in these early, ignorant days.

The journey began with Molloy on a hill-top not far from a town, crouched in the shadow of a rock 'like Belacqua, or Sordello, I forget', and watching two men, A and C, converge, meet and part on the country road below. As an outsider Molloy considers their progress. He meditates on their business, on whether they are acquainted and what they intend, answering each query with a logical proposition, the only method for the alien who observes and speaks of the society from which he is excluded. The identity of the two men remains a conjecture. One is short and the other tall; both wear greatcoats and C has a cocked hat and stout stick which Moran admires when he meets him in the second part of the novel. From their appearance it is possible they were characters in a previous book—Art and Con Lynch or perhaps Mercier and Camier, for both pairs are suggested by the description. Molloy, however, thinks of them in Christian terms. He remembers them later as 'my two thieves' and perhaps associates them with those other representatives of God's arbitrary attitude to man, Abel and Cain.

Molloy spends the night on the hill and when he wakes towards noon ('I heard the angelus, recalling the incarnation, shortly after'), he decides to visit his mother. Gathering up his crutches—one leg has already stiffened beyond use—he fastens them to the cross-bar of his bike and sets out. Although he finds cycling a delicious experience and 'was no mean cyclist, at that period,' the journey is slow and painful:

> every hundred yards or so I stopped to rest my legs, the good one as well as the bad, and not only my legs, not only my legs. I didn't properly speaking get down off the machine, I remained astride it, my feet on the ground, my arms on the handle-bars, my head on my arms, and I waited until I felt better.

He reaches the outskirts of his town and is rudely arrested by a policeman, apparently because this method of resting infringes some obscure bye-law. He is taken before a sergeant who questions him, in vain, about his identity and threatens him with a cylindrical ruler. Molloy cannot be certain that his mother lives in this town or that her name is identical with his, but he is confident that if she is found it will be near the slaughterhouse for he remembers the 'raucous, tremulous bellowing' of the cattle. The interrogation is inconclusive and Molloy, outwardly chastened, is set free that afternoon. His release is as mystifying as his arrest was alarming. Like Joseph K. he finds the law incomprehensible. 'Had I,' he wonders, 'without my knowledge, a friend at court?'

He cycles along the canal bank out into the country again. He watches the donkeys heaving the barges through the unruffled water and then sinks into a ditch where he nibbles the grass and spends the night (or perhaps several, his sense of time has grown confused). He remembers, however, a morning when he awoke to see a shepherd and his dog standing over him. Molloy asks him where he is taking his sheep but the man leads his flock away without replying. Molloy returns to the town which seems even less like the right one than before. He runs over a dog and is about to be torn to pieces by the bystanders when the dog's owner, a woman named Lousse, intervenes. She takes him home with her and Molloy watches while she buries the dog. Then he falls asleep in a room with barred windows. When he wakes he finds himself shaved, washed and scented with lavender. He has been given a nightshirt and there are indications, which turn out to be correct, that he will remain with Lousse 'a good while'.

In Lousse's house the atmosphere is heavy and dream-like: all Molloy's attempts to describe his stay there end in confusion. She has the unreality of a distorted enchantress before whom the mind crumbles into darkness. Lousse seems to adopt him as a substitute for the dog though Molloy implies that her interest was sexual. However, he is impotent and Lousse never forces him: 'all she asked was to feel me near her, with her, and the right to contemplate from time to time this extraordinary body both at rest and in motion.' She lets him roam in the garden, dress as he likes and keep whatever hours he pleases. She offers to feed and house him so that his 'remaining days would glide by without a care', and is herself content to peep at him from a distance. Nevertheless Molloy remarks that only men come into her garden which is surrounded by an intimidating, glass-topped wall. It seems he was constrained by Lousse, and Molloy obscurely suspects her of sapping his will to escape with poisons; but when he does leave he is not molested and the wicket gate leading into the road is unlocked.

Molloy's condition now deteriorates rapidly. He has lost his bicycle and is restricted to his crutches. Shaken by St Vitus' dance he considers settling in a blind alley and even makes an abortive attempt at suicide. He travels to the seashore, replenishes his stock of sucking stones and sees a group of women, one of whom separates herself from her companions and approaches him. He lives for a while in a cave but the image of 'my mother...blunted for some time past, was beginning now to harrow me again' and he starts back inland. He skirts a swamp and enters a forest where his progress becomes slower and slower. His good leg is now more painful than the other which itself has begun to shorten. He hears a voice ordering him to continue and the babbling, ceaseless churn of words within rises to a crescendo of minute debate as the darkness of 'these giant fronds, where I hobble, listen, fall, rise, listen and hobble on' appears unending. The last human being he sees is a charcoal burner, 'sick with solitude probably', who offers Molloy a resting place in his hut. Molloy, however, resents the intrusion and methodically kicks the man to death by swinging backwards and forwards pivoted on his crutches. Soon he can only crawl and drags himself along on his stomach, hooking his crutches into the undergrowth and using them as grapnels. He covers fifteen paces a day in this manner, sometimes murmuring 'Mother' to encourage himself, and on one occasion hears the sound of a gong in the distance. At last he tumbles out of the forest, which he is sorry to leave, into a ditch on the edge of a plain from where 'I fancied I saw, faintly outlined against the horizon, the towers and steeples of a town.' A voice tells him that help is coming and it is apparently from this ditch that he is brought to his mother's room, there to write the story we have just read.

The second part promises at first to be a more coherent and reliable document. It is told in precise sentences by Jacques Moran, the only hero since Belacqua to be given a Christian name, and his meticulous concern for detail and rectitude portends an accurate, if fussy, account. His story begins one Sunday morning in Summer. Moran is seated in the well-tended garden of his suburban house when a messenger, Gaber, disrupts his rest with instructions to take his son, also named Jacques, and go in search of a man named Molloy. Gaber is the intermediary between Moran and his employer, a mysterious and distant individual called Youdi. Moran appears at first to be some kind of private detective whom Youdi orders to trace a variety of individuals —among them some of Beckett's earlier heroes. When he finds them Moran acts on Youdi's instructions and sometimes makes a report on the affair when he returns home. It is his report which we are reading now.

Moran resents Gaber's intrusion. It prevents his attendance at last mass and means he will have to solicit private communion. The order to take his son with him is also annoying. He feels that his son lacks respect for him despite the repressive nature of his education which is founded on the principle *sollst entbehren*. When they do depart his son's compliance is only ensured by Moran himself pocketing the knife that is his son's most treasured possession. The whole affair is disquieting. Moran ('I so sly as a rule'), is not sure of his quarry's name and cannot remember what Gaber ordered him to do once he is found. He therefore climbs into bed because it is there that he best follows the 'falsetto of reason' through the dark labyrinth of his mind, 'its paths as familiar as those of my garden.' For Moran too the mind is a place and:

> It is lying down, in the warmth, in the gloom, that I best pierce the outer turmoil's veil, discern my quarry, sense what course to follow, find peace in another's ludicrous distress.

Yet this time peace avoids him. Molloy, far from being a stranger, is an old familiar menacingly present within Moran himself. The latter conjures up his image. The negative he receives is imprecise and frightening. Molloy appears like the awesome shadow of the figure in part one, a huge, shaggy, dark and shapeless creature angrily pounding about within Moran until the latter feels himself 'nothing but uproar, bulk, rage, suffocation, effort, unceasing, frenzied and vain'. Moran becomes confused and anxious and finds it painful not to understand, he who until this moment organized his world with absolute confidence. The private communion which Father Ambrose gives him brings no relief. It mingles with his stew, spoilt by the delay, and both lie heavy on his stomach. Then, just before the journey begins, Moran is crippled by a sharp pain in the knee and he leaves his house filled with misgiving.

The journey itself is a disaster for Moran and its end as indefinite as Molloy's quest for his mother. Moran, sadly thinking of the peaceful world he leaves behind, calls it 'the long anguish of vagrancy and freedom'. Soon after the start his leg becomes useless and he sends Jacques into the nearest town to buy a bicycle. The boy is away three days and in his absence Moran, who is holed up in his tent on a hill, receives two visitors. The first is C, still dressed in his greatcoat and carrying his stick. Moran gives him a piece of bread, watches him eat it with pleasure and sees him depart with obvious reluctance: 'I wished I could have been in the middle of a desert, under the midday sun, to look after him till he was only a dot, on the horizon'. The next day he breaks himself off a stick that resembles C's and is poking the fire with it when a second man interrupts him to ask if anyone has passed that way. From the description his quarry is clearly C. Moran, however, refuses to answer. He dislikes this man as much as he admired the first and when he refuses to move out of Moran's way, Moran clubs him to death with the stick.

When Jacques returns they struggle forward on the bicycle. But Jacques gradually revolts against his enfeebled father's control until one night he disappears with the bike and most of the luggage. Moran remains isolated in the country until Gaber reappears and orders him to return home, assuring him that Youdi is not angry but sitting laughing to himself and saying 'life is a thing of beauty...and a joy for ever'. Moran asks: 'Do you think he meant human life?' but Gaber has already vanished.

Physically Moran now resembles Molloy as he first appeared on the hill-side. With the support of his umbrella he stumbles back through wind and snow towards his house. Like Molloy he apparently passes a whole winter on the journey and arrives home in the spring. He finds his house deserted, the electricity cut off and his once well-tended garden in ruins. His hens have died and all that remains of his hive is 'a dry light ball. It crumbled under my fingers.' Father Ambrose is shocked by his appearance but Moran makes no attempt to restore either himself or his property. He spends May and June in the garden and promises himself that once he has finished his report he will leave again. He has crutches now so it should be easier. Once more the narrative ends with its beginning.

The two monologues of *Molloy* are as masterly a construction in form as the two acts of *Godot* or the four parts of *Watt*. They complement each other in character, style, incident and setting, and the second part, far from being a tired reflection of its more vigorous predecessor, provides an essential extension of the narrative and a commentary on the earlier section. For example, both heroes meet with a shepherd in the course of their journey. Molloy's shepherd sees him in a ditch where he has been nibbling the grass, cause, Molloy supposes, for the shepherd to mistake him for one of his flock trapped in the brambles. Molloy therefore excuses the intrusion and puns grimly on the idea of being 'a black sheep'. The shepherd, having assured himself on Molloy's identity (at least he is not a sheep) moves off in silence. In the second part Moran and his son are cycling down a hill when they too encounter a shepherd and his dog. Around them stray a flock of black sheep. Moran dismounts and tentatively approaches the shepherd. He longs to say 'Take me with you, I will serve you faithfully, just for a place to lie and a little food', but all he manages is a weak question as to his whereabouts. Here again the shepherd does not speak. He points out his reply with the stem of his pipe and then, losing interest as Moran lapses into silence, moves his flock away into the evening. This second incident gains from the first and reflects back on to it a significance that was originally but barely suggested. The Christian implications of 'shepherd', hinted at in Molloy's jest at being a black sheep (or the sacrificial victim:–Abraham and Isaac are also envoked through the brambles that imprison him) and therefore outside the flock in the shepherd's care, is made explicit by Moran. He distorts an echo of Christ's words to the disciples, inverting the situation and speaking them himself. In a moment of despair he asks of the human shepherd what the divine shepherd asked of man, once again emphasizing the disinherited nature of the hero.

Many such details are repeated. The reappearance of C has already been remarked and a close reading of the text provides an extensive list of parallels benefiting through their mutual interaction. Molloy speaks of a son he may have forgotten; Moran is a father who loses a son. Molloy carries a rusted clasp-knife; Moran puts a similar knife belonging to his son into his pocket. Both men are troubled by their testicles which 'hung a little too low;' attach their hats to their collars with a shoe lace; rest their stiff legs to dislodge the clots and express the pleasure they would receive by describing their bicycles. (Molloy: 'To describe it at length would be a pleasure.' Moran: 'I would gladly describe it, I would gladly write four thousand words on it alone.') Molloy tells us that the man who collects his writings calls every Sunday and is always thirsty. Gaber comes twice to Moran: on both occasions it is Sunday. The first time he drinks his host's Wallenstein and on the second 'announced he was dying of thirst'. It is likely therefore that Molloy's visitor is also Gaber and that perhaps the man who marks his papers is the elusive Youdi, or that Moran is also a writer on commission, an idea that will be developed shortly. Thus Moran's journey which begins shortly after a gong has been struck in his house, a sound heard by Molloy just before help arrived, seems at first to be a prosaic account of what Molloy conveys with greater power and imagination. The winter in the woods feeding off berries and crawling through the undergrowth, which is common to both narratives, would be simply explained away if one could assume that Molloy's account is an imaginative reconstruction of the report written for Youdi by a younger and more coherent Moran. However, such an assumption would emphasize the series of parallels to the exclusion of the remainder of the novel and, as we shall see, is untenable. The parallels amplify, they do not explain.

Nevertheless the framework of the two parts is integral to the novel's construction which, as John Fletcher first suggested, was inspired by *Pilgrim's Progress*. Once again Beckett reveals an inclination to follow the early English novelists and on this occasion definitely improves on the borrowed framework of Bunyan's two parts. Where Bunyan originally wrote his work in one part, adding the second pilgrimage only on the public success of the first, Beckett, with the additional experience of three centuries of novel writing, creates both monologues in a reciprocal alliance, the one inconceivable without the other. Mrs Christian was a luxury; Moran is a necessity. Moreover Bunyan's words are implicitly echoed by Molloy: 'there is no need to despair, you may scrabble on the right door, in the right way, in the end.' Gaber takes the place of Bunyan's Evangelist and Molloy's arrest and subsequent treatment at the hands of an enraged populace is reminiscent of the pilgrims' seizure in Vanity Fair. Both Molloy and Moran directly recall Bunyan's famous gateway. Molloy escapes from Lousse and Moran begins his journey, by passing through a wicket-gate into the world beyond. However, Moran's re-entry into his garden at the end of the novel points the circular, hopeless nature of their pilgrimage in search of the Self against Christian's discovery of paradise. Christian, as John Fletcher has written, 'is promised fatigue, pain, hunger, nakedness, and darkness on his way; these are the lot also of Molloy and Moran.'[22] But for Christian, though he may err and become lost, there is only one road to the Celestial city, for Molloy there are many. 'All roads were right for me, a wrong road was an event, for me.' All roads are now equally right or, if one prefers, equally wrong. There is no longer even a straight and narrow path to paradise, simply a multitude of arbitrary roads to failure or the universal road to...Nought.

Although Moran retraces Molloy's journey in detail and deteriorates to a condition similar to that in which Molloy began there is little in common between the characters of the two heroes or in their approach to the world. Moran might be Molloy's *alter ego*. Certainly his pedantic inquiries show the failure of the rational mind to understand or even contact the burgeoning, expansive world of Molloy, whose nature accords with the irrational and the infinite. Molloy seems almost timeless, a creature who shambles towards us like the terrifying image of Yeats' *The Second Coming*. He inspires dread and reduces both logic and morality to the compost-heap or dead-end alley in which he first made love and now would like to live. His 'I', with its dwelling 'deep down...somewhere between the mud and the scum', exists in a world where all values seem ground into the dust and dirt of supreme indifference. 'And deep down it was all the same to me...I didn't give a fiddler's curse,' he exclaims, having just expended all his energies on the monumental saga of the sucking stones. Yet out of this 'sordid, malodorous, obscene Calvary-procession from womb to refuse-dump',[23] as Richard Coe describes it, emerges a figure who is magnificent even as he disgusts and by whose side Moran is like a mangy hyena scuttling in the penumbra of his shadow. For Molloy, despite his outcries of hatred, does care. Molloy has suffered the worst that life can inflict and is still suffering, mentally and physically; his disgust and contempt only hide his pain, and his indifference, like the metaphysical anguish of Camus' *Caligula*, is the result of his tragic experience. Molloy, in spite of his disregard for traditional moral responses, is altogether a more human being than the self-important, self-satisfied and malicious Moran. He includes within himself the whole human experience and is, as we shall see, a powerfully poetic and mythopoetic creation.

In appearance Molloy is uncouth. Besides the decay of his legs he is toothless, covered with scabs, long-haired and has a grubby beard. He dresses in the by now traditional manner of the derelict clown: bowler hat pushed firmly down over his brow, long uncomfortable boots, trousers and greatcoat. His appetite is small and in the forest where he has become inseparable from the vegetation he finds the berries on the trees quite sufficient. He denigrates the body, however, because he believes it valueless and mocks its functions because it is condemned to decay.

Molloy is also a defunct scholar, probably of languages for he quotes in Latin and French and makes allusions to Kaspar David Friedrick, Balzac, Leibnitz and Geulincx. He provokes others on sight partly because his habits and appearance outrage them but also because, like Watt, he seems to threaten the prepared and established arrangement under which they exist. All Beckett's heroes (his one heroine, Winnie, is the exception,) act as catalysts against the Proustian subterfuge of habit. At one level Molloy simply outrages the established system. He steals Lousse's silverwear, considers love 'a mug's game' and regards with complete indifference those values, such as the will to live, which others consider important. He is also, however, a scapegoat, encouraging assault merely by his presence. Individuals turn away from him in silence or if they do speak it is in a tone 'compounded of pity, of fear, of disgust'. Molloy's alienation, which is unsolicited, leads him to call his fellow men They and to consider their habits with irony. He sleeps during the morning because that is:

> ...the time to hide. They wake up, hale and hearty, their tongues hanging out for order, beauty and justice, baying their due. Yes, from eight or nine till noon is the dangerous time. But towards noon things quieten down, the most implacable are sated, they go home, it might have been better but they've done a good job, there have been a few survivors, but they'll give no more trouble, each man counts his rats... Day is the time for lynching, for sleep is sacred, and especially the morning, between breakfast and lunch.

At their best They will only try to draw him back into the 'game, the jollity' like the social worker who approaches Molloy in the police-station and against whose 'charitable gesture there is no defence'. At their worst They will threaten him with cylindrical rulers or seek to kill him, like the 'bloodthirsty mob of both sexes and all ages' that surround him when he accidentally runs over the dog. Thus when Molloy at the end hears a voice promising him help he greets it with an ironic, objective tolerance but no enthusiasm: 'well, I suppose you have to try everything once, succour included, to get a complete picture of the resources of their planet.'

Molloy's appearance alone, however, does not explain the disquieting and compelling effect of his image on the reader. His huge, massy bulk journeying across forest and plain, crouched on the mountain-side or in a cave on the seashore, troubles the imagination with the ultimate impenetrability of an archetype. Out of the monologue emerges a series of images, of a man with arms outstretched, trapped in a wood, or seated alone on an eminence overlooking the sea, that stand immense and clear in the reader's mind and yet seem at the edges to conceal a still greater significance. Molloy appears both as a character with a story to tell and the embodied shape of a series of responses and uncertainties until now concealed within the reader. It is the awesome shape itself that Moran later responds to, but in the reader Molloy gradually emerges as a creation in whom Beckett has combined several mythical strands. He reaches down into the reader's own subconscious and disturbs a series of suggestions and approximate analogies which reveal themselves and progress in mythical patterns. It is Beckett's achievement to have allowed these patterns to discover themselves, and to have integrated the evidence so completely into the narrative that it is not only almost impossible to separate it from the text but also becomes apparent as if Molloy himself was unaware of its presence and, like the reader, did not understand that his own subconscious was also engaged in the monologue.

The principal themes which Molloy uncovers are Christ's sacrifice on the cross and the ancient story of the wanderer, exemplified in the tale of Ulysses. He speaks specifically of his journey as a Calvary. It starts, one remembers, with the sound of the angelus on the hillside overlooking 'my two thieves' as if that night were Molloy's Gethsemane. The following day he rides on his bicycle (in place of an ass)[24] into the city and is arrested. It closes with Molloy lying in a ditch and gazing at a distant city which recalls both Bunyan's Christian looking up from the River of Life and Christ on the cross beholding a heavenly Jerusalem.

The journey also opens with a symbol of birth. Molloy hears the 'awful cries of the corncrakes', the sacred bird of Artemis, goddess of birth to which Beckett also alludes in *Waiting for Godot*, just as he intends to begin the search for his mother. The journey itself, however, is accompanied by images of death. Molloy, clearly dying, drags himself homeward towards the ghastly, hag image of his mother. He wishes to end the exile from himself at the source and understands that death is not merely the end but a new beginning: that he was born dead and is now completing the circle that returns him to his birth into death. As he journeys he recalls having sailed upon the ocean and as he gazes over the waters a young woman comes towards him as Ulysses was once approached by Nausicaa. He relates his adventures with much of the cunning and invention for which Ulysses was famous. In the police-station he narrowly escapes the sergeant who is the Cyclops of this Odyssey only to sink becalmed into the Circe-like captivity of Lousse. She keeps him a prisoner 'perhaps by spells' as her ancestress once enchanted Ulysses. Moreover she has a dog which Molloy kills and from his window he watches the moon, one of the few events he records while he is with her. Dog and moon are attributes of wayside enchantresses including the classical goddess of the underworld, Persephone, whose realms were visited by Ulysses. Lousse would seem to have disturbed these unconscious sources in Molloy's apprehensive mind. She recalls, in both guises, the death-like embrace to which the mythical hero is drawn; an impression that finds support in the chill, dream atmosphere of her house.[25]

The inner landscape of Molloy's journey is reflected in the countryside he crosses. He tells his story in what he calls 'the mythological present' and his imagination transforms what is clearly once again the area around Dublin into the backcloth that will sustain his narrative. Molloy always speaks of its appearance, its weather and its customs as if he knew them only long ago: 'things have perhaps changed since my time.' He refers to it as 'the island' and inflates what Moran calls an 'administrative' area not in excess of five or six square miles, into the plains, mountains, forest and ocean of his story which gains in power through the emotive qualities of these words. Bally, the county town of Ballybaba, where Molloy was born, is intersected, like Dublin, by two canals, but from a distance he imagines it to be a walled town with towers and ramparts.

The unimaginative Moran sees nothing of this. Carefully appraising the journey before him he describes Bally as a small market town or village neighbouring the canton of Turdybaba (principal town Turdy: all the names are Anglo-Saxon obscenities) where he himself lives. Ballybaba, which Molloy it seems has never left, consists of bogland, a few copses, some fields and a little strangulated creek which its inhabitants, few in number, consider to be of great beauty. This disparity in their descriptions immediately reveals the difference between the two men, one that is also illustrated in the style of their narratives. Molloy's has the elemental simplicity, grandeur and obscurity of the non-literary epic. It is written in only two paragraphs, broken into short pauses by the comma which determines the pace and rhythm. The comma is used as the pause is in speech, for emphasis, to separate mental interjections from the actual story, perhaps to occupy the interval while the speaker smiles. The second part is told in a more cultivated tone and with a far greater awareness of what is implied.

Even the closing section where Moran has almost become Molloy is normally sentenced and paragraphed. Hugh Kenner has compared Moran's tale to the *Aeneid* which similarly retraces the framework of a former journey and again substitutes a civilized consciousness for the more primitive, myth-making imagination of its predecessor. However, the two parts also approximate (in the naming of the heroes as well as in their style) to the dual influence under which Beckett writes. The punctilious Jacques Moran hunting down the anarchic Molloy does so in a monologue that is distinctly French in inspiration. The rational impulse to precision in the second part which attempts to trace and imprison the violent, dark substance of the more natural (and Irish) first part would seem to be yet another example of Beckett's art commenting on itself as well as successfully conveying the demands upon technique within the subject of the novel.

Moran, as he first appears, is an unpleasant time-serving wage-earner living in the suburbs of a small country town. He has all the self-induced sense of importance and propriety of the provincial bourgeois which Beckett detests. He is scrupulous in his religious duties, lacks a sense of humour and insists on his son's obedience and respect which he himself has done so little to deserve. Moran cannot understand why his son is so quiet with him and talkative with his companions; he deliberately forces him into deceit and in general treats him as callously as his own masters, those he fearfully calls 'They', treat him. Moran is prosaic: he detests the imagination, is proud of 'being a sensible man' and organizes his house with a stultifying precision. He walks 'with delicate steps, almost mincing, congratulating myself as usual on the resilience of my Wilton'; insists that meals are punctual; and carries a large bunch of keys, one to each drawer in the house, on a massive chain. No mention is made of his wife until, to escape the wrath of a farmer who accuses him of trespassing, he invents the story of his pilgrimage in a straight line to the Madonna of Turdy, where he hints that she died in childbirth. In dress too he is meticulous. For the journey he selects, from an extensive wardrobe, a pepper-and-salt shooting suit, plus-fours, black boots and an old straw boater.

Unlike Molloy whose life is lived almost entirely in 'that inner space one never sees' Moran is 'patiently turned towards the outer world as towards the lesser evil'. He, alone of Beckett's heroes, willingly faces the 'blooming confusion' and the alienation he has achieved is self-imposed. 'I don't like men and I don't like animals', he explains. Molloy discourses at length upon the orifices of the body whereas Moran educates his son to a 'horror of the body and its functions'. He is misanthropic, terrified by the brutal circumstance of existence which Molloy intuitively understands and even by the notion of freedom in a journey which will separate him from the contrived regimen he has erected against life. He speaks with emotion of being:

> ...banished from my house, from my garden, lose my trees, my lawns, my birds...and all those things at hand without which I could not bear being a man, where my enemies cannot reach me, which it was my life's work to build, to adorn, to perfect, to keep.

Moran is the creature of his possessions as well as a creature of habit: one on whom the Proustian stasis has descended.

But Moran and his world are affected by the presence of Molloy. Even before he sets out on his journey Moran receives uneasy intimations of a less rational life and is troubled by the image of a darker, more forbidding existence within himself. Moran's hunt for his quarry in which he gradually changes into the dimly discerned figure he once recoiled from in horror, is both a fable of the individual's search for identity and an account of the artist's personal exploration of his subconscious.

Moran is already acquainted with the subject of Gaber's instructions:

> Molloy, or Mollose, was no stranger to me. If I had had colleagues, I might have suspected I had spoken of him to them, as of one destined to occupy us, sooner or later. But I had no colleagues and knew nothing of the circumstances in which I had learnt of his existence. Perhaps I had invented him, I mean found him ready-made in my head...For who could have spoken to me of Molloy if not myself and to whom if not to myself could I have spoken of him.

Molloy it seems must be an invention of Moran, the man engaged to write of him. Here the significance of Gaber being the same man that visits Molloy becomes more pertinent. Moran receives his commission which includes a written report. It is, moreover, not the first. He has already, he cannot remember when, been engaged to track down 'a gallery of moribunds' that exist 'in my head..Murphy, Watt, Yerk, Mercier and others', and on several occasions has written of them. It seems very possible that the second monologue is in fact an examination of Beckett's own artistic process: of how, suddenly compelled to write on an as yet unclear subject, the author turns inward and slowly brings him out of the 'slow and massive world, where all things move with the ponderous sullenness of oxen, patiently through the immemorial ways', assuming many of his characteristics as he does so.

This supposition becomes more credible as Moran unfolds his

monologue. The figure he discerns within himself is very similar to the hero of the first part. He pants, sways to-and-fro like a bear and 'seemed to be crashing through jungle'. Although he is 'just the opposite of me, in fact,' Moran is almost sorry when he loses sight of him. His task is to recapture this man and bring him into the open and then, as Edith Kern first suggested, to turn 'little by little a disturbance into words'. Moran's report on Molloy therefore, which will fulfil this obligation, performs the artistic event as it was described in *Watt.* Molloy ('him who has need of me to be delivered, who cannot deliver himself'), the source of this disturbance, must be dislodged from Moran's mind by Moran himself and then written about.

In achieving this end the rational intelligence of Moran extracts Molloy from deep within his subconscious and in so doing becomes involved in the vast universe through which the latter moves, where:

> All is dark, but with that simple darkness that follows like a balm upon the great dismemberings. From their places masses move, stark as laws. Masses of what? One does not ask. There somewhere man is too, vast conglomerate of all of nature's kingdoms, as lonely and as bound[26].

The rational Moran, however, does not create. He is only able to report on a being too immense for the mind to encompass and about whom no investigation is possible. Moran, as he explains, is 'paid to seek'; the quarry awaits his arrival and 'comes away. His life has been nothing but a waiting for this.' But the irrational nature of this quarry enables Moran to glimpse only the beginning, the end remains problematical:

> What I heard...was a first syllable, Mol, very clear, followed almost at once by a second, very thick, as though gobbled by the first, and which might have been oy as it might have been ose, or one, or even oc.

Once again the hero is halted by the nothingness into which the Self disappears. The Self, or the nature of Molloy, which Moran locates in the gloom within, is incomplete. Like the goal of the ever-recurring decimal which must some time reach zero, he cannot discover what follows the first evident syllable. Or as Hugh Kenner writes; somewhere 'between $1\frac{169}{408}$ and $1\frac{70}{169}$ we may expect the root of two to exist, though we should not expect to find it.'[27] The Self too exists in a similar interstice of nothingness: the hero knows it to be there even though it appears impossible. It is in this interstice, or as Belacqua would say 'Beethoven pause', that Molloy exists, perhaps as the zero at the end of the decimals—as Nothing.

As a man Moran suffers from this ignorance but as the artist whose task it is to complete his report his pain is redundant. In a passage which is characteristic of Beckett's own approach to his art Moran explains the value of his endeavours. He sees them as their own justification which will survive the artist himself and reaches the Proustian conclusion in its most obvious form, that art redeems life and the work of art is greater and beyond the transient vehicle who acted as intermediary for it:

> For what I was doing I was doing neither for Molloy, who mattered nothing to me, nor for myself, of whom I despaired, but on behalf of a cause which, while having need of us to be accomplished, was in its essence anonymous, and would subsist, haunting the minds of men, when its miserable artisans should be no more.

When Moran returns from his search he has united himself with this antithetical self. He becomes his opposite. Moran ends not only crippled in his legs but indifferent to religion, undismayed by the ruin of his house and independent of the contrived microcosm he had been so reluctant to leave. Moran who had once 'found it painful...not to understand' now accepts his ignorance: he has exchanged his time-bound existence for the irrational, timeless Self he had sensed in his subconscious, or at least for an intimation of it. But to achieve the terrible freedom that is his legacy from Molloy Moran has first to recognize the man he would like to be and then to actually kill the image of his old self.

This he manages during the two visits which occur while his son is away buying a bicycle. The first is from C who stares in silence at Moran for some time before he asks for a piece of bread. 'His face was pale and noble', remarks the misanthropic Moran, 'I could have done with it.' This revealing emotion of Moran's directs his actions. He offers the man fish rather than bread even though his food is running low, looks admiringly at his stick and is sorry when he leaves. The next day, however, his behaviour is very different. The second man like Moran, is searching for another and his rude, self-important attitude is reminiscent of Moran's own character particularly towards the beginning of his monologue. His appearance is also similar:

> He was on the small side, but thick-set. He wore a thick navy-blue suit (double-breasted) of hideous cut and a pair of outrageously wide black shoes...This dreadful shape seems only to occur in black shoes... but all this was nothing compared to the face which I regret to say vaguely resembled my own...

Moran coldly clubs the man to death with his stick, so recently cut in imitation of C's: then, bending over the body, he remarks with satisfaction—'He no longer resembled me'.

Only now does Moran reconcile himself with the image of Molloy. As if in sympathy with his decision the massive bunch of keys, one to every compartment of his old life, falls apart. Moran ceases to oppose his double and in renouncing his own limited 'I' ('I have been a man long enough,...I shall not try any more') he gains a broader and more human dimension. However, although he has achieved a 'sharper and clearer sense of my own identity' it seems likely to prove a sterile victory. He has reached not the end but the beginning of the Calvary without end that Molloy has long since entered upon. Moran, as he blows out his lamp and goes into the garden, is as yet unaware of the tragic doctrine of guilt, suffering, time and decay which Molloy begins to evolve in the first monologue and which is resumed with ever less hope by his successors, Malone and The Unnamable.

IV

For the man whose first wish is to 'finish dying' everything else is at best superfluous, at worst an annoying distraction. In Molloy's monologue the Beckett tramp appears to have become nothing more than a projection of ultimate indifference. Even his surroundings are now a minor concern:

> But it's a change of muck. And if all muck is the same muck that doesn't matter, it's good to have a change of muck, to move from one heap to another a little further on, from time to time, fluttering you might say, like a butterfly, as if you were ephemeral.

However, Molloy's monumental disdain is only a façade against the contingencies of the external world. Within, in the arena of his mind, he discovers the business of dying to be more difficult than he at first imagined, and he becomes deeply concerned with his endeavour to cease where the possibility of an end appears to recede.

Molloy's indifference is really the lassitude of a man for whom:

> The last deception has perished
> Which I believed eternal[28]

It is the barren tedium that surrounds despair in the mind of one who has aspired to meaning and found nothing, one who has demanded a purpose and an end in the universe of which he is a part and received as answer only the spectral movement of decay. From his bed Molloy retraces the destruction of his body which, like a true Cartesian machine, only operates at the command of the brain: 'my feet...never took me to my mother unless they received a definite order to do so.' The sight of this decrepit machine agitates a feeling of physical disgust and causes him to savagely revile its odorous functions. His revulsion, however, is the obverse reaction of his indifference: he hates because his condition is inescapable and therefore reserves his most potent scorn for the unwitting cause, his mother 'veiled with hair, wrinkles, filth, slobber', and for the sexual act itself in his affair with Edith.

Once again the body is understood to be separate from the mind. Their interaction is inexplicable and the mind is exempt from the otherwise universal process of decay. Molloy describes his mind as 'the best part of me', and with the cessation of physical ability it becomes a still more finely attuned instrument. Molloy's final disintegration, however, occurs only after the failure of an ingenious but vain attempt to surmount the problem of dualism. As Hugh Kenner has suggested, the bicycle in Beckett's world has a significance which exceeds its vehicular function.[30] In Cartesian terms the body is an imperfect machine: Descartes could neither analyse the control of the mind over this machine or imagine a perfected machine which would not decay. The Beckett hero seems to overcome this lasting dilemma by riding a bicycle. Cyclist and machine appear inseparable in a perfected tableau which creates the ideal body. For the machine itself is a masterpiece of technical, functional and geometric ingenuity produced by the intelligence of the rider who sits astride it, his mind visibly controlling and directing the matter by which he moves:

> The intelligence guides, the mobile wonder obeys, and there is no mysterious interpenetration of function.[30]

This mechanical Houyhnhnm is the climax of the hero's active life. Once he loses it he is limited to unsatisfactory substitutes like his crutches. He is forced to accept the distasteful inadequacy of his body. It explains why both Molloy and Moran would rather write about their bicycles than about anything else. Like Belacqua, none of the succeeding heroes can 'on any account resist a bicycle'.

Molloy, however, is a reluctant and tormented Cartesian. He rejects the world not because he is idle but because he is conscious of the vacuity of an existence that is denied a complete immortality. Like the tradition of anguished men who proceeded him (Leopardi, Unamuno,

Nietzsche) he finds no consolation in the alternative solutions of reason. His mind, he is aware, is of value only in the particular:—'For the particulars, if you are interested in the particulars, there is no need to despair...It's for the whole there seems to be no spell.' Molloy detects the absurdity of those substitutes with which reason has replaced immortality. In *The Tragic Sense of Life* Unamuno denounces the rationalist consolation:

> Must I declare to you again the supreme vacuity of culture, of science, of art, of good, of truth, of beauty, of justice, of all these beautiful conceptions, if at the last, in four days, or in four million centuries—it matters not which—no human consciousness shall exist.[31]

Such concepts are nothing to the man who has lost the certainty of the 'last deception'; who seeks with all his energies to rediscover a dimension of the Self that will *be* for ever. This is the meaning of Molloy's indifference: of why he has long refuted his learning and abandoned all traditional ethical standards. Of his former disciplines only mathematics still retains an influence on him for its effortless, ultimately meaningless permutations help to reduce the external world of sucking stones and farts to the nothingness where they belong. His longing is to reach the purity of his own irreducable Self and the quest for intellectual certainty is nothing but 'a prick of misgiving, like one dying of cancer obliged to consult his dentist'.

But this search is made more difficult by the body on which he is so reluctantly dependant. Self-knowledge is almost impossible because bodily decay cuts him off from the most elementary sensory divination. It is a miserable catalogue of failure. His eyes are seldom open and if he does perceive anything there is a time lapse before recognition. His hearing is good but he has difficulty in forming speech into intelligible units and he tastes and smells things 'without knowing exactly what'. In addition his memory is poor: he does not recognize his own town and writes that he is liable to confuse 'several different occasions'. The world recedes from him, space becomes relative and time indefinite until he admits that:

> ...even my sense of identity was wrapped in a namelessness often hard to penetrate...already all was fading, waves and particles, there could be no things but nameless things, no names but thingless names.

There is nothing left to him but the ruinous desolation of the 'place' in his skull, a place which, he says, is not the kind one goes to but where one finds oneself. He attempts an image of this place and in so doing draws one of the most terrifying portraits of contemporary isolation; a poetically accurate reconstruction of the anchorless, derelict waste through which the mind now moves:

> I listen and the voice is of a world collapsing endlessly, a frozen world, under a faint untroubled sky, enough to see by, yes, and frozen too. And I hear it murmur that all wilts and yields, as if loaded down, but here there are no loads, and the ground too, unfit for loads, and the light too, down towards an end it seems can never come. For what possible end to these wastes where true light never was, nor any upright thing, nor any true foundation, but only those leaning things, forever lapsing and crumbling away, beneath a sky without memory of morning or hope of night.

The silence of this hopeless world is penetrated at intervals by the tormenting 'far whisper' of the hypothetical imperative. It is the rustle of the imperative that tears him from the place where he is and urges him onwards though, as he remarks, 'nearly all (the imperatives) bore on the same question, that of my relationship with my mother'. At their instigation he begins the search. It is a journey back to the source, to his beginnings. He is looking, not for a human figure but for a meaning at the most probable of all possible moments in his 'enormous history', the moment that separates his present existence in time from his earlier existence in union with the Self. It is why he returns, when all else has collapsed about him, to the centre and seeks refuge in his mother's room, which, as Edith Kern suggests, reminds one of the search for those Mothers of Being who—according to Nietzsche—preside over 'the innermost heart of things'.[32] This impulse to return is not new:

> ...all my life, I think I had been going to my mother, with the purpose of establishing our relationship on a less precarious footing...And when I appeared to give up and to busy myself with something else, or with nothing at all any more, in reality I was hatching my plans and seeking the way to her house.

When he arrives at her room she is no longer there but during the search he has, like the tragic hero, been stripped of all his externals. Molloy becomes 'unaccommodated man' and in the process learns, as did Lear, the fundamental truths of his world. Despite his lack of personality and the disintegration of his senses he is always aware that 'something is taking its course'[33] and the apparent, though often incomprehensible, laws by which this change is made create the universal, human residue of the novel.

He begins by acknowledging the sense of Arsène's monologue which Watt, so concerned with his positivist explanations, ignored. Man is born to suffer, he is wedded at birth to a reasonless pain and decay that is unchosen and without a certain end. He is, again the image is taken from Descartes, a:

> Watch wound and buried by the watchmaker, before he died, whose ruined works will one day speak of God, to the worms.

The remark is filled with a uniquely poignant irony for the great watchmaker who fashioned the most intricate of machines from clay is now dead and it was Descartes who unwittingly began to kill the image of the artificer in the mind of his creature. In the aimless existence that is left over, gratuitous suffering provides the hero with the only certain evidence that he continues to live. As the Unnamable says 'I know my eyes are open because of the tears that fall from them unceasingly'. They fall without cause in a suffering that is nameless. 'What makes me weep so? From time to time. There is nothing saddening here. Perhaps it is liquefied brain.' They are the tears of humanity shed on humanity's behalf; tears that well over from an intimate experience of the terrible words, also spoken by Unamuno:

> If the death of the body...and of the consciousness merely involves a return to the absolute unconsciousness...then our toil-worn human race is nothing but a fatidical procession of phantoms, going from nothingness to nothingness...[34]

If one had to define the nature of this sadness it would be in the words with which Solon replied to the pedant who asked him, when he saw him weeping for the death of his son: 'why do you weep thus, if weeping avails nothing?' Solon answered 'Precisely for that reason—because it does not avail.' The hero has, in fact, rediscovered the first truth of Greek tragedy also divined by Nietzsche as the wisdom of Dionysus, that not to be born is man's only good. Thus before his mother Molloy's attitude is similar to Ivan Karamazov's before God. Where Ivan wonders how anyone can forgive God for the suffering he has caused, the hero asks the question: how can anyone take the responsibility for birth? For without love and procreation all this suffering, decay and death would be avoided. As Hamlet, in a similar moment of despair, cried out—'We will have no more marriages'.[35]

Nevertheless Molloy is alive and the discovery that life is a *via dolorosa* is nothing to the one which succeeds it. Molloy senses that in being born he has been excluded from an ideally timeless existence. He is in exile from an inner reality and disconnected from his own essence, his Self. Life is accompanied by an obscure feeling of guilt. 'It's my fault,' says Molloy, but what fault is it unless it was birth itself? With a primitive, childlike adjustment he comes to sense that he is being punished and therefore that he must have sinned, most probably against his imperatives. 'For I have greatly sinned at all times, greatly sinned against my prompters,' says Molloy, and Moran feels a need to 'crave forgiveness' yet 'forgiveness for what?' This notion is to have grave implications for the later heroes, but for the moment Molloy longs only to be reunited with the lost part of him. His journey back to his beginning is a search for an escape, for an end. However, the nearer he gets to the end the farther it recedes. Logically he knows it must be approaching for having left one's beginning there is nowhere else to go, yet it sends forward no sign and his progress, if that is what it can be called, is in appearance a circle, not a line from A to B, just as the end of his story is also his beginning. He has encountered, in short, the tragic dilemma of man trapped in time.

Molloy knows that one day be began, that Mag expelled him into the world 'through the hole in her arse'. As she did so he became the prisoner of time: the servant of the finite time of the body and the exile from the infinite freedom of the Self. As he says:

> My life, my life, now I speak of it as something over now as of a joke which still goes on, and it is neither, for at the same time it is over and it goes on, and is there any tense for that?

Birth is the beginning of a series to which there seems no end. Unlike Mr. Knott's servants whose arrival and departure is strictly determined, Molloy notices with horror that his mother did not die when he was born and that now he must be nearly as old as she is. One end of the series is closed while the other might extend to infinity. Death, the apparent conclusion, is not the opposite of birth for if it merely obliterates life then it destroys everything (and this is impossible if the soul is 'a mote in the dark of absolute freedom' and therefore cannot be obliterated) or, if life persists beyond death then the hero continues to be divorced from himself and in search of an end. The only birth and death which can have any significance to the hero will be the one that ends his exile and that, if it occurs, will be both a birth and a death.

Thus death becomes irrelevant. Molloy remarks with surprise that he is still alive ('that may come in useful') but at other times speaks of himself as already dead ('it is only since I ceased to live that I think of these things'). It is not death he fears but the nothingness of an exile without a conclusion. He writes, not to store up his existence against decay, but to eliminate everything that might intrude between himself and the elusive end. Sometimes he gives in and consoles himself with words. He tries to define his exact position:

> The fact is, it seems, the most you can hope is to be a little less, in the end, the creature you were in the beginning and the middle...

and uses language to create an appearance of finality:

> All I know is what the words know, and the dead things, and that makes a handsome little sum, with a beginning, a middle and an end, as in the well-built phrase and the long sonata of the dead.

The words cannot imprison the Self, time or space. Like death they can only settle on temporary phenomena and pronounce, with meaning, an end on things that are seen to die. On the Self there can be no such conclusion for though it has a beginning and a middle that may be dreamt over again in art, it persists as a waiting which is beyond the compass of language—as Vladimir and Estragon painfully discover.

How then is the exile to conclude? The answer is the dreadful, tragic paradox of Beckett's world. (And paradox is not a sign of intellectual imprecision: it marks, in the modern world, the split between the reasons of the heart which Pascal showed to be much more than vague feelings, and the dictatorial reasons of the mind). If there is an end there must be a beginning and therefore a series, a rigid determinism before and after which insists on an absence of freedom. From what we know of the Self this is intolerable for the Self is nothing if not free and cannot be immured forever in the determinism of a series. However, not to end is equally intolerable because it implies that the Self has no escape from time and will never be reunited with the whole that is essentially timeless. 'It is for the whole there is no name.' This is the legacy Molloy passes to his successors, and Malone's stories and the Unnamable's torrent of words are both attempts to speak the name which will resolve the particulars in a silence where one need speak no more.

SEVEN: THE TRILOGY: 2

To human kind fate has appointed only dying.

LEOPARDI[1]

I

'MALONE DIES' is the epitome of the novel and perhaps the most appealing work Beckett has written. Certainly it is the most approachable among the later novels. Malone's situation is simple. Confined to his bed and awaiting death he occupies the interim by writing: what we read is the result of his meditations and inventions. The novel begins at the point where *Molloy* left off. The journey is over and the hero unable to leave the room he has taken so long to find. It ends with the arbitrary intervention of death. Malone could, he declares, 'die today, if I wished, merely by making a little effort. But it is just as well to let myself die, quietly, without rushing things.' He will die, he says, 'tepid, without enthusiasm', and imagines that he has quite enough with which to concern himself before the arrival of his 'old debtor'—the death which life owes him.

Like Molloy he doesn't know how he arrived at the room but he is certain he is in neither a hospital nor an asylum. It is an ordinary room from which he can hear 'the peaceful sounds of men at large, getting up, lying down, preparing food, coming and going, weeping and laughing ...All I know is that the living are here, above and beneath me. It follows at least I am not in the basement.' He presumes the room is his own, perhaps a legacy from its last occupant. It contains a cupboard he has never looked into and a window near to his bed through which he can see the sky and into a room in the house over the way.

In one corner his possessions are heaped, of exactly the kind one would expect a successor of Molloy to cherish. There is a sucking stone, 'a little silver knife rest,' (like the one Molloy stole from Lousse), a boot, a club 'stained with blood', the bowl of a pipe, half a crutch and the cap of a bicycle bell—all that remains of the wonderful machine. With him in bed, is a stick that he uses both to root amongst these possessions and to draw to his bedside the table upon which a withered hand once a day places his food (it is soup) and a clean chamber pot. The stick has replaced the bicycle and crutches as an essential extension of his body. Like his predecessors he analyses the mystery of dualism but his comments are less frenzied. He accepts the limitations of decay and does not hope to move from the bed in which he sits (as Descartes too once sat and meditated) naked, toothless, hairy and impotent. His sight and hearing are very bad but fortunately his arms 'once they are in position, can exert a certain force'. Thus he is able to regulate the temperature of his bed by increasing or diminishing the blankets with which he has been provided ('They have thought of everything'), and satisfy his needs with the help of the stick. For though he may sometimes err and 'give my body the old orders I know it cannot obey', the stick overcomes his incapacity and forms his only link with the world about him. His body itself is so useless and remote that it might be at an infinite distance from his brain. As he describes it, with the expected Cartesian bias:

> My feet, which even in the ordinary way are so much further from me than all the rest, from my head I mean, for that is where I am fled, my feet are leagues away. And to call them in, to be cleaned for example, would I think take me over a month, exclusive of the time required to locate them...My fingers too write in other latitudes and the air that breathes through my pages turns them without my knowing.

So, when the stick, with which he has been trying to force the bed across the floor and out of the room, slips from his hand out of reach, it is a momentous event. It might now, he says, be as far from him as the equator. Even his possessions are beyond the limits of his world: he is as successfully marooned in his bed as ever Crusoe was on his desert island.

There are only two other events during the entire novel that similarly affect Malone's actual condition. Firstly the old woman suddenly disappears and no one comes with food or empties his pot. Malone therefore is forced to consider the possibility of his dying of starvation 'after having struggled successfully all my life against that menace' rather than of old age. However, he does not think this likely for looking at his ghastly, shrivelled flesh he ironically observes: 'There is a providence for impotent old men, to the end. And when they cannot swallow any more someone rams a tube down their gullet, or up their rectum, and fills them full of vitaminized pap, so as not to be accused of murder.' Secondly, a short time before he dies, he is visited by a man wearing a black block-hat and a black suit of antiquated cut with a ruler in the breast pocket. He announces himself with a blow on Malone's head and the latter wonders if he is not the undertaker annoyed at coming too early. But Malone cannot articulate the question even though the man bends down to listen, and neither can he hear what the man says: 'His mouth opened, his lips worked, but I heard nothing.' The man stays about seven hours, looking through Malone's possessions or standing silently by the bed occasionally poking the bedclothes with his tightly-rolled umbrella. Malone thinks that he is searching for his exercise book and hides it, though when the man has gone he writes twenty-one questions down to show him should he return again in the morning. 'Strange need,' Malone remarks of these questions, 'to know who people are and what they do for a living and what they want with you':—as if the answer to such questions would establish anything fundamental about another human being's identity.

Apart from these occurrences Malone is free either to meditate on his past, to dream through again the life already lived, or to tell his stories. It is quickly apparent, however, that the calm Malone imagines himself to have reached at the beginning of his narrative is only an illusion. But a few lines after declaring that he will die tepid he speaks in the familiar Beckettian tone of outrage, using words almost identical to those with which Watt arraigned the intolerable series of birth and death and the passing of the seasons: 'I forgive nobody. I wish them all an atrocious life and then the fires and ice of hell and in the execrable generations to come an honoured name.' The room, of course, approximates to the inside of his head. On one occasion he deliberately hints that 'these six planes that enclose me are of solid bone', and that everything he describes is to be located somewhere in this ratiocinating dome. And now that his body has entirely deserted him it is in this crumbling silence alone that he can live, listening to the 'faint sound of aerial surf that is my silence', or peopling the silence with the doings of his characters. He announces at the start that henceforward he will only play, that he will tell himself stories which will be '...neither beautiful, nor ugly, they will be calm, there will be no ugliness or beauty or fever in them any more, they will be almost lifeless like the teller.' He has even given himself a time-table which ought, he considers, to be adequate for the time that remains to him. In the words of Chateaubriand, one of the first to turn inwards in self-contemplation, consciously remembering the life almost ended, it will be 'a work destined to beguile for me the boredom of those last, lonely hours which nobody wants and which one does not know how to employ.'[2] One glimpses in the trilogy the end of that shift in values which occurred when Rousseau and Chateaubriand introduced the primacy of self-consciousness into literature.

There are to be four stories:

> One about a man, another about a woman, a third about a thing and finally one about an animal, a bird probably...then I shall speak of the things that remain in my possession, that is the thing I have always wanted to do. It will be a kind of inventory...I have also decided to remind myself briefly of my present state before embarking on my stories.

However, this plan soon collapses. Nothing is written either about the animal or the thing. The man and the woman are placed in the same story which the man dominates and the inventory, which develops into an obsession agitated by the fear that he might die before it is completed, intrudes into the narrative whenever his attention wanders. Still more important he does not succeed in remaining calm. The stories, it will become apparent later, are not simple entertainments as he likes to pretend in the beginning but an endeavour with a crucial, metaphysical purpose. The life of his hero becomes confused with his own personal memories which obstinately errupt into the placid narrative exterior. His attempt 'to live and cause to live, at last, to play at last and die alive' is destroyed by the dead world of the ancient night in which Molloy existed and where Malone finds himself again in 'darkness, long stumbling with outstretched arms' at the mercy of every sombre meditation that enters his skull.

Thus the leisured pace of the narratives are broken into by the jagged, fragmentary sentences of Malone's personal despair. As in *Endgame* or *Waiting for Godot* where Hamm and Pozzo respectively, assume a deliberate tone for their stories, *Malone Dies* is written in two distinct styles. Moreover the two strands of the novel are also separated by the contrast between Malone's random and eclectic thoughts and the reasonably straightforward progression of the narrative. Unlike Molloy Malone does not always return to his point of departure after each mental interjection but hobbles from one dissociated concern to another. His story, on the other hand, proceeds from the youth of its hero through middle-age towards a senescence comparable to Malone's own. Despite frequent unaccountable changes of time and place between individual episodes it remains close to fiction's old laws of cause and effect and only departs from them when Malone senses the approach of death and in a paroxysm of hatred destroys almost all the characters.

However, not all his memories are violent and disturbing and Malone recalls, at intervals, his ancestry in the closed world of Beckett's novels. Molloy is constantly envoked ('now that I speak of a forest I vaguely remember a forest') even to the almost exact reproduction of his words: 'I do not remember how I got here. In an ambulance perhaps, a vehicle of some kind certainly.' Then, as he studies the stars in the patch of sky outside his window Malone remembers his existence under the persona of Murphy: 'gazing at them one night I suddenly saw myself in London. Is it possible I got as far as London?' He also recalls Mr Endon and the Mercyseat—'with the insane too I failed, by a hair's breadth'—and still more pregnantly, the butler who committed suicide in the flat above Celia: 'there was the old butler too, in London I think, there's London again...it seems to me he had a name.' On this occasion it is Beckett himself, rather than the hero, who is remembering, for Murphy was no longer with Celia when the butler died. Fiction and reality are closely intertwined and it is Beckett, not Malone, who interrupts to say of the butler: 'I cut his throat with his razor.' Other memories are less confusing. Twice he alludes to 'that bloody man Quin' who may be Caper Quin of *More Pricks Than Kicks* and recollections of the French stories are frequent. Malone has a photograph of the donkey on which he once rode and mentions the phial of sedatives that was prominent in *Le Calmant*. Moreover when his hero, Macmann, watches the cabs passing across Dublin Malone thinks of the time he too was conveyed from lodging to lodging in *The Expelled*, and as he thinks of the sea breaking on the shore in the mouth of the cave where he was almost happy, he speaks of that brief moment of tenderness between himself and the donkeyman, of him who 'took me in his arms and told me to stay with him always, who gave me his place and watched over me'. The landscape that Malone describes in his story is clearly once again that of *Molloy*: the Irish countryside round Dublin. He portrays his hero lost on a plain between the mountains and the sea, and rootless in the city of Dublin itself. Nearby is the asylum of St John of God, the harbour of Dun Laoghaire from which the patients set out on their excursion, and the hills west of Carrickmines where the stone-cutters live and about which author and character enjoy their moment of Proustian remembrance. In effect *Malone Dies* subsumes the earlier novels. For the hero who meditates in bed has, in his consciousness, all that the Beckett clown ever experienced and can relive this past as it comes back to him. He lives in the shadow of an end that dwarfs his former activities and only what he cares to set down at this moment of being 'born into death' can have any significance. Malone is intent to abandon this past which reappears in fragments throughout his story; to reach the end where 'it will be all over with the Murphys, Merciers, Molloys, Morans and Malones, unless it goes on beyond the grave.' Leaving aside the ominous threat of those last seven words one becomes aware that this novel is in the nature of an epilogue to the hero's previous existence. Malone is abandoning the dimension in which the former heroes lived and as he does so lets fall a few comments on the continuing world outside his room, the last he hopes he will be called on to make.

This farewell is, for the most part, contained within Malone's story. The latter describes the life, from boyhood to insane old-age, of its hero who is at first called Saposcat, or Sapo for short. Sapo is the 'eldest child of poor and sickly parents...a great cylinder endowed with the faculties of cognition and volition', and in the account of his childhood Beckett, via Malone, satirizes the bourgeoisie, its concepts, attitudes and assumptions, in the traditional centre of its strength, the family. Sapo's first years are spent watching and listening to the conversations of his parents, introspectively brooding on the 'babel raging in his head' or wandering in the fields near his house, wondering 'how he was going to live, and live vanquished, blindly, in a mad world, in the midst of strangers'. Like his creator he feels alienated from the people about him, especially from his parents. Malone himself declares explicitly '—the living. They were always more than I could bear', and describes this part of his story as 'a last effort to understand, how such creatures are possible.' As he portrays Mr and Mrs Saposcat the gulf between them and the ideal of the Beckett hero is obvious. Succinctly their preoccupation with money and health, the one obliterating the other depending on which ever they choose to strive for, is presented: 'He (Sapo) often heard them talk of what they ought to do in order to have better health and more money.' To become comfortably off Mr Saposcat would have to work at night and at the weekends, but if he did so the already precarious balance of his health would be ruined. On the other hand to preserve his health is to preserve his poverty: as in *Murphy* the law of the quantum of wantum is still in control of destiny. Their position is worsened by the stupidity of their pre-occupations and conventions. Malone describes, with unanswerable irony, the eternally repetitive nature of their thoughts and conversation:

> The life of the Saposcats was full of axioms, of which one at least established the criminal absurdity of a garden without roses and with its paths and lawns uncared for.

and with a ruthless accuracy he displays the complete poverty of their characters and lives which lack any emotional, intellectual or spiritual content:

> Starting from a given theme their minds laboured in unison. They had no conversation properly speaking. They made use of the spoken word in much the same way as the guard of the train makes use of his flags or his lantern.

However, the most repulsive aspect of their human poverty, is illustrated in their attitude towards their eldest son. Sapo's childhood is an apt preparation for the disinherited adult who ends his life in a lunatic asylum at Stillorgan. Sapo is not an intelligent child and regularly fails his examinations. Instead of working he hides his books under a stone and goes to visit the Lamberts, a family of peasants with whom he is friendly. The Lamberts too are poor though the father is much sought after as a 'bleeder and destroyer of pigs'. The orgy in which he indulges during the traditional slaughtering season every December and January suggests a French origin for the family (known in the French version as Les Louis) and this has been confirmed by Beckett himself who says he drew them from a family he knew when he was in the Vaucluze. The mother has the doubtful peasant virtue of extreme thrift and the son and daughter share the same bedroom. 'Incest was in the air,' writes Malone, but actually it is the father who provides the threat which Mrs. Lambert saw coming 'with indifference'. During his visits to the farm Sapo rarely speaks, and a lonely, obdurate silence is common to the house as in this poignant image of father and son just after the death of their mule:

> There they sat, the table between them, in the gloom, one speaking, the other listening, and far removed, the one from what he said, the other from what he heard, and far from each other. The heap of earth was dwindling, the earth shone strangely in the raking evening light, glowing in patches as though with its own fire, in the fading light.

Perhaps it is this undemonstrative silence that attracts Sapo for he prefers their company to the niggling conversation of his parents. If he does not speak he leaves the Lamberts little presents that are accepted in a comparable understanding silence, and when he decides to leave home the daughter is the only person in whom he confides.

His parents know nothing of these attachments. All their conversations end in an 'unbridled dream' which assumes that Sapo will distinguish himself for no other reason but to be able to help the financial burden of an ever-growing family. The Saposcats' life is directed towards the moment when the elder son's departure as a wage-earner will balance the arrival of the annual birth, a process that will continue until there are no new births and the aged Saposcats can enjoy a prosperity for which they will then have no use. Sapo's succeeding life, therefore, is not to be wondered at when at the outset he is the centre of the selfish delusions with which his parents surround him. Faced with the evidence of his intellectual backwardness ('they wondered if it was not the mark of superior minds to fail miserably at the written paper and cover themselves with ridicule at the viva voce') and knowing nothing of his personality or his inclinations they are blind to any consciousness other than the fulfilment of their own narrow desires which they hope to perpetuate through him. Arbitrarily they allot him a destiny: it is a common story:

> They did not know why he was committed to a liberal profession. That was yet another thing that went without saying. It was therefore impossible he should be unfit for it.

but of course, he was.

When Sapo leaves home Malone loses sight of him for some years and does not resume the story until his hero is middle-aged. Sapo, 'this patient, reasonable child' as Malone had called him at first has now become a derelict, rootless tramp much nearer to the erstwhile character and condition of his author. Malone feels that Sapo is no longer a suitable name for his creation and changes it to Macmann, thus emphasizing his kinship with Beckett's other heroes. He is seen sitting on the bank of the Liffey in a position 'like that of the Colossus of Memnon' (Malone too is well-educated), his back to the river where the gulls 'swoop ravening about the offal' with dreadful cries. He is looking towards the busy streets, at the mad world which as a boy he feared to enter, and through his eyes Malone portrays the anonymity and loneliness of city life. It is Beckett's most sustained diatribe against what Heidegger termed 'Forfeiture', the drab, impersonal vacuity of man's everyday exchange: life without a centre lived in the boring, mechanical repetition of spiritless gesture and debased, inhuman contact. In tone and imagery the passage is similar to Eliot's description of the modern city in *The Waste Land* and *Burnt Norton*. It is the

> ...violet hour, when the eyes and back
> Turn upward from the desk, when the human engine waits
> Like a taxi throbbing waiting,...[3]

Macmann watches the 'evening hour that strives/Homeward',[4] in which people are disgorged by the offices, shops and day-light rendezvous into the street where they cluster together uncertain how to part or where to go and yet incapable of achieving even the smallest measure of human contact which would anyway be inevitably denied:

> The doors open and spew them out, each door its contingent. For an instant they cluster in a daze, huddled on the sidewalk or in the gutter, then set off singly on their appointed ways. And even those who know themselves condemned, at the outset, to the same direction, for the choice of direction at the outset is not great, take leave of one another and part, but politely, with some polite excuse, or without a word, for they all know one another's little ways. And God help him who longs, for once, in his recovered freedom, to walk a little way with a fellow-creature, no matter which unless of course by a merciful chance he stumble upon one in the same plight. Then they take a few paces happily side by side, then part, each muttering perhaps, Now there will be no holding him.

A few, like Eliot's typist, seek refuge in unsatisfactory love-making. Others go to transitory gatherings in pub, hall or cinema. Most remain solitary. If they have gone out they may return in a cab drawn by a horse destined for the shambles in the not too distant future. Malone forms his portrait of a solitary traveller in a cab into a complex image for our modern loss of individuality and for the seizure, or collapse, of will and desire. City life has reduced man to an unreasoning acceptance of his insignificance and his impotence. Malone's traveller continues blindly on his way, as empty as all the other citizens that pass him in the night, accompanied only by a dull ache that hints at the spiritual loss he has suffered:

> But the passenger, having named the place he wants to go and knowing himself as helpless to act on the course of events as the dark box that encloses him, abandons himself to the pleasant feeling of being freed from all responsibility, or he ponders on what lies before him, or on what lies behind him, saying, Twill not be ever thus, and then in the same breath, But twas ever thus, for there are not five hundred different kinds of passengers.

Malone does not describe Macmann's own feelings in this situation or whether or not he was attempting to make some contact with one of the crowd. He is diverted into speaking of himself once more and when he returns to his hero it is to find him out in the country lying prostrate in a crucified position on the ground in an effort to keep at least half of his body sheltered from the heavy rain that is falling. Malone comments on his hero's failure as a street-cleaner and gardener, the two occupations he has been driven to in order to continue 'coming and going on the earth'. Actually Macmann did not particularly wish to keep on coming and going but was obliged to do so 'for reasons known to who knows God alone'. At this point the author interjects—

> ...to tell the truth God does not seem to need reasons for doing what he does, and for omitting to do what he omits to do, to the same degree as his creatures, does he?

and so is distracted from his purpose yet again.

When he returns to Macmann it is to locate him in The House of St John of God which Wylie mentioned in *Murphy*. From Belacqua, who declared his heart to be in Portrane Asylum, onwards Beckett's heroes have demonstrated an almost hereditary interest in mental hospitals. Murphy imagined for a time that he had found what he was searching for at the Mercyseat; Watt ended his career in one, and it is likely that it was an asylum from which the hero was discharged in the story, *The End*. John Fletcher points out that:

> ...where Swift compared the insane to the sane to ridicule the antics and conceit of the latter, Beckett is interested in the insane in their own right; for him...they have a kind of honesty and innocence that those with pretension to sanity completely lack: they are men who, living absorbed in their own world, are uncorrupted by the world of men.[5]

Beckett evidently shares the sympathies, if not the compulsion, of his characters. When he was living in London during the nineteen-thirties he visited Bethlem Royal Hospital at Beckenham and his close observation of the mentally sick is evident in the descriptions of the inmates who accompany Macmann on his outing with Lady Peddle. The mental institution is the ultimate refuge of all his characters who 'live vanquished on a mad world, in the midst of strangers'. In an asylum they are no longer hounded back into the game by the hale and hearty inhabitants of whom they ask nothing better than to be left alone. It is the real world which appears insane to the hero (and in general, to Beckett himself) and he eventually resolves the problem of his alienation by entering the so-called world of the mad.

In the asylum Macmann is placed in the care of an old woman named Moll who is as ill-conditioned, physically, as Macmann himself. It is in this episode (and in an earlier passage where Malone describes what he sees in a window over the way) that Beckett brings his treatment of love and procreation to a climax of revulsion. The plays that follow make, though in a subdued tone, a plea for companionship and tenderness, if not for love.

From his bed Malone sometimes raises his shaggy head to look out into the street and to observe the house which faces his own. Through one of its windows he is able (like the beetle man in Dostoyevsky's *Notes from the Underground*) to follow the existence of his fellow-men unbeknown to them. On one occasion he sees a man and a woman making love against a lighted lamp, their shadows forming an exaggerated parallel of the scene on the curtain. It is a splendidly controlled passage which contains not only Beckett's disgust and irony at the act of love—as in *Molloy*—but also an intimation through the pain of that act, of the pain that will inevitably follow in the unthought of being that is its effect. This time the hero's disgust is coupled with a pitying realization that the two people are striving, unsuccessfully, to forget their individual lonelinesses in the union of their separate identities.

Malone sees them:

> standing up against each other behind the curtain...they cleave so fast together that they seem a single body, and consequently a single shadow. But when they totter it is clear they are twain, and in vain they clasp with the energy of despair, it is clear we have two distinct and separate bodies, each enclosed within its own frontiers, and having no need of each other to come and go and sustain the flame of life, for each is well able to do so, independently of the other.

Man, even at the most intense moment of his aspiring love that reaches out to grasp and enfold an other, is condemned to live within the solitary confinement of his own skin.

For a few moments Malone is unaware what they are doing. He thinks they are perhaps trying to keep out the cold (which of course in a sense they are) but because they are lightly clad he realizes that this cannot be the case. Then comes understanding:

> Ah, how stupid I am, I see what it is, they must be loving each other, that must be how it is done...They have loved each other standing, like dogs. Soon they will be able to part. Or perhaps they are just having a breather before they tackle the titbit. Back and forth, that must be wonderful. They seem to be in pain.

There are no illusions in Malone's view even though it would seem he has only experienced love at the remove of a voyeur. It has no imposed spirituality. It remains a straightforward, unromanticized biological fact and human beings driven to extremes of isolation and passion perform it, not even as human beings but 'like dogs'. As Proust demonstrated, the act of physical possession is a paradox for the possessor retires at the end having possessed nothing. The moment of fulfilment is neither joyous nor transcendent; it is seen as a moment of pain. Man is created in pain and from the moment of his conception pain and sorrow attend him on earth.

Beckett's conception of love is similar to the first stage of Unamuno's thought on that subject in *The Tragic Sense of Life*. Love for Unamuno is the most tragic thing of all; it is the handmaiden of despair for despair drives one to love and the discovery that even love is insufficient returns one to an even greater despair. Love, for Unamuno, is 'death's brother':

> It is suffering flesh, it is suffering, it is death, that lovers perpetuate on earth. Love is at once the brother, son and father of death, which is its sister, mother and daughter. And thus it is that in the depths of love there is a depth of eternal despair.[6]

The eternal despair of disillusioned love is the worst of agonies, and Malone thinks it foolish even to attempt love knowing that this will be the result. Yet Malone's description of the two beings emphatically individual even at the moment of maximum interpenetration of being, has a compassion and a universality that Molloy, in his description of his affair with Edith, had not. Malone, and behind him Beckett, are here witnesses to the end of a framework of conceptions that have prevailed for some hundred and fifty years. For as a result of the breakdown of religious communication and the individualization of social life love was given a paramount importance as the sole remaining means of communication. This was a distinctly nineteenth-century manifestation, apparent in the ideal fabrication of Shelley's *Epipsychidion* and also in the legendary effect of the sorrows of Goethe's *Werther* on the public of his time. Love assumed the greatest importance as a way of communication and salvation in a world that appeared awry. It was seen as a chance to break through the loneliness of individuation and fuse one fragmentary soul with another in the belief that, though the world itself might be in chaos, two people together can discover in their unity the talisman of happiness. The world, so the legend ran, might be transcended by love—or to be more mundane, escaped. In the words of the song—'There's a place for us, somewhere'. Yet love, which expressed the desire of the infinite in humanity, rapidly discovered limits, and as the infinite can in no way be confined, humanity was repulsed back upon itself. The deception perished and humanity was left either to see in love a profound despair, as did Unamuno, or to hate the illusion that failed, as does Beckett. It is Proust, Beckett's antecedent, who describes love as time and space made perceptible to the heart, and this analysis points to exactly the anguish of a non-transcendent love. The microcosm is always aware of the relative immortality of the macrocosm from which it is excluded. Though his lovers clasp one another with the energy of despair, Malone notices that they are inexorably twain. Love has lost its validity as a substitute for religion:— or as one of Celine's characters remarks 'Love is a poodle's chance of attaining the infinite.'

The other passage on love in *Malone Dies*, this time an extended episode in the life of Macmann, is almost certainly the strangest affair of the heart in literature. It is a bravura extension of the factual grotesque, profoundly ironic and wildly amusing yet consumed by an acid bitterness that is the grotesque's substitute for the catharsis of tragedy. It belongs with those works such as Goya's etchings and the bitumen scrawled paintings of his last years, wherein hatred and violence are barely tempered by the palliative of the ludicrous.

In the asylum the responsibility of cleaning both Macmann and his room falls upon Moll, 'a little old woman immoderately ill-favoured of both face and body'. After some time a strange feeling arises in her towards her charge, a feeling which one would describe as the beginning of love were not the condition of the two of them so physically bizarre and repulsive:

> And she contemplated with tenderness the old bewildered face relaxing, and in its tod of hair the mouth trying to smile, and the little red eyes turning timidly towards her as if in gratitude or rolling rowards the recovered hat, and the hands raised to set it on more firmly and returning to rest trembling on the blanket. And at last a long look passed between them and Moll's lips puffed and parted in a dreadful smile, which made Macmann's eyes waver like those of an animal glared on by its master and then compelled to look away.

Despite the grotesque situation tenderness trembles on the perimeter of the writing. It threatens to immerse the scene in a real poignancy and Malone is forced to add in a caustic and deprecating tone: 'End of anecdote.'

The relationship advances rapidly and a kind of intimacy springs up between the two derelicts. This intimacy 'led them to lie together and copulate as best they could,' an attempt in which they counter severe difficulties partly because of their great age and also through their previous inexperience. They are both impotent yet nevertheless manage somehow 'in striking from their dry and feeble clips a kind of sombre gratification'. At this stage Moll is the most demonstrative of the two and frequently exclaims 'Oh would we had but met sixty years ago!' While Macmann remains somewhat unimpressed at gaining at this late stage in life, and so unexpectedly, 'some insight into the expression two is company.'

Nevertheless he progresses in learning the arts of love partly instructed by the embarrassed and gauche letters Moll writes him. Their whole affair is an assault on the conventions of romantic love and in particular on the love stories one sees in weekly magazines. Every event finds its parallel in the romantic myths which these stories perpetuate and the description of the impact of the affair on Macmann's mind might be transferred, in essence, with little adjustment to the common fare of railway bookstalls. The only addition is the violent irony with which Malone describes his hero's struggles. Even the details are accurate, such as the letters (tied up with ribbon of course) which are kissed when read and hidden under the pillow. In them Moll consoles herself and Macmann with the thought that though their time is brief their love has not time to grow cold as it would in youth, and she congratulates them both on achieving what they do achieve in such a state of decay. 'Let us make the most of it, there are pears that ripen only in December' is her refrain, and she emphasizes that love is more than the flesh and their love is truly innocent—they have preserved themselves for each other.

The affair then moves into its second phase. Macmann has got used to Moll's 'blobber lips, gums which sucked and long yellow canine bared to the roots' and he warms to her. Her habit of letting her upper lip spring back upon her gums with a smack excites Macmann as much, writes Malone, as the sight of a woman's garter and thigh inspire a younger man. He begins to dominate their relationship and take the initiative in the petting. But even as he does so, feeling desire for Moll for the first time, she begins to lose her feelings for him. She starts to smell and reveals symptoms of pregnancy. She vomits all over the floor; her hair falls out and her complexion turns a deep yellow. Despite this development 'the sight of her so diminished did not damp Mac's desire to take her, all stinking, yellow, bald and vomiting, in his arms'. However, she begins to actually repulse him. Her thoughts are evidently elsewhere and Macmann, subjected for the first time to a woman's caprice, despairs. He is seized by a frenzy and belabours his chest, the pillow and the mattress, writhing about the bed and crying out for her to take pity on him to such an extent that Moll leaves. The romance is over, and eventually a man comes to him and says that Moll is dead and that from now on he is to be Macmann's keeper.

During the latter stages of this affair Macmann is torn by all the plaints of the disappointed lover. He watches Moll's smallest actions and is driven towards neurosis by the interpretations which he places on them. Moreover the affair follows the pattern traced at greater length by Proust: the one love fading as the other ripens. It is impossible they should fuse at a moment of equal momentum for, in Sartrian terms, it involves the clash of two *pour-soi*'s each regarding the other as an object, or *en-soi*. The result is a battle wherein each attempts to dominate, to extend itself, if not to infinity, at least over the province of an other, and this is impossible for each is, in its own personality, a *pour-soi*, or Self, that cannot be encompassed. Thus the result is always a sickening see-saw between the hope of exaltation and the reality of suffering, which is either deeply tragic or absurd. Malone sees it as absurd and crushes love's pretence with irony and hatred. Yet in spite of the surface revulsion of the physical elements in the episode, one finishes it not entirely certain that the author has been able to withhold all compassion from the two lovers. For, though lovers and therefore perpetrators of the cardinal sin, they are also suffering human beings themselves seeking some form of warmth and contact. The passages of frenzy, such as the description of Macmann bundling 'his sex into his partner's like a pillow into a pillow slip', are undermined by the tenderness apparent in such moments as Moll's first affectionate glance at her charge. The hatred has that tone of desperation which comes from uncertainty and there is an anticipation here of the desire for companionship which is clearly present in the plays.[7]

II

The stories which Malone tells himself have other, and more important, purposes than he at first declares. Like Molloy, Malone is tortured by his own lack of identity, by the elusive Self that is inexplicably tied to a dying animal. The death which Molloy awaited has now almost come, but the imponderables remain for the living being caught in 'the lingers of evaporation'. The Self continues to be not an ideally timeless centre but a cloud of mystification and Malone is also obsessed by a death towards which he is outwardly indifferent. The end becomes not less but more crucial to the understanding the nearer it approaches and his labours with pencil and notebook are a way of passing the time only in a metaphysical sense.

For Malone all the usual means of self-definition have broken down. As he describes himself he reveals his unsuitability for even the most localized organization of experience. He has receded so far from the world that though 'All my senses are trained full on me...I am no prey for them.' He has lost himself within himself. His 'stupid flesh' does not feel pain; there is an interval between experience and cognition; and when he does receive a sensory message either from within or from the world beyond his bed, he can no longer form it into meaning:—'the noises of nature, of mankind and even my own, were all jumbled together in one and the same gibberish.' The mind also fails him in this search: 'Somewhere in this turmoil thought struggles on, it too wide of the mark. It too seeks me, as it always has, where I am not to be found.' Both thought and feeling cannot discern in which inward chamber his 'I' lives, that 'I' which has enquired and desired all his life and yet which is no more recognizable near the end than it was in the beginning. Moreover now there are additional obstacles. Time has ceased to be meaningful ('In a flicker of my lids whole days have flown'); memory is indistinct; the future becomes confused with the past and the present with them both so that life and death can at moments appear synonymous: 'Perhaps I expired in the forest, or even earlier.'

In this mess of imprecision Malone discovers two possibilities. He can examine the meaning of suffering which is the one certainty to survive the decay of his body, or he can employ fiction in the search in which his own enfeebled qualities have already failed.

Malone is more deeply aware of suffering than any previous hero. He is fascinated by its inexplicable action upon the individual and comes to see gratuitous suffering as a means to the discovery of identity. What attracts him is that suffering, like life, seems causeless and that to follow suffering back towards its origin is as valuable a journey towards a primal reality as was Molloy's search for his mother's room. In his story he brings Macmann to a desolate plain where he lies on the ground, arms outstretched to form the shape of a cross, beaten by a pitiless rain. It is perhaps the ancient significance of this position that suggests the idea of suffering to him yet it also introduces an imponderable, for the incessant rain falls on everything else as well as upon Macmann. Malone notices that there is no connection between punisher and punished: Macmann has not offended the rain which discomforts him and the means of punishment does not explain its cause which seems reasonless. Their association is gratuitous:—'as if there existed a relationship between that which suffers and that which causes to suffer.' Suffering therefore is a partner to the Self, a causeless refugee in the world of time cut off from the Void of which it is a part. Needing apparently nothing for it to be, suffering must, like the life of the Self in time, be in exile from the Void until its discomfiture is over. People do wrong, says Malone, to search for a cause in the offal of everyday reality, in what is nearest to hand:

> People are never content to suffer, but they must have heat and cold, rain and its contrary which is fine weather, black skin and sexual and peptic deficiency for example, in short the furies and frenzies happily too numerous to be numbered of the body including the skull and its annexes, whatever that means, such as the club-foot, in order that they may know very precisely what exactly it is that dares prevent their happiness from being unalloyed.

Suffering is not a rational entity that can be framed in an explanation which connects it to an evident cause. If it has a cause it is, as with life, in the beginning and Malone sees that, coming as it seems to from the same source, it is perhaps the only connection he has with his own Self, and a proof that he is continuing to be.

However, Malone also realizes that to see suffering as evidence of a Paradise that has been lost is to see it as a punishment, or more exactly, an atonement. If life on earth is suffering it is the atonement for some sin long past: it is the end term of a series that began at birth, perhaps even before. Or, more exactly, as 'the ideas of guilt and punishment were confused together in his mind, as those of cause and effect so often are in the minds of those who continue to think,' the punishment is not caused by the sin but creates the need for a sin. In an enclosed world like that of the trilogy punishment may precede guilt and atonement compel the sufferer to attribute a reason for his fall into a time-bound Purgatory. As Malone describes Macmann:

> And without knowing exactly what his sin was he felt full well that living was not a sufficient atonement for it or that this atonement was in itself a sin, calling for more atonement, and so on, as if there could be anything but life, for the living.

The only sin that Macmann remembers, however, is 'the memory, more and more galling, of his having consented to live in his mother, than to leave her.' At last one recognizes the drift of these discussions and the obsessive hold which they have on the hero's mind. Life exists that suffering exists and one suffers for the sin of having been born. It is once again the Greek tragic vision but this time impregnated with the Christian ideal of a Calvary, and a haunting echo of that most hideous debate, original sin. Beckett's creatures are as helplessly predestined to suffer as Milton's Adam was to fall, and in arraigning the poet for his injustice one is only revolting against the terms of one's own existence, painfully illustrated in the fate of the hero. Theology apart, both Milton and Beckett (and one might add the Old Testament prophets in whom the Christian tradition comes closest to tragedy) create an image of a reality that underlies all the immediate causes of suffering. One's birth may be arbitrary but in the act of 'consenting' to live one is condemned both to sin and to suffer. In Beckett the suffering will cease only when life itself ceases and its end will signify a return to the lost paradise of the Self, that Self of which it is a tenuous reminder throughout life. Thus suffering is important to the Beckett hero in a manner analogous to its place in the life of many Christians. It is a symbol of their exile in the world but an affliction to be embraced with joy. As Dante portrays the souls in Purgatory welcoming the worst if it will bring them nearer to Paradise, so Beckett's heroes too seek to suffer more. The attitude of Clov in *Endgame* corresponds closely to the Christian ideal of suffering through atonement:

> I say to myself—sometimes, Clov, you must learn to suffer better than that if you want them to weary of punishing you—one day. I say to myself—sometimes, Clov, you must be there better than that if you want them to let you go—one day.

With the almost mechanical pathos of Beckett's later heroes Clov believes that if he can suffer still more the time of his release might be brought forward. It is a notion those in the *Purgatorio* would have easily comprehended. Despite the advance of technology and science the hero finds more that is fundamental to his experience in those mythical patterns of guilt, suffering and atonement which sustained his ancestors and were explored in the first of all tragedies, The Fall of Man and the *Oresteia*. However, there is one essential reservation. Where the Christian hoped and the Greek perfected, the Beckett hero now begins to understand that the end he aspires to is hopeless and impossible: time itself slows down.

In his writings Malone seeks to abandon his own personae, the faulty appearance that cloaks his Self, and enter that of another creature. He dreams of making an end wherein 'on the threshold of being no more I succeed in being another'. His own senses and intelligence, for so long misdirected, are now incapable of locating that Self which has receded from the world until, as he says, 'I would be lost in the eye of a needle, I am so hard and contracted.' Therefore he attempts in fiction what he cannot achieve in life. He sees in writing a remote chance of apprehending his identity at the moment of death. The plan is ingenious. Incapable of movement his notebook becomes his life: nothing exists that is not written in its pages, so that when he loses his pencil he observes 'I have spent two unforgettable days of which nothing will ever be known.' (As in *Murphy* the pun can truly be said to have been 'in the beginning,' and points to the elusiveness of meaning). Moreover, in appreciating the distance between his real Self and the existence he is living as 'Malone', he sees that his life in time is like that of the fictional hero. Unlike Molloy who rarely distinguished between the 'I' that wrote and the 'I' he had lost, Malone does not see the two as necessarily identical. It is only one of many selves that he can assume, no more exact a definition of identity than his creations Macmann and Sapo who are as accurate portraits of his inward 'I' as his original pseudo-self, 'Malone'. What he seeks to do is to create one of these other selves, so avoiding the imprecision and the failure that would be certain if he relied on his own senses and intelligence for an inward search. He creates Macmann so as to 'slip into him...in the hope of learning something'. If he can write of an other he can perhaps regard the essence of his Self in the other's image: turn his vital *pour-soi* into an *en-soi* that he can observe without frenzy or passion. Particularly he might be able to correspond his invented Self, Macmann, with his Self as 'Malone' in the moment of death and so leave his true Self distinct and free. In that moment where temporal and infinite meet his real 'I' will be separated from these pseudonyms, unsullied by their contact and so at liberty to enter into the timeless nature of its own being. As he describes it, he seeks to 'die alive'.

But this attempt at a monumental objectivity fails because fiction so easily becomes another type of 'autobiography.' To distinguish between memory and invention is a difficult process in one whose notions of time and place are easily confused. The idea torments Malone. 'I call that playing,' he writes after an early episode—'I wonder if I am not talking yet again about myself. Shall I be incapable, to the end, of lying on any other subject?' He threatens his enterprise by alternating a passage of fiction with his own reflections. At one point he says he recalls nothing of his life up until the present moment, at another he amuses himself by inventing 'those lost events'. But where his memory is so imprecise the extraction of the superfluous from the essential, the true from the imagined, is impossible. Clearly much that Macmann endures has already been suffered by the dying Malone. This interchange between invention and experience makes the novel as a whole into yet another study of the nature of fiction.

Malone therefore is called back from the Self he seeks to enter to the Self he has always lived with, often by the words themselves. 'There I am forgetting myself again. My concern is not with me but with another...Of myself I could never tell.' He loses patience with language, the precarious serenity on which his forgetting depends is threatened, and the narrative exhibits the familiar insults against epistemology:—'In his country the problem...no I can't do it...What truth is there in all this babble...how false all this is.' The words, of course, betray his intentions. 'Invent. It is not the word. Neither is live. No matter.' But he has a deeper understanding of this process than his predecessor: 'There is no use indicating words, they are no shoddier than the wares they peddle.' Gradually he abandons the delusion of objectivity. Sapo, whom he had described as 'unsullied by my presence,' becomes Macmann. The French influence apparent in the earlier, more objective descriptions of Sapo and the Lamberts gives way before the intrusion of Macmann who forces his way up from a more personal and intimate Irish substratum. Malone admits his failure. His stories, those cerebral games with destiny, were all in vain for 'I was still breathing in and out the air of this earth.' To be successful he would have had to seal this air in jars as tight as those that contain the miracle of Proustian remembrance and this would be to relinquish one victory over time for another. As he decides at last:

> Yes, a little creature, I shall try and make a little creature, to hold in my arms, a little creature in my own image, no matter what I say,...

But if the stories cannot help him to reach himself they do have another purpose, one that in *The Unnamable* is to become the most vital need of all. As he waits for his end Malone notices that time becomes irrelevant. Day and night merge into a single monotone phenomenon; dusk follows dawn without an interval and the distinction between one and the other becomes meaningless. For Malone is in search of infinity, the union of his personal infinity with that of the universal nothing, and that is like tracking the recurring decimal. Although he is sensible that for the end to be approaching time is passing, it comes so slowly that it does not effectively decrease. Infinity is continually approached yet remains as distant. With horror Malone realizes that for as long as he is in time he can have no end and that to be freed from it he must make an end: 'Perhaps there is none, no morrow any more, for one who has waited so long in vain.' This cry, though muted in the comparison, is no less anguished than Nietzsche's discovery of the death of God. It is also the terrible and inevitable successor to such knowledge.

Malone therefore finds himself in the infinite silence of those places that so terrified Pascal, that limitless, empty void which has no reason to be but is. Malone, and the Unnamable after him, know that to exist in such a place they must somehow annihilate time, must stop the just perceptible rustle of its passage that sounds in the silences between the words, like some thousand grains of sand displaced upon the sea-shore without the evident assistance of wind or man. There lies the importance of the stories. (Or of mathematics: the meaningless playing with figures that can reduce something to almost nothing if used by an expert like Malone. He remembers how he used to count for the sake of counting and then divide by sixty. 'That passed the time. I was time.') In fiction one can invent a cause and its effect, and manipulate the changes of beginning and ending from which one is precluded in life. In addition one can describe even such insignificant things as a hat or a coat in such detail that the foreground of the world is entirely filled by this mania for exactness.

Yet time will not end. The silences that consume the dialogue of Estragon and Vladimir threaten the writer at each full stop. Soon, to close a sentence will be to encourage despair. Time cannot be killed by words or numbers and therefore neither can Malone die into life as he desires. His death will never be real until time dies and that is never. There was a beginning, there is a waiting but to the waiting there is still no end:

> he who has waited long enough will wait for ever. And there comes the hour when nothing more can happen and nobody more can come and all is ended but the waiting that knows itself in vain...

For Beckett there is nothing more but this moment to write about, and in the succeeding novels and plays he returns but rarely to the world of the living which Malone here takes leave of. From now on there is nothing but the silence and a voice, sometimes two voices, continuing in a vain effort to drown that silence and bring the waiting to an end. Beckett's own books are the record of this hopeless endeavour.

EIGHT: THE TRILOGY: 3

To be is to be perceived.

BERKELEY

I

'THE UNNAMABLE' is the inevitable and terrifying end to all Beckett's previous novels. It is the most painful of his works, one that has, in the best sense (that of honesty and need), abandoned literature. *The Unnamable* describes the grey, formless limbo into which the hero passes at death. It is most probably only the inside of his distant skull where he is bound in time and words. In the interval between this work and *Malone Dies* the hero died. The crisis occurred off-stage as befits an event of only marginal importance. For such is death. It has solved nothing. The hero, as he feared, did not find in death the longed-for annihilation he was seeking and once he becomes accustomed to the change (he has been in Purgatory just long enough to know it is 'the same place as always') he discovers his anguish has increased. There are now no distractions. He has left the world of sucking stones and bicycles for one where he is compelled to think of his own disappearing reality without pause, and thinking to speak. If he ceases for a moment from this terrible imposition the silence of the infinite spaces rushes in upon him and swells his mind with the agony of nothingness.

The novel has no beginning or end except the arbitrary start and finish lent it by print and paper. All the appurtenances of fiction have been abandoned. The 'I' that speaks, at last distinct from its vice-existers, is simply a voice inescapably perceiving its own continuance, the voice of the creature who has been concealed behind and spoken through Murphy, Watt and Malone from the beginning. He had slipped into them in the hope of learning something about his real Self. Now he is reduced to this unknown, hesitating 'I' and lacks even the minimal physical appearance of his immediate predecessor. He is truly 'unnamable'—there is nothing but a voice to identify and that can only be done in terms of what it is not—not-Malone, not-Molloy, not-Moran etc.

The Unnamable opens with three questions which recall Belacqua's troubled interrogation of the Otto in *Dante and the Lobster*: 'Where now? Who now? When now?' The succeeding monologue is his attempt to answer them, to define himself and his condition in terms that will restore him to the ideal (not the temporal) silence of his true Self. Shortly after the start he abandons paragraphs and when, in despair, he recognizes the full difficulty of his task, punctuation as well. The book tumbles forward under the impetus of the all-powerful, meaningless words, in an anarchy of atoms, growing ever more frenzied and unrestrained. It matters little to the hero what he says so long as he speaks above the silence. All words are as important that are not *the* words which explain himself, and the breathless torrent (which seems even more urgent with the comma snatched between each phrase) cascades onwards to its hopeless finish. For hopeless it is. Again, finite weapons (words) are supposed to imprison the infinite; the solution has never been more desperately needed, it has never seemed more impossible. What emerges are fragments: chips of meaning, short descriptions, changes of direction, stories rapidly abandoned, all vomited out into a whole that defies the restraining techniques of criticism. There are no characters or story. Everything has been abandoned for there is nothing *but* the voice and its agony does not end. Assumptions or conclusions are invidious about a document such as this which can be experienced only in the totality of itself. Any attempt at discussion must necessarily remain incomplete, as incomplete as the book itself which ends with the hero still crossing what is only the minute threshold of eternity:...'I don't know, I'll never know, in the silence you don't know, you must go on, I can't go on, I'll go on.'

However from what the Unnamable says a few certainties emerge. The latter either bear on the place he takes himself to be in or concern those he calls his 'delegates', enfeebled descendants of the earlier heroes who occasionally contribute a little to the story, or supply the Unnamable with information he would otherwise lack. Whether he is in an actual place or not is difficult to ascertain: 'I have been here, ever since I began to be...this place was made for me, and I for it, at the same instant.' Yet at other times it seems to be a waste, a zone where one day he found himself, which is neither hot nor cold ('strange hell that has no heating') and probably without limits. There is 'nothing nocturnal here.' The light is grey, at first murky then opaque, and he wonders whether he himself generates luminosity into it or if he is the centre of a lamp turned on by someone far distant from himself. It seems likely that he is in the midst of this 'place' (though perhaps in infinity each thinks himself the centre; Hamm is also concerned whether or not his chair is in the exact middle of the stage). His body, which he feels has the 'shape and consistency of an egg' is 'incapable of the smallest movement.' His eyes, he knows, must be open from the tears that fall unceasingly ('They must be as red as live coals') and now they will no longer close. Nor is he deaf: 'That I am not stone deaf is shown by the sounds that reach me. For though the silence here is almost unbroken, it is not completely so...After so long a silence, a little cry, stifled outright.' He imagines himself 'gazing before me like a great horn-owl in an aviary,' and knows that 'I am seated, my hands on my knees, because of the pressure against my rump, against the soles of my feet, against the palms of my hands, against my knees.' Like the other heroes his head is covered with pustules though this time he is hairless. All the parts of the body which obtrude from the trunk are falling off: 'why should I have a sex, who have no longer a nose? All those things have fallen, all those things that stick out, with my eyes, my hair...I am a big talking ball.' (This last quotation is typical of the ghastly humour which characterizes his monologue, ironically reminding one on this occasion of those rubber toys which, when knocked down, immediately bob back up into their old position through their absence of feature.)

Both his knowledge of the world of men and his memory are, he declares, very limited. How limited, however, remains throughout a disturbing problem. Near the beginning he asks himself: 'These notions of forbears, of houses where lamps are lit at night, and other such, where do they come to me from?' He is puzzled by the idea of being indebted for his information to persons whom he cannot remember having met, and wonders if his knowledge is not innate. But it seems he was once instructed in those subjects on which others place so high a value and which the hero, from Belacqua onwards, has seen so little purpose in. His recollection of life at Bally firmly establishes his descent from the previous heroes:

> They...gave me the lowdown on God. They told me I depended on him, in the last analysis. They had it on the reliable information of his agents at Bally I forget what, this being, according to them the

> place where the inestimable gift of life had been rammed down my gullet. But what they were most determined for me to swallow was my fellow creatures...They gave me courses on love, on intelligence, most precious, most precious. They also taught me to count, and even to reason. Some of this rubbish has come in handy on occasions, I don't deny it, on occasions which would never have arisen if they had left me in peace. I use it still, to scratch my arse with.

Like Molloy's comments on *The Times Literary Supplement*, the Unnamable views his learning with a mixture of disgust, boredom and contempt. In his opinion both the world and man are valueless. Life excluded from the whole is, in Hamm's words, 'an extraordinary bitter day... zero by the thermometer'.[1] Thus all his instruction cannot acquire value in a world that is worthless to start with. If man is no more than a zero no amount of multiplication can increase or change his situation. Therefore he scorns the information with which he has been indoctrinated for without it he would never have suffered the agony of learning its emptiness. Nevertheless he later tries to offer up his old lesson, all that he now considers important in his previous life, for at least it is speaking. The summary is familiar:

> But now I shall say my old lesson, if I can remember it. Under the skies, on the roads, in the towns, in the woods, in the hills, in the plains, on the shores, on the seas, behind my mannikins, I was not always sad, I wasted my time, abjured my rights, suffered for nothing, forgot my lesson. Then a little hell after my own heart, not too cruel, with a few nice damned to foist my groans on, something sighing off and on and the distant gleams of pity's fires biding their hour to promote us to ashes.

Yet if he himself has always been bound to this place where 'there are no days' and which was made especially for him, how can he recall anything beyond it? The answer is with his 'mannikins'. All his knowledge (such as the notion of time—'years is one of Basil's ideas') he claims to have received from his vice-existers or delegates. They have told him 'what I know about men and the ways they have of putting it'; it is they who have made his 'appearances elsewhere.' From them he has learnt that in the world of men one is never alone. He ironically reviles humanity for its 'aptitude for happiness' in the face of reality and mocks the efforts which it employs in its quest for love ('there's a carrot never fails...you love as many times as necessary, as necessary in order to be happy'). At one point he compares himself to man's first benefactor, Prometheus, in whose exile he notices certain similarities to his own, but hastily insists that 'between me and that miscreant who mocked the gods, invented fire, denatured clay and domesticated the horse, in a word obliged humanity, I trust there is nothing in common.' Humanism, like knowledge, is only a way of multiplying the zeros.

Early on in the monologue the Unnamable mentions Malone. He is familiar with all the previous heroes for it is they who wandered through the world on his behalf: 'I believe they are all here, at least from Murphy on.' He regards himself as their creator and calls them 'my troop of lunatics.' At times he is quite specific: he alludes to his stick, to the piano-tuners in *Watt*, to a lobster that was 'lepping fresh' and, despite the contradiction it makes with his previous remarks, to his being born in Bally. Malone appears in person: '...he passes before me at doubtless regular intervals...a few feet away, always in the same direction.' In doing so he helps the Unnamable out of a peculiarly illogical situation. The latter imagines himself to be in a timeless world, in the eternity which succeeds life. In such a world movement, thought or personality are a contradiction. There ought to be no 'I', especially if it has physical remains, and yet the Unnamable is precisely this impossible 'I' in an infinite space. He is thinking being shaped like an egg in a non-temporal universe: in short a logical contradiction. Malone's appearance, which seems to follow some regulated cycle in time, helps to resolve the imponderable of at least this dimension. It is just possible that infinity could be made up of an infinite number of finite time sequences. The Unnamable believes that time is circular, without beginning or end but with repetitions continued into eternity, and each revolution of Malone about the motionless Unnamable separates one cycle from another. Thus it is conceivable that he should exist, excluded from the infinite, within eternity itself.

However, this is the last occasion on which the Unnamable receives any definite aid from one of his vice-existers. The final novel of the trilogy marks an important change in the relationship between the 'I' that creates and the selves it has assumed during the previous fifteen years. The latter are no longer welcome diversions. He has only to think of them to be angry: 'the time I've wasted on these bran-dips, beginning with Murphy, who wasn't even the first, when I had me on the premises, within easy reach.' He cannot bring himself to name them 'who told me I was they.' They, he realizes, are a threat to himself of whom he should have spoken all along. Unlike Malone who nurtured Macmann and hoped, with the assistance of his story, to shave away everything superfluous surrounding his identity, the Unnamable finds that only his own words are important. Release will come, if at all, with a statement about himself, not through another. Therefore his vice-existers are the first obstacles he has to face in this new world:

> All these Murphys, Molloys and Malones do not fool me. They have made me waste my time, suffer for nothing, speak of them when, in order to stop speaking, I should have spoken of me and of me alone... I thought I was right in enlisting these sufferers in my pains. I was wrong. They never suffered my pains...Let them be gone now, them and all the others, those I have used and those I have not used, give me back the pains I lent them and vanish, from my life.

Yet what confuses the reader is that though the Unnamable would dissociate himself entirely from his vice-existers much of the monologue is devoted to them. He introduces two new ones, Basil (who turns into Mahood: 'Decidedly Basil is becoming important, I'll call him Mahood instead.' The Unnamable thus aligns him with the other members of what he calls this 'sinecure handed down from generation to generation, to judge by their family air.') and Worm. In spite of his efforts he is often to be caught taking 'myself for the other', and the distinction between the 'I' and its vice-existers has grown almost imperceptible. Malone distinguished Macmann as 'he' and varied the pace and style of his monologue to accommodate the different material. In *The Unnamable* all the speakers are merged together under a single, embracing 'I' so that it is often impossible to tell where one section ends and another begins. Occasionally the Unnamable inserts 'still Mahood speaking' or 'Mahood dixit' into the text but such comments are too infrequent to reveal much.

Moreover, Mahood and Worm are important to the Unnamable despite his almost sadistic impatience with their offerings. In addition to keeping him informed about the world of the living, Mahood helps him to occupy another fragment of eternity each time he resumes his story. The latter is far more disjointed than Macmann's. It describes his journey, from Java, to a small rotunda, apparently in Paris,[2] behind which his family are clustered awaiting his arrival as if in a state of siege. Partly because he has only one leg but also because he travels in ever-decreasing spirals inwards towards the rotunda, he makes slow progress. Those within follow his course as they would trace a strange planet, watching his orbit through the cracks in their wall. But before he arrives they all die, 'carried off by sausage poisoning, in great agony.' He therefore spends some days in a fury of revulsion, grinding the ends of his crutches into the decomposing entrails, especially 'the two cunts...the one for ever accursed that ejected me into this world and the other, infundibuliform, in which, pumping my likes, I tried to take my revenge.' He likes to think 'that it was in my mother's entrails I spent the last days of my long voyage,' before he sets out again propelled violently backwards into another orbit, this time of ever widening spirals.

Just as Molloy-Malone ended his journey in the bed in his mother's room, so Mahood reaches a final stasis—this time in a jar outside a restaurant:

> For of the great traveller I have been, on my hands and knees in the later stages, then crawling on my belly or rolling on the ground, only the trunk remains (in sorry trim), surmounted by the head with which we are already familiar,...
>
> Stuck like a sheaf of flowers in a deep jar, its neck flush with my mouth, on the side of a quiet street near the shambles, I am at rest at last.

In this grotesque situation Mahood's remnants anticipate the incarcerated heroes of the plays: Nag and Nell in their dustbins, the three voices of *Play* in their urns, or Hamm bound to the centre of his universe in his armchair and allowed to monarchize his little scene, a gross and fallen counterpart to Shakespeare's kings. Nothing more is to be expected of Mahood except perhaps the volume of speech which is his substitute for physical movement. The early heroes spoke little but were constantly in motion. Belacqua engaged in his 'boomerangs out and back', Cooper in *Murphy*, who could not sit down, both used words sparingly, but the later heroes need to fill the vacuum left by the crumbling away of movement with an uninterrupted stream of speech.

Mahood is also the culmination of his predecessor's attempts to eliminate everything superfluous to the Self. He has experienced all three stages of their existence—motion, decay and stasis—and his grotesque end is an image of the invalid solution they laboured for. His senses have abandoned him, his body is reduced to an immobile shell stripped of its numerous extensions, and although he has not reached his true Self he still hopes that in time he may achieve the paring away of all that intrudes between himself and the featureless mote in eternity he longs to become:

> Faith, that's an idea, yet another, mutilate, mutilate, and perhaps some day, fifteen generations hence, you'll succeed in beginning to look like yourself, among the passers-by.

Mahood's final situation in which he is covered by a tarpaulin in winter and where the proprietress, Madeleine, occasionally rubs his naked skull with ointments, is also an image of that backward birth, the attempt to 'Die alive,' which Malone was seeking. Once again myth provides a background to the hero's condition. Dieter Wellershoff writes:

> This horrifying picture seems like a grotesque version of the last stations of the cross. The jar, or urn, is an allusion to the tomb, and Madeleine, who rubs the skull of the torso with ointment, recalls Mary Magdalene, who went to Christ's tomb with her ointments. And again death appears as birth backwards. The jar that has swallowed the torso up to the head is the archetypal image of the Great Mother taking life back into herself.[3]

If one adds to this the memory of Proust's vases suspended outside time and then compares it to the image of Winnie buried in the earth in *Happy Days*, one appreciates the unity of Beckett's work, from first to last, and how almost all his books depend on this one image. Murphy's chair, Malone's bed, Mahood's pot are the centres of their narratives where temporal and infinite meet.

However, though Mahood is immobilized he is no nearer to the Self than Molloy or Malone, for the Self is not only motionless but timeless and dimensionless as well. Moreover, Mahood has merely replaced motion by speech which in turn implies thought:

> The Self alone escapes, or rather stands outside, this tyrannical régime of motion, time and thought. Hence its dilemma. It dare not think about itself, and yet to know itself, it cannot help but think. To think, to be, to be even in thought, is to give the initial impulse to that motion which, henceforward, can never be brought to rest. Thus for the Self to think about the Self is to destroy itself. It can, as always, be defined only in terms of what it is not.[4]

Therefore Mahood becomes as useless to the unnamable 'I' as his previous vice-existers. He is only another of those about whom the 'I' speaks when he should have been speaking of himself. What he needs is a vice-exister who is not, a nothing comparable to the Self that evades him. For this purpose he discovers Worm.

Worm is the most extreme description of that foetal urge which has obsessed Beckett ever since his first book. He is a 'tiny blur, in the depths of the pit,' pure existence that has as yet no life or personality. He is, for he has been conceived, but he is nothing—'the one outside of life we always were in the end, all our long vain life long.' He has 'come into the world unborn, abiding there unliving, with no hope of death': life, if one likes, in the womb for, ironically, 'it would be his life-warrant to stir from where he is.' He has no sense or intelligence, can make no distinctions either about himself or other phenomena and thus, in not defining himself as all the previous heroes have attempted to do, he does not tell the lie which is spoken each time the Self, which is nothing, turns itself into an object (which it cannot possibly be) for discussion. The concept of the lie, which the Unnamable introduces into his monologue—'It's a lie,' he says continually—again points to a rewarding comparison with Sartre's *L'Être et le Néant* with its notion of *mauvais foi*. For Sartre individual consciousness is a *pour-soi*. The universe about this consciousness, all that is or the *en-soi*, is positive for its quality is its being there. Consciousness, or the *pour-soi*, which organizes all that is (the *en-soi*), must therefore be negative for it is outside the positive realm of being. It cannot conceive itself for if it does so it turns itself into an object in the way the Beckett hero, in speaking of himself as of an other, must immediately become an other and not himself. The *pour-soi*, furthermore, can only define itself in terms of what it is not. For the *pour-soi* to state something positive about itself would be to tell a lie, or an act of *mauvais-foi*; it can only separate itself by a series of negatives from the universe of *en-soi's* which surround it. In Sartre's words the *pour-soi* 'is its own not being.'

Thus, as we have mentioned before, the *pour-soi* approximates to the Beckettian Self. It is also embodied in the image of Worm, the hero's attempt to create a vice-exister who is at the same time as he is not. How can he be therefore? The answer is in Sartre's conception of *L'autre* or the Other, which is also suggested in *The Unnamable* ('The Other advances towards me. He emerges as from heavy hangings, advances a few steps, looks at me, then backs away.') Being looked at is fundamental to Sartre's description of human relationships. The Other too is a *pour-soi* in himself, and therefore unknowable to himself, but looked at he becomes an object. Similarly 'I', when looked at, become an *en-soi*, an object definitely located within time and space in the Other's universe. 'I' exist, though unknowable to myself because the Other perceives me. Therefore Worm can be: 'Feeling nothing, knowing nothing, he exists, nevertheless, but not for himself, for others, others conceive him and say, Worm is, since we conceive him.'

However, if the Unnamable, masquerading as Mahood, is to reach the Selfhood embodied in Worm, he must not only conceive him but become him as well. Yet the difference between Worm's non-being and Mahood's existence in a sentient world, conscious that he is conscious, merely emphasizes the impossibility of this attempt. What must happen, the Unnamable decides, if he is to become what he really is (i.e. Worm) is not for him to assume the guise of Mahood and try to enter Worm's negative world, but for Worm to be given one element of consciousness whereby he might become an Other and perceive Mahood. Worm is therefore endowed with hearing. Mahood sees the chance and starts forward to intercept Worm's opportunity of recognition: 'Quick, a place. With no way in, no way out, a safe place. Not like Eden. And Worm inside.' It is of course a failure. Worm who hears is no longer the same Worm who was nothing, but an Other, trapped in time and space by Mahood's reciprocal perception. Worm has become an *en-soi* in Mahood's temporal universe.

The Unnamable is forced to conclude that 'Mahood won't get me out, nor Worm either.' They, like his previous vice-existers, threaten his Selfhood by absorbing his suffering and identity into their own. 'It's a lot to expect of one creature', he considers, 'that he should first behave as if he were not, then as if he were, before being admitted to that peace where he neither is nor is not, and where language dies that permits of such expressions. Two falsehoods, two trappings, to be borne to the end, before I can be let loose, alone, in the unthinkable, unspeakable.' What he wants is a language whereby he can only speak of himself, 'of me alone,' for ever more. But the Unnamable is bound by words as well as time, 'I'm in words, made of words...I'm all these words,...with no ground for their settling,' and this search involves him once again in the problems of language. In the last, torrential pages of the novel he searches in vain for a pronoun by which to speak about his real Self. Continually other names interfere, Moran, Malone, Mercier, Molloy, but 'their day is done'; they never spoke but through his agency. When he starts on a fresh story he substitutes 'he' for their names only to insist

> it is not he, it's I, or another, or others, what does it matter, the case is clear, it is not he, he who I know I am, that's all I know, who I cannot say I am, I can't say anything,

He tries other pronouns for this absent voice, as Watt tried words on things as a woman does hats, but they are not successful: 'it's the fault of the pronouns, there is no name for me, no pronoun for me, all the trouble comes from that.' He never even begins his real story, the one that will define himself and set him free. When the novel breaks off he is still on the threshold where it is certain he will remain, as he is, for eternity, Unnamed because there is in language no word to describe his Self. All pronouns and vice-existers are equally futile for the Self, once named, ceases to be itself and becomes a projection of his insufficiency:

> I never spoke, I seem to speak, that's because he says I as if he were I, I nearly believed him, do you hear him, as if he were I, I who am far, who can't move, can't be found..

Here language comes as near as it can to expressing nothing. The Unnamable's real Self only seems to speak because his apparent Self, that being shaped like an egg, is compelled to use the pronoun 'I', whereas 'he', the apparent Self, is not 'I', or the real Self at all. Nowhere in Beckett is the tragic incapacity of language so clearly illustrated for in this statement even the 'I' that explains it never spoke except as a derivative of the 'he,' is itself the 'he' describing its own failure to evolve a language for the Self.

II

The Unnamable's search for the lost language of his Self is filled with contradictions. The most obvious of these are his inability to keep silent about his vice-existers and the way he slips into Mahood's story to pass the time, despite his decision to speak only of himself. But this is only the beginning. Having reduced his world, so he believes, to the personal 'me' or 'I' he discovers a need for at least one other. Like the hero of the *Nouvelles*, the Unnamable is caught in the universal, human paradox which sends one in search of an other even though to find him will solve nothing. The hero abandons the detested society of his fellow men only to discover a need for recognition in his isolation. Beckett's heroes, in their situation as individual beings, are forced to accept Berkeley's doctrine, that *esse est percipi*, and see in the Other the only assurance of their own existence. It is a need with far-reaching implications for though at first straightforward, it soon develops into the frightening, Sartrian realization that hell is other people (*L'Enfer, c'est les autres*) and then into the cosmic system of master and slave which Beckett explores in *How it is*.

The Unnamable, once he has banished Mahood, has no sense of time, knowledge of the world he has left, or awareness of the one he is in. Worst of all he has no sense of his own Self. As a pure Self which cannot, by its nature, either define or perceive its own essence, the Unnamable can only rely on the Other to locate him in time and space. One of his pleasantest fancies is that of a man who will notice him exactly as he dies (so accomplishing, simultaneously, his two fundamental needs, the one to know he was, the other to cease to be):

> Perhaps some day some gentleman, at the precise moment when my last is favouring me with a final smack of the flight of time, will exclaim, loud enough for me to hear, Oh I say, this man is ailing, we must call an ambulance! Thus with a single stone, when all hope seemed lost, the two rare birds. I shall be dead, but I shall have lived.

Without such recognition or its equivalent, he must continue to doubt his existence. He even hopes never to die until he has received the assurance 'that I was really there, such as a kick in the arse, for example, or a kiss, the nature of the attention is of little importance, provided I cannot be suspected of being its author.' What the Unnamable wants is, again in Sartrian terms, *being for others*. He seeks to obtain acknowledgement of his own being from the Other who will act as mediator between him and himself. Being looked at will give him solidity for he will be in an other's world; as Sartre writes, 'the road of interiority passes through the Other.'

Such a situation was feasible in terms of Worm who, though perceived by others was himself oblivious to their gaze. The Unnamable, however, though he will know he exists, will at the same time know he is being looked at and so be reduced to the limits of a material object. He will become an *en-soi,* the slave of the Other who uses him to prove (by being other than he is) that he himself exists. In that moment the Unnamable will lose the freedom of his *pour-soi* which is the essential prerequisite of the Self and become a prisoner in the Other's gaze. He can, it seems, either know he exists or hope for release without such knowledge but he cannot enjoy both. Either way is agony to him and this dichotomy of need, though only implied in *The Unnamable*, becomes an important aspect of the plays where it encourages the ambivalent feelings of love and hate between the recurring pairs. It is implicit in Clov's inability to leave Hamm, in Winnie's need for the silent Willy, and helps to explain what has kept Vladimir and Estragon together for so long despite their continual threats to part. Furthermore it is the foundation of the infinite series of torturers and tortured in *How it is* which describes poetically the cruel basis of all human relationships as seen by Sartre. For Sartre, sadism and masochism are the impulses which govern the attitude of one human being to another and they arise from this essential need to be perceived. Depending on one's approach to the Other, one either seeks to gain an ascendancy over him, fixing him more firmly in the time and space of one's own perception, which is a form of sadism, or else one attempts to accommodate oneself to the Other's perception which is a form of masochism. In either case there is conflict which explains the suitability of such a view to drama, and though Beckett is only examining the edge of this problem in *The Unnamable* it seems essential even now to be aware of its implications for it is the development he saw and chose to follow after the present book had apparently brought him to 'a situation that I can't extricate myself from.'[5]

This need to be perceived is not confined to the merely-human. It rapidly takes on a metaphysical significance which involves the creation —or at least the contemplation of the creation—of an extra-human system of observers. And as with all hierarchies of omnipotence it is founded on the human sensibility to suffering, guilt and pain.

In *Malone Dies* the hero examines suffering and comments on the rationalizing human need to assign a cause to what is seemingly gratuitous. The Unnamable also connects the idea of suffering with his exile in time and considers it as a possible way to release: 'I'm not suffering enough yet, it's not yet my turn, not suffering enough to be able to stir...' However, in a world where even the opiate of mathematics has failed, such a notion, open on all sides to the incommensurables of the void, is no longer sufficient in itself. In a world without God and without a First Cause man finds himself lonely and abandoned: worse, he is forced to accept both his own meaninglessness, his potentiality for multiplying the zeros, and the complementary meaninglessness of the world which sustains him. Therefore to rediscover a purpose in this endless Calvary which alone makes it possible for him to bear and speak of his condition he invents a hierarchy of tormentors to conceal that his torments are gratuitous.

It is a monstrous projection of Berkeley's doctrine of perception and of Sartre's concept of the Other. He imagines 'a whole college of tyrants' to whom he must testify until he dies. He is 'possessed of no utterance but theirs', and in being pressed into speaking as an expiation for a crime which apparently never ends until 'they' decree it, he now comes to identify his crime with his punishment: 'this is my punishment, my crime is my punishment'. There is not even the need to attribute the cause to birth for life merely prolongs sin into eternity which is for always a crime and a punishment.

However, if the Unnamable is necessarily trapped in an eternity of being perceived, his masters must be confined to a similar period of perceiving: 'To be on the watch and never to sight, to listen for the moan that never comes, that's not a life worth living either.' So they themselves must be responsible to yet an other ('The everlasting third party') who has taught them how to torment him ('they know how to cause suffering, the master explained it to them') and who punishes them if they relax their attentions. The need to belong to a purposeful universe entails an ever-expanding system of suffering perceptors.

This 'sporting God' behind the college of tyrants, who is the source of the Unnamable's pain, is Descarte's malignant deity become a horrible reality. Like the evil genius that Descartes imagined, he is 'as powerful as he is cunning' and 'has used all his zeal to deceive me.'[6] Beckett, still the suffering Cartesian, has put the torments of hell back where they belong, inside man's head, and the tormentor of the *Meditations* who delights in laying traps for man's credulity therefore provides another of those apt and ironic correspondences that exist between the works of these two men, the one at the beginning, the other at the close, of modern rationalism. It is apt because the Unnamable, like Descartes, has reduced the universe to his mental processes and both their sporting Gods are inventions of the mind. It is ironic because confident rationalism destroyed the old and so created the need for this new God born in the mind. The weapon of his destruction was assertive doubt, a purely mental occupation; the punishment, also mental, is to be condemned to uncertainty, caught in the perpetual tension of the need to know and the impossibility of knowing. 'My great and good master...his will be done,' says the Unnamable with irony, but what his will is he cannot say. Perhaps, the hero asks in desperation, no one has done anything; the entire formulation has no meaning but just is. In a moment of sublime compassion he absolves not only himself, but his torturers too, from causing the reciprocal agony of perception in which they live eternally:

> It's all a bubble, we've been told a lot of lies, he's been told a lot of lies, who he, the master, by whom, no one knows,...the master's not to blame, neither are they, neither am I, least of all I, we are foolish to accuse one another, the master me, them, himself, they me, the master, themselves, I them, the master, myself, we are all innocent...it's nobody's fault.

Yet this gratuitous condition cannot sustain his doubt for ever. He is unable to believe that no one is responsible for his terrible situation or that his master will never release him. So he continues to listen for 'the words of my master, never spoken, Well done, my child,...you may go, you are free, you are acquitted, you are pardoned, never spoken;' and to search for the atonement which will lead him to his Self: 'Let him inform me once and for all what exactly it is he wants from me,... assuming he exists and existing hears me.'

It is to answer this question that he introduces the idea of a pensum:

> Yes, I have a pensum to discharge, before I can be free, free to dribble, free to speak no more, listen no more, and I've forgotten what it is. There at last is a fair picture of my situation. I was given a pensum, at birth perhaps, as a punishment for having been born perhaps, or for no particular reason, because they dislike me, and I've forgotten what it is. But was I ever told?

Imprisoned in time and space the Unnamable picks upon the most incontrovertible, single fact of his exile from the Self, his persisting thought, and imagines that to be the punishment he must complete before he can be free. In the silence where he sits, staring before himself into the grey limbo, he seeks 'to hit upon the right pensum somewhere in this churn of words.' This, he believes, is what his master is waiting for him to do. Yet, like his master, the pensum is only an illusion he has invented to give meaning to the silence. As long as he believes in a pensum he can imagine an end approaching and not admit to his eternal solitude, but without it he returns to being a meaningless voice in a nothing rushing towards zero:

> All this business of a labour to accomplish, before I can end, of words to say, a truth to recover, in order to say it, before I can end, of an imposed task, once known, long neglected, finally forgotten, to perform before I can be done with speaking, done with listening, I invented it all, in the hope it would console me...

Only now, in admitting to the falseness of both master and pensum, does the Unnamable reach the tragic centre of his predicament, though tragedy seems an all too exalted and hopeful concept against which to describe it. His is a voice obliged to speak 'knowing that it lies... knowing itself useless and its uselessness in vain, not listening to itself but to the silence that it breaks,' and this voice cannot cease unless the whole of existence itself contrives an end. It does not even seem to be his voice any longer but one which has taken possession of him and filled him with words:

> It issues from me, it fills me, it clamours against my walls, it is not mine, I can't prevent it, from tearing me, racking me, assailing me. It is not mine, I have none, I have no voice and must speak, that is all I know, it's round that I must revolve.

Like Beckett's description of writing in the *Three Dialogues* speech is an obligation (and perhaps, knowing the fundamental unity of Beckett's thought, it is possible to see an explanation of his own, personal obligation here, the need and the nothing to write—writing is for him where suffering, guilt and expiation find their centre) but one which no longer promises 'the long clear sigh of advent and farewell,' the birth into death the hero has been waiting for so long.[7] It is in vain he exhorts it to stop or speaks of its existence as a mistake that should never have occurred: it is precisely its existence which demonstrates the eternal nature of his exile:

> Ah if only this voice could stop, this meaningless voice which prevents you from being nothing, just barely prevents you from being nothing, and nowhere, just enough to keep alight this little yellow flame feebly darting from side to side, panting, as if straining to tear itself from its wick, it should never have been lit, or it should never have been fed, or it should have been put out, put out, it should have been let go out.

The ability to speak has become scarcely less frightening than the silence it opposes for, like most extreme antagonisms, the one would not exist without the other and both prevent the extinction which he is seeking.

The ideal of this eternal voice is to 'speak and yet say nothing.' If he could say nothing he would be nothing. He wonders 'would it not be better if I were to keep on saying babababa?' but, knowing the treachery of language, wisely decides against it: 'it seems impossible to speak and yet say nothing, you think you have succeeded, but you always overlook something, a little yes, a little no, enough to exterminate a regiment of dragoons.' Thus, for example, if he did achieve a moment's ideal silence he would not be at peace but immediately have to consider what kind of silence he was keeping.

And so to his final subterfuge. If he cannot say nothing then perhaps he can try to say everything. Though words are rational and temporal it might be possible to tumble them out in such a deluge that the whole universe would become submerged in them. He decides to try and annihilate time and space with their own weapon, language, by freeing the latter from all meaning and context. It is a solution discovered in despair and its possibilities are dubious but perhaps, and this is what he hopes, he might stumble across that absent combination which will define himself, or that language, freed from its moorings, will resolve itself into the speech of that greater silence which all the heroes have searched for in vain. It is almost inconceivable that this should be so but, though the hero is now certain that the Self cannot be discovered, he is equally sure that somewhere, in a world to which he is for ever denied access, it does exist. It is the square root of 2 once again; that which both is and is not.

Whether the Unnamable ever succeeds or not remains unknown.

When the novel breaks off he is still only discovering the implications of this new attempt, trying to subordinate meditation, stories and inventions into a language which is as yet unused to the irrational outrages he seeks to perform upon it. The trilogy ends with the Unnamable striving to reach the great silence of the Self by explaining, in words, the silence of the infinite spaces of time. If the incredible happens 'it will be because the words have been said, those it behoved to say, no need to know which, no means of knowing which, they'll be there somewhere, in the heap, in the torrent.' In that torrent he is bound, a voice, entirely alone and trapped within himself, circling round and round waiting, waiting for the end. And this could go on to infinity. Literature is scarcely ever so terrifying as in these closing pages which more than any others reveal the pitiless, metaphysical anguish of the individual caught in his impotent hope:

> I'll wake, in the silence, and never sleep again, it will be I, or dream, dream again, dream of a silence, a dream silence, full of murmurs, I don't know, that's all words, never wake, all words, there's nothing else, you must go on, that's all I know, they're going to stop, I know that well, I can feel it, they're going to abandon me, it will be the silence, for a moment, a few good moments, or it will be mine, the lasting one, that didn't last, that still lasts, it will be I, you must go on, I can't go on, you must go on, I'll go on, you must say words, as long as there are any, until they find me, until they say me, strange pain, strange sin, you must go on, perhaps it's done already, perhaps they have said me already, perhaps they have carried me to the threshold of my story, before the door that opens on my story, that would surprise me, if it opens, it will be I, it will be the silence where I am, I don't know, I'll never know, in the silence you don't know, you must go on, I can't go on, I'll go on.

Here are all his torments: the silence, the words that will not say the last of him, the pain, the guilt, the longing and the inevitable, perpetual failure of desire. But no analysis or discussion can do justice to the compassion with which these pages are filled or to their heartrending, disinherited poetry. Such treatment must await the time when the trilogy is recognized beside the Elegies of Rilke and *A` la recherche du temps perdu* as one of the great achievements of the spirit in this century—and by then such discussion may have become superfluous.

NINE: THE LATER FICTION

'Sullen we lie here now in the black mud.'
This hymn they gurgle in their throats, for whole
Words they can nowise frame.

DANTE[1]

IN *The Unnamable* Beckett appeared to have reached an impasse—at least where the writing of fiction was concerned. Faithful to his declaration in *Proust*, that the only true development for the artist is a contraction, a continual descent ever deeper into himself where the work of art is neither created nor chosen but exists for his discovery, a law of his nature, Beckett pursued his hero until nothing remained but the voice, the silence and eternity. In book after book the hero had been stripped of all his possibilities, losing first society, then his learning, senses, substance and even the illusion of an identity and a language in which to speak. At the end of this ordeal he is so close (and yet so essentially distant) to uniting himself with the nothing he has been striving to reach that he leaves the author little space or material from which to make a fresh departure. With dogged honesty Beckett contracted his world, never refusing or ameliorating the often terrible implications that emerged from his inward exploration, only to find that:

> The French work brought me to the point where I felt I was saying the same thing over and over again. For some authors writing gets easier the more they write. For me it gets more and more difficult. For me the area gets smaller and smaller...At the end of my work there's nothing but dust...In the last book, 'L'Innomable', there's complete disintegration. No 'I', no 'have', no 'being'. No nominative, no accusative, no verb. There's no way to go on.

It seemed, in fact, that if he were going to continue he would have to merely add to the Unnamable's final incoherent outpouring; either that or become one with the intolerable silence itself.

Nevertheless, like his hero, Beckett does go on. His obligation to write finds new expression in the theatre where it is probable the most valid of his recent work has been done. The plays, which have brought him prominence, were all, with the exception of *Waiting for Godot*, written after *The Unnamable*. For a time at least (his drama now seems also to have reached an impasse) the new form introduced fresh possibilities and other ways of treating his old preoccupations. However, he never entirely abandoned fiction and during the last fifteen years there have been four[2] known attempts to pass beyond the trilogy. It is with these works that this chapter is concerned, and therefore, in order to retain the three-part framework of this study, it is necessary to violate a strict chronology for the first time.

In general these recent fictions make few additions to the world which, in *The Unnamable*, Beckett has refined almost out of existence. The author is not so much concerned with broadening his canvas or changing what has been essential in the preceding novels, but with retranslating the obstinate residue left by the trilogy into more meaningful and coherent terms. The hero reached his final incarnation in the grey limbo of the Unnamable and Beckett seeks neither to alter the dreadful terms implicit in that situation nor to negate any stage of the journey there. What is sought is a form and a language that will adequately convey the naked non-Self within its denuded, wasted universe. There is, therefore, a change of emphasis. His later fiction is not as tense or despairing as *Watt* and the trilogy. It becomes important for what it is in itself, a painfully wrought construction in language where form is inseparable from content and the style of saying of greater concern than what is said.

The thirteen *Textes pour rien* (*Texts for nothing*—1950) which Beckett himself considers a failure, clearly prolong the inquiry of *The Unnamable*. They are more vague and disjointed than the novel, meditations of the 'I' from those interstices where nothing is more apparent than something. The text stands midway between fiction and poetry, a form of extended prose poem in which the voice makes its convolutions in search of meaning aware of its impotence and predestined to establish nothing. On the page the thin stream of the voice mesmerizes the reader by its Proteus-like ability to enter and assume a hundred successive mental possibilities; off the page one remembers only its meaningless, incessant interruption of the silence.

The 'I' of the *Texts* is searching for an identity it can call its own. It lacks even Mahood's featureless trunk but rather than rejoice in the final disappearance of the physical, anticipated for so long, it desires a body in which to clothe the voice and follow its progress. The voice, which is condemned to speak, has sunk into a region of darkness forever excluded from the world of light. There it discovers a vague nostalgia for the place it has left and anxiously awaits the reports of its delegates who bring it information of their own lives up above. However, though their descriptions of Paris and Dublin revive its memories this service has a double edge. The vice-existers speak only about themselves. The 'I' that narrates remains as ignorant as ever about itself. In consequence the need to know what it is and where it is becomes desperate. But fortunately the division of the universe into light and dark enables the 'I' to believe itself perceived by those in the world above, as if those in the light existed to peer down into the obscure abyss where the voice is trapped and witness its positive identity.

But if the 'I' has this consolation it is the only one. Everything else has been resolved into a nothing which lacks all certitude. Time has fallen into an empty void of duration where it is impossible to separate one event from another; it is no longer certain whether the voice which speaks is alone or one of many from which it is indistinguishable; and without a body the 'I' neither knows where it is, nor if it is distinct from the objects it assumes surround it. At times it recalls its old appearance in the world of man, as Molloy in the forest for example, but these memories have ceased to contain any significance. Such a reality which at the same time is irredeemably divorced from all reality, denies any importance to what is said or written. Words are an uproar in the head without any meaning in the world to which they are applied. Where there is no knowledge they are all arbitrary, incapable of saying anything more than the sound which falls upon a second of nothingness. 'My unnamable words,' the voice calls them. Here, where language has ceased to encourage the hope of one day discovering that final cadence in which all will be said, is Beckett's failure to go on beyond *The Unnamable*. 'The only way one can speak of nothing', he wrote in *Watt*, 'is to speak of it as if it were something.' The *Texts* fail through the absence of this something.[3]

Beckett's next work of fiction was not in French but English, the first time he had used his native language for an original departure since *Watt* in 1944. The attempt, as the title implies, was not a success. A passage called *From an Abandoned Work* was first read as a dramatic monologue on the radio in 1957, and later published with no attempt to provide it with either a context or an end.

It describes three days in the life of its hero who is a throw-back to the still-active derelict Beckett was concerned with in *Molloy* and the French stories. He (again nameless) is expelled from his parents' house, apparently to his mother's sorrow. From a window she watches him pick himself up out of the road and start into the country. As he walks he speaks about himself, his education, his gradual loss of physical co-ordination and, perhaps more illuminatingly, about the family he leaves behind. On the second day he is attacked by a family of stoats, and on the third he meets an old roadman named Balfe of whom he had gone in terror when a child. 'Now he is dead and I resemble him,' the hero says with resignation. But how he degenerated into the wild, anarchic creature who is telling this narrative is not shown. The passage concludes with the hero 'up in the bracken lashing about with the stick,' heading out into the country where the 'great ferns, like starched, very woody, terrible stalks, take the skin off your legs through your trousers.' One recalls Molloy and can only assume, from having read the other French monologues, that his future will take him to Malone's room and then to the Unnamable's eloquent stasis.

As an addition to Beckett's works its importance is slight, but it is interesting to observe the effect of English upon material which until now has been approached in French. *From an Abandoned Work* lacks the precision and sinew of the originally French monologues. The writing is more consistently evocatory. In English words tend to rediscover that sense of meaning and fluidity which the *Texts,* for example, lacked. The language no longer possesses the aridity of which Beckett complained after *The Unnamable* but there is also a corresponding lack of density. Moreover it seems that Beckett could only retain this vitality by returning to the dilemmas which confronted him when he began to write in French. Short of recreating everything, from the *Nouvelles* to *L'Innomable,* in his native language, in the hope that at the end of that process he would find the impasse clear and himself able to go on, this way too very quickly impressed its futility upon him.

It is also interesting to observe the tone of this fragment. Despite the hero's usual assurance that he regrets nothing, the note of regret is continually raised throughout the monologue. There is a new resignation and pathos in his approach to his condition, very different from the violent denunciation of life in the French novels. He even says he can sometimes 'weep for happiness as I go along and for love of this old earth that has carried me so long and whose uncomplainingness will soon be mine.' Though the Unnamable might dismiss that last phrase as an enormous self-deception it nevertheless is important to hear it said. For the first time since *Murphy* poignancy and tenderness, rather than savage disgust, becomes evident in the writing. Furthermore, it is possible to see the cause of this change, in the present work, as the result of a momentary lapse into overt introspection by the author himself. The obvious pain in the son's desertion of his mother, followed very shortly by the memory of his dead father, might involve Beckett himself:

> Fortunately my father died when I was a boy, otherwise I might have been a professor, he had set his heart on it. A very fair scholar I was too, no thought, but a great memory.

His own independence in Paris was ensured by an annuity of two hundred pounds a year upon his father's death, which helped him to live free of the academic world he detested, but also apart from his mother whom he visited for one month each year until her death—except during the Occupation. That his decision was not free of guilt seems apparent in a sentence shortly after these lines: 'I asked her for the money, I can't go back on that now, those must have been my last words to her.' Possibly his return to English was an obscure catalyst reminding Beckett of the past, of what might have been, but his hero's memories are abruptly severed on the dark side of revelation.

However, *From an Abandoned Work* shares this resignation and mildness with the plays to which it is contemporary. Indeed, its affinity with *Krapp's Last Tape* is too great to be dismissed as coincidence. In the play there is the same nostalgia for a lost past in which memory is envoked in a rich sensuousness of language. Krapp also thinks back to his mother, in his case to remember her death in an obsessional mixture of guilt and sorrow, and he alternates moments of angry self-disgust with elegiac recollections of a life which has not fulfilled its first promise. 'A good woman might have been the making of me,' thinks the hero of the prose monologue where Krapp monotonously replays the tape of a year which once seemed to presage success. It is almost certain that Beckett abandoned the novel in favour of the play, retaining its best features and thereby creating, through the retrospective medium of the tape-recorder, one of his most compelling dramas.

In 1961, when it seemed that Beckett had definitely abandoned fiction as a creative possibility, he confounded his critics by publishing

Comment C'est (*How it is*). It is almost certainly the strangest novel ever written, looking at first sight more like a rough draft than a published typescript. It consists of individual blocks of language, in skeletal paragraphs of varying length (though usually with about five lines to each) which are often repetitious and without even a minimal concession to the traditional foundations of fiction. It is also quite different to Beckett's own earlier novels. Though it re-examines many of the old problems it does so in original terms, employing fresh techniques and prompted by new tendencies within the hero himself. Yet, paradoxically, the change is consistent with what has gone before. Instead of seeking to free language from its rational context in a deluge of meaningless words, the hero of this new novel begins from the opposite position. He strips his speech of all main verbs, conjunctions and definite articles in an attempt to convey the essential reality of his situation within as limited a framework as possible. Language is given no opportunity, or so he thinks, to adopt its own meanings and departures: all at once there seems a possibility, perhaps in the empty spaces between the groups of words, of understanding the elusive reality of this forbidding and negative universe. However, before the formal and linguistic implications of this novel can be studied, it is necessary to examine the description it presents of that universe, and see it against the tradition of which it is a part.

How it is is in three sections of equal length. The first describes the hero's world and how he travels towards Pim whom he meets at the beginning of the second part. The latter describes their life together and the third, to retain the symmetry, describes what happened after Pim. 'How it was after Pim how it is' says the hero, though the English lacks the pun on *comment c'est—commencer* in the original title. The latter is perhaps the cruellest of all Beckett's jokes about finitude and the Self expressed in the occasional illogicisms of language. Each section concludes with a similar statement but in this novel there is no hope of a beginning or end. The hero knows what even the Unnamable never admitted, that he has failed to escape from the eternal duration of time, and the three parts of the story reflect this knowledge. Time past, present and future is cyclical and all three sections repeat themselves into infinity. Though, in the midst of his story, the hero may speak of the past as over and the future as still to come, in reality all three parts occur simultaneously for they are eternally present in his mind and only the illusionist tricks of language allow him to speak as if they are isolated events in a steadily unfolding series. Therefore it is easy for him to mistake material relevant to one part when writing another ('something wrong there,' he laments continually) for each fragment is only an arbitrary moment of eternity 'realized provisionally in the present in one of its infinite repetitions.'[4]

The hero, who later calls himself Bom in order to remain distinct from Pim, is no longer a writer but a speaker, buried in a pitch dark world of mud and slime. To the end it remains unclear whether the voice we hear is his own or, like the language it uses, something imposed on him from the outside. He is possessed, he says at the opening, by a 'voice once without quaqua on all sides then in me when the panting stops tell me again finish telling me invocation,' but the words he speaks do not belong to him: 'I quote...as I hear it.' The panting, which only ceases when the voice begins, is comparable to Nagg's tears in *Endgame*. Unlike the earlier heroes Bom cannot speak continually and the silences between the paragraphs are filled with the gasping sound of his exertions in the stagnant mud. Apparently both words and pants are noted by an omnipotent scribe (a fearful reflection of the Christian recording angel) who is kept aware that something is still taking its course by the perpetual alternation of these two noises. The ambiguity, however, in the first of the hero's telegrammatic comments, which later assume a mathematical concision, probably arises from his intent to separate his real from his apparent self. What he utters are 'scraps of an ancient voice in me not mine' by which he means the same voice, old these thirty years, which is not his true one but which he has always been reduced to using, each time describing yet another variation about the text that he was born to: 'my life last state last version ill-said ill-heard ill-recaptured ill-murmured in the mud brief movements of the lower face.' On the first page, therefore, Bom aligns himself with that sinecure of moribunds which precedes him and warns the reader to expect little new material in what follows.

The first part, in which the hero describes his condition, is dominated by the mud, warm, wet and steaming up into the dank, odourless air. It covers the landscape and the hero crawling across it in layer after layer of cloying filth, infesting his hair, eyes and mouth but never loosening its grip to allow him to sink below the surface and suffocate. It is the most revolting of all Beckett's images, a symbol of universal meaninglessness and impotence which in its own way is as powerful and suggestive as, for example, the Chancery fog of *Bleak House*. It is the natural outcome of Molloy's indifference and savage disgust. The intelligence which annihilated all values, feelings and finally itself, reducing them and the world in which they are sustained to the same level of worthless, loathsome abundance, was comparable to the fury of the Old Testament prophet or Christian mystic appalled by a Godless world. The mud of *How it is* is the spiritually empty counterpart to Ezekiel's valley of dry bones where nothing is because God is not, and the tormented human drags himself forward 'into the black night of boundless futurity' only certain of his lack of hope. So Bom moves, ironically remarking the quintessence of his condition and the needs which still enervate him: 'when the great needs fail the need to move on the need to shit and vomit and the other great needs all my great categories of being.' Around his neck is the cord of a small jute coal-sack, filled with tins of sardines and tunny, that he eats with disinterest and often throws away half-finished and covered with mildew. When he wants to drink he dips his tongue into the moist mud itself. Like Malone and his notebook, the hero found the sack just when he needed it, and he sometimes attempts a ludicrous jest about its contents, imagining a 'celestial tin of miraculous sardines sent down by God' to keep him alive and praying one week longer. Even the rats have deserted him this time ('I've sickened them'): his only diversion is to struggle ahead towards Pim, a progress which, in eternity, is not a progress but which yet seems, when one considers the enormous difficulties it involves, as momentous and heroic a journey in its own terms as the voyage of Odysseus:

> I turn on my side which side the left it's preferable throw the right hand forward bend the right knee these joints are working the fingers sink the toes sink in the slime these are my holds...
> push pull the leg straightens the arm bends all these joints are working the head arrives alongside the hand flat on the face and rest
> the other side left leg left arm push pull the head and upper trunk rise clear reducing friction correspondingly fall back I crawl in an amble ten yards fifteen yards and halt

Out of the epistemological poverty of this denuded universe Beckett contrives, as if poetry exists in ratio to its absence, a fusion of the detailed scientific tradition of the novel (for the sheer quantity of information it contains this passage stands comparison with Defoe) and the elemental purpose of the epic, embracing them both in these dislocated, insistent fragments. In the reiteration of certain phrases ('vast tracts of time...murmur in the mud') the voice assumes the rhythm and intensity of poetry returning to the original, primitive nakedness of language. It is the most complete and desperate break with the late nineteenth-century tradition so far attempted yet even in disclosing the failure of the 'incantation towards the miracle' it reaffirms the spiritual needs which forced literature into its recent extremities.

To find a valid comparison for this poetry of squalor one has to return to Dante. Dante gave Beckett the first of his images from which all the later novels derive and the affinity he feels towards the Italian poet is again evident in many of the later fictions and plays. It was Dante who, in Cantos vi and vii of the Inferno, first imagined an eternity of mud. His description of the wrathful and the gluttonous who 'gulp the marish foul,' floundering in 'the black mud' and tormenting their companions clearly anticipates Bom's condition and his later relations with Pim:

> And I, staring about with eyes intent,
> Saw mud stained figures in the mire beneath,
> Naked, with looks of savage discontent,
>
> At fisticuffs—not with fists alone, but with
> Their heads and heels, and with their bodies too,
> And tearing each other piecemeal with their teeth.[5]

Bom refines these tortures, adding a can-opener to the human armoury, and gives them a semblance of a purpose which Dante's damned lack. Therein lies an essential difference between the two worlds. The wrathful suffer according to a rigid determinism of guilt and suffering caught up in a meaningless activity. The hero of *How it is* suffers gratuitously because he is an exile from a world where that same determinism has vanished, but by clinging to an illusory purpose even he manages to retain a hold on the edge, not of Hell, but Ante-Purgatory.

Nevertheless the distinction is so fine as to be almost non-existent and at bottom it is unimportant because the idea of a static hell for the guilty and a hopeful purgatory for the penitent has ceased to be meaningful. Images from both of Dante's regions stand side by side in *How it is*. The hero often speaks of 'life the other above in the light said to have been mine,' sometimes with a kind of sarcastic nostalgia at the pleasure he receives from his memories. In this he is one with the tortured of the *Inferno* who beseech Dante for news of the world they have left—much as the Unnamable or the 'I' of the *Texts* send their vice-existers in search of the knowledge from which they are excluded. Moreover the damned frequently recall 'the life where the light beams,' it is part of their punishment, but those in the *Purgatorio* with their aspirations all heavenwards, have no time for recollection: that is with the exception of Belacqua.

The hero of *How it is* has not lost his resemblance to the idle figure, crouched in the lee of the rock, but a change has occurred. He describes himself now as 'Belacqua fallen over on his side tired of waiting forgotten of the hearts where grace abides asleep.' He has no stories with which to beguile his time, no vice-existers, or the desire for them, to live in his stead, and claims 'I haven't been given memories this time images.' However, as if this lack would sever him too violently from his ancestor the images all bear on his life in the light. The distinction between image and memory lies in the irregular appearance of the former, as if a curtain hiding Bom from the light were momentarily brushed aside, and in his inability to retain them as long as he wants. Like the voice they seem to come to him from without. These images sometimes refer to his mother. In one he sees himself die again while an old woman sits knitting in a chair; in another he returns to his childhood and sees his mother's face. They are sitting together 'on a veranda smothered in verbena' and she chides him for making a mistake in the apostle's creed.[6] At other times they refer to the life already lived in the previous novels; to the basement flat in *Le Fin* and to *Fingal*, one of the stories in *More Pricks than Kicks*, where a man, woman and dog walk on a hill-top near Leopardstown racecourse. The image presents the quintessence of the earlier story, even down to the sandwich which they eat in alternate bites.

In spite of the deterioration in his condition the hero feels little of the anguish which tormented his predecessors. This is perhaps the most remarkable change. The Belacqua who has grown tired of waiting has resigned himself to eternal futility. He endures without hope, laboriously fulfilling the demands of the place where he finds himself, and even introduces noticeable shades of happiness into his activities. He never worries himself with the old questions; how he arrived or where he is going, but accepts the infinite present and adapts himself to its hopelessness much as Winnie evokes Proustian habit: 'my good moments', he intones like a refrain as she repeats 'Ah happy days.' He thinks with wonder of 'the humanities I had my God' and delights in tracing their remnants: 'it's not said where on earth I can have received my education acquired my notions of mathematics astronomy and even physics they have marked me that's the main thing.' He notices a deterioration in his sense of humour but this is compensated for by fewer tears, and he is still not incapable of making a joke, usually ironic, either about the world of men or God's obvious neglect of him here. Moreover it seems a new world of sensuous delight is open to him. He takes pleasure in little comforts such as the smell of a tin of fish ('irreproachable distant perfume of laurel felicity') or his freedom to wipe his face clear of mud with his hand: 'it's a resource when all fails images dreams sleep.'

In part two Bom reaches Pim whose presence has all along given the first section an illusion of purpose. The hero has centred all his dreams of human companionship on Pim and until now has spoken as if in their meeting the locked selves will be released and the incredible mystery of communication will suddenly flower. However, the reality is very different, as horrible a description of human relationships as even Beckett himself has written. Bom's original conception of an ideal love degenerates into a ghastly reality wherein lover and beloved have become torturer and victim. Were it not for its treatment which presents 'the attempt to communicate where no communication is possible' as the 'simian vulgarity...horribly comic' that[7] was described in *Proust*, the passage would be all but unreadable.

Pim too is bound in the mud and Bom only discovers which way round he is lying by digging his nails into Pim's buttock and noting the spot where he cries out. Bom, who for the moment is dumb, is amazed to learn that his companion can sing and therefore, imagining that he can also speak, sets about training him in an art he has forgotten through disuse. It is an arduous and painful process which involves Pim being dug in the back and arse with the can-opener, beaten on the head with Bom's fist and scored in the armpits with his nails. It is also a very rational process, working stage by stage towards perfection by stimulus and disencouragement, Pim often performing the wrong function to Bom's precise and violent command but each time learning from his mistakes. Gradually the cries of pain develop into rational language. At the end of his training Pim is able to distinguish between a series of commands which allow Bom considerable freedom in what he asks of his companion:

> table of basic stimuli one sing nails in armpit two speak blade [of opener] in arse three stop thump on skull four louder pestle on kidney five softer index in anus six bravo clap athwart arse seven lousy same as three eight encore same as one or two as may be

It is fortunate for them both that they 'use the same idiom' for the period of Pavlovian instruction over, communication proper begins.

In this stage the dumb Bom is reduced to imprinting his questions with the nail of his right index finger on Pim's backside ('as in our civilization I carve my Roman capital'), stabbing Pim with the tin opener to see whether or not he has understood. He asks about Pim's life in the light and is told of his wife's death, caused by their loveless existence together. That is the only event to stand out against the journeys and slumbers, in hiding from mankind, that echo the experience of the older heroes. The remainder of Bom's questions apply to their life together and especially to whether or not he is loved by Pim:

> ...if he loved me a little if Pim loved me a little yes or no if I loved him a little in the dark the mud in spite of all a little affection find someone at last someone find you at last live together glued together love each other a little love a little without being loved be loved a little without loving answer that leave it vague leave it dark

The desire to know if one is loved, like the need to know if one is perceived (of which it is a part), becomes an obsession, the existence of which demonstrates love's failure. If love existed it could not be mistaken and Bom's questions which reveal his fevered search for identity, certainty and an end to his loneliness, show that it does not. His impossible dream of an everlasting companion who will abandon his own identity and comfort him, degenerates into the ugly reality of Sartre's description of all human relationships. Bom grows disgusted with Pim's whining subservience and yet angry when he does not receive the expected answer.

Gradually their subjects of conversation, never great in number, are exhausted and they lie side by side in the mud, Bom too weary to ask, Pim too weak to move away: the experiment is over. Throughout Pim has acted as the slave, accommodating himself to Bom's demands and whispering his answers into his tormentor's ear, so close to him that the bristles on his lip tickle the other's chin. He has in fact made himself into the Sartrian object which the other manipulates for his own purposes, showing no more regard for Pim's humanity than he would for an inanimate machine. However, the idea of a talking machine which responds to clearly defined stimuli cannot be simply dismissed as an unhealthy product of a mind infected by contemporary ideas on the psychological cruelty of human relations. Beckett, if he does have a source, always finds the germ for his images in the confident beginnings of the tradition to which he belongs, not in its exhausted end. A supreme confidence, moreover, often conceals a dangerous shortsightedness over the eventual outcome of its assertions and it is this which enables Beckett to so consistently re-examine Descartes with the ironic knowledge of experience. The latter is once again Beckett's source when he describes Bom's method of instructions. In the fifth section of the *Discourse on Method* Descartes writes:

> ...we can certainly conceive of a machine so constructed that it can utter

> words, and can even utter words in relation to bodily actions that cause some change in its organs. Thus, if we touch it in one spot, it may ask us what we want with it; if we touch it in another, it may cry out that it is hurt, and so on.[8]

Aware of this relationship to Descartes one sees again that Beckett's oblique vision which connects source and result within this rational tradition, provides a more devastating, if less sensational, comment on its failure than the sometimes extravagant statements made by many of his contemporaries. Though it would be irresponsible to charge Descartes with having directly inspired the pitiful waste of human feeling apparent in *How it is*, the juxtaposition of the two images allows Beckett to suppose an inherent tendency towards such a masochistic and sadistic dehumanization, as existing at the root of the rational approach and only recently made evident.

Nevertheless the meeting with Pim is not a complete failure. Though communication itself is impossible, the presence of the Other gives purpose and meaning to Bom's existence in the mud. Without Pim he even doubts himself, with him he at least achieves a limited degree of self-definition which is why he reiterates the sparse physical aspects of their life together so often and in such detail:

> his right cheek to the mud his mouth to my ear our narrow shoulders overlapping his hairs in mine human breath shrill murmur if too loud finger in arse I'll stir no more from this place I'm still there

It is Pim who locates him in time and space, who affirms that he is 'still there,' and this feature, the need for perception, is the one which Bom develops into the enormity of a universal system, founded on logic, in part three.

At the beginning of the final section Bom is deserted by Pim who moves onward in search of another whom he will torture. Bom meanwhile lies in the mud 'struck numb with stupor' and awaits the arrival of a fourth who is already approaching him. This time Bom will be tormented, learn to speak, and love will fail again before the time comes for him to move on and rediscover Pim. From this original, unending sequence the hero then creates an infinite series of men, all trapped like Pim and himself in the mud in groups of four, where each is only aware of the one ahead whom he will torture and the one behind who catches and torments him. In the pauses between half are waiting and half moving, the earthly pattern of journey and stasis is maintained even here. This final, monstrous projection of logic and mathematics ('I always loved arithmetic it has paid me back in full') is based upon the fundamental need to be witnessed, and this demands that the duality of torturer and victim be enacted in turn by both parties. If only one were tortured there would be a lack, an absence of active, self-defining perception on his part; of necessity he must both impose his own identity on another and prove tractable when the other makes the same demands on him. But as the two desires cannot be satisfied simultaneously the need for the series is created. Only in this way can the terrible reality which, the hero says, is a reflection of life up above in the light, be described: a reality where:

> each one of us is at the same time Bom and Pim tormentor and tormented pedant and dunce wooer and wooed speechless and reafflicted with speech

To the hero it is inconceivable that any member of his series should go in want either of torment or the ability to torment. It is also necessary that nothing which takes place in the mud should escape notice. Therefore his world is provided with a hierarchy of overseers who no longer appear as the tyrannical masters of the trilogy but as a comforting guarantee to the continuing stability and justice of his condition. There are two to each figure in the mud, one listening and the other recording. His movements are entered in a blue notebook, his mutterings in a yellow and his comments in a red. To these scribes, or rather to the ever-lasting third party behind them:

> the spectacle on the one hand of a single one among us towards whom no one ever goes and on the other of a single other who never goes towards anyone it would be an injustice and that is above in the light

The hero takes comfort in this justice which will never permit a failure of perception in either direction. In this world, so 'exquisitely organized' compared to the one above, logic has provided for all extremities. Though one no longer hopes for release, one is safe in the knowledge that justice will not fail, that one will never be left in doubt to search for a companion in order to know if one is: 'at the instant I reach Pim another reaches Bom we are regulated thus our justice wills it.'

It is because this justice is so precise and undeviating that the novel only needs three parts and two names to describe the universal interaction of perceptor and perceived. A fourth part, describing Bom's instruction and torture would be superfluous for it would repeat exactly the process recorded in part two: only one of the names would be different. Similarly Pim's journey in search of another would repeat part one. As the hero says: 'having already appeared with Pim in my quality of tormentor part two I have not to take cognizance of part four in which I would appear with Bom in my quality of victim it is sufficient for this episode to be announced.' Merely by calling himself Pim and the one who torments him, Bom, the whole episode becomes re-interpretable in the new situation. Nothing changes 'but the names and hardly they two are enough nameless each awaits his Bom nameless goes towards his Pim.' Therefore if the reader still remains curious about the substance of this fourth episode the hero says he has no objection if 'cognizance then of the present communication be taken backward.'

However, at this moment, when the hero appears to have consolidated this universe in a book which perfectly reflects the logical framework on which it is built, Beckett destroys everything in one of the most daring gestures of iconoclasm ever attempted. The eternal, dark and silent world where the hero is imprisoned in the mud, where countless millions of other men also lie, tormented and tormenting, is infinite. According to the hero justice logically demands that the series must therefore also be infinite to avoid the chance of a single member going unperceived. Injustice, the contrary of logic, is inconceivable under these conditions. The metaphysical necessity on which the book is founded presents the hero with a simple choice: 'either I am alone and no further problem or else we are innumerable and no further problem either.' His human necessity, the child of his loneliness and the inability to know himself, encourages him to suppose the latter but as he continues to shore up the whole elaborate system on which his faith depends, the unavoidable truth constantly threatens and finally, in a moment of weariness, overwhelms him: the rational can never control and encompass the infinite. His whole structure is a logical impossibility in which finite weapons are again—as in Watt's confrontation with Mr Knott— repelled by the enormity of the void: his system building is revealed as the childishness of the rational intent on imposing a reason upon a world that is unreasonable. Unable to suffer the ache of nothingness his despair invented it all, including Pim: 'all these calculations yes explanations yes the whole story from beginning to end yes completely false.' There never was any journey or waiting, Pim or Bom: he created it all, scribes, sacks, tins, images, recollections of his mother, to break the silence and lend eternity the semblance of a meaning reduced to comprehensible units of time. The final pages are filled with a furious questioning which dismisses everything except the voice that speaks and the mud which is spoken to:

> only me yes alone yes with my voice yes my murmur yes when the panting stops yes all that holds yes panting yes worse and worse no answer WORSE AND WORSE yes flat on my belly yes in the mud yes the dark yes nothing to emend there no the arms spread yes like a cross no answer LIKE A CROSS no answer YES OR NO yes

That alone is real: that is how it is. As in the final section of *Ulysses* the reiterated *yes* rises to a crescendo of affirmation. But Molly Bloom praised life: here the hero is affirming his precarious corner in nothingness. With that single despairing, yet defiant collapse of a structure laboriously and lovingly erected throughout one hundred and fifty pages Beckett leaves the reader not simply contemplating Nothing, that he has often done, but holding it between his hands as well.

Nevertheless *How it is* does exist, as a printed book if not as a meaningful addition to the earlier novels, and it is perhaps in this solidly physical dimension that its real achievement is to be found. In *Proust* Beckett speaks of the creative process as one wherein the artist acquires his text for the artisan to translate. That he did not separate artist and artisan but saw them as two parts of a single creator becomes evident in the novels, particularly in *Molloy*. In the latter Moran, commissioned to track down the hero of the first part, speaks of Molloy as someone already present within himself and whose life has been a waiting for Moran to arrive and deliver him 'who cannot deliver himself'.[9] Here Moran clearly performs the second part of the creative act as seen by Beckett: that of the artisan who translates an already existing subject into distinct and recognizable terms. This is what Beckett himself attempts in *How it is*. The new syntax, the obvious importance of symmetry and the appearance of the book itself reveal the ascendancy of the artisan. *The Unnamable* was still created by the artist, refining the text which had occupied him throughout a life-time, into its essential terms, but once those final terms were reached nothing remained for the author but the discovery of new ways of expression, in short the perfect language for the translation of the text.

Beckett comes closest to this language in *How it is* which is why it appears the major achievement in his later fiction. The panting voice, speaking against enormous opposition, uses a language that approximates to the movement of the mind struggling to form ideas, and lacks every sign of prolonged meditation. Each fragment seems instantaneous, uttered from necessity and entirely without an impression of the effort it cost the author during its formation. It is a language without precedence in literature: indeed it is the style (or 'absence of style') of urgent communication beyond literature for which Beckett long ago perceived the need. Yet the very condensation and precision of these dislocated chunks, so forbidding at first reading, gives them the force and clarity of genuine poetry, as for example, here where the hero is describing his own death:

> my head where is my head it rests on the table...she sees I am not sleeping the wind blows tempestuous the little clouds drive before it the table glides from light to darkness darkness to light
>
> that's not all she stoops to her work again the needle stops in midstitch she straightens up and looks at me again she has only to call me by my name get up come and feel me but no
>
> I don't move her anxiety grows she suddenly leaves the house and runs to friends

By the emphatic absence of any attempt to convey more than the simplest physical detail in this scene Beckett succeeds in suggesting the whole unspoken complexity of feeling. To infiltrate obvious emotion into this image would blur the control it is given by the angular, rhythmic phrases set in groups that remind one of verses in the Bible. Above all the passage is concerned with bypassing the tissue of supposed responses which surround an event such as death, in order to reach the central, incontestable fact itself. It seeks to extract order from the chaotic and express the true stature of that lonely moment. In this it is, like all great poetry, essentially realistic, not a part of the spurious realism of the faithful-to-life but a true expression of the subject restored to itself outside the dispersion of time and freed from the human will to assimilate it into the lifeless pattern of the usual.

However, content and poetry do not possess the same value for the artisan as they do for the artist. The former is not concerned with what is done but how it is made. In *How it is* the demolition of the contents in the final pages leaves the reader with nothing but the elaborate architecture on which they were raised. Throughout the novel the artisan's delight in this architecture is as evident as the despair of the artist who wrote the trilogy is conspicuous by its absence. Beckett has here extended the implications of his comment on Joyce, that Joyce is not writing about something; he is writing something. He abandons the illusion of meaning even if it has the solidity and purpose which life lacks and creates his something in the more obvious terms of an object, a book that is one hundred and sixty pages long with the print arranged unusually but attractively on the paper and exactly reflecting, in its structure, what is written—though the latter signifies nothing.

How it is suggests that in any further novel by Beckett the artist will have no place. This supposition has recently been reinforced by the publication of *Imagination Dead Imagine*, a thousand-word text in which two embryonic figures who inhabit a world of blinding light and dark, heat and cold, are described in sparse and clinical geometrical terms. The text contains enough material for a full-length novel, and most of the old preoccupations are apparent, but the ascendant artisan, intent on discovering a satisfying medium, subordinates everything—which is meaningless anyway—to the new, refined framework. This process is quite consistent with the earlier novels which were themselves conceived as more than expositions of their contents. *Watt*, for example, and *Murphy* used all the resources of print footnotes, musical notation, blank spaces and addendas, to facilitate the actual act of creation. But once what was written ceased to signify it was natural that how it is written should assume first importance. You can cut away a picture but the frame remains and it is the latter which concerns Beckett now.

PART THREE

THE PLAYS

I. THE THEATRE

BECKETT'S aesthetic concerns itself with failure. To write is to fail, a self-imposed necessary doom, for man is unknown and unknowable, his existence a logical impossibility encircled by Nothing. He is, but he should not be, and any attempt to lend him a meaning is an act of bad faith. It sets about him a metaphysical order which is not there. This is the agony of Beckett's situation. As a writer, language traps him into defining a meaning where one no longer exists. He has only to write the first person singular of the verb 'to be', to establish the most questionable of all possible hypotheses. Beckett's novels are founded upon a profound despair of language, for words cannot be trusted to remain a tool in the hands of the artisan. They have their own organic existence which threatens to overthrow the elaborate attempt to speak of *nothing* as if it were *something* with a betrayal at the source. They set up their own systems, begin stories and define meanings in such a way that the *something* begins to exist in its own right. By the end of the trilogy the dichotomy of which Beckett speaks in the *Three Dialogues*, the obligation to write and the nothing to write, becomes irreconcilable. The hero is forced into repeatedly denying a valid meaning to his words: Beckett is left with a voice in the void that can never know itself, must find itself, has only words with which to achieve this and yet lies in every word it speaks.

Beckett's decision to turn to the theatre arose from this situation and looking back, with the recent example of *How it is* for confirmation, it appears the only direction in which a development was possible. In drama there was a chance that the two crucial problems on which the novels foundered, the distrust of language and the need to be perceived, could be resolved. For the theatre is more than language. When asked about the contradiction which must exist if one continues to write under the conviction that language cannot convey a meaning, Beckett replied, '*Que voulez-vous, Monsieur? C'est les mots; on n'a rien d'autre.*[1] In fiction this is so, the cruel truth at which the trilogy ends, but drama has no such restrictions. In the theatre, or at least in the theatrical tradition with which Beckett aligns himself, language is only one vehicle among many and not the most important. The total meaning of a performance includes mime, silence, decor and above all action, that which is actually seen to take place by an audience. This promises a firmer reality than a subjective monologue written and read in isolation: perhaps on the stage the reality behind the words may be revealed by the action which often contradicts their literal meaning. For example the stage direction which concludes both acts of *Waiting for Godot:*

> EST: Well? shall we go?
> VLAD: Yes, let's go.
> They do not move.

The theatre allows Beckett a double freedom; the opportunity to explore the blank spaces between the words and the ability to provide visual evidence of the untrustworthiness of language.

The theatre is also a method of communication, between actor and audience and, if there are two, between the actors themselves. The world of *The Unnamable*, reduced to the lonely voice of its protagonist, created the need for an Other not only, it seems, to define the hero in time and space but also to provide genuine companionship:

> the need came on me, for someone, to be with me, anyone, a stranger, to talk to, imagine he hears me, years of that, and then, now, for someone who knew me, in the old days, anyone, to be with me, imagine he hears me, what I am, now.

Even though the essential isolation of the speaking voice may not alter, its need to feel itself being heard has become undeniable. In *Happy Days* the silent Willie is a necessity. Although his hat alone is visible he must be there to succour Winnie. What love ever existed between them is unimportant beside the fact that if she, in the usual Beckettian sense, is a person through the medium of thought translated into words.

she must have ears to receive those words. Any other situation would be absurd. Moreover, if she is to sustain her illusion of happiness she requires his company:

> just to know that in theory you can hear me even though in fact you don't is all I need, just to feel you there within earshot and conceivably on the qui vive is all I ask

She, and all the other characters in the plays, dread the awful collapse into silence and uncertainty which would occur if they were alone. Their ability to exist depends upon an Other whom they use with shameless self-indulgence as a barrier against the void, not caring what the Other hears or says so long as he prevents the terrible intrusion of nothingness. Furthermore there remains the hope, despite the evidence to the contrary, that given a juxtaposition of persons the locked selves may at last flower like the miracle of Proustian memory, that communication will be a possibility and with communication a chance that the Self, real and indivisible, will at last appear. *Waiting for Godot*, the drama of non-communication, depends upon the tension that it may not always be so, that something valid will be said that will release the waiting tramps—perhaps through the intervention of Godot himself. This situation is essentially dramatic for through their demands on each other the characters exist in conflict. The pairs in the plays, Vladimir and Estragon, Pozzo and Lucky, Clov and Hamm, are as firmly bound to one another as Ulysses and Diomed or Ugolin and Roger in *The Inferno* ('The perfect pair, like Dante's damned, their faces arsey-varsy,' says Mrs Rooney), and their relationships are complex. At times the eternal couple, tormenting and tormented, they show at others a moving tenderness and compassion. They are brought together by solitude—even the overlord Pozzo needs companionship: 'I cannot go for long without the society of my likes'—only to find themselves imprisoned in a mutual dependency they would desperately like to break. This is, however, at least in the first plays, an expansion of the world of the novels which introduces, despite still enormous limitations, a new area of possibility on which Beckett himself has also commented:

> Hamm as stated, and Clov as stated, together as stated...in such a place and in such a world, that's all I can manage, more than I could

A creative form, however, presents its own conditions. Beckett's turn to the theatre involved him in an entirely separate discipline, one he had never attempted before,[2] and his success depended as much on the use he made of this form as on the preoccupations he brought to it. In the first part of this section therefore, some attempt is made to understand the interpenetration of form and subject, particularly in relation to *Waiting for Godot*, for where, as in Beckett, they correspond so exactly the content relies upon the dictation of the form.

The plays, like the novels, reduce both the historic and formal elements of their genre to the essential. *Waiting for Godot* presents the audience with a platform, the stage, to represent a country road, a tree (later identified as a weeping willow but easily mistaken for a bush or shrub) and a time of day, evening. This is all one needs: sumptuousness is a luxury. The barren area, lit up before the auditorium, could be any road, any tree, any evening, but unpeopled it seems especially naked: man is needed to complete the scene. The two who appear, dressed as tramps and uncertain whether or not they have arrived at the right place, bring a variety of objects with them, boots, carrots, bowler-hats and a piece of rope. They are the actors, detailed to pass the next two hours by any form of improvisation in which they may or may not make use of the objects to hand. The audience accepts the situation and waits, as the tramps wait, for something to happen. What this is cannot be stated explicitly but when one of them says 'We're waiting for Godot' it temporarily satisfies the audience. Both parties are confined in the wooden O of theatricality which relies upon expectation. The theatre is an acute reflection of Beckett's obsession with waiting for an end, or perhaps for an event; for Godot to come, Lear to enter with Cordelia dead in his arms or Oedipus to step from the palace, his eyes bloody and sightless.

While the hero who will transfigure the action remains off stage the tramps help the evening along with the resources of vaudeville: the dirty story, trousers which fall down, a song, and some incompetent clowning. As in the Music Hall they refer to the audience ('that bog,' says Vladimir,...'Not a soul in sight!') and on one occasion include them in the action:

> EST: Charming spot. (He turns, advances to front, halts facing auditorium.) Inspiring prospects. (He turns to Vladimir.) Let's go.
> VLAD: We can't.
> EST: Why not?
> VLAD: We're waiting for Godot.

In this exchange, the first mention Godot receives, the music hall technique not only fixes the audience within the evening's entertainment but also in the universal state of waiting outside the theatre which the play reflects. Vladimir's 'We' applies to audience and actors alike (in the French text the sentence 'On attend Godot' is more inclusive) and establishes them both, at the beginning, in the same anguished condition. Not to realize this shared predicament, which the tramps' commentary on the action reveals, is to limit and endanger the comprehensive meaning and image of the play. There is no escape. The tramps remind the audience that what they are seeing tonight is not unique; that a performance was also enacted here last night: 'What did we do yesterday? In my opinion we were here,' and that tonight's entertainment is not the last:

> We'll come back tomorrow.
> And then the day after tomorrow.
> Possibly.
> And so on.

Each night they begin again, attempt again and repeat again the failure of tonight, a failure that cannot be dismissed as a mere entertainment for it has the reality of life. And this reality is not conveyed as a photographically accurate representation of life but within the nature of the performance itself. Not only are the tramps here every night, an audience—any audience, it does not matter—chooses to join them and so wait for their time to pass.

At one moment in *Waiting for Godot* this mutual expectation appears to be redeemed from improvisation by the entrance of Pozzo. Here, it would seem, is the real actor, an imposing figure who makes his entrance conscious of its effect and with none of the timid uncertainty and inconclusiveness attached to the tramps. Bestriding the stage he declaims:

> POZZO: (*terrifying voice*): I am Pozzo. (*silence.*) Pozzo! (*silence.*) Does that name mean nothing to you? (*silence.*) I say does that name mean nothing to you?

At his first entrance Pozzo has no doubts; he knows who he is and the audience, who, like the tramps, probably mistake him for Godot, believe that the waiting will now be resolved. For several minutes he sustains the illusion. With the aid of his vaporizer he recites a speech describing the fall of night. This is the true performance, patiently studied and rehearsed, frequently spoken and owing nothing to the improvised passages that have been offered earlier in the evening. It is lyrical, prosaic and vibrant, uses dramatic pause and a variety of accepted theatrical gestures ('hand raised in admonition; he raises his eyes to the sky') to increase its effect. Afterwards the artiste asks his audience, represented by Estragon and Vladimir, 'How did you find me?', thanks them for their automatic enthusiasm and concedes: 'I weakened a little towards the end, you didn't notice?' The general effect, however, has been disappointing; as Estragon says: 'I've been better entertained.' Pozzo is not Godot as the second act makes clear. The evening is not saved for he needs the tramps as the audience needs them and Lucky needs him; it is another of those chains of cause and effect which have dominated the individual's freedom since *Murphy*. The deadening repetition of dialogue and action is demonstrated in the theatrical situation itself. If the necessity of being seen compels the actors to return before an audience night after night, the audience, for the moment the tyrant or witness, comes because it too is committed to wait. And if, during the evening, any progress is made (as, for example, Estragon's discovery of a new pair of boots) the next night returns them to the same point on the circle once again.

This correspondence between life on the stage and life in the auditorium has a further resonance. In *Endgame* Hamm, as the name implies, a ham actor, performs certain set speeches which are scheduled to be spoken at intervals during the evening[3]. 'I'm warming up for my last soliloquy,' he snaps at Clov who has mistaken his purposes. In these speeches where he uses rhetorical effects like Pozzo and Mr Rooney, Hamm is not concerned with the truth of what he says but with the style in which the story is told. As in *Malone Dies* where the author's shifting feelings towards his material were written into the text, so here Hamm murmurs 'nicely put that'; 'There's English for you'; 'A bit feeble that'; and like Malone searches for accuracy of expression. Hamm's narrative, describing the last stages of life on earth, is an attempt to save life from insignificance by putting it into the constancy of art, even though he is at the same time conscious that his task is pointless: 'I'll soon have finished with this story (Pause). Unless I bring in other characters...the whole thing is comical, I grant you.' The performance is again a game and Hamm, Pozzo or Krapp with his tape-recorder watch and listen to themselves playing, aware that they are only involved in somebody else's entertainment:

CLOV: Why this farce day after day?
HAMM: Routine.

In this dimension life, for Beckett, consists of pretence. The actors on the stage reveal reality itself as pretending or a game: they perform in earnest what the audience lives, a long space of time that at best is filled with entertainment.

In one of their exchanges on the evening in progress Vladimir and Estragon introduce the foundation of their theatre:

VLAD: Charming evening we're having.
EST: Unforgettable.
And it's not over.
Apparently not.
It's only beginning.
It's awful.
Worse than being at the theatre.
The circus.
The music hall.
The circus.

Dressed as they are their affinity to the clown is obvious; and in turning to the theatre Beckett returns his hero to his natural environment. There seems a curious justice in this homecoming for the hero, in appearance at least, is closer to that knowledge of reality and being for which he seeks than at any time since *Watt* and *Molloy*. In his perceptive essay on Beckett's plays, Robbe Grillet observed:

> All the creatures that have passed before us [in the novels] were only there to deceive us: they occupied the sentences of the novel in the place of that elusive being who always refuses to appear, the man who cannot enter into his own existence, the man who can never succeed in being there.[4]

Suddenly, in the theatre, all this is changed, for whatever the value of the introspective, exploratory monologue the theatre alone naturally reproduces the actual, physical reality of man, his condition, as Heidegger says, of *being there:*

> The essential thing about a character in a play is that he is 'on the scene': *there.*[5]

What *Waiting for Godot* presents us with is exactly this; two men who are halted one evening by a country road. 'You did see us, didn't you?' one of them asks the boy who ostensibly comes from Godot himself; they have kept their appointment, they were there.

Any interpretation which does not start from, insist on and return at the end to this fundamental certainty detracts from the purpose of what we are watching, a complex metaphor as inexplicable as life and which is only sustained by the archetypal dramatic images it employs. *Waiting for Godot* is nourished by the traditions of the theatre. In its limited number of actors, its crisis (Pozzo's blindness and Lucky's deafness) off stage, and the expectation of a *deus ex machina* who on this occasion does not appear, it recalls the Greek theatre, just as *Endgame* (see below) is performed in a Shakespearian world of reference. With the symbolic tree in the background and the ritual dance, the dance of the net performed by Lucky, it also reveals elements of the Japanese Noh play, but the most persuasive influence is the tradition of the non-literary theatre. In *Peer Gynt* the hero strips away the layers of skin from an onion which represents for him the human creature whose essence he has been seeking all his life: he finds nothing. *Waiting for Godot* begins at the centre of the onion and remains there, largely because it is founded upon the universal significance of the hobo-clown.

The tradition of the clown, we have already noticed, is retraceable to the same origins as its apparently more respectable counterpart, tragedy. Theatre emerged from a popular heritage at once religious and coarse: the death and sublimation of the year-god, Dionysus, being celebrated by a chorus of worshippers who, in their intoxication, often lost their wisdom and apprehension in blatantly phallic entertainment. Ever since the popular rites and festivals of the Hellenic world were translated into the enduring structure of Greek drama two strands, the literary and the anti-literary, have coexisted under the general title, theatre. It is usually assumed that the literary theatre evolved from Aeschylus and incorporated the serious, moral and religious elements of the old festivals while the popular tradition appropriated the physical, bawdy and farcical and was consequently of lesser importance. Nevertheless each has its own validity and though at certain times one or the other strand has been predominant those ages are accounted the greatest in which the two are seen to fuse most completely. Such an age was that of Shakespeare which drew heavily for its extent and vitality on the tradition of the juggler, clown, acrobat and fool. It was, moreover, this popular tradition, working outside the playhouse, which secured the difficult transition of drama from the ancient to the modern world when its literary counterpart had ceased to exist. In this passage from the Roman Mimus through Medieval drama and on to the *Commedia dell' Arte* it remained close to its archetypal beginnings. For this reason individual dramatists such as Plautus and Molière have found it a source that liberates the often exhausted forms in which they work. However, this anarchic fringe was eventually compelled by an unprecedented strength in its literary counterpart, to seek refuge in areas of the theatre mistakenly dubbed 'illegitimate', the circus, the music hall and the boulevard. Distrusting language especially when, as in the modern tradition of the well-made play, it performs under the illusion of infallibility, it was from these sources that Beckett and the other dramatists of the absurd took their forms. Straining towards a new purity, and establishing the primacy of the image, they have, in recent years, restored the theatre to its lost unity wherein the religious and the irreverent once again combine to confront man with his ultimate reality.

Beckett's sympathy with the pure, non-literary theatre is evident in the particular and the general structure of his plays. Lucky's famous speech with its confusion of garbled knowledge recalls the Doctor in ancient farce while the improvisation of the two tramps suggests the endless semantic speculations and misunderstandings of the *Commedia dell' Arte*. Likewise the couples who suffer and cause to suffer re-echo the simplicity of the eternal dramatic types, the father and son, master and slave, king and serf, or, if one likes, Punch and Judy, and each has his own set-piece to perform, an exact and well-tried *lazzo* such as the exchange of hats in *Godot* or Clov's repeated misadventures with step-ladder and telescope. In the plays the ceaseless linguistic permutations of the novels are replaced by equally pedantic and mechanical physical permutations. If language does threaten to assert itself, its pretensions are burst by the pratfall. At times the pratfall works from within language itself as in Pozzo's inflated speech which portends, in the beginning, to be the definitive speech we have come to the theatre to hear: after leading his audience to a climax of expectation he cannot sustain the illusion and gloomily concludes—'That's how it is on this bitch of the earth.' More frequently, however, it is solely physical and often disgusting. It deflates the platitudes and expressions of sentiment with which the characters clothe their isolation, as for example here where Vladimir and Estragon, out of habit and the boredom of their condition, attempt a reconciliation:

> EST...(*Est lays his hand on Vladimir's shoulder*): Come Didi. (*silence.*) Give me your hand. (*Vladimir turns.*) Embrace me! (*Vladimir softens. They embrace. Estragon recoils.*) You stink of garlic.
> VLAD: It's good for the kidneys. (*silence. Estragon looks attentively at the tree.*) What do we do now?
> EST: We wait.

The pratfall returns them to the painful level of reality from which they will begin another 'little canter' towards the same end. This is the clown's weapon, the undignified, ceremonious collapse of human pretension, a levelling down from the upright to the horizontal. In

Act II of *Godot* the tramps, Pozzo and Lucky all stumble and fall together to form a pile of bodies centre stage. It is the universal pratfall, a crude knockabout reminiscent of Jarry's *Ubu Roi*, where the master lies with his servant and they are joined by the tramps of whom Pozzo remarked with irony in the first act: 'You are human beings none the less!...Of the same species as Pozzo. Made in God's image!' And as it is unlikely that the audience in the theatre would remember this previous observation, Beckett is careful to repeat its significance, once again stressing their inclusion in what they see. It is, after all, an arrival, another of the infrequent certainties created by this evening's entertainment:

VLAD: We've arrived.
POZZO: Who are you?
VLAD: We are men.

Detached from history and society Vladimir and Estragon have time to be men. Though they are sharply individualized, have their own past and are concerned, in the present, with the vagrant's usual preoccupations—what to eat; where to sleep (Vladimir admires Estragon for discovering a good ditch); beatings and the state of their boots—they achieve a universal dimension. Like Edgar and the Fool who lead Lear to the innermost heart of things from where he receives his vision of unaccommodated man, they present a commentary on life and a definition of man: humanity considered in its residue, stripped of the 'robes and furr'd gowns [which] hide all'[6] and left facing itself. Beckett's achievement, like Shakespeare's, is to join this cruel comedy to the sphere of myth and religion.

Here perhaps, the long-felt but obscure relevance of *King Lear* to the drama of the absurd becomes clear. In their particulars *Lear* and *Godot* are comic, it makes their pathos bearable. The Fool's gibes and Gloucester's 'suicide' are of the same grotesque order as the tramps' expectations which end in the pratfall. But more especially, in the scenes on the heath where the old king and his companions have reached the hub of despair, it takes refuge in the agonized illogicality of the clown, the perilous area where so much contemporary literature is to be found. In the words of Gunther Anders: 'Farce seems to have become the last asylum for compassion, the complicity of the sad, our last comfort.'[7] *Lear* is tragic at the close when the king, chastened and wise through suffering, is reunited with Cordelia only to lose her again, but in the central scenes where language dispenses with logic and discursive thought and moves in despair towards the unconceptual fragments of the poetic image, it anticipates the tragi-comic situation of Beckett's theatre:

> that mysterious situation before which, although horrified, we laugh. We laugh but are paralysed with horror. We laugh but our eyes are wet.[8]

The condition inspires the choked laughter of which Kant wrote: 'the result of an expectation which, of a sudden, ends in nothing.' Both *Lear* and *Godot* are saturated in this nothing, a void that falls away before the characters. In Cordelia's reply it is the catalyst to Lear's tragedy; the Fool councils the king to live with it; and when Edgar rushes from the hovel Lear greets 'the thing itself' with a string of negatives. In *Godot* it swirls like mist, intangible between the sentences, asserts itself at every pause and overpowers the landscape and the characters on it: 'You couldn't describe it,' Vladimir says of the place, 'It's like nothing.' Only the clown, it seems, has the resources to exist in this condition. 'Can you make no use of nothing, nuncle?'[9] the Fool asks Lear who, still ignorant, replies (as might that debased relic of the tragic stage, Pozzo, who also stumbled when he saw) 'Nothing can be made out of nothing'. This is precisely the clown's endeavour—and the writer's whose subject is Nothing. He alone has the resilience to endure because he accepts the right to fail; it is the title he was born to. And from this failure there emerges, not a victory but the slender, far more painful, triumph of continuance which repeats its affirmation when the impressive towers and kingdoms of the hero are compounded with indifference. This is the clown's secret, a little of which escapes into the following description, by Beerbohm, of the American Dan Leno:

> That face puckered with cares...that face so tragic, with all the tragedy that is writ on the face of a baby monkey, yet ever liable to relax its mouth into a sudden wide grin and to screw up its eyes to vanishing point over some little triumph wrested from fate, the tyrant; that poor little personage so 'put upon' yet so plucky with his squeaking voice and his sweeping gestures; bent but not broken, faint but pursuing; incarnate of the will to live in a world not at all worth living in.[10]

This similarity extends beyond their use of the clown. Both *Lear* and *Godot* abandon discursive speech and base their language on patterns of concrete images. Neither in the scenes on the heath nor in the tramps' exchanges is the drama concerned with telling a story, conveying information or illustrating a didactic premise: at the centre of nothing such attempts would be meaningless. Both are in search of a personal sense of being and for that words are inadequate. The result is a terrible simplicity. When his reason crumbles, the fragments of Lear's understanding break loose into the poetry of madness where, as in the feigned madness of Edgar and the Fool, his thought is expressed through the free association of the image. Behind the collapsed syntax the unconceptual meaning which he discovers beneath appearances is expressed in insistent, hallucinatory images wherein opposites are reconciled and by a strange inversion his insanity is the source of logic —for example here, where his search for justice joins the two recurring visions of lust and cruelty:

> Thou rascal beadle, hold thy bloody hand!
> Why dost thou lash that whore? Strip thine own back;
> Thou hotly lust'st to use her in that kind
> For which thou whipp'st her.[11]

Lear's insight runs towards the wisdom of the clown who often uses false syllogism and the inherent contradictions of language—whereby the apparent innocence of a word or phrase will revolt against its habitual sense—to express his fearful knowledge. His own fool provides abundant examples in his songs, riddles and bitter gibes and warnings. And in the central scenes where the trio of madmen pursue, beneath the pitiless fury of the storm, their excavations in search of the 'cause in nàture' drama passes beyond the needs of the plot and enters a larger synthesis. The images are interwoven like music, intent, beyond the immediate dramatic effect, on creating a total impression which cannot be reduced into any terms but its own. As Granville Barker wrote about the 'lunatic mummery' of the mock trial to 'anatomize Regan':

> Its effect depends upon the combination of the sound and meaning of the words and the sight of it being brought to bear as a whole directly on our sensibility. The sound of the dialogue matters almost more than the meaning. Poor Tom and the Fool chant antiphonally; Kent's deep and kindly tones tell against the higher, agonized, weakened voice of Lear. But the chief significance is in the show.[12]

The individual characters give way before the impersonal poetry of pure theatre which returns to a deeper meaning than language can express. On the heath we are again conscious of the intuitive mysterious source of drama where: 'The structure of the scenes and the visible imagery reveal a deeper wisdom than that which the poet himself is able to put into words and concepts.'[13]

This is where *Godot* and the theatre of the absurd begins. At the root of Beckett's drama is the image as it appears in the central act of

King Lear. Just as the novels present the basis of fiction, the man writing in a room, so Beckett's drama is founded upon a complex poetic image in which it is possible to pass behind the level of conceptual thinking. Beckett's is a theatre of situation, of what is there, as opposed to the theatre of events in sequence. There is no extension in time or space, as there isn't on the heath; there is only a contraction and a descent ever deeper into the meaning of the original statement. Beckett dismantles the elaborate three-act play of convention and in its place presents us with the essence of that play reduced to a metaphor or image. Thus *Godot* is built around the simple act of waiting, *Endgame* on an end-of-the-world situation inside a skull, and *Happy Days* upon memory and time. In effect what we witness is the intense centre of a play, extended over an entire evening but which ideally should be comprehended in a single moment as an abstract painting seeks to impress the reality of an object upon the eye without its diffusion in the necessity of recognition. It is *Lear* reduced to the insanity on the heath, Hamlet at the grave side, and Richard II in his prison cell; an attempt to hold up the central reality against its dispersion and change in the varied demands of plot, structure and language.

But if it is impossible, in terms of the theatre, not to translate the immediacy of the image into the extension necessary for a dramatic presentation, Beckett at least ensures consistency by binding the whole in a classical purity of form. In all his plays the scene remains unchanged, the central character(s) leave the stage, if at all, only for a moment, and particular images reflect the irreducible meaning of the whole. The tramps' exchanges return to the silence and waiting visible in their condition but even in their attempts to speak a meaning into their situation the words merely emphasize their impotence, as for example in the passage on 'all the dead voices' or here where they discuss suicide:

> VLAD: What do we do now?...
> EST: What about hanging ourselves?
> VLAD: Hmm. It'd give us an erection.
> EST (*highly excited*): An erection!
> VLAD: With all that follows. Where it falls mandrakes grow. That's why they shriek when you pull them up. Did you know that?
> EST: Let's hang ourselves immediately!

In their situation suicide, a definite gesture, is positive, but like all their actions it ends in impotence, a conclusion this image (which the Lord

Chamberlain caused to be struck out of the English edition) illustrates better than any other. To achieve the enervation necessary to produce life—even the mockery of a shrieking mandrake is that—they must first kill themselves. Its absurd pathos reflects the circle of futility which is demonstrated by the larger context of the play in general. Similarly in *Endgame*, the lingering dissolution of a world at zero which it describes is also the substance of Hamm's narrative, a performance within the play, and of the anecdote of the madman who saw in nature nothing but ashes.

In these plays, the perfection of form in which Beckett seeks to enclose the purity of the image is, like *Lear*, part of a larger synthesis. Aided by their theatrical heritage his tramps rediscover the poetry of the theatre which resides, not, as Eliot mistakenly conceived, in the creation of a special linguistic vehicle that would convey heightened emotion, but in the mysterious result of the fusion of language, action and scene into a single inseparable structure. The individual at moments of great stress and emotion does not, as Eliot stated in *Poetry and Drama*, always express himself in poetry. In the extremity of his suffering Lear's mind seeks to loosen the bonds of rational syntax and speak in prose, a fact which Beckett (and Buchner before him) are almost alone in recognizing. Language falls drastically short of the depths of anguish: Lear is reduced to the undignified expedient of helpless repetition—'And when I've stol'n upon these sons-in-law, Then, kill, kill, kill, kill, kill, kill.'[14] Yet on the heath he reaches a dimension of poetry quite beyond the formal polished verse of Act I where language was given the eminence which allowed Goneril and Regan to deceive Lear. The haunting, antiphonal cadences of the two tramps, filled with inadequately expressed misery, belong to the same dimension:

Silence

EST: Where shall we go?
VLAD: Not far.
EST: Oh yes, let's go far away from here.
VLAD: We can't.
EST: Why not?
VLAD: We have to come back tomorrow.
EST: What for?
VLAD: To wait for Godot.
EST: Ah! (*Pause.*) He didn't come?
VLAD: No.
EST: And now it's too late.

VLAD: Yes, now it's night.
EST: And if we dropped him? (*Pause.*) If we dropped him.
VLAD: He'd punish us. (*Silence. He looks at the tree.*) Everthing's dead but the tree.

......

EST: Didi.
VLAD: Yes.
EST: I can't go on like this.
VLAD: That's what you think.
EST: If we parted? That might be better for us.
VLAD: We'll hang ourselves tomorrow. (*Pause.*) Unless Godot comes.
EST: And if he comes?
VLAD: We'll be saved.

The silences, questions without question marks (or unanswered unless by the questioner), and the very evident tenderness powerless to effect itself, are more eloquent than the feeble words wearily employed to re-examine alternatives that, the audience is aware, do not exist. But, as the lights are dimmed for the fall of night and the pathetic tree beneath which the tramps are standing, is silhouetted against the dark blue back-cloth we recognize this as the real poetic theatre of our time. However:

The image is a moment of time realized in depth. In Beckett's theatre past and future, as they troubled the novels, give way before the eternal present of perception. But, just as the novelist's monologue is bound by the necessity of writing, so in the theatre the character on stage is trapped in the convention of drama. His 'being there' releases him from the deceit of language into the prison of time, the time not only of this evening's performance but of all the succeeding nights (and revivals) when he must reappear at the same place, in the same clothes and speaking the same words. If, by appearing before an audience, the Beckett hero re-establishes his physical existence—an advance on the almost total ignorance of *The Unnamable*—it is only to become immersed in what Mayoux termed the 'unceasing haemorrhage of time.'[15]

In an essay on Beckett's drama Jacques Guicharnaud cleverly related the incomplete world of these plays to a description, by Rémy de Gourmont, of Maeterlinck's theatre:

Hidden in mist somewhere there is an island, and on that island there is a castle, and in that castle there is a great room lit by a lamp. And in that room people are waiting. Waiting for what? They don't

> know. They're waiting for someone to knock at their door, waiting for their lamp to go out, waiting for Fear and Death. They talk. Yes, they speak words that shatter the silence of the moment. And then they listen again, leaving their sentences unfinished, their gestures uncompleted. They are listening. They are waiting.[16]

Without the mist and an echo of Maeterlinck's vague period symbolism this passage might indeed apply to Beckett. It anticipates both the tramps' weary expectation of Godot and the vast, domed room where Hamm and Clov also wait for the slow minutes to mount up into a life and therefore a death that will set them free. 'Outside of here it's death,' Hamm says: inside the feeble wick of life splutters pathetically before it dies, like old Mother Pegg, 'Of darkness,' and they are one with the extinguished universe. 'I see my light dying,' Clov tells Hamm when the latter asks him what he does in his kitchen. 'It can die just as well here,' is the reply; everywhere there is death and everyone is waiting 'for their lamp to go out'. But in the eternal present of the theatre it is precisely this end that is withheld. The heroes of the plays are fixed in the perpetual cycle where each night begins and continues to the moment where the last night stopped. They are condemned to pause forever in the stasis where the curtain leaves them, eternally approaching and never entering the future beyond. They wait for Godot or the knock on the door of which Gourmont wrote, but both are impossible so long as time remains. What they seek to complete is the arbitrary series begun by birth, to reach that end where time is no more and where their present unreality is changed into the certainty of their own identity and existence. What, in fact, they seek is to be reunited with the Self they know *must* exist outside time in the union of their personal infinity with that of the timeless void.

But this, as the trilogy illustrated, is what they cannot do. Creatures of time whose thought and language stress their finite condition, they are unable to enter the essential reality which is infinite. Logical impossibilities they exist where they should not, islands in infinity, sensible that for the end which must be approaching time is passing and yet that it doesn't effectively decrease. At the end of the trilogy the Unnamable is caught on the threshold of his story while immense periods of finite time, which he can only imagine as spirals, repeat themselves throughout eternity. It is this situation which the theatre reflects in miniature and that dominates Beckett's plays. The inescapable coils of finite time where the confused and helpless Self revolves in exile are present in the mound of days that threatens, but never allows, Winnie a final death; on the spools of memory where Krapp's life turns today the very moment of yesterday; in the musical confinement of *Play* where only the intervention of the author temporarily silences the three voices; and especially in the image and structure of *Waiting for Godot*.

2. WAITING FOR GODOT

In *Godot* the image is the waiting. The play offers us two tramps, Vladimir and Estragon, standing by a country road. They were there, so they tell us, last night; they are there tonight, for we can see them; and they intend, if a person named Godot does not arrive, to come back tomorrow: this also is confirmed, by the poster in the foyer. This is what the play, at a variety of levels, informs us; it is what we ourselves witness, and if, at the final curtain, we take something more away from the theatre, that is another token of the need we share with the characters for a meaning and a purpose in time. We will have joined the tramps, at whom we laughed, in their obstinate endeavour to erect a structure of words and ideas, actions and habit, over the timeless void. For this sympathetic and embarrassed laughter is aroused by the knowledge that their endeavours are futile. Like them our minds wish to create a meaning that will maintain itself in the desolation of nothing, but as perceptors we are compelled to acknowledge the essential comedy of a construction of words over what is not there. Our laughter refers to the breakdown of illusion which the tramps strive, without success, to conceal, and the weary refrain of their verbal mirage ends by emphasizing the absence of what they are waiting for: Godot will not come.

In relation to the time in which the tramps wait, Godot resembles the God defined by Jarry, who is 'the tangenital point of zero and the infinite.'[17] He is the final term of the series along which all Beckett's heroes are travelling, the end which completes the whole and determines the sense of what has gone before. Already the tramps have idled their way towards the timeless moment where Godot is to be found. But if they seem only a stage away from the end where 'peace enters in, to the soul of the incurious seeker,'[18] it is an illusion created by their immobility. Time has not stopped though on occasions that is how it appears (Vladimir tells Pozzo that it has but he is mistaken), it has merely slowed down. The closer they get to the end the more insignificant each day seems—as the numbers towards the decimal point grow steadily more meaningless—but at nightfall the end still eludes their grasp and will continue to do so for as long as they pursue the infinite with the useless weapons of the finite exile in time.

Their waiting is like any waiting for an event to take place, an arrival or a departure, when the present moment assumes a kind of hallucinated reality. As in a train travelling from A to B and pausing, unscheduled, at C, the unexpected interruption in time—which remains equal in progress or delay—suspends the traveller in the middle of nowhere acutely conscious of the minutes that are slipping away. 'That passed the time,' Vladimir says, after Pozzo's first visit. 'It would have passed in any case,' Estragon replies, but Vladimir will not relinquish his point: 'Yes, but not so rapidly.' Time is only sufferable when it is given the illusion of value, like the elaborate social web of induced significance which Pozzo brings to the first act and which masks the abyss he is tragically introduced to, in the second. Thus the tramps embark on their games with words, and when one of these 'little canters' fails them they hurriedly erect another to take its place. Vladimir imitates a mannikin or 'squirms like an aesthete'; they play at Pozzo and Lucky; permute their hats; do their exercises; examine their boots or start an artificial conversation: 'let's contradict each other...let's ask each other questions...let's abuse each other':

> They turn, increase the space between them, turn again and face each other.
> VLAD: Moron!
> EST: Vermin!
> VLAD: Abortion!
> EST: Morpion!
> VLAD: Sewer rat!
> EST: Curate!
> VLAD: Cretin!
> EST (*with finality*): Crritic!
> VLAD: Oh!
> He wilts, vanquished, and turns away.
> EST: Now let's make it up.
> VLAD: Gogo!
> EST: Didi!
> VLAD: Your hand!
> EST: Take it!
> VLAD: Come to my arms!
> EST: Your arms?
> VLAD: My breast!
> EST: Off we go.
> They embrace, separate, silence.
> VLAD: How time flies when one has fun.

Estragon, who is the more easily satisfied of the two in these diversions, remarks: 'We always find something, eh, Didi, to give us the impression that we exist?' But, however long they sustain each departure, its eventual collapse into nothing is certain. Even as they speak the tramps are aware of the impossible task they have forced upon language, and if the words themselves do not puncture the illusion it will be destroyed in another way. It can be as rapid as a pause into silence which immediately leads to the question, 'What do we do now?' or Estragon's sudden cry, 'God have pity on me!' And when the game does break down it invariably ends in cruelty or human rejection. Moreover, within the context of infinity their activity—any activity—is meaningless and progress impossible. 'Nothing to be done,' Estragon says in the words with which the play opens. Once again Beckett, his own best critic, comments on his creation and informs the spectator of exactly what the succeeding work will demonstrate. Nothing ends in this infinity which is composed of an infinite number of periods of finite time for ever repeating themselves. This is demonstrated by the principle of renewal in the conventions of drama, and in the structure and dialogue of *Godot* itself. The second act repeats the first: both open with the tramps coming together again after the night, end with their motionless withdrawal, and are punctuated, in the middle, by Pozzo and Lucky on their journey. *Waiting for Godot* is founded on Beckett's dual obsession of journey and stasis. And if, during the interval, five adjustments are made (Pozzo goes blind, Lucky dumb, the tree flowers, Estragon's boots are changed and Lucky gains a new hat), such things are the logical imponderables of Beckett's world which show that something is still taking its course in time. Neither is the tree's movement from winter to spring, apparently in a single night, a subject for credulity. It only moves fast in relation to the tramps, reminding us that objective time proceeds indifferent to their anguish, and that unless one approaches experience with Vladimir's desperation of the rational it does not matter, in infinity, whether it takes months or minutes to complete the change. Unfortunately, most of us do and therefore, like Vladimir, are dismayed that nothing ends except by the arbitrary (but aesthetic—another act would have unbalanced the form) intercession of the author. Everything reaches into infinity, like the circular song of the dog (also sung in *Watt* and *The Unnamable*) which opens the second act and reduces Vladimir to despair. Sentences remain unfinished; stories (for example, of the Englishman in the brothel) are interrupted; Lucky is not allowed to complete his harrowing speech; and thoughts, like the speculation on the two thieves, or actions, like the twice-introduced attempts of the tramps to hang themselves, are never carried to a conclusion but founder against the surrounding darkness into helpless uncertainty, confusion and silence. 'Nothing happens, nobody comes, nobody goes, it's awful,' Estragon laments, beautifully.

It is in these silences that the tramps suffer. Jean Anouilh described *Waiting for Godot* as 'a music hall sketch of Pascal's Pensées performed by the Fratellini clowns.' This describes the play's fusion of bleak tragedy and knock-about as well, perhaps, as any single observation could, but it is improbable if at that time (the first performance in Paris) this insight was related to Beckett's thought in general. The monologue on Proust is again of assistance here. Of the many fragments in Pascal which might have been introduced into this discussion, that which most obviously applies to *Waiting for Godot* is where Pascal describes the agony of man at rest.

> Nothing is so insufferable to man as to be completely at rest, without passions, without business, without diversion, without study. He then feels his nothingness, his forlornness, his insufficiency, his dependence, his weakness, his emptiness. There will immediately arise from the depths of his heart weariness, gloom, sadness, fretfulness, vexation, despair.[19]

Pascal describes exactly what happens to the tramps throughout the evening. Each time the dialogue lapses because there is no true dialectic of thought flickering across it they are exposed not only to the nothing without but also to the emptiness within, a dual exposure in which they encounter the suffering of being. The tragi-comic nature of *Godot* is sustained by the vagaries of habit on which the tramps rely. The regression into habit where the game of meaning is played, creates the comedy; the reaching out towards each other for companionship which is rejected, and their recognition of their condition as it really is, create the tragedy. Pascal's words describe the result of the two conflicting principles about which Beckett wrote in *Proust*:

> Suffering represents the omission of that duty (i.e. habit) whether through negligence or insufficiency, and boredom its adequate performance. The pendulum oscillates between these two terms: Suffering —that opens a window on the real and is the main condition of the artistic experience, and Boredom...that must be considered as the most tolerable because the most durable of human evils.[20]

In *Godot* it seems to be accepted that to try to avoid the suffering of being is no longer the crime it was once considered to be in the novels:

where the pain is so great that evasion is a necessity. But the absolute victory of boredom which might succeed in eliminating all significance, is withheld: 'This is becoming really insignificant./Not enough.' In spite of their patter the tramps continue to hear, in the silences, the 'dead voices' (Esslin suggests the voices of the old heroes) who thought and pursued the Self to the corners of anguish where Nothing dwells: 'To have lived is not enough for them./They have to talk about it./To be dead is not enough for them.' And Vladimir who, as we shall see, suffers more deeply than Estragon from the Cartesian cross which will not let his mind find peace, adds: 'What is terrible is to have thought.' He is unable to abandon the habit of reason which encourages the expectation of an answer even though, he is aware, it has 'long been straying in the night without end of the abyssal depths.' It is this lingering intelligence, riven by doubt, which condemns the tramps to suffer Pascal's inward emptiness. Their nobility lies in their persistent search for meaning; their tragedy in the impotence of the intelligence to overcome the incommensurables that surround it.

The waiting reduces everything in time to the same level of significance—or insignificance. But within the limits which this situation creates, the tramps are two distinct individuals, each with his own character and interests. Their shared condition is the ground on which their fundamentally opposed natures enter into the conflict, or tension, that is necessary to drama: at no time, though this has been asserted, is the shrewdly balanced dialogue interchangeable from one to the other. Estragon explains one essential difference when he tells Pozzo: 'He has stinking breath and I have stinking feet.' Vladimir's preoccupation, which is mental, and Estragon's, which is physical, are reflected in the distinct smells which disgust Pozzo. Of the two Vladimir thinks more and is therefore more eloquent: his anguish is intellectual. Consequently he appears to be the stronger. It is Vladimir who implies he once dealt with Godot, assures Estragon they are in the right place ('He said it was here') and dispenses the food—turnips, carrots and radishes—which is in his charge. He is more cultured than his companion: he quotes Latin and searches his memory for the correct word, unlike Estragon who is content with the first that appears. It is Vladimir who tries to make polite conversation with Pozzo while Estragon listens or follows his own thoughts. But Vladimir's thinking is fallible and exposes him to greater anguish than Estragon. When they discuss the idea of hanging themselves Estragon sees at once that Vladimir, who is the heavier of the two, may break the bough, but Vladimir has to have it explained to him as if he were a child and then says, 'I didn't think of that.' And it is Estragon who often destroys his painfully built intellectual certainties: 'Nothing is certain when you're about'—(with the stress on the first word). Vladimir's head is a 'charnel house' of dead ideas, and when he needs to think he takes off his hat and peers inside as if looking for something—a pantomime of the intellectual's hollow crown. When Lucky leaves his hat behind Vladimir exchanges it for his, perhaps prefering other men's ideas to his own. Above all he lives according to the rationalist tenet which exhorts him to 'be reasonable, you haven't tried everything yet. And I resumed the struggle.'

Vladimir is also capable of thinking of others whereas Estragon is only concerned by his own pain. He is outraged by the sores which the rope has made on Lucky's neck and remonstrates with Pozzo when the latter says he is on his way to sell his servant at the market: 'And now you turn him away? Such an old and faithful servant...After having sucked all the good out of him you chuck him away like a... like a banana skin. Really...' But as it proves intellectual compassion is not boundless: Vladimir's sympathy is for the suffering of the moment. When, a few lines later, Pozzo gives way to grief Vladimir turns on Lucky in an identical manner: 'How dare you! Such a good master! Crucify him like that! After so many years! Really!' Estragon meanwhile, is more interested in Pozzo's discarded chicken bones. He is more petulant, stubborn and egotistical than Vladimir. He sulks like a child, sitting inert on the mound while Vladimir paces restlessly about with his eyes searching the horizon as if the answer to his agony might be found there. His imagination is spontaneous and he habitually personalizes the universe; thus when he talks of Christ it is not surprising to find him identifying himself with him or that he claims, looking at his rags, to have been a poet. When Pozzo asks his name he replies, 'Catullus.' Vladimir reads the Bible for instruction, Estragon for the coloured maps of the Holy Land: 'The Dead Sea was pale blue. The very look of it made me thirsty.' His suffering is physical, as with his boots, or emotional, but he still delights in the body and in physical coarseness as when Vladimir (who despises it) has to relieve himself. Then he stands in the middle of the stage and enjoys the spectacle. Estragon is also more naturally a victim—he is the one kicked by Lucky and beaten by the nameless 'they'—and in his innocence of thought seems to be more beloved by whoever it is who introduces the several mysterious acts of grace into the evening. In the first act he struggles to get his feet into his boots; after the interval they have been replaced by a pair a little too large. (Beckett told Harold Hobson: 'One of Estragon's feet is blessed, and the other is damned. The boot won't go on the foot that is damned; and it will go on the foot that is not.)[21] Finally, Estragon is closer to timelessness than Vladimir. All landscapes are now the same to him and his memory is incapable of reaching back even to the previous day ('I'm not a historian'). Once completed an event is forgotten; 'day' means nothing to him any longer; and in his mind, which makes no distinction between events in time, his thoughts belong to the infinite number of repeated present moments in which they are spoken. Thus he is easily pleased by their improvizations and when he is, is confident for the tomorrow of which he cannot form any real conception, unlike Vladimir who dreads the always coming of the night.

The dialogue in which the tramps attract and repel, demand and reject, possess and elude one another, expresses a friendship which is situated 'somewhere between fatigue and ennui'.[22] They have been together many years and their pasts were once more promising than their present state suggests. Vladimir, who uses memory to enforce whatever bond it is binds them to each other, recalls a time when they still belonged to society:

> In the 'nineties, hand in hand, from the top of the Eiffel Tower, among the first. We were respectable in those days. Now it's too late. They wouldn't even let us up.

On another occasion they were grape-harvesting in the Macon country when Estragon threw himself into the Rhone. Vladimir fished him out and his clothes dried in the sun. Now, however, their friendship is the Proustian desert of habit, loneliness and recrimination:

> VLAD... (*joyous*): There you are again. (*indifferent.*) There we are again. (*gloomy.*) There I am again.

The words destroy Vladimir's original innocent pleasure in Estragon's presence, reducing him first to the boredom in which they were last together and then to a sudden understanding of the unsolvable question. 'You see,' Estragon tells him, 'You feel worse when I'm with you. I feel better alone, too.' Each feels closer to his own Self without the other who reminds him of his imprisonment in time. They remain unknown and unknowable to one another but prefer to continue a relationship which repeatedly stresses their inviolable isolation, rather than separate and endure the inescapable self-perception of life alone. Both feel pain and call on the other to recognize their suffering but neither is capable of penetrating to the other's being: Vladimir suffering intellectually is a spectacle for Estragon; Estragon suffering physically is beyond Vladimir's comprehension:

EST (*feebly*): Help me!
VLAD: It hurts?
EST: Hurts! He wants to know if it hurts!
VLAD (*angrily*): Nobody ever suffers but you. I don't count. I'd like to hear what you'd say if you had what I have.
EST: It hurts?
VLAD: Hurts! He wants to know if it hurts!

Suffering doesn't ennoble or create a human solidarity; it is unsharable and it brutalizes. When he is kicked Estragon spits at Lucky and later, when the latter is incapable on the ground, belabours him with fists and feet. Again, when Estragon calls on God for pity, Vladimir, his friend, is excluded from the plea:

EST: ...God have pity on me!
VLAD (*vexed*): And me?
EST: On me! On me! Pity! On me!

Like all who love, or are close to another, they are adept at wounding. Rejection is followed by counter rejection and Estragon's selfish wants encourage Vladimir to sarcasm and bitterness.

Therefore perhaps they should part. Estragon considers it many times which in itself hurts Vladimir's feelings. The two tramps, one who wants to go and the other to stay, embody the two fools who were within Molloy. 'If we parted. That might be better for us...' Estragon conjectures; 'Then why do you always come crawling back?' Vladimir answers him in pique:—'I don't know.' But despite the suffering which sets a distance between them, and the other's presence which emphasizes their essential loneliness, there is also a profound need which can sometimes transform the irritations of hatred into tenderness and their anger into a compassion which is close to love. Vladimir needs someone to listen to him explain the conflicting evidence in his head ('Go on, Gogo, return the ball, can't you, once in a way?') and the childlike Estragon wants protection from himself and others: 'When I think of it...all these years...but for me...where would you be...? You'd be nothing more than a little heap of bones at the present minute.' It is always the tormentedly articulate Vladimir who makes the initial advance and Estragon who at first repels him. But the latter's need is not the lesser simply because it is more difficult for him to express. Indeed on two occasions he manages adequately. In the first act when

Estragon falls asleep Vladimir is left alone and lonely. He is no longer perceived for sleep is a temporary escape into nothing that emphasizes the isolation of him who watches. Therefore he wakes Estragon up:

EST: Why will you never let me sleep?
VLAD: I felt lonely.
EST: I had a dream.
VLAD: Don't tell me!
EST...Who am I to tell my private nightmares to if I can't tell them to you?
VLAD: Let them remain private.

The need is everyone's but Vladimir cannot bear another's nightmare in addition to his own. (However, in the second act when Estragon sleeps again, Vladimir sings a pathetic lullaby, takes off his coat and puts it over Estragon's shoulders, and runs to comfort him and hold him in his arms when he wakes up terrified by the visions which pursue him even in sleep.) Then, as Vladimir comes to greet him at the opening of act two, Estragon utters a cry which, more than any other, expresses the conflicting nature of their life together: 'Don't touch me! Don't question me! Don't speak to me! Stay with me!'

Pozzo and Lucky are representatives of the ordinary world from which the tramps are excluded. 'We've lost our rights?' Estragon asks. Vladimir prefers to say 'We've waived them.' Even the tramps wish to assert their importance as free agents by insisting that their exclusion is voluntary. By contrast with Pozzo and Lucky, however, it is the tramps' lives which appear normal. The former create a metaphor of society, not as it is but as the tramps might see it, with the social structure reduced to an essential distinction between master and slave. Since Hegel this division in human relationships has coloured man's approaches to society and to his fellow men in both serious and popular thinking, and the basic separation into two classes is a convenient one for drama, particularly as here where Beckett is concerned with the traditional couples of the non-literary theatre where such a distinction has always existed. Hegel's original premises can, with care, be used in describing the relationship between Pozzo and Lucky and its original impression on the tramps, but only (and this is crucial) if one remembers that Beckett's ends are not Hegel's ends, and that his own individual preoccupations will, in the second act, supersede the impression which is made by their first entrance.

In *The Rebel*, Camus writes that, for Hegel, 'Fundamental human relations are relations of pure prestige, a perpetual struggle to the death, for recognition of one human being by another.' It is fortunate for Hegel's system, Camus continues, that there have always existed two types of consciousness:

> ...one of which has not the courage to renounce life and which is therefore willing to recognize the other kind of consciousness without being recognized itself in return. It consents, in short, to being considered as an object. This type of consciousness which, to preserve its animal existence, renounces independent life, is the consciousness of a slave. The type of consciousness which by being recognized achieves independence is that of the master...
>
> Undoubtedly the master enjoys total freedom first as regards the slave, since the latter recognizes him totally, and then as regards the natural world, since by his work the slave transforms it into objects of enjoyment which the master consumes in a perpetual affirmation of his own identity. However, the autonomy is not absolute. The master, to his detriment, is recognized in his autonomy by a consciousness which he himself does not recognize as autonomous. Therefore he cannot be satisfied and his autonomy is only negative. Mastery is a blind alley.[23]

This analysis applies in depth to the Pozzo-Lucky relationship. In a world like that of *Godot* where man awaits a revelation, or at least the intimation of a revelation, Pozzo, the master, is the nearest approach to what is absent. He appears all powerful, dominating the stage by his gestures and his inflated language. Life, for Pozzo, is important. When he enters he still values the body (witness the provisions he has brought with him for the journey); he is capable of enjoying sensual delights and depends upon a collection of cherished possessions (his Kapp and Peterson, vaporizer and watch). Pozzo recalls the feudal lord of the manor, self-consciously magnanimous in his disposal of time and charity. He condescends to recognize Vladimir and Estragon, who are on his land, as fellow men though he regrets the road is open to all, and when Estragon unashamedly asks for the chicken bones, remarks that in theory the bones go to the carrier. Pozzo's is a fixed and well-regulated world in contrast to the stationary confusion of the tramps where everything is in flux, and his behaviour echoes the image which the tramps have of Godot (so does his name). Not surprisingly they at first mistake his identity:

> EST: Is that him?
> VLAD: Who?
> EST (*trying to remember the name*): Er...
> VLAD: Godot?

EST: Yes.
POZZO: I present myself: Pozzo.
VLAD: Not at all!

Pozzo, in fact, is a temporal substitute for Godot: he is the man who has taken it upon himself to act as if the answers are known, who lives exclusively in terms of power, and whose existence is circumscribed by time. Lucky, it seems, is fortunate in his having found this substitute. His bondage is an alternative to the tramps' unbearable waiting.

However, Pozzo's power is hollow. Like Hegel's master he does not recognize his servant whom he calls 'pig' or 'hog', and has to turn to others, even to the tramps, for recognition. 'The road seems long when one journeys alone': Lucky is discounted... 'I cannot talk in a vacuum.' But it is his speech which reveals his inward emptiness. In the first act, before he has been overtaken by the reality of his position in time, he speaks in platitudes ('From the meanest creature one departs wiser, richer, more conscious of one's blessings') or elevates the simplest remark into an exaggerated performance to conceal the insignificance he prefers not to see. Thus, when Vladimir asks him a question which, as an appeal to another, is the most precious form of linguistic contact, Pozzo prepares his answer like a teacher or a priest. He twice sprays his throat with the vaporizer, then groups the audience about him in anticipation and finally, having once forgotten what was originally asked of him, spells out the answer with pedantic logic. It is a mockery of all attempts to impart knowledge. If Lucky has found a substitute Godot, Pozzo avoids the tramps' waiting by filling his life with illusion. Pozzo on his journey, clings to his condition: the tramps who remain where they are, are always seeking to change theirs.

It is Lucky who, like Hegel's slave, has transformed the world for his master and given Pozzo what intelligence and culture he now possesses. 'But for him all my thoughts, all my feelings would have been of common things...Beauty, grace, truth of the first water, I knew they were all beyond me.' The rope which binds Lucky to Pozzo also ties the master to his slave, and in the second act Pozzo no longer drives but follows him. Lucky is now a puppet who performs to peremptory commands. He dances, sings, recites and thinks *for* Pozzo, and his personal life has been reduced to basic animal reflexes: he cries and he kicks. But once, we have Pozzo's word for it, he was a better dancer and capable of giving his master moments of great illumination and joy: 'He used to be so kind...so helpful and entertaining...He even used to think very prettily once.' However, this has changed: 'now...

he's killing me.' Pozzo has Lucky not only to act as carrier but also to underline his own reality and Lucky's thinking is now not the rationalist consolation it once was but total scepticism which illuminates the agony beneath appearances. When he speaks he is Pozzo's tormentor: he reminds him of the reality which his whole life is an endeavour to avoid.

This becomes apparent in Lucky's great speech which terrifies the other characters because it foretells the extinction of the world. Lucky posits 'the existence of a personal God' with a white beard (like Godot: human imagination is limited) 'who loves us dearly with some exceptions for reasons unknown...and suffers like the divine Miranda with those who for reasons unknown but time will tell are plunged in torment.' Despite His presence and the labours of all the authorities, it is discovered 'that man...in spite of progress...man in short...man in brief...wastes and pines...abandoned...and...for reasons unknown... (continues) to shrink and dwindle into the great cold the great dark...' The authorities, whose names Lucky quotes in this parody of a master's oral, bent on establishing 'beyond all reasonable doubt' the exact truth about man (though 'for reasons unknown' recurs like a refrain: more reasons are unknown, than known in rationalist thinking) discover that in spite of all the researches of science, the intuition of the artist, the physical culture of sport and the endurance of the earth, everything is condemned to waste into the great dark of nothing. This is the only certainty which his intelligence has discovered, and though most of the works to which Lucky refers withdrew from this conclusion or were left unfinished, it is, for him, inescapable. 'Science and reason,' writes John Moore, 'can only end in doubt and contradiction when they deal with ultimate questions or offer us geological and astronomical pictures of the running down of the universe.'[24] Lucky's knowledge of this ends in despair and his thinking in the agonized incoherence of his speech which, with its devaluation of art, progress, religion and science, anticipates the extinguished world of *Endgame*.

The change which has overtaken Pozzo and Lucky by the second act is not, however, simply a comment on the inevitable deterioration of the master-slave society, as has been asserted, though Pozzo's blindness does create a tragic image of his earlier refusal to see human existence as it really is. Rather it belongs to the larger context of Beckett's treatment of man in time. When he first appears Pozzo is still firmly immersed in normal time. He even carries a watch and checks the length of his journey by it: time is valuable and not to be wasted by waiting under a tree for night to fall:

POZZO (*he consults his watch*): But I must really be getting along if I am to observe my schedule.
VLAD: Time has stopped.
POZZO (*cuddling his watch to his ear*): Don't you believe it, sir, don't you believe it.

For the tramps nothing noticeable is taking place, but for Pozzo 'night is charging and will burst upon us—Pop! Like that!' However, he has not been long in the tramps' presence before a change takes place. At first he notices that 'All subsides. A great calm descends... Pan sleeps,' and then, like Moran who was also on a journey that contacted the irrational, he starts to lose his possessions, first his pipe, then his vaporizer and finally his watch. When this happens he experiences difficulties in remembering what he has just said and his hold on what he insists is reality begins to weaken. During the interval the process is completed. In the time since 'yesterday' he has gone blind and Lucky dumb, and their miserable procession across the stage introduces a new meaning into an established image: ''Tis the time's plague, when madmen lead the blind'.[25] Even Estragon is surprised at the rapidity of the change. 'Since when?' he demands to know; it is he, not Pozzo, who now seeks to establish some reason into time. Pozzo's great cry which provides the answer, contains all of Beckett's pent-up anguish over man in time: in our conception is our end and yet we have to live it out to this dreadful conclusion which men are powerless to alter:

> Have you not done tormenting me with you accursed time? It's abominable. When! When! One day, is that not enough for you, one day like any other day, one day he went dumb, one day I went blind, one day we'll go deaf, one day we were born, one day we'll die, the same day, the same second, is that not enough for you? (Calmer.) They give birth astride of a grave, the light gleams an instant, then it's night once more.

When Vladimir says that he and Estragon waived their rights rather than lost them, he is consciously adopting an importance which he does not possess. The tramps are anxious to establish their independence. 'We're not tied?' asks Estragon:

VLAD: How do you mean tied?
EST: Down.
VLAD: But to whom? By whom?
EST: To your man.
VLAD: To Godot? Tied to Godot? What an idea! No question of it. (*Pause.*) For the moment.

The tramps, like those in the society from which they are excluded, want to believe that their individual decisions change things and that these decisions are made without duress. But, despite their apparent freedom as outcasts, their condition is as circumscribed as Pozzo's. This is evident in their waiting. They need Godot to give a meaning to their universe: they depend on his arrival, and so long as Godot does not come to resolve their waiting everything that happens is only provisional.

Godot, because he exists for the tramps and directs the course of the evening in progress, is as real a character as any of those we see. By the kind of logical reversal which appeals to Beckett his absence demonstrates his presence and dominates the play in which he fails to appear. It is as if Hamlet were, one night, to remain off stage though the courtiers prepare for his entrance and continue to expect his arrival. Although he is, at best, a dimly remembered acquaintance, and Estragon 'wouldn't even know him if I saw him,' a general image of Godot does emerge during the evening. To the tramps he lives in the capitalist world of family, agents, correspondents and bank account. They identify his power with what is most familiar to them in the only world they have experience of: authority. But to the boy who brings his messages Godot has a white beard and his life is occupied by the far older mastership over the sheep and the goats. In another of the contradictory divisions of punishment and grace which occur in this play Godot beats the brother who cares for the sheep and favours the goatherd. His behaviour, if not strictly accurate, has a precedent: 'And he shall seat the sheep on his right hand but the goats on his left.'

This, among other allusions, suggests an interpretation of Godot in terms of the first three letters of his name. The latter is a bilingual pun on God and water, the two lacks which the hero craves in his isolation and spiritual thirst.[26] But though *Waiting for Godot* is rich in Christian imagery and symbolism it is not more prevalent than, for example, in *Molloy* or *The Unnamable*. If Godot is God then Beckett's irony is unusually heavy (Vlad: 'What does he do, your master? Boy: He does nothing, sir.') and besides, Beckett's characters are all certain that God, as such, does not exist. Like many sensitive members of their civilization they are haunted by his absence or not-being (Est: 'Do you think God sees me?') but it is the absence of a certainty rather than of a specific manifestation of a Godhead, which disturbs them. The proof of Godot's existence is another mockery of the rational determination to find a meaning. He is because he is not ('Let's go./We can't./Why not?/We're waiting for Godot.') which like Hamm's deductions in

Endgame call on one to speak or pray to that which is not there: 'The Bastard! He doesn't exist.' Beckett employs Christian imagery, like Faulkner in *Light in August* or Albee in *Who's afraid of Virginia Woolf*, to broaden his effects. As he has said: 'Christianity is a mythology with which I am perfectly familiar, so I naturally use it.'[27] Thus in the passage where Vladimir and Estragon discuss the two thieves crucified along with Christ, his intention is not to suppose the withered tree to represent the cross without the saviour and the tramps as the co-sufferers, but to examine again the curious polarity of human life. 'Remark', says Pozzo of his relationship with Lucky, 'that I might just as well have been in his shoes and he in mine. If chance had not willed it otherwise.' In the theatre of life there exists this strange disposal of approval and disapproval, or blessedness and damnation, it is difficult to know what, which applies to Estragon's feet as well as to Cain and Abel or the two thieves. This has preoccupied Beckett since *Dante and the Lobster* and in the passage in question it is the irrational distribution of justice that Vladimir is concerned about, why one of the thieves called right and the other wrong and was punished, not with Jesus and salvation. Vladimir regards the Bible as a document to be verified, not as the repository of the word of God, and is tormented by the discrepancies which exist between the four Gospels ('The four of them were there—or thereabouts, and only one speaks of the thief being saved...why him rather than the others?') .What Vladimir seeks is not the Christian solution that ends either in heaven or hell but simply, as he says, to be saved 'From death!' which extinguishes all meaning. That one of the thieves succeeded in finding a way round death is what compels his imagination, never who saved him. Thus to see Godot as the lost God of Christianity ignores the tramps' thinking throughout the play. It also reduces Beckett's cosmic cry of anguish to a particular complaint. Godot's existence is the result of man's inability to be a nihilist: he is the creation of man's profound need for meaning. When man is shown, as here, to be incapable of accepting his own insignificance in a slowly dying world, and of realizing that his suffering is meaningless, Godot is the necessary unknown at the end of the series who is introduced to justify existence by the rational leap into the dark. He is the missing quantity in the universe which the tramps can define in no other way, the answer to the unanswerable question who would, if he appeared, integrate the world that is always disintegrating and restore man, out of meaninglessness, into meaning.

But what or who Godot actually is, is really of no importance. It is the waiting, not an arrival, that the play is about. The tramps, because they are human, are prepared to wait for ever even though Vladimir, in a rare moment of honesty towards the end, admits that the wait is in vain. And we, the audience, are likewise constrained and in our own refusal to accept insignificance readily act in collusion with them. The search for some significance in the absent Godot which avoids the reality of the waiting we have witnessed, demonstrates this. As always Beckett secretes away the words which clearly express the basic situation and enlarge it into its universal implications. When Pozzo falls and calls for help Vladimir says:

> To all mankind they were addressed, those cries for help still ringing in our ears. But at this place, at this moment of time, all mankind is us, whether we like it or not.

On attend Godot: not only the tramps but the audience who they represent during the performance. Out of what he calls 'this immense confusion,' Vladimir seeks to establish the residue of what he has experienced this night. And in his words, which can tell little about an event that Estragon will have forgotten tomorrow, and which no one hears because Estragon is again sleeping, the anguish and boredom of his waiting in time are suddenly raised on to that level of awareness, which Aristotle termed recognition, wherein man perceives his true condition:

> Tomorrow, when I wake, or think I do, what shall I say of today? That with Estragon, my friend, at this place, until the fall of night, I waited for Godot? That Pozzo passed, with his carrier, and talked to us? Probably. But in all that what truth will there be? (Estragon, having struggled with his boots in vain, is dozing off again. Vladimir stares at him). He'll know nothing. He'll tell me about the blows he received and I'll give him a carrot. (*Pause.*) Astride of a grave and a difficult birth. Down in the hole, lingeringly, the grave-digger puts on his forceps. We have time to grow old. The air is full of our cries. (He listens.) But habit is a great deadener. (He looks again at Estragon.) At me too someone is looking, of me too someone is saying, He is sleeping, he knows nothing, let him sleep on. (*Pause.*) I can't go on. (*Pause.*) What have I said?

Immediately afterwards the boy arrives to say that Godot will not be coming tonight. 'What am I to say to Mr Godot, sir?' he asks. Vladimir hesitates and then says, 'tell him...that you saw me.' Like Hamlet or Othello he wishes the truth about himself to be reported at the end. 'Absent thee from felicity'[28] or 'I pray you, in your letters,/When you shall these unlucky deeds relate,/Speak of me as I am:'[29] the hero strives, even with his expiring breath, to set the record straight at the end, and Vladimir is no exception. In the moment of being reported to Godot perhaps what we have seen will be, for an instant, and not have been in vain.

3. ENDGAME

Criticism often forgets that the theatrical text is not self-reliant but depends, when the writing is finished, upon the forces aroused by its presentation before an auditorium of temporarily associated individuals. *Waiting for Godot* is liable to suffer from these forces in its transfer from study to stage. The presence of the hobo-clown tends to introduce an element of miserabilism into Beckett's first play, and both the ambivalent use of Christian myth and the obscure significance of Godot himself when separated from the general context of Beckett's work, reinforce the effect of the unfortunate associations which surround the modern clown. Years of affectionate circus appearances have diluted his once incisive nature and accustomed audiences to expect from him a diffuse, reassuring pathos. Audiences have a habit of extracting what they demand from a performance, whether or not what they seek is there in the text, and *Godot* emerges from such a conflict through an atmosphere of nostalgia and even religious regret which is at odds with Beckett's intentions. That it does emerge justifies his choice of medium but the temptation to a false pathos (or its comic counterpart, bathos) is there, as is the opportunity to indulge in a Christian interpretation of the rich but indefinite Biblical imagery. In contrast *Endgame* offers no such opening. It has a tautness and power which makes its brevity as exhausting as many three act-dramas. A masterpiece of contraction, it is probably Beckett's most individual work; it is also his finest play.

Endgame is fixed in a cruel reality yet bears the aura of an apocalyptic vision comparable to that of the insane engraver recounted by Hamm. It is a unique, a terrifying insight into the loveless skull of the human world at the close of its career. The material within the text, however, is bewilderingly complex. *Endgame* can be approached on an embarrassing number of levels, from the conflict of generations or the perpetual struggle with time, to chess or Shakespearian analogy. Beckett's remarkable achievement (perhaps the most remarkable in all his exactly formed constructs of words, especially as here the process is invisible) is to integrate his material so completely that, in the theatre, the impact is total and simultaneous. Imagery applied to one level is also relevant to one or more other, with such reciprocal effect that meaningful criticism of any aspect in isolation is almost impossible. Nevertheless, two approaches are obvious and necessary. One is to examine the various underlying patterns of borrowed reference on which the play is built. The other is to speak of the content as a further and new, expression of the author's thought and art. Here the former approach is taken first, though the reader unacquainted with the text might prefer to reverse the order should he need a more general impression of the play in the beginning.

In *Endgame* the presence behind the plays becomes evident for the first time. As Descartes dominates the novelist's solitary mental world, so the time-imprisoned characters of Beckett's theatre are as they are through the, at first, curious ubiquity of the Greek philosopher, Zeno. Like Beckett Zeno is concerned with the quarrel between the mortal microcosm and the relatively immortal macrocosm, and by the permanent separation of a finite being in time and space from the surrounding universe. For, convinced of the reality of this universe, he not unusually sees the essence of reality as infinity. He demonstrates this rift by means of a heap of millet. If one takes a finite quantity of millet and first pour half of it into a heap; then take half of what remains and add that to the heap, and continue in this way until all the millet is brought into a single pile once again, one will discover that, although in an infinite universe the heap could be completed, this will never happen within the limitations of the finite, for the closer the heap approaches to completion, the slower it actually increases. This is obvious material for Beckett, providing him with an analogy for his own search for an end, the attainment of the Self or some release from the terrible chain of cause and effect.

Endgame depicts the last stages of this struggle with the heap of days. The universe, it seems at first, has been entirely destroyed. The holocaust has come, apparently with a whimper and not a bang as the dramatically-conscious Hamm would have liked, and the extinct world rolls through nothing towards Nothing, the only witnesses of its past sealed within the domed room on stage, outside of which is death. Those inside wait for the end that has so far eluded them, longing for the heap to be completed. In the opening words of the play Clov turns towards the audience and explains how near they are to the end:

> Finished, it's finished, nearly finished, it must be nearly finished. (*Pause.*) Grain upon grain, one by one, and one day, suddenly there's a heap, a little heap, the impossible heap.

They are on the verge of timelessness. Even more than for the tramps in *Godot* time passing goes unindicated ('What time is it?/The same as usual'); days are reduced to indeterminate periods ('it's a day like any other day') and are only separated by the ritual removal of the dust-covers from the two ash-bins and from over Hamm, at the beginning of each performance. This, as Kenner writes, is another indication that 'what we are about to witness is a dusty dramatic exhibition repeated and repeatable.'[30] Hamm takes up Clov's statement that *it* is nearly finished; this is one of the refrains which run through the play and bind the different levels to one another. His story, which he has been telling himself all his days, is 'nearly finished'. On another occasion he asks Nagg with exasperation: 'Have you not finished? Will you never be finished?' and then enlarging the reference—'Will this never finish?' Or, in a quieter moment of the many thousand they spend together, he enquires of Clov: 'Do you not think this has gone on long enough?' As with other of the general observations which are made during the evening ('We're getting on...This is slow work...This is deadly.') it refers directly to the state of the evening's performance. It is also, however, a comment on time and on life itself, and illustrates the profound interpenetration between theatre and life. The words are exact and metaphysical, an inquiry which might legitimately be made by any member of the audience, and a serious, almost the crucial, question. But as a question it is valueless; Hamm already knows the answer. If the past means 'that bloody awful day, long ago, before this bloody awful day,' and the future, reunited with the Self, is not yet (Clov: 'Do you believe in the life to come?' Hamm: 'Mine was always that.'), then the present is that in which nothing really finishes, 'the end of the day like any other day,' through which in the general slowing down of the world we are made aware that 'something is takings its course'. And though this something may be characterized as the approach of death, the process of decay or a heart dripping in Hamm's head, what we in fact hear are the accumulating seconds which, like Zeno's heap, will never be completed. As Hamm ends his great speech:

> Moment upon moment, pattering down, like the millet grains of... (he hesitates)...that old Greek, and all life long you wait for that to mount up to a life.

The structure of *Endgame* is founded upon a personal interest that Beckett last exploited in the description of Murphy's service as night-warder at the Mercyseat. There the hero played endless games of chess with the amiable schizophrenic, Mr Endon. Hamm's often to be repeated first words—'Me (he yawns) to play'—fix him as the mover of the piece now beginning and the play as a whole in the context of chess. The idea of life as a game, to be played and passed by inventing vice-existers or telling stories, has been common to Beckett's work since *Malone Dies*. Now, however, its significance is extended. In *Endgame* the characters not only play but are played with: Hamm is both player and chess piece, to be exact the threatened king. He dominates the action from his throne in the centre of the room, directing the activities of his subordinates. But he is also helpless in his chair on castors. Like the king in chess Hamm's movement is limited in any one direction, and he relies on Clov to push him round his confined kingdom: 'right round the world'.

This is the first of many significances given the domed room: a chessboard where Hamm is guarded by his attendant pieces. Nagg and Nell in their dustbins appear to represent imprisoned pawns while Clov, with his restricted movement ('I can't sit') and the more specific reference ('And your rounds? When you inspected my paupers. Always on foot?/Sometimes on horse.') resembles the knight. To move beyond the inner boundaries of the nine-square area which the king commands exposes Hamm to danger: 'Outside of here it's death.' He lives in anxiety, concerned for his own security and reliant upon Clov to protect him against a sudden assault. At Hamm's call Clov, with increasing resentment, comes from his kitchen (a cubical chess square: 'ten feet by ten feet by ten feet, nice dimensions, nice proportions') to spy through the windows with his telescope, inspecting the board for signs of a threatening movement. All seems safe, however, and Hamm's fears ludicrous and groundless. There is nothing in the surrounding desolation to effect the gradual exhaustion which overtakes Hamm's forces, who, like the pieces in a real chess game, are struck from the board one by one. It is a game of reduction (to which Hamm is resigned); at the end the board is almost empty, 'There are no more... bicycle wheels...coffins...sugar-plums...pain killer...pap...tide... navigators or rugs.'

This is as Hamm wants it. His opponent is not human but time and against the latter one seeks to lose, to be eliminated into Nothing, not to win and continue a perverse encounter without hope:

> Old endgame lost of old, play and lose, and have done with losing... Since that's the way we're playing it let's play it that way...and speak no more about it...speak no more.

In this game to win is to lose, to shed the life imposed at birth, and until near the end Hamm succeeds. Everything living, like the rat and the flea, is quickly exterminated; one of his pawns, Nell, appears to have died, and each successive end adds another grain to the heap, when in dismay Clov, on a routine inspection through the window, sees a small boy sitting on the ground outside. This is what Hamm has been fearing: an irrational intrusion of life into this world of death which would renew the possibility of meaning and so destroy the patient exercise in destruction which he has been engaged in. Clov demands the gaff, intending to go out and kill the child, but now that his fear is confirmed Hamm is curiously possessed and tranquil. The child's appearance seems a miracle; such a birth from Nothing cannot be exterminated like the rat in Clov's kitchen. (Here, unaccountably omitted from the English version, Hamm murmurs 'La Pierre levée' in memory of the resurrected Christ, and then a still earlier recollection of Moses gazing at the promised land: 'Il regarde la maison sans doute, avec les yeux de Moise mourant.') There is no possible reply to this inexplicable event and Hamm concedes the game. His pawns immobile, himself in check from the boy, he gives Clov his freedom: 'It's the end, Clov, we've come to the end. I don't need you any more.'

But the game is not in fact over. Hamm has lost his attempt to lose everything to time but not the game as a game of chess. The end is not checkmate but stalemate, as it must be against an adversary as negative as time. The finite and the infinite remain apart in an unalterable stasis; Hamm, like the Unnamable, is unable to go on yet also unable to finish. 'Let's stop playing,' Clov demanded earlier, but this is a game one cannot leave in the middle. Like Murphy's original move against Mr Endon, the conventional, P—K4 which was 'the primary cause of all his subsequent difficulties,' birth into time projects man into a series (or a universe) where he is without meaning, the plaything of forces he cannot penetrate yet with just enough ability himself to take an active part in the game. At the end Hamm can neither lose nor win, for, of the boy, if 'he exists he'll die there or he'll come here. And if he doesn't...,' while his one remaining piece is at the door about to abandon him but for the moment immobile. Therefore, until tomorrow Hamm makes a temporary close by reversing the opening. He covers his face with the large, blood-stained St Veronica handkerchief and remains motionless. Against time this stalemate can exist for eternity.

During one circuit of his kingdom, Hamm pauses against the wall 'Do you hear? (he strikes the wall with his knuckles)...Hollow bricks ...All that's hollow.' The rounded room with its two small windows high up in either side like eyes, presents a remarkable image of the inside of the skull where man is bound. Through the windows, or eyes, they look out at the grey waste of a reasonless universe; inside they struggle with the last hollow tenets of rationalism: 'No one who lived thought as crooked as we.' But this empty circle has still another dimension, one that introduces a third area of reference to join Zeno and chess and complete the structure on which *Endgame* is built. Until now Shakespeare has not been explicitly evoked by Beckett's characters although his presence is suggested in the dramatic structure of *Godot*. Hamm needs no precedent: 'My kingdom for a nightman!' he shouts across the empty stage, confusing in one image chess and Richard III, the Shakespearian king within whose temples is the hollow and mortal crown of the skull known to Henry IV, Henry VI and Richard II. There, as in the realm where Hamm exerts his power:

> ...keeps death his court, and there the Antic sits,
> Scoffing his state and grinning at his pomp.
> Allowing him a breath, a little scene
> To monarchize, be feared and kill with looks.[31]

However, it is not the histories but the Shakespeare play most conscious of itself as a play which underlies *Endgame—The Tempest*. 'Our revels now are ended': Hamm ironically repeats Prospero's words, broadening their implication to include not only the mock action represented on the stage but also the serious collapse of life in the world which the play represents as real. Prospero too, in spite of his magic powers, was trapped in the determinism of the play and had to pray for release:

> And my ending is despair
> Unless I be reliev'd by prayer...
> Let your indulgence set me free,[32]

He ruled an island from his cell (This cell's my court'), the same place where Ferdinand and Miranda played at chess and the actors vanished nightly into thin air. Hamm likewise is 'the master of a full poor cell'[33] where he is both despot and dependent on those he rules, and where Clov, about to leave, remarks: 'I open the door of the cell and go.' Hamm has dreams of a paradise over the hill, the home of Flora, Pomona and Ceres, which recalls the Masque in *The Tempest*. But Hamm is 'a toppled Prospero'.[34] His powers have been crucially enfeebled, and Paradise is only one of the many things he remembers with regret but can no longer summon into being. His gaff, which resembles Prospero's staff, the symbol of his dignity and strength, is not powerful enough to move his chair round the room, and it is rendered entirely useless by the boy's appearance. At the end he discards the gaff as Prospero broke his staff and buried his book. For both of them the game is over: now 'Every third thought shall be my grave.'[35]

While Hamm participates in only one role, Prospero, *Endgame* so reduces Shakespeare's original abundance that Clov must play three: Ariel, who also receives his freedom at the end of an irksome day's service, Miranda and Caliban. Prospero asks Miranda (Act I, sc. 2) if she can remember 'a time before we came unto this cell'[36] and is surprised to learn that she recalls 'rather like a dream than an assurance',[37] images of another place. So Clov can speak of old Mother Pegg and remembers the education he was once given into life—when there was still a world to live in (*Endgame* p. 50). A more explicit parallel exists, however, in the passage where Hamm questions Clov about their arrival in this place:

> HAMM: Do you remember when you came here?
> CLOV: No. Too small, you told me.
> HAMM: Do you remember your father?
> CLOV (*wearily*): Same answer. (Pause.) You asked me these questions millions of times.
> HAMM: ...It was I was a father to you.

It echoes Prospero's lengthy opening catechism with Miranda 'who/ Art ignorant of what thou art.'[38] Material borrowed from the original —a mysterious past we expect to be clarified and the uncertainty of parentage—is joined to Beckett's own recurring obsessions. The actor playing Clov wearily speaks out against the convention which demands these questions receive nightly attention, whether here or in Shakespeare, and reasonably asks the dominating parent what purpose they can possibly serve. Miranda also queried Prospero's intention:

> ...you have often
> Begun to tell me what I am, but stopp'd
> And left me to a bootless inquisition.[39]

It seems that Prospero, despite his magic, has also been silenced by the same impossible answer that eludes Hamm as it has eluded Beckett's earlier heroes. Who is it that can tell me what I am? Clov, like Miranda, or the Unnamable by Worm, remains unenlightened by Hamm.

Nevertheless, if the pathetic tenderness in Clov's nature perhaps owes something to an unconscious association with Miranda, Caliban's grudging anger and spite are more usually apparent. Clov performs

Caliban's tasks. Hamm cannot live without him as Prospero could not avoid using Caliban:

> But, as 'tis
> We cannot miss him; he does make our fire,
> Fetch in our wood; and serves in offices
> That profit us.[40]

Hamm secures Clov's obedience by withholding the combination of the larder which is the ostensible reason why Clov doesn't kill him. He always obeys Hamm's whistle, a more obvious but no less effective means of command than the mysteries with which Prospero surrounds himself, coming at once from the kitchen to peer through the windows, push the chair or unbottle Nagg and Nell. Also like Caliban, Clov has suffered the inadequacies of education. Hamm and Prospero share a zeal for instruction: as the latter expresses himself to Caliban:

> I pitied thee,
> Took pains to make thee speak, taught thee each hour
> One thing or other, when thou didst not, savage,
> Know thine own meaning, but wouldst gabble like
> A thing most brutish, I endowed thy purposes
> With words that made them known.[41]

An admirable intention, prompted by fine sentiments; but the rational attempt to extend learning falters in both cases, either through circumstance (with Clov) or inherent opposition from the pupil (with Caliban). And common to both is a particular failure in the area of language. Neither Caliban nor Clov find that meaning in language which apparently satisfies their masters. Yesterday, to Clov, is that bloody awful day before today, but these concepts of time—days, weeks or years—have lost their essential meaning. As definitions of temporal experience in infinity they convey nothing to him, but without an alternative he is compelled to employ them when they appear in the conversation: 'I use the words you taught me. If they don't mean anything any more, teach me others, or let me be silent.' And so Caliban: for him language does not define the universe into intelligible units but disintegrates the original oneness of the island as it was before Prospero's intrusion. To Caliban Prospero is one of those self-assured bringers of light who introduce darkness into the mind, like the honest or outraged citizens who gave the hero of the trilogy those 'courses on love, on intelligence, most precious,...They also taught me to count and even to reason.'[42] In Prospero's opinion the island, before his arrival, was in a state of cruel anarchy, but if there was confusion it went unperceived by Caliban. Prospero has removed his innocent ignorance and replaced it with the rudimentary incoherence of thought; a dubious benefit as were the courses which the hero received. The Unnamable places the conflict in its true perspective: 'Some of this rubbish has come in handy on occasions, I don't deny it, on occasions which would never have arisen if they had left me in peace'.[43] Language does not explain Caliban's purposes to him; above all words do not make him 'know thy own meaning.' In his rethinking of the original text, therefore, Beckett takes exception to Prospero's suggestion—made to both Miranda and Caliban—that with his assistance they can come to know themselves. As Caliban replies to the already quoted speech of Prospero:

> You taught me language; and my profit on't
> is, I know how to curse; the red plague rid you
> For learning me your language.[44]

Hamm, Clov, Nagg and Nell also benefit from the ability to use language as a curse, against one another, God ('The bastard') and the indifferent universe. To Hamm, Nagg is the 'accursed progenitor... accursed fornicator,' the hated and unforgiven arbitrary author of his existence:

> HAMM: Scoundrel! Why did you engender me?
> NAGG: I didn't know.
> HAMM: What? What didn't you know?
> NAGG: That it'd be you.

Generation incriminates against generation, often punishing one another with inhuman treatment that is expressed in phrases of great brutality and ugliness. 'Have you bottled her?' Hamm asks Clov of his mother in the dustbin: 'Are they both bottled?' And when Nagg and Nell's conversation becomes tedious: 'Clear away this muck.' Hamm is suddenly afraid he has not made Clov suffer enough, and when Nell appears to die there is no grief ('Go and see if she's dead./Looks like it.') An individual death, normally a theatrical climax, is lost in the universal decay where one death more signifies nothing. Tears are for the living—as in *Lear*: 'We came crying hither...the first time that we smell the air we wail and cry.'[45] The inhumanity and curses of *Endgame* are one aspect of the hatred for life which the play expresses, a result of human outrage over the inescapable fact of decay and death. As we shall see when Hamm argues the case against life in his curtain speech, all this might have been prevented had the first generation been more responsible.

But Hamm's is not the only cruel nature although he curses more frequently than the others. When, as a child at night, Hamm cried out in the dark for someone to recognize him, Nagg and Nell moved out of earshot and continued to sleep. The father was cruel before the son and hopes again for an opportunity to ignore Hamm when the latter needs him. He receives, and takes, this chance when it occurs at the end of the play. This conflict between generations (an adjunct to the class struggle in the pattern of contemporary history) introduces one further consideration which it is perhaps permissible to treat here. The hatred felt by the survivors for their accursed progenitors has its parallel in history. Nagg and Nell recall a time when they once rode a tandem together, the summit of harmony achieved between man and his bicycle:

> NAGG: Do you remember?
> NELL: No.
> NAGG: When we crashed on our tandem and lost our shanks.
> (*They laugh heartily*)
> NELL: It was in the Ardennes.
> (*They laugh less heartily*)
> NAGG: On the road to Sedan.

Beckett is usually explicit. Why Sedan, unless one recalls Napoleon III's defeat there in 1870, when European history was abruptly diverted and plunged, uncontrolled ('Lost our shanks') towards totalitarianism and nuclear destruction? Nagg and Nell who linger on only in the extent of their memories, unable to adapt themselves to changing circumstances, did not know they would engender the unfeeling generation of Hamm who destroys life without care for human loss and whose power, though now proscribed, still dominates Clov. This interpretation of the play as a historical fable reviewed from after the holocaust is too slender a notion for Beckett to stress, but it seems not improbable to suggest that the inescapable process which it describes is assisted, perhaps unconsciously, by an idea of historical determinism.

Hamm as director of the action is in the position of Apollinaire's Tiresias:

> His universe is the play
> Within which he is God the creator.[46]

He is the hammer who beats Clov (fr. clou) Nagg (Ger. Nagel) and Nell (Eng. Nail) and, like Pozzo, he exercises a feudal authority. He speaks of his domains and his paupers, dispenses the victuals and was, when a living world existed, court of appeal for those in his region. In his story Hamm forces the man who comes begging for food to take back to his dying son, down on to his knees and keeps him there in supplication while he lectures him, refusing, though his granaries are full of corn, to commit himself to a positive answer. That was in the past, however. Now Hamm's tyranny is limited to the stuffed dog which gives a less troublesome response than the human ('is he gazing at me?...imploring me') or to Clov. Like Vladimir and Estragon they complement one another, Hamm confined to his chair unable to stand and Clov always in motion unable to sit. As Hamm says: 'Everyone his speciality'. They are incompatible yet condemned by the unpitying bond which holds them together, to torment and suffer. They loved one another 'once', they say, but Clov will not touch Hamm's hand in farewell and when Hamm asks him for 'A few words...to ponder... in my heart,' as a token of their friendship Clov speaks to himself. Hamm tells Clov to go or to kill him but Clov cannot, and Clov threatens to leave, is told he may leave, but does not; they are inseparable:

> HAMM: Why do you stay with me?
> CLOV: Why do you keep me?
> HAMM: There's no one else.
> CLOV: There's nowhere else.

The finality of these two replies, however, leaves the foundation of their relationship unexplained. Why, for example, does Clov always obey Hamm? There seems no reason why he should not live beside his blind master and neglect his duties with impunity. The answer to this question provides a solution which reconciles the conflict between the need for an Other and the hatred of his presence in Beckett's work as a whole. When Clov asks Hamm to explain for him the nature of his continuing loyalty, the reply seems, in the situation to be obviously ironic: 'perhaps it's compassion. (Pause). A kind of great compassion.' But Clov doesn't query the word. Like Beckett's first hero, Belacqua, who shed no tears for the young girl run down by a bus and instead devoted his pity to 'the nameless multitude of the current quick',[47] Hamm is referring to the inhuman compassion of human solidarity which concerns itself with all who are born into the suffering of being, not to the individual who, like Lady Pedal in the last scene of *Malone Dies*, comes between the witness and her pain and belittles the universal reality of which she is only a part.

Nagg and Nell are also bound to one another, though in their case the bond is memory. 'Ah yesterday,' Nell repeats elegiacally, anticipating

Winnie's refrain in *Happy Days*. While Nagg is telling the old Vaudeville standby of the Jewish tailor and a pair of trousers, Nell has returned in time to the day after their engagement when they went rowing on Lake Como. Like the Proustian moment: 'It was deep, deep. And you could see down to the bottom. So white. So clean.' In the present, however, they are limited to Malone's bodily fundamentals and both of them concentrate on the vulgarity of the physical, Nell on what remains of erotic habit, Nagg on his stomach. 'What is it my pet?...Time for Love?' are Nell's first words as, straining over the rims of their dustbins, they attempt to bring their lips together. It is horribly comic, according with Nell's own comments that repeat the substance of Arsene's definition of laughter in *Watt*:

> Nothing is funnier than unhappiness, I grant you that...Yes, yes, it's the most comical thing in the world. And we laugh, we laugh, with a will, in the beginning. But it's always the same thing. Yes, it's like the funny story we have heard too often, we still find it funny but we don't laugh any more.

Nell explains the effect which *Endgame* has on an audience. Just as at the beginning of the play Clov guffaws briefly at each of the figures which he undrapes, and later agrees with Hamm that they can no longer laugh 'at this farce from day to day', so the spectator is tricked into an emotional response that suddenly ends in silence—there is nothing there to laugh at.

The small sensuous adjustments Nagg and Nell introduce into their lives cushion them against reality. Pleasure is to be gained from scratching oneself on the rim of the dustbin or by retreating into memory, the waste ground of habit, rather than by contemplating their present dissolution. Hamm and Clov also practise a form of complicity with their surroundings in which they seek to avert their sufferings. Clov's determination to find a purpose which doesn't exist is expressed each time he tells Hamm 'I'll leave you, I have things to do.' Then he retreats into his kitchen where he stares at the wall. Hamm, who knows there is nothing to be done, mocks him: 'What do you see on your wall?...Naked bodies?'[48] And Clov admits it is empty; he only watches himself die. When they are both dead his ruthless dream of order will be realized:

> I love order. It's my dream. A world where all would be silent and still and each thing in its last place, under the dust.

Then there will be no more picking up and putting down, servitude will be over, the impossible heap completed.

Hamm's complicity is more involved than that of his companions. In his case the association of guilt and responsibility, blindness and suffering, leads to a response which is fundamentally tragic. It is implied but never clearly stated that the characters helped themselves into their present situation. When all about the sound was of a world collapsing their crooked thinking allowed Hamm to take satisfaction in the extinction of the surrounding country ('I inquired about the situation at Kov, beyond the gulf. Not a sinner. Good.') and refuse help to those who came to him for sanctuary, on the principle that 'You're on earth, there's no cure for that.' But his is not the tragedy of hubris (though Hamm is proud). There was not a single mistake made by a great nature in a moment of divided consciousness, as in *Macbeth* or *King Lear*, from which all that follows takes its course. In *Endgame* as in Job or Aeschylus, the tragedy was inevitable: connected to the mechanism of fate a world disintegrates and Hamm is committed to follow: the action precludes free will. From this situation, it is sometimes argued, there cannot be tragedy, only the gloomy pathos of man as victim (or a helpless pawn which the universe engages in chess. If, as science has proved, the world will end and time cancel out every trace of human significance, then we are, in fact, a meaningless game to pass the time. This is the action of fate, stripped of religious mystery, that *Endgame* presents). But man is free either to acquiesce and condone the power that crushes him or to rebel and live in the complete knowledge of his condition. If, like Job, he resists then the situation is tragic; Beckett's heroes, aware via Geulincx and the crawling slave, of the negative possibilities of freedom, usually attempt to live in ignorance induced by habit. Troy may burn and Paradise is lost while Belacqua sits dreaming beneath his rock; as Clov says, 'The universe is extinguished though I never saw it lit.'

Hamm too has attempted to lose himself in habit. He escapes into dreams of love-making in the woods (when there were woods); attaches himself to the old questions ('I love the old questions (*with fervour*) Ah the old questions, the old answers, there's nothing like them!'); and now that the end has almost come he fears the change it will introduce: 'And yet I hesitate to end.' But there are moments when he cannot sustain his complicity and in these intervals when habit fails Hamm is thrust unwillingly into tragic awareness where he sees the truth of what he has desperately been trying to ignore. His story, 'my chronicle' he calls it, is a fictionalized autobiography like Beckett's own novels, in which he flatters his egotism and puts forward his biased version of the collapse into zero. It is designed to affirm his innocence in the face of the guilt he evidently feels towards his conduct at that time. Occasionally this guilt escapes him: 'All those I might have helped,' he murmurs, and then turns to Clov to confirm him in his deceit. 'I was never there,' he insists. 'Absent, always. It all happened without me. I don't know what happened.' Clov's reply, however, punctures this feeble alibi:

> When old Mother Pegg asked you for oil for her lamp and you told her to get out to hell, you knew what was happening then, no?

Hamm's life is an exhausting endeavour to maintain a balance between knowledge and suffering on the one hand and habit on the other, and when he fails, as here, he is exposed to the merciless vision of tragedy. Job's confrontation with God repeats an angry, 'Why?' 'Why am I so punished?' Hamm, at his most lucid, demands to know (anguished) 'What's happening?' It is then that he questions the presence of decay and death in the world.

This second confrontation, of man with time, is at the centre of the tragic experience. The conflict between time, which is indifferently engaged in the destruction of the living world, and man, who looks for meaning in this reasonless dissolution, introduces 'the anguish of the marrow/The ague of the skeleton,'[49] that thirst within the individual for his personal immortality or, as Unamuno insisted in the preposition which he took from Spinoza and set at the beginning of *The Tragic Sense of Life*, the endeavour of everything in so far as it is in itself, to persist in its own being. And now the individual complaint which Hamlet directed against nature beside Ophelia's grave, the inevitable return of the living to dust, has been transformed by science into the certainty of an eventual end to the universe in time. 'A time will come' Leopardi wrote in *The Song of the Wild Cock*:

> when this universe and nature itself will be extinguished...Of the entire world and of the vicissitudes and calamities of all created things there will remain not a single trace, but a naked silence and a most profound stillness will fill the immensity of space. And so before ever it has been uttered or understood, this admirable and fearful secret of universal existence will be obliterated and lost.

It is an unpleasant truth which the mind contrives to ignore. What the eye sees as vital and healthy is only a covering for ashes and decay. 'I once knew a madman,' Hamm says to Clov:

> who thought the end of the world had come. He was a painter—and engraver. I had a great fondness for him. I used to go and see him, in

> the asylum. I'd take him by the hand and drag him to the window. Look! There! All that rising corn! And there! Look! The sails of the herring fleet! All that loveliness. (*Pause.*) He'd snatch away his hand and go back into his corner. Appalled. All he had seen was ashes.

In *Endgame* which begins in the silent world of Leopardi's poem, man's anguish before death is presented even more powerfully than in *Hamlet* or Webster. Despair and outrage combine to emphasize this sense of mortality at the expense of Beckett's usual concern with the imprisoned Self, and the result is a complex pattern of related phrases and memories, united in theme and imagery, which create a vision of the end of the world. The universe outside the sealed rotunda is crumbling away as in the reductive process of a chess game; those inside are left staring into the terrifying abyss of unmeaning, compelled, in spite of their declared indifference, to undertake the tragic search for a purpose to justify their existence in the oncoming void. This attempt, which is Beckett's not Hamm's, to descend with complete lucidity into a knowledge of absolute human insignificance, in the hope that some shred of meaning which is not illusion, will be found there, is our next, and last, concern.

When asked to describe in one word, what everything is, Clov replies, 'Corpsed.' We hear of individual deaths, like Mother Pegg's, and particular instances of sterility, like Clov's seeds which will not grow. Nagg loses a tooth: it is part of the long decline into old age ('But we breathe, we change! We lose our hair, our teeth! Our bloom! Our ideals!'), one of the minute adjustments within decay which alone shows that something is taking its course: 'We too were bonny—once. It's a rare thing not to have been bonny—once.' This is the expectation of everything in time, and Hamm, who has already experienced it, takes a grim relish in describing to Clov what he must shortly endure. One day he will go blind, another day he will be paralysed, and then, one day when he wakes up from a little sleep, he will find himself as Hamm is now:

> Infinite emptiness will be all around you, all the resurrected dead of all the ages wouldn't fill it, and there you'll be like a little bit of grit in the middle of the steppe.

Hamm is, in fact, using Clov as a pretext to describe his own condition. This is the agony of the man who is condemned to wait on the ledge before Paradise throughout eternity. Unlike Belacqua in the shadow of his rock, who could see the heavens revolving with a purpose and therefore was content to dream in the secure knowledge of a prescribed end to his exile from God, Hamm cannot anticipate his release from time. In his world the moments move so slowly that astral time, the sun, moon, stars, seasons, are all compounded in the same, general colourlessness. The world seen from the window is unchanging: the waves are 'lead' the sun 'zero' and the landscape a 'light black. From pole to pole'—or, as it is not included in the logical inconsistencies which obstruct man, at the end of the series, 'zero...zero...and zero.' Hamm asks Clov if there is anything on the horizon. 'What in God's name could there be on the horizon?' he answers with exasperation. God is not there and where He is not there is nothing. The logic is traditional. Hence when they pray it must be in silence. Hamm insists on this propriety to that which is not, who is perhaps without, a part of the greater silence from which they are eternally excluded.

If life is as it appears to Hamm then its existence is intolerable and ought not to be permitted. Hamm, more extreme than Ivan Karamazov, returns the ticket of life, not the ticket to heaven. He has no pity for suffering humanity or rather his pity, like his compassion, is taken to a logical extreme where the individual has no place and the conclusion is extinction. To feed the dying is to encourage life to continue. Therefore Hamm tells the man who comes begging assistance for his child.

> ...you want him to bloom while you are withering...He doesn't realize, all he knows is hunger, and cold, and death to crown it all. But you! You ought to know what the earth is like, nowadays, Oh, I put before him his responsibilities.

This denial of life is quite within the remorseless dialectic which Hamm opposes to his situation: the complete negation of meaning. Until now Beckett's work has always presupposed the possibility of meaning, though its extent and sense remains in doubt. Although traditional categories and values are dismissed in a ruthless extermination of illusion, the intention remains to elicit something from nothing. In *Godot*, for example, the tramps are as far removed from conventional nihilism as it is possible to be. Their waiting, in opposition to all the evidence, is for a meaning to be discovered to them, and when they are undeceived in one assumption they adopt another and continue the search. But in *Endgame* the characters are terrified of finding this 'admirable and fearful secret' of which Leopardi wrote. So near at last to being timeless they have abandoned the concept of their own significance as the final possible illusion which can come between them and the surrounding nothing. 'We're not beginning to...to...mean something?' Hamm asks with concern; if they do mean something it must be in relation to something outside themselves for their own gratuitous impotence is self-evident. This reappearance of meaning is their constant fear: they cannot endure to start again now that they are almost 'beyond knowing'. Therefore when Clov discovers a flea in his trousers it must be destroyed. For, if it is 'Laying' and not 'Lying' doggo, as Clov mistakenly asserts in his fumbling use of language which forces the latter into a somersault of meaning that restores the threat of renewed life, then 'We'd be bitched.' For, 'humanity might start from there all over again,' in which case Hamm's attempt to eradicate the illusion of meaning would be a failure. A rational being might evolve who would start interpreting what he saw like the audience ('Wouldn't he be liable to get ideas into his head if he observed us long enough?'). Then, as Hamm says, with ferocious irony, 'perhaps it won't all have been for nothing.'

Thus, when the boy appears ('A potential procreator') Hamm is lost. The inexplicable introduction—from where?—of life into a dead universe restores the possibility of meaning and therefore the need for its discovery. Meaninglessness as Hamm attempted it is impossible so long as oblivion, which empties life of significance, continues to be obscured by new life that demands an explanation. *Endgame* reverts at the end to the reasonable percentage of the two thieves. There is nothing or something and man's suffering intellect is denied knowledge of either. Where it differs from Beckett's previous work is in the desperation with which the situation is presented. At the final curtain Hamm is left with nothing to do but wait for whatever it is to take its course. 'The end is in the beginning and yet you go on.' Life takes place in this 'and yet' where Hamm, his furious despair replaced by resignation, resumes the game he lost by being born.

4. ALL THAT FALL

Beckett's preoccupation with a Self made from language leads him naturally to the dimension of radio. The survivor of the trilogy, bereft of his body and alone in the void, is only certain of his own continuing reality through the words he speaks and his need to speak. 'I'm in words, made of words, other's words,' says the Unnamable. Man is man by virtue of thought—i.e. speech: so long as man is, words are. This is what the radio play demonstrates. The author creates both the physical reality of a character and the universe about him with nothing but words and sounds. Old Mrs Rooney, Mr Slocum and his car, the sheep in the fields and the ditch which separates them from the road are all in the words that spill from the loudspeaker into the silence where they vanish: 'this dust of words.' 'What way am I facing?' asks blind Dan Rooney: 'You have turned aside and are bowed down over the ditch,' replies his wife. Ditch and figures are suddenly there, but only until a voice resumes and another reality is momentarily present.

However, the power of words to build up an illusory world which the listener might come to identify as actual is so great that this drama must always warn against itself. When even the silence can become populated ('Do not imagine, because I am silent, that I am not present, and alive, to all that is going on,' says Mrs Rooney, after others have been conversing around her) there is always a danger that the provisional nature of this existence in time will be forgotten. Words which can create an aural landscape including Foxrock station and Leopardstown racecourse in Broadcasting House threaten to endow nothing with more than the appearance of something. Therefore Mrs Rooney is made to comment on her nature as a composition of the words of another, namely Beckett himself. The latter deliberately allows her to speak outside her character and prompts her to notice the inconsistency:

> Do you not find anything...bizarre about my way of speaking. (*Pause.*) I do not mean the voice. (*Pause.*) No, I mean the words. (*Pause. More to herself.*) I use none but the simplest words, I hope, and yet I sometimes find my way of speaking very...bizarre.

Yet, in another sense, the Nothing has never been more apparent than in this construction of words for radio. Whatever the period of time described by fiction the whole is reclaimable when the end is reached merely by turning back to the first words, read often days, maybe weeks, before. They have remained as they were, in print on the page. Even in the theatre minutes of silence are filled by action or, when the stage is deserted, by the scene itself. But these words and sounds which orchestrate Mrs Rooney's journey to the station one Saturday afternoon in June (for once the time is specific); her tiring wait for the twelve-thirty down from the city which is delayed; and finally the long trudge home guiding her blind husband along the road neither he nor we can see without her, appear out of silence, translate themselves, on an instant, into time and then, expended, die. And from the silence into which they go there is no recall: once formed they are lost, for ever. *All That Fall* is made out of another man's words which summon cartwheels, bicycles, cars and human beings up from the void itself:

> MRS ROONEY: Oh, Mr Tyler, you startled the life out of me stealing up behind me like that like a deer-stalker! Oh!
> MR TYLER (*playfully*): I rang my bell, Mrs Rooney, the moment I sighted you I started tinkling my bell, now don't you deny it.
> MRS ROONEY: Your bell is one thing, Mr Tyler, and you are another.

When he rides away into the silence our ears cannot penetrate or define, Mr Tyler loses his only reality, the reality of a voice, a squeaking brake and a bicycle bumping painfully on a deflated back tyre. So long as Mrs Rooney does not recall him in her conversation he is now enveloped once more in the Nothing from which the words have just taken him. Thus a surprising irony is added to his innocent curse at 'the wet Saturday afternoon of my conception.'

These words in which everything is created only to cease the moment after, reinforce the atmosphere of transience which fills the play. Both the landscape and figures are saturated in the process of death and dying. Among her first words Mrs Rooney asks, with emotion, 'Will it hold up?' and what follows answers her in the negative: the future is decay. The countryside is one where old women, alone in ruinous houses, listen to 'Death and the Maiden' on their gramophones, where the trees are losing their first bloom and the ditches, even in Summer, are filled with rotting leaves 'from last year, and the year before last, and from the year before that again.' Mrs Rooney describes herself as 'just a hysterical old hag I know, destroyed with sorrow and pining and gentility and church-going and fat and rheumatism and childlessness'; Mr Rooney, already blind, looks forward to going deaf and dumb; and their daughter, Minnie, whose death Mrs Rooney remembers in broken sobs, would if she had lived be: 'In her forties now... I don't know, fifty girding up her lovely little loins, getting ready for the change...' that anticipates the end. She hears the same lament from those she meets along the road: from Christie, the carter of dung:[50] ('How is your poor wife? No better, Ma'am. Your daughter then? No worse.'); from Mr Tyler, of his daughter: 'They removed everything, you know, the whole...er... bag of tricks. Now I am grandchildless; and from the young boy, Jerry: 'How is your poor father? They took him away, Ma'am. Then you are all alone? Yes, Ma'am.' Those more fortunate are given a quick death without the misery of decay, like the hen which strays in front of Mr Slocum's car:

> MRS ROONEY: Mind the hen. (*Scream of brakes. Squawk of hen.*) Oh, mother, you have squashed her, drive on, drive on!...What a death!

> One minute picking happy at the dung on the road, in the sun, with now and then a dust bath, and then—bang!—all her troubles over. All the laying and the hatching. Just one great squawk and then...peace.

But whether rapid or prolonged this death is certain, the one incontrovertible fact established in the ignorance of birth: 'It is suicide to be abroad. But what is it to be at home, Mr Tyler, what is it to be at home? A lingering dissolution.' Even the non-human is not exempt from the latter. Mr Slocum's car ('All this morning she went like a dream, and now she is dead') and Mr Tyler's bicycle, are both subject to the same inescapable decline which infects the living creature who made and uses them: 'Now if it were the front I should not so much mind. But the back. The back! The chain! The oil! The grease! The hub! The gear! No! It is too much!'

The pattern of words and imagery on which *All That Fall* is composed, is expressed through a language which is itself sterile and embalmed. Avoiding both the brief, painful interjections of the two tramps in *Waiting for Godot* and the unceasing monologue employed by Henry in *Embers* Mrs Rooney speaks in elegant sentences that are capable, as Kenner remarks, of a 'fine rhetorical finesse':[51] 'Let us halt a moment and let this vile dust fall back upon the viler worms.' In a finely ironic passage the characters reveal that they are aware they use an impotent vehicle:

> MR ROONEY: ...Do you know, Maddy, sometimes one would think you were struggling with a dead language.
>
> MRS ROONEY: Yes indeed, Dan, I know full well what you mean, I often have that feeling, it is unspeakably excruciating.
>
> MR ROONEY: I confess I have it sometimes myself, when I happen to overhear what I am saying.
>
> MRS ROONEY: Well, you know, it will be dead in time, just like our own poor dead Gaelic, there is that to be said.

No trace of urgency enters this exchange despite the protestations of concern. The language absorbs its melancholy subject into the poised, unruffled phrases as elsewhere it soothes the misery of decay. *All That Fall* is unique among Beckett's works in that instead of acting as a catalyst, language becomes a palliative to the suffering of being. The tendency of words to create, from their own organic existence, another and disturbing meaning to the one intended by the speaker, is here restricted to the episode in which Mr Slocum helps Mrs Rooney into his car. But even there the sexual significance contained in the sounds and exclamations that accompany their physical exertions, suggest a fulfilment which can never be achieved. It is a sterile departure: 'We're past the age.' However, two issues remain which language cannot subdue or inter.

The first is the death of the child, the terrible pivot on which the whole play turns. Despite several inquiries made as she waits at the station Mrs Rooney is unable to learn what causes the train to be fifteen minutes late on a thirty-minute run. Therefore, as she and her husband make their way home, she appeals to him for the missing explanation: '...you must know, Dan, of course, you were on it. Whatever happened?...Was it at the terminus? Did you leave on time? Or was it on the line?' But Dan is curiously reluctant to reply ('I have never known anything to happen'), evading an answer either by anger or by telling her his own story of the day's events which is narrated with the same emphasis on effect as, for example, Hamm's narrative, and with the same distortion of fact for the purpose of style. However, at intervals, he interrupts himself to ask his wife 'Did you ever wish to kill a child? (Pause.) Nip some young doom in the bud,' or to confirm the account he is giving her: 'You say nothing? (Pause.) Say something, Maddy. Say you believe me.' His disquiet is so evident that Mrs Rooney wonders if he is not ill—worse than usual that is—but the mystery is not resolved until the last lines, and then not by Dan himself. They are overtaken by Jerry, sent by the station master to give Dan a ball he is supposed to have dropped. At least it looks like a ball but when Mrs Rooney asks him what it is he avoids a direct reply and tries to drag her away from Jerry before she can ask the reason for the delay:

MRS ROONEY: What was it, Jerry?
JERRY: It was a little child, Ma'am.
(*Mrs Rooney groans.*)
MRS ROONEY: What do you mean it was a little child?
JERRY: It was a little child fell out of the carriage, Ma'am. (*Pause.*) On to the line, Ma'am. (*Pause.*) Under the wheels, Ma'am.
Silence.

The effect is complete and shocking. The sudden reality of the child's death erupts into the elegiac complaint the kindly words have been composing, and with a single phrase from Jerry's innocent lips, destroys it. Nothing in what has been previously spoken prepares us for the dreadful words 'under the wheels'. Of course, the question of Dan Rooney's guilt is immediately raised but it is no longer relevant. Was he, as appears likely, lying when he said: 'I had the compartment to myself as usual. At least I hope so, for I made no effort to restrain myself?' Mrs Rooney, by her groan, seems to have anticipated it. Yet no answer is given and nor is one expected: what possible truth of accusation could mitigate this inflexible reality? The child's death is more than the living who are witness to it, and they return the only suitable reply—silence. This is one reality language cannot engulf; as Kenner writes:

> It is too terrible for apothegm, epigram, cadence, or plaint. The dead language with which she (Mrs Rooney) struggles and from which she wrests the satisfactions of eloquence is suddenly defeated by something intransigently alive: a death.[52]

Finally the language is not proof against the author's personal anguish. *All That Fall* is moved by the same anger at the intolerable fact of death which was present in the finer pages of *Watt*. Here Beckett reveals the universal human dimension that strives beneath the rational examination of man in time as it is explored in the other plays: the grudge which the mortal microcosm bears the comparatively immortal macrocosm. The preacher's text from which the title is taken is to Beckett and Mrs Rooney alike, evidently false: 'The Lord upholdeth all that fall and raiseth up all those that be bowed down.' Just after these words are spoken there is a silence and then Mrs Rooney and Dan 'join in wild laughter'. The Lord does not raise up the child who falls beneath the wheels or repeal the gratuitous misery, suffering and death to which all the other characters are condemned. 'Love, that is all I asked, a little love,' says Mrs Rooney, but in this world where each is locked in his own silent despair even a helping hand is beyond call. No one helps another out of sympathy, thanks consist of curses and aid, if it comes, is the result of ulterior calculation:

> MRS ROONEY: Your arm! Any arm! A helping hand! For five seconds! Christ what a planet!
>
> ......
>
> MISS FITT (*resignedly*): Well, I suppose it is the Protestant thing to do.
>
> MRS ROONEY: Pismires do it for one another. (*Pause.*) I have seen slugs do it.

At these moments of rupture Mrs Rooney's cries barely conceal the author's own outrage. A God who conceives such a world in the full consciousness of what he has created must either, in his desire to hear the cries of another, be the most monstrous of tyrants, or else and this seems the more likely as he continues to refrain from extending an upholding hand, he is not there. The sounds of this Saturday afternoon in June belong to an extinguished world falling towards Nothing yet certain, as Mrs Rooney says, not to reach it 'in our lifetime'; and our cries, like the words from the loudspeaker, are uttered to the silence of the cosmos where we wait alone:

> All is still. No living soul in sight. There is no one to ask. The world is feeding. The wind scarcely stirs the leaves and the birds are tired singing. The cows and sheep ruminate in silence. The dogs are hushed and the hens sprawl torpid in the dust. We are alone. There is no one to ask.
>
> Silence.

5. KRAPP'S LAST TAPE

Krapp's Last Tape—again the title brings together dung and time—is the most remarkable monologue in the language. It contains Beckett's last comment to date on that particular aspect of man's relationship with time originally examined in the opening pages of his first book: the ever-changing identity of the Self which is in a constant process of decantation from the future to the past. *Krapp*, Kenner writes, is 'a last bitter parody of those vases celebrated in "Proust", where the lost past is sealed away'.[53] As in the novels Beckett's concern with man's changing identity in time and words leads him to abandon the vulgarity of a dialogue which negates 'the irremediable solitude to which every human being is condemned',[54] and to create a form in which the hero is alone with his unrelated selves once more. To do this in the theatre rather than through the novel he had first to surmount one of the theatre's most stringent limitations; not to be aware of this is to underestimate the extent of Beckett's achievement.

The dramatist has always had to find a solution as to how the form he uses, which takes place in the visible present, can incorporate material from the past. Once drama ceases to rely on the public memory embodied in myth there are only two usual solutions. The first is to open with an exchange between two characters who, in the course of their conversation, inform the audience of what has happened up until the present. This was Ibsen's method, used with such effect in *Rosmersholm* and *John Gabriel Borkman*. The second, more dangerous because it cannot be performed within the terms of the action as can the former, is for one character to separate himself from the action, call another aside and tell him everything. This is what Shakespeare did in *The Tempest* and risked Prospero being thought a bore. Neither of these methods, however, was feasible for Beckett who began with only one character, yet he fashioned a vehicle which manages to combine, not only the background which drama normally requires, but also the Proustian past of an individual in time. Moreover, it gives unprecedented freedom to the dramatic monologue:

> In *Krapp's Last Tape* the soliloquy has found, for the first and probably the last time, a form which combines the immobile mask and the mobile face, mime and speech, monologue and dialogue and offers all their various resources to one performer.[55]

The absolute simplicity introduced by the presence of the tape-recorder which sets the past to dialogue with the present could only be used once: *Krapp* is, and will remain, unique.

There are three Krapps in the play itself though many more are locked away on their spools in the drawer. The first we see. He is an old, sordid, wearish man, dressed in rags and living alone in his den where a single light falls on a table supporting the tape-recorder and a well-thumbed, battered ledger. There are remnants of the clown in his appearance, a white face and a large red nose (and in the banana skin over which he inevitably falls) but he is also still Belacqua 'condemned as always to live again in the dream-reality of the instantaneous present'.[56] For, on the tape-recorder, he has captured the essence of his past, or that part of it he considers worth reliving. On the spools are the selves which are other through the passing of time, speaking in different voices to the figure on stage but unquestionably his ancestor. One, to whom the bodily Krapp is particularly attracted, lived some thirty years ago when he was 'aged' thirty-nine; this is the voice we hear. The latter in its turn recalls 'that young whelp' of a former year whom he finds it hard to believe he really was. Indeed Krapp is none of them. He has become the purely verbal creature on the tapes, the sum of these words caught in the cycles of eternity. The tape-recorder has rendered the Proustian equation obsolete for the past no longer depends for its life on the vagrancies of memory. It is there on the spools, relived by pressing a button, and though the voice may declare 'Here I end,' the tape has only to be rewound to commence again at the same place. The words, once spoken, exist for ever, always in the present and always there; the silence alone, sometimes recorded by mistake, belongs to a separate dimension—the speechless nothing.

Although 'other' than the man we see, the voice on the tape anticipates him in many details. Krapp has three obsessions, drink, sex and bananas (in his hands an evident sexual substitute). On the spool of his thirty-ninth year the voice records that he was, intellectually, 'at the crest...of the wave' though even then needing to warn himself against the number of hours spent on licensed premises, the bananas he eats ('Have just eaten I regret to say three bananas and with difficulty refrained from a fourth') and the time consumed by his 'engrossing sexual life'. However, the misanthropic creature on the tape possesses certain illusions which the Krapp who has now capitulated to the worst of his cravings, laughs at with vehement disgust. There is, for example, the future of his magnum opus and his attempt to describe what he calls 'The vision at last', a vision that seemingly proved false for when the voice begins to describe it Krapp stops the tape:

> clear to me at last that the dark I have always struggled to keep under is in reality my most—(Krapp curses, switches off, winds tape forward, switches on again.)

When he comes, at the end of the play, to record his entry for this year, he speaks in a coarse vernacular that contrasts with the polished sentences of the old tape. His intellectual activity is now confined to reading a page of *Effie Briest* a day, imagining himself content with her among the dunes of the Baltic; his happiest moment among the last half million has been to revel in the word 'Spooool!'; and to comment with disinterest on the fate of his book:

> Seventeen copies sold, of which eleven at trade price to free circulating libraries beyond the seas. Getting known. (*Pause.*) One pound six and something, eight I have little doubt.

However, it is not for any of these reasons that Krapp chooses to replay this particular tape. What makes it so remarkable—and *Krapp* itself in the general context of Beckett's work—is its delineation of love, first in the tender description of his mother's death which is poignantly imprisoned on the tape to be recounted at will—'Moments. Her moments, my moments'—and then in a description of physical love between man and woman. This latter passage, which Krapp calls his 'Farewell to love,' describes an experience of human contact which for once is neither a vulgarity nor horribly comic. It is perhaps the one moment in his life which was not an illusion, and where a meaning endures despite the fact that love fails as always to fulfill its promise and annihilate time. Exceptionally, in Beckett's work, this love is not sordid nor condemned as irrational—as in Molloy's affair with Edith—but returns to the 'music, MUSIC, MUSIC' of *Murphy* where Krapp, as Coe suggests, finds a strange peace and stillness in which time quivers on the threshold of oblivion. This is the nearest any of Beckett's characters come to the end they search for, and its memory endures even when the tape runs on into the silence of Nothing:

> She lay stretched out on the floorboards with her hands under her head and her eyes closed. Sun blazing down, bit of a breeze, water nice and lively. I noticed a scratch on her thigh and asked her how she came by it. Picking gooseberries she said. I said again I thought it was hopeless and no good going on and she agreed, without opening her eyes. (*Pause.*) I asked her to look at me and after a few moments—(*Pause*)—after a few moments she did, but the eyes just slits, because of the glare. I bent over her to get them in the shadow and they opened. (*Pause. Low.*) Let me in. (*Pause.*) We drifted in among the flags and stuck. The way they went down, sighing, before the stem! (*Pause.*) I lay down across her with my face in her breasts and my hand on her. We lay there without moving. But under us all moved, and moved us, gently, up and down, and from side to side.

6. EMBERS

Beckett's later works, particularly in the theatre, derive much of their power from a remarkable integration of content and form: to this generality, however, the second radio play, *Embers,* is a puzzling exception. It lacks the sure control of emotion, the absolute command of its medium, and the resonant language which enabled *All That Fall* to develop from a haunting plaint upon decay into a universal statement of man's anguish without God. For once the theme does not seem to have found an adequate vehicle and the structure disintegrates under the too-human cry of loneliness the words are unable to absorb. *All that Fall* remains in art: in *Embers* the chaotic pain of life shows through the artisan's attempt to give it coherence.

As in *Krapp* an old man is heard remembering the past. For most of the play there is only one voice, Henry's, alone with its memories. He is sitting by the sea, at the place where his father took his last fatal swim, talking constantly in a vain endeavour to drown the roaring of the waves. Their sound, it seems, threatens his own longing for extinction with the eternal promise of life. By a startlingly obvious use of the medium it is as if the loudspeaker opens a door on to the interior monologue of another, through which we can hear not only his private thoughts and the fictions into which he distils his personal grief, but also the sounds which accompany them and the voices of the dead speaking to him as they did when alive, in the coils of his memories. Thus when his thoughts require the sound of horses' hooves they are amplified upon the speaker, and when he remembers his life with his wife, Ada, her voice returns to continue the dialogue interrupted by death. For that she has experienced the minor death of the body there is little doubt, though the details in which she betrays her changed dimension are all insignificant: once again the unimportance of an end which is only an illusion is stressed. 'I have lost count of time,' Ada tells Henry, who is still concerned with placing the past in the context of years. She cannot see the beach where Henry is sitting ('is there anyone about?') without his words to describe it; asks after her daughter, Addie, as if there is no longer contact between them; and, when Henry can find nothing more to say to her on this occasion, tells him, 'I think I'll be getting back,' at which she disappears without a sound from the shingle and leaves Henry calling after her into the void where her presence is intangible and as impossible for him to grasp as the silence itself. But though she may be absent she will never reach that final extinction which death pretends to be but is not, while Henry continues to need 'someone who knew me, in the old days,' and tries to satisfy that need in memory.

Henry is mainly concerned to recall his father and Ada, seeking to establish in his mind the communication he failed to achieve with them in life. With the former he is not very successful. He remembers how the conflict between his own introspective nature and his father's healthy vitality reached its climax on the night of the latter's death when he failed to persuade Henry to join him in the evening swim he 'took once too often. You wouldn't know me now,' Henry says to his presence, 'you'd be sorry you ever had me, but you were that already, a washout, that's the last I ever heard from you, a washout.' The antipathy between them was so great that Henry is not surprised when his father doesn't answer. Ada, however, will always talk to him: 'conversation with her, that was something, that's what hell will be like, small chat to the babbling of Lethe about the good old days when we wished we were dead. (Pause.) Price of margarine fifty years ago.' In her company whole episodes are relived, mostly relevant to the child which Henry blames for their failure in marriage—Addie's music lessons, her riding lessons which Henry bitterly resented, and their struggles to have her in the first place. Only once is there a memory of happiness, when Ada's nagging 'dont's' unclasp a Proustian evocation of the first time they made love to a sudden crescendo in the waves upon the shore:

> ADA: Don't wet your boots.
> HENRY: Don't, don't...
> Sea suddenly rough.
> ADA (twenty years earlier, *imploring*): Don't! Don't!
> HENRY (twenty years earlier, *urgent*): Darling!
> ADA (twenty years earlier, *more feebly*): Don't!
> HENRY (twenty years earlier, *exultantly*): Darling!

However, the memory, like the moment itself, does not last: Henry and Ada are no closer now than they were in life. 'You needn't speak,' he pleads with her. 'Just listen. Not even. Be with me.' But this is the impossible demand of one human to another exacted by the solitude in which he is condemned to live. Ada leaves him without understanding and certainly not fulfilling what is at once the most minimal and the most urgent of his needs: the sympathetic presence of another.

To fill this absence Henry falls back upon the old expedient of 'stories, years and years of stories,' in particular one about two men, Bolton and Holloway. In contrast with Hamm's narrative this is not a performance. How the story is told is not important to Henry: what matters is the suffering within himself that makes its creation a necessity. It becomes evident, as we overhear him compose the inadequate words, that they are an attempt to express his own condition beneath an ill-disguised appearance of fiction. Into this tale in which Bolton, 'an old man in great trouble,' calls out his friend and doctor, Holloway, in the middle of an icy winter night, not because he is ill but because he is alone, Henry puts all his own isolation and desire for companionship. He does this with great imaginative sympathy and the ending, where Bolton does not receive the recognition he has longed for throughout the night, is the more painful because it is clearly Henry's loneliness which is the subject:

> Then he suddenly strikes a match, Bolton does, lights a candle, catches it up above his head, walks over and looks Holloway full in the eye... Not a word, just the look, the old blue eye, Holloway: 'If you want a shot say so and let me get the hell out of here.' (*Pause.*) 'We've had all this before, Bolton, don't ask me to go through it again.' (*Pause.*) Bolton: 'Please! (*Pause.*) Please! (*Pause.*) Please, Holloway!' (*Pause.*) Candle smoking and guttering all over the place, lower now, old arm tired, takes it in the other hand and holds it high again, that's it that was always it, night, and the embers cold, and the glim shaking in your old fist, saying, Please! Please! (*Pause.*) Begging. (*Pause.*) Of the poor. (*Pause.*) Ada! (*Pause.*) Father! (*Pause.*) Christ! (*Pause.*)

All Bolton, Henry and Beckett ask is a movement of sympathy in response to a look but this is what Holloway, Ada, and in the last plea, Christ, are unable to give. They turn away in horrified silence from this appeal to what is also their own wretchedness, while the forsaken speaker turns back upon himself and the unrecognized word falls into the gulf between. The play, however, has now ceased to be effective. The uneasy fusion of monologue, narrative and recollective dialogue is shattered by a human reality for which there is no reply. Henry cannot find the language to communicate the incommunicable and he ends in halting pairs of words which seek to dismiss what has just occurred:

> Holloway covers his face, not a sound, white world, bitter cold, ghastly scene, old men, great trouble, no good.

Then he takes out his pocket-book and examines the emptiness of his companionless life: 'All day all night nothing.'

7. HAPPY DAYS

Zeno's impossible heap of finite time now fills the centre of the stage. An otherwise unbroken view of plain and sky is dominated by a mound of scorched grass and earth where Winnie (for the first time, with the exception of Mrs Rooney, the central figure is a woman) is embedded. There she remains throughout the evening, gradually consumed by the time which holds her prisoner. At first her arms are free: the earth only reaches to her waist and she is able to turn slightly in the direction of Willie who, we discover later, lies hidden asleep behind the mound. But in the second act it has risen to her chin and movement is confined to the opening and closing of her eyes. At the start she can still occupy herself with her possessions which are scattered on the ground about her; after the interval even they are beyond her reach and her sole activity is, of course, speech.

Winnie talks unceasingly, about herself, her memories and her situation. As in *Endgame* time has almost mounted to an end and there is no longer a distinction between day and night. The daylight is endless, night will never come. She is roused in the 'morning' by a bell which rings again—a shrill, piercing sound from out of nowhere—when it is 'time' to sleep. In the waking interval she is exposed to a merciless sun against which her decorative beak-handled parasol (Beckett's directions are, as always, explicit) is inadequate protection. Perhaps this is hell itself for where the impossibility of an end has reduced death to insignificance the hero no longer remarks an event that is only a transition into still greater cycles of recurrent time. Winnie speaks of 'this hellish sun...this blaze of hellish light,' and her state, more terrible than the dead world of *Endgame* because it is further along the impossible series and therefore more limited and futile, appears as the visual presentation of an isolated corner of Dante's Inferno. Like the Violent against God, Nature and Art she is confined to a burning desert under a rain of perpetual fire, visible first from waist to head like the Heretics in their burning tombs, and then from forehead to neck like the Traitors Dante saw in the Lake of Cocytus.

However, the most terrible aspect of Winnie's condition is her happiness itself. Because it contrasts so strangely with what we actually see, her refrain 'Ah, Happy Days!' is at first gently amusing, but unlike the clown who perseveres in the knowledge of inevitable failure, Winnie achieves 'happiness' through resignation and not in spite of her condition. Her optimism, 'our pernicious and incurable optimism' Beckett calls it in *Proust*, is not courage nor a virtue: it is her way of joining the situation and reducing its imponderables to a palatable dimension 'in the haze of our smug will to live'.[57] The earlier heroes placed a value on suffering. They connected it with the Paradise that had been lost at birth and sought, like Clov, 'to suffer more,' for in those moments when the mortal microcosm is open to the suffering of being it is most deeply aware of its existence and perhaps closer to the hidden reality of the Self. But Winnie, like Pozzo who surrounded himself with an elaborate social web, favours complicity with the universe that punishes her and blinds herself to reality: 'How can one better magnify the Almighty,' she asks, 'than by sniggering with him at his little jokes, particularly the poorer ones?' The torment of the search is over. Winnie is content with any truth, words or occupation so long as they do not disturb her happiness. As she excuses herself:

> One does it all. (*Pause.*) All one can. (*Pause.*) 'Tis only human. (*Pause.*) Human Nature...Human weakness...Natural weakness...

The ensuing sterility is a grimmer experience to witness than the lingering dissolution of *Endgame* or *Godot*. This world too is filled with cries. Winnie hears them about and within her but, as Vladimir said, 'Habit is a great deadener.' Winnie embodies the dialectic of habit which Beckett first described in *Proust*, that sprawling compromise effected between both the individual and the world and the individual and himself—'the guarantee of a dull inviolability'.[58] Her indifference is impregnable. The day begins with a prayer of thanksgiving (her speech is filled with half-remembered hymns and Biblical texts: 'Oh, I know it does not follow when two are gathered together...Lift up your eyes to me, Willie'), and from then until she sleeps again everything is 'wonderful.' She amuses herself with her story, about a girl, her doll and a mouse; reads the inscription on her toothbrush which takes up the major part of the first act; succeeds in learning the definition of 'Hog' (thanks to Willie), at which she remarks with satisfaction that 'not a day goes by...without some addition to one's knowledge however trifling;' and has at her disposal the bag containing her possessions. The latter reveals the small shifts of diversion and content with which the creature of habit can be satisfied. The bag alone bears looking at, from the front, sideways or back to front, and, as with Malone, her love for the 'little portable things' which remain to her, amounts to an obsession. With these remnants of her femininity, the lipstick, mirror, nail-file, brush and comb, habit subjugates eternity itself. Just as the condemned man buttons his trousers before leaving his cell, so Winnie combs her hair and reddens her lips, cleans her spectacles and arranges her hat while all around the universe is falling into Nothing. In fact, the only time her composure is disturbed is by an omission in her routine toilet; otherwise she can accommodate herself to the most painful realities: 'The heat is much greater. (Pause.) The perspiration much less. (Pause.) That is what I find so wonderful. (Pause.) The way man adapts himself. (Pause.) To changing conditions.' The irony is, of course, deliberate and in this instance crushing. Observing the speaker 'stuck up to her diddies in the bleeding ground' and then appreciating the disparity between her words and her condition, one feels that Beckett, like Proust, has little regard for man's much lauded adaptability. The countless treaties in which the individual subject adjusts itself to the universal object do not, in their view, make all best in the best of possible words—nor as Winnie incants, is it 'Wonderful'.

Like Hamm Winnie takes pleasure in the old words and succumbs to the temptation which, since Watt, the hero has resisted, the desire to make them into a pillow for the head. The hero of the novels mocked his incomplete and useless learning and sought, like Dante's damned 'the stark death of knowledge in us,' but Winnie clings to the relics of her previous reading for there the content, like the forgotten author, has been refined out of existence. Nothing remains to disturb her intellectual composure. 'What is that unforgettable line?' she asks herself with equanimity, and later:

> What are those exquisite lines? (*Pause.*) Go forget me why should something o'er that something shadow fling...(*Pause. With a sigh.*) One loses one's classics. (*Pause.*) Oh not all. (*Pause.*) A part. (*Pause.*) A part remains. (*Pause.*) That is what I find so wonderful, a part remains, of one's classics, to help one through the day.

As here Winnie often employs the old units of time that have lost their meaning in the context of eternity. When one is waiting, as she is, for 'the happy day to come when flesh melts at so many degrees and the night of the moon has so many hundred hours,' the concepts whereby man places himself in time and space and satisfies the demands of cognition, have all collapsed. But, unlike Malone for whom the prospect of a morning awaited in vain was intolerable, or the Unnamable who needed to rediscover some movement of objective time, Winnie continues to use these empty terms for she cannot imagine an alternative to this dead language which operates spontaneously. She remembers them with affection, reserves a special smile for their use—'At the end of the day. (Smile.) To speak in the old style. (Pause.) The sweet old style. (Smile off.)'—and is not even concerned when they and the other overworked expressions she relies upon, suddenly fail her. This is perhaps the most complete evidence of the degree of complicity and indifference which she has achieved. For the tramps in *Godot* the lapse into silence and the longing for night to come was the source of their deepest anguish; but Winnie has buried the terror of Nothing within routine as certainly as she herself is immersed in the heap of time:

> words fail, there are times when even they fail...What is one to do then, until they come again? Brush and comb the hair, if it has not been done, or if there is some doubt, trim the nails if they are in need of trimming, these things tide one over.

It is this accurate reflection of normal human expediency before life itself, expressed in the sterility of worn cliché and habitude, that explains the peculiar, irksome depression this play arouses. On this occasion Beckett explores the anguish of man in time, unable to end, in an image built out of man's daily capitulation to habit in the ordinary affairs of life. Out of the exceptional image and situation set up upon the stage and which commands our first attention there emerges this secondary theme, a realistic portrait of man's mundane, everyday complicity. It is Winnie's routine gestures and pat phrases that provide a foundation for the vast image of infinity. They enable Beckett to control the enormous tracts of time we are asked to consider, and when Winnie adjusts herself to her condition with glib sophistication or by exclaiming 'Thank heaven for small mercies' it is ourselves we recognize evading reality. Hence our guilt and our discomfort: her complicity is our own.

However, to sustain the dull inviolability of her world, Winnie is bound to consider one necessity over which habit has no control. As in all Beckett's later works the problems of identity, perception and companionship are among the most important raised in this play. Not only is Winnie convinced of the existence of a benevolent overseer who regulates the sun which burns her and the bell which rings ('Someone is looking at me still. (Pause.) Caring for me still. (Pause.) That is what I find so wonderful. (Pause.) Eyes on my eyes.'); she also has, and needs, Willie. His indifference, if it is possible, is greater than Winnie's. Helplessly infirm he passes the entire play, apart from the last moments, behind the mound; his grey, pustule-covered head alone occasionally visible. There he sleeps, reads his newspaper or looks at his collection of pornographic postcards which he prefers to the 'sadness after song' of sex. Winnie's remarks are all addressed to his silent back and she often encourages him to 'come round this side... and let me feast on you.' But whether they were ever truly in love is uncertain: Winnie herself is dubious. Like the earlier heroes, with the exception of Krapp and perhaps Murphy, she is unable to decide if what she herself has experienced is the same as what she knows to have been so highly praised in speech and print. And when at last Willie does move towards her, grotesquely swaying and crawling up the side of the mound in a top hat and morning suit, his hand stretched out towards her and a gleam of desire in his eye, she turns the vitriolic tongue of outraged femininity on him.

But Willie's presence is more important to Winnie than his love. He only speaks to her directly on two occasions, once at the end to weakly say her name as he used to say it when they were first married, and once to define the word 'Hog', perhaps applying it to his own role as husband: 'Castrated male swine reared for slaughter.' Otherwise for long stretches of the play he is so silent that Winnie wonders if he might not be dead. This last, however, she usually considers unlikely, even impossible, for though he need not speak to her he must be there to hear: 'I used to think that I would learn to talk alone...but no...Ergo you are there.' She cannot conceive of a situation in which she, whose person is made of the words she speaks, could exist if there were no one nearby to know she is speaking, and therefore to recognize her presence. It does not matter to her whether Willie responds to what she says nor if he troubles to turn its ceaseless flow into sense, just so long as he is there and she is happy that she is not in the absurd position of speaking to the deaf void. Even Winnie is aware that were Willie to disappear she would be compelled to acknowledge the infinite nothing:

> So that I may say at all times, even when you do not answer and perhaps hear nothing, something of this is being heard, I am not merely talking to myself, that is in the wilderness, a thing I could never bear to do—for any length of time. (*Pause.*) That is what enables me to go on, go on talking that is. (*Pause.*) Whereas if you were to die—(*Smile*) to speak in the old style (*Smile off*)—or go away and leave me, then what could I do, what could I do, all day long, I mean between the bell for waking and the bell for sleep? (*Pause.*) Simply gaze before me with compressed lips.

The danger is already present that, in the following plays, returns Beckett to the impasse where the trilogy ended. Winnie needs Willie as Bom needed Pim, if she is not to discover the terrible, skull-bound isolation of the Unnamable. Moreover this is beyond the control of habit and her anxiety is seen in her constant need to refer herself to him. Willie's presence, which gives her protracted life its only meaning, is hers by providence and might as inexplicably be removed. Therefore when Willie does reply to one of her questions with the single word 'it,' it is with some truth that she replies 'this is going to be a happy day.' She is not yet exposed like her successors, to the impossible situation Beckett wrote of in the *Textes pour rien*.

8. PLAY

In *Play* Beckett is returned to the impasse of *The Unnamable*. His characters are again bound in time on the threshold of an eternity they will never enter, condemned to relive the past (Belacqua's image still persists) in the impossible hope that they will sometime tell that unknown version of their story which will satisfy 'the everlasting third party'—himself probably deceased—and set them free.

The three characters of *Play* present a visual image of Mahood's final stasis. They are fixed in three identical grey urns about one yard high, their necks held fast by the mouth of the urn. Unable to turn their heads they stare into the auditorium throughout the play, their aged faces almost part of the urns, expressionless like their faint, toneless voices. Beckett's directions are explicit for this image of the backward birth by way of a tomb into the life from which man is excluded by the first helpless expulsion into time. He suggests the actors kneel throughout as if they also are to be punished in a ghastly parody of worship, and stresses that the light which provokes them into speech must come from a single spot as best 'expressive of a unique inquisitor.'

The three voices speak their separate versions of a mutual obsession as mechanically as a fugue, each impervious to the presence of the other two. They have no names, simply the designations M, W1 and W2 which aim at anonymity but also stand for all men and women who have, like them, been caught up in a three-part love affair. Joined, in the life now past, as the three corners of love's eternal triangle (the emphasis here is on eternal), they are trapped for ever, side by side, condemned to repeat for ever the fragments of their shared past but ignorant that they are still accompanied by the other two figures in their individual recollections. 'To think we were never together' the man remarks during the evening, oblivious to the horrible irony of their perpetual joint imprisonment. If there is a comparison to be made in literature it is with Sartre's *Huis Clos*, but there a man and two women, unknown to each other in life, are brought together to torment one another in death; in *Play* the torment occurred in life and the eternal now at which they have arrived is the lonely anguish of memory without end: 'At the same time I prefer this [in the urn] to...to the other thing [life]. 'Definitely. There are endurable moments.'

The playing out of this familiar situation is one more example of Beckett's breaking down to its essence a much-used convention of literature and then using the residue for his personal preoccupations. The structure of the play demonstrates the movement of finite time within infinity as it was explained in the first pages of *The Unnamable*: vast tracts of time eternally repeated, each cycle beginning and ending at the same words which mark the furthest progress possible along the never-to-be-ended series. The dialogue once spoken repeats itself exactly according to what Beckett called in *Proust*:

> the beautiful convention of 'da capo'...a testimony to the intimate and ineffable nature of an art that is perfectly intelligible and perfectly inexplicable.[59]

When it reaches the same point a second time the words would begin again, but after the first phrase the author mercifully intervenes to impose a temporary halt for which the only purposeful necessity is that, until the next night, the transport facilities of his audience are almost exhausted. Analogy with the 'ineffable' art, music, best describes the effect of *Play*. Although each voice is used as an instrument to follow its own score, picking its way among the débris of memory and allowed to speak its recollections with just so much colour as is compatible with its individual character, their personal and separate timbre combines to orchestrate their mutual theme. Each in itself is only capable of one side of the triangle but, after the tutti opening, the texture is polyphonic, an interweaving of voices that comment on, underline and enlarge the statements of one another in the purity of their individual expression that is unsullied by the vulgarity of intercourse. At the close, the listener, though he has not separated each strand from the others, receives a total impression to which they have all contributed, an appropriate harmony of the dismal affair in which the characters once participated.

The affair was unexceptional. From the moment when the man tried to escape his tired marriage and odious professional commitments by taking a mistress, it followed a course which many more elaborate novels and plays have also described without adding to what is shown here. The wife soon began to 'smell her off him'; there were painful recriminations when the wife accused the man, hired a private detective, threatened to kill herself, and confronted the mistress in an old rambling house reminiscent of *Watt*. (And where the servant is again Erskine, still 'coming and going on the earth, letting people in, showing people out'—the eternal servant. As in *All That Fall* where the Lynch twins are revived, Beckett reminds us that even the minor characters in his early books continue to be.) The man renounced the mistress, was forgiven by the wife who 'suggested a little jaunt to celebrate, to the Riviera or our darling Grand Canary,' and then, predictably, returned to the mistress, this time to elope with her. But once desire was translated into habit, exactly as Beckett described the Proustian analysis of love in his first book, their relationship too, became jaded, and the man concludes his recollections by imagining the two women contentedly drinking tea together, happy with their shared memories he can no longer disturb.

Memory of this old affair provides the structure but not the real purpose of *Play* which is, like *The Unnamable*, to answer the persistent questions, Where now? Who now? When now? Memory is the dialogue of nothingness and in the 'hellish half-light' which provokes speech it is the characters' one resource: they cannot, however, take it seriously. Speaking of his previous life the man remarks: 'I know now, that was all...play', but what then is the meaning of 'all this? And when will this become the same?' All three characters admit that life was senseless yet there appears to be 'no sense in this...either, none whatsoever'; though this does not prevent them from making the 'same mistake as when it was the sun that shone, of looking for sense where possibly there is none.' Thus they are driven to search for whatever it is that keeps them where they are, as always connecting the idea of a punishment with the fact of their suffering. It leads, of course, to the concept of a tormentor from whom they try to learn what it is he wants them to do: 'I can do nothing...for anybody...any more...thank God. So it must be something I have to say. How the mind works still.' And as everything that can be said has already been spoken: 'is it that I do not always tell the truth, is that it, that some day somehow I may tell the truth at last and then no more light at last, for the truth?'

This is again the impossibility with which the Unnamable struggled: the knowledge that to speak is to lie, that it might be better to stare ahead with sightless eyes murmuring babababa into eternity, but that while life exists one must say something which, whatever the words, exclude one from 'the long clear sigh of advent and farewell'.[60] Before the cycle begins again the characters in *Play* echo the repudiation of the doctrine of guilt and suffering adopted by Clov and Malone: 'Penitence, yes at a pinch, atonement, one was always resigned, but no, that does not seem to be the point either.' What consoled one in the life above is no longer possible: resignation cannot outlast eternity, it belongs in that place where death seemed to promise an end, and resignation is necessary if one is to wait patiently, like Belacqua, until suffering has effaced the guilt perhaps introduced at birth. Such an idea, the Unnamable sees from the grey waste to which he passed at death, is an illusion that depends on a certain end. Remove this end as he has been witness to the failure of death (here the characters of *Play* are compelled to agree with him) and it becomes meaningless. There is no cause, no purpose, no tormentor: all is gratuitous and so it will remain. Thus when the mistress asks the familiar questions: 'Is anyone listening to me? Is anyone looking at me? Is anyone bothering about me at all?' it is the wife who has the final word: '...all is falling, all fallen, from the beginning, on empty air. Nothing being asked at all. No one asking me for anything at all.' They are playing, as the novelist tells his stories, a pointless game with unending time of which they are the playthings.

AN END

At the moment of death, the succession of his works is but a collection of his failures. But if those failures all have the same resonance, the creator has managed to repeat the image of his own condition, to make the air echo with the sterile secret he possesses.

CAMUS[1]

IN *Cascando*, the short piece for radio which follows *Play*, there are two voices, the Opener and the story teller. The Opener opens and closes the stories which are told by the low panting Voice, and in this particular work the narrative is about a man named Woburn. Woburn has left the shed in which he lives and is out walking, waiting anxiously for night to fall. He wears the 'same old coat...same old broadbrim... jammed down,' and carries the 'same old stick.' His choice of ways is also familiar, 'right the sea...left the hills,' and so is the landscape of giant aspens across which he stumbles until he falls at last 'face in the mud...arms outstretched' among the dunes. It is, of course, the same old hero of the trilogy, *From an Abandoned Work* and the French short stories whom the Voice has revived after prompting from the Opener. This time, he believes, *will* be the last: when Woburn's story is finished there will be 'no more stories...no more words'. But, the Opener says, what he presents is only 'An image, like any other.' It is one more of the stories on which, in spite of people's incredulity, he has been living...'till I'm old.'

For once, and only once, Beckett's own presence enters directly into his mature work. This is the sole comment he has allowed himself on the nature of the stubborn enterprise he has been engaged in for almost half a century and which is still continuing though it is doubtful if, in the future, he will do more than explore further the situations and pre-occupations that have concerned him in the past. But this is as it should be and in harmony with the description of the artistic process as it was set down in *Proust*—the descent, behind appearances, to the Idea, or, as Beckett has written elsewhere, the meditative result of 'a head abandoned to its ancient solitary resources.' To try and extract some general philosophy from these works is both an impossibility and an affront to the books themselves. They stand as they are, not as tracts but testimony to the integrity and devotion of a vision that has spared itself nothing in the attempt to state what it sees and not what it thinks it ought to see. This is the source of their remarkable unity and also the aesthetic cause of any 'pleasure' one receives from them.

Beckett is frequently arraigned on two charges: that he is a perverse 'messenger of gloom' and that he writes only of the extraordinary in terms of unnecessary complexity. It is not entirely irrelevant to ask why Beckett should be easy, cheerful and reassuring or even, as he did himself in the essay on Joyce, why art should be without difficulty: 'The time is not perhaps all together too green for the vile suggestion that art has nothing to do with clarity, does not dabble in the clear and does not make clear.' The purpose of his art, as he understood it in *Proust*, is not to explain but to contemplate; the will, he stated, is not a condition of the artistic experience. This art does not suppose to solve and make plain but to discover and perhaps to comprehend—by perception and intuition, not by the intelligence. And if the subject of his contemplation withholds a meaning then the duty of this art is not to impose one but to remain in doubt. A resolution is comparable to believing that all is well with the world—which it obviously isn't. Thus the boy in *Endgame* may or may not be a sign of resurrection, Beckett's point is precisely this, he doesn't know and will not presume. He cannot accept either the dogmas of belief or the reasons of science ('The men, women and children of science have as many ways of kneeling to their facts as any other body of illuminati') and denied a certainty he refuses to take any of the irrational leaps into a faith which might tempt him. He refuses, in fact, to commit what Camus called 'philosophical suicide': the attempt to transcend the facts implicit in the only universe he has experience of, by denying the reality of what he perceives with a single leap up to the ultimate it would be convenient to find elsewhere. In Beckett one remains with an ignorance that does not pretend to be otherwise and it is this, easily mistaken for obscurity, that discomforts the reader.

Furthermore, his art cannot be judged irresponsible or idiosyncratic because it does not apparently concern itself with the social or political circumstance of its time. It is precisely because the destructive forces of the twentieth century have given the lie to progress, reason, stability, perfectability and simplicity that Beckett subscribes to none of them and his writing is as it is. Beckett does not write of the hydrogen bomb or of Dachau but he does portray in a unique poetry, and with an even more unique truthfulness the cruelty, suffering and helplessness which is the human climate of a world in which the bomb exists and such events take place. Beckett's art abandons 'the plane of the feasible' where subjects such as these are treated directly and in the inhuman passages in his writing, as when Watt feeds the young rats to their parents or the Unnamable stamps his crutches into the entrails of his dying family, seeks for the essence that precedes them.

Ultimately, however, even these preoccupations are like 'the act of a dying man forced to see his dentist.' The one fundamental behind all of Beckett's work is the ancient tragic knowledge which has been revived by the absurd, of man's solitude, imprisonment and pain in an intolerable universe that is indifferent to his suffering. Beckett is, if in these conditions the word retains a meaning, a pessimist, which is to say he writes what he considers to be true and not what he knows is diverting. This is not a criticism of a right or wrong approach: only a test of where one places the value in life. The world in which Beckett begins to write is without unity, clarity, rationality or hope, and where man, absurdly conscious that he is conscious and bound to die, feels himself alone and a stranger in a place which itself will one day cease to exist. From this confrontation between the unreasonable silence of the universe and the human need to be and to be known, there arises that futile revolt against existence; the anguished rebellion of the spirit against Apollinaris's three necessities, the abject necessity of being born, the hard necessity of living and the sharp necessity of dying, which is constant throughout his work.

It is, moreover, the actual creation of this work which constitutes the final dimension of his revolt. The man who, like Beckett, continues to create despite his awareness of these conditions is, as Camus writes in *The Myth of Sisyphus*, 'the most absurd character'.[2] The conflict between the world's irrationality and man's hopeless desire for unity is most acute in the artist who, having once believed in his near omnipotence is now forced to recognize his almost total impotence. Yet there remains—Beckett is almost alone in recognizing—the right to fail. Creating, or not creating, changes nothing, and the words which are written will remain at best, only a hesitant approximation of those finer words which, if they do exist, continue to elude his need. But if he persists in this endeavour which he knows to be futile he will have sustained his consciousness in the face of the universe and its absurdity. The artist is his own clown. For him too, his perseverance is his dignity and his failure the emblem of his unextinguished revolt. For Beckett it is the writing, not the writer nor the reader, that ultimately matters:

> a cause which, while having need of us to be accomplished, was in its essence anonymous, and would subsist, haunting the minds of men, when its miserable artisans should be no more.

BIBLIOGRAPHY

1. WORKS BY BECKETT

(For a comprehensive bibliography including Beckett's numerous and uncollected translations, reviews, and variants of work in progress, the reader is referred to John Fletcher: 'The Novels of Samuel Beckett' pp. 234-248.
The following is restricted, with a few exceptions, to works discussed in the text).

A. POETRY

Whoroscope. Paris (The Hours Press) 1930. Reprinted in *Poems in English*

Echo's Bones and Other Precipitates. Paris (Europa Press) 1935. Reprinted in *Poems in English*.

Poems in English. London (Calder) 1961.

B. FICTION

More Pricks Than Kicks. London (Chatto and Windus) 1934. 'Dante and the Lobster' reprinted in the *Evergreen Review* Vol. 1, No. 1 (1957); 'Yellow' reprinted in *New World Writing*, No. 10, November 1956.

Murphy. London (Routledge) 1938. Reprinted New York (Grove Press) 1958; London (Calder) 1963. French trans. Paris (Bordas) 1947; (Minuit) 1953.

Watt. (written 1942-44). Paris (Olympia) 1953. Reprinted New York (Grove Press) 1959; London (Calder) 1961.

Molloy. Paris (Minuit) 1951. Translation by Patrick Bowles in collaboration with the author, Paris (Olympia) 1955. Reprinted New York (Grove Press) 1955; and in *Three Novels* (Calder) 1959.

Malone meurt. Paris (Minuit) 1951. Translation, by the author, *Malone Dies*, New York (Grove Press) 1956; London (Calder) 1958, reprinted in *Three Novels* (Calder) 1959.

L'Innomable. Paris (Minuit) 1953. English translation, by the author, *The Unnamable*, New York (Grove Press) 1958; *Three Novels* (Calder) 1959.

Nouvelles et Textes pour Rien. Containing thirteen short texts, dated 1950, and three short stories, dated 1945; 'L'Expulse'; 'Le Calmant'; 'La Fin'. Paris (Minuit) 1955. 'La Fin', translated by Richard Seaver in collaboration with the author as 'The End' (Evergreen Review, Vol. 4, No. 15, 1960, pp. 22-41). 'L'Expulse' translated by Richard Seaver and the author, as 'The Expelled' (*Evergreen Review*, Vol. 6, No. 22, 1962, pp. 8-20); 'Text for Nothing' 1, translation by the author, in *Evergreen Review*, Vol. 3, No. 9, 1959, pp. 21-24.

From an Abandoned Work. (First heard on the B.B.C. Third Programme, 14 December 1957); *Evergreen Review* No. 3 (1957); London (Faber) 1958.

Comment c'est. Paris (Minuit) 1961. English translation, by the author, *How it is*, New York (Grove Press) 1961; London (Calder) 1964.

Imagination Dead Imagine. London (Calder) 1966.

No's Knife, Collected Shorter Prose 1947-1966 (includes English versions of 'Nouvelles et Textes pour Rien', 'From an Abandoned Work'; and three later texts, 'Enough'; Imagination Dead Imagine'; and 'Ping'), London (Calder) 1967.

C. THEATRE

En attendant Godot. (Theatre Babylone, 5 January 1953); Paris (Minuit) 1952. Translation by the author, *Waiting for Godot*, New York (Grove Press) 1954; London (Faber) 1956.

Fin de partie. (Royal Court, London, 3 April 1957). Paris (Minuit) 1957. Translation, *Endgame*, by the author, London (Faber) 1958; New York (Grove Press) 1958.

Acte sans paroles I. (Mime, music by John Beckett; Royal Court, London, 3 April 1957); Paris (Minuit) 1957. Translation, by the author, as *Act Without Words I*, London (Faber) 1958; New York (Grove Press) 1958.

All That Fall. (B.B.C. Third Programme, 13 January 1957). London (Faber) 1957; New York (Grove Press) 1960. French translation by Robert Pinget: *Tous ceux qui tombent*. Paris (Minuit) 1957.

Krapp's Last Tape. (Royal Court, London, 28 October 1958). *Evergreen Review*, No. 5 (1958). London (Faber) 1959; New York (Grove Press) 1960. French translation, by the author, *La Dernière Bande*. Paris (Minuit) 1959.

Embers. (B.B.C. Third Programme, 24 June 1959). London (Faber) 1959; New York (Grove Press) 1960. French translation, by the author and Robert Pinget: *Cendres*. Paris (Minuit) 1959.

Act Without Words II. New York (Grove Press) 1960.

Happy Days. (Cherry Lane Theatre, New York, 17 September 1961). New York (Grove Press) 1961; London (Faber) 1962. French translation, by the author, *Oh les beaux jours*. Paris (Minuit) 1963.

Play. (First performance in German at the Ulmer Theatre, Ulm-Donau, 14 June 1963) London (Faber) 1964.

Words and Music. *Evergreen Review*, No. 27, November 1962, pp. 33-43. London (Faber) 1964.

Cascando. (First broadcast in French on R.T.F. 1963 with music by Marcel Mihalovici), English translation, by the author, in *Evergreen Review* No. 30, May-June 1963, pp. 47-57, and Faber 1964.

Eh Joe. (First televised July 1966 by the B.B.C.), with *Act Without Words II* and *Film* (awarded Tal Prix Filmcritica at the Venice Film Festival in October 1965). Faber 1967.

Come and Go. (Playscript). Calder, 1967.

D. CRITICISM

Dante...Bruno. Vico...Joyce in 'Our Exagmination round his Factification for Incamination of Work in Progress'. Paris (Shakespeare and Co.) 1929; reprinted London (Faber) 1961.

Proust. London (Chatto and Windus) 1931. Reprinted, New York (Grove Press) 1957, London (Calder) 1965.

Three Dialogues. (By Samuel Beckett and Georges Duthuit). *Transition Forty Nine* reprinted, London (Calder) 1965.

E. TRANSLATIONS

Anthology of Mexican Poetry. (Compiled by Octavio Paz). London (Thames and Hudson) 1958.

The Old Tune. (B.B.C. Third Programme, 21 August 1960). Translation of *La Manivelle* by Robert Pinget. *Evergreen Review*, Vol. 5, No. 17, pp. 47-60, March-April 1961.

F. KNOWN UNPUBLISHED WORKS

Dream of Fair to Middling Women—novel in English written *c*.1932.

Premier Amour—short story in French written in conjunction with the three published *Nouvelles* about 1945.

Mercier et Camier—unfinished novel in French, written *c*.1945. (Two extracts, translated by Hugh Kenner and R. Federman have been published in *Spectrum*, Vol. 4, No. 1, pp. 3-11, Winter 1960.)

Eleutheria—play in three acts in French, written *c*.1947-48.

2. CRITICISM (Selected)

Anon: 'Messenger of Gloom: A Profile'. *The Observer*, 9 November 1958.

Anon: 'Paradise of Indignity'. *T.L.S.*, 28 March 1958, p. 168.

Abel, Lionel: 'Joyce the Father, Beckett the Son'. *New Leader* (New York), 14 December 1959.

Anders, Gunther: 'Being without Time: On Beckett's play, "Waiting for Godot" ' in *Samuel Beckett. A collection of critical essays*. Prentice Hall (New York) 1965.

Barbour, Thomas: 'Beckett and Ionesco'. *Hudson Review*, Vol. XI, No. 2 (Summer 1958).

Bowles, Patrick: 'How Samuel Beckett sees the Universe'. *The Listener*, 19 June 1958

Brooke-Rose, Christine: 'Samuel Beckett and the Anti-Novel', *London Magazine*, Vol. V, No. 12, December 1958.

Butler, Michael: 'Anatomy of Despair'. *Encore*, May-June 1961.

Calder, John (Ed.): 'Beckett at Sixty'—a celebratory symposium of reminiscence and criticism for Beckett's birthday, Calder 1967.

Chambers, Ross: 'Samuel Beckett and the Padded Cell', *Meanjin Quarterly* (Melbourne) 1962.

'Beckett's Brinkmanship. *AUMLA 19* (Christchurch N.Z.), May 1963. Reprinted in *Samuel Beckett: A collection of critical essays*, Prentice Hall 1965.

Cmarada, Geraldine: 'Malone Dies: A Round of Consciousness' in *Symposium*, Vol. XIV, No. 3, Fall 1960.

Coe, Richard: *Samuel Beckett*. Oliver and Boyd, London 1964.

Cohn, Ruby: 'A Note on Beckett, Dante and Geulincx'. *Comparative Literature*, No. 12, 1960.

'Samuel Beckett, Self-Translator'. *P.M.L.A.*, December 1961.
'Watt in the Light of "The Castle".' *Comparative Literature,* No. 2, 1961.
Samuel Beckett: The Comic Gamut, Rutgers University Press 1962.
'Philosophical Fragments in the Works of Samuel Beckett'. *Criticism*, Vol. VI, No. 1 (Winter 1964). Reprinted in *Samuel Beckett: A collection of critical essays,* Prentice Hall 1965.

Cruikshank, John (ed.): *The Novelist as Philosopher: studies in French fiction 1935-60.* Oxford 1962. (*Beckett* by Martin Esslin.)

Driver, Tom: 'Beckett by the Madeleine' in *Columbia University Forum*, Vol. 4, No. 3, pp. 21-25, Summer 1961.

Duckworth, Colin: 'The Making of Godot'. *Theatre Research*, Vol. VII, No. 3, 1966.

Ellmann, Richard: *James Joyce*, Oxford 1959.

Esslin, Martin: *The Theatre of the Absurd.*
(Ed.) *Samuel Beckett: A collection of critical essays*, Prentice Hall 1965. (Critical Introduction).

Fletcher, John: *The Novels of Samuel Beckett*, Chatto and Windus 1964.
The Private Pain and the Whey of Words: a survey of Beckett's Verse in Samuel Beckett: a collection of critical essays'. Prentice Hall 1965.
Samuel Beckett as Critic. 'The Listener'.
Samuel Beckett's Art, Chatto and Windus 1967.

Fraser, G. S.; 'Waiting for Godot' in *English Critical Essays, Twentieth Century* (*Second Series*), selected by Derek Hudson. O.U.P. 1958.

Friedman, Melvin: 'The Novels of Samuel Beckett: an amalgam of Joyce and Proust'. *Comparative Literature*, Vol. XLL, No. 1 (Winter 1960).

Gilbert, Stuart (ed.): *Letters of James Joyce*, London 1957.

Gray, Ronald: 'Waiting for Godot: a Christian interpretation'. *The Listener*, 24 January 1957.

Gregory, Horace: 'Prose and Poetry of Samuel Beckett'. *Commonweal LXXI*, No. 5 30 October 1959.
'Beckett's Dying Gladiators'. *Commonweal Vol. LXV.* Reprinted in *Dying Gladiators and Other Essays*, New York (Grove Press) 1961.

Grossvogel, David: *The Self-Conscious Stage in Modern French Drama,* New York (Columbia University Press) 1958.
Four Playwrights and a Postscript: Brecht, Ionesco, Beckett, Genet. Ithaca, New York (Cornell University Press) 1962.

Guggenheim, Peggy: *Out of this Century*, New York (Dial Press) 1946.
Confessions of an Art-Addict, London 1960.

Guicharnaud, Jacques: *Modern French Theatre from Giradoux to Beckett*, Yale University Press 1961.

Harvey, Lawrence: 'Art and the Existential in En attendant Godot'. *P.M.L.A.*, Vol. LXXV, No. 1 (March 1960).

Heppenstall, Rayner: *The Fourfold Tradition*, London 1961.

Hobson, Harold: 'Samuel Beckett, Dramatist of the Year'. *International Theatre Annual* No. 1. (Calder) London 1956.

Hoeffer, Jacqueline: 'Watt'. *Perspective XI*, No. 3, Autumn 1959. Reprinted in *Samuel Beckett: a collection of critical essays*, Prentice Hall 1965.

Hoffmann, Friedrick J.: *Samuel Beckett; the language of Self.* Crosscurrents—Modern Critiques, Southern Illinois University Press, 1962.

Karl, F.: 'Waiting for Beckett: Quest and Request'. *Sewanee Review*, Vol. LXIX, 1961.

Kenner, Hugh: *Samuel Beckett: a critical study*, New York 1961, London (Calder) 1962.
'The Beckett Landscape'. *Spectrum*, Winter 1958.
'The Cartesian Centaur'. *Perspective XI*, No. 3, Autumn 1959.
Flaubert, Joyce and Beckett: the Stoic Comedians, Boston 1963.

Kern, Edith: 'Drama Stripped for Inaction'. *Yale French Studies No. 14,* Winter 1954-55.
'Moran-Molloy: the hero as author'. *Perspective,* Vol. XI, No. 3, Autumn 1959.

Kott, Jan: *Shakespeare Our Contemporary,* London (Methuen) 1967.

Jacobsen, Josephine (with William R. Mueller): *The Testament of Samuel Beckett,* New York 1964, London 1966.

Leventhal, A. J.: 'The Beckett Hero' in *Samuel Beckett: a collection of critical essays,* Prentice Hall 1965.

Mauriac, Claude: *La littérature contemporaine,* Paris 1958. Translated by Samuel Stone as *The New Literature,* New York 1959.

Mayoux, Jean-Jacques: 'The Theatre of Samuel Beckett'. *Perspective XI,* No. 3, 1959.
'Samuel Beckett and Universal Parody' in *Samuel Beckett: a collection of critical essays,* Prentice Hall 1965.

Mercier, Vivian: 'Samuel Beckett and the Sheela-na-gig'. *Kenyon Review,* Vol. XXIII. Spring 1961.

Metman, Eva: 'Reflections on Samuel Beckett's Plays' in *The Journal of Analytical Psychology,* January 1960. Reprinted in *Samuel Beckett: a collection of critical essays,* Prentice Hall 1965.

Mintz, Samuel: 'Beckett's "Murphy": A Cartesian Novel'. *Perspective XI,* No. 3, 1959.

Montgomery, Niall: 'No Symbols where none intended'. *New World Writing,* No. 5, New York 1954.

Moore, John: 'A Farewell to Something'. *Tulane Drama Review,* V, No. 1, September 1960.

Nadeau, Maurice: 'Humour and the Void' in *Samuel Beckett: a collection of critical essays,* Prentice Hall 1965.

Noon, William: 'Modern Literature and the Sense of Time'. *Thought,* Vol. XXXIII, No. 131, Winter 1958-59.

Pritchett, V. S.: 'Irish Oblomov'. *New Statesman,* 2 April 1960.

Pronko, Leonard: 'Avante-Garde: the experimental theatre in France'. *University of California Press,* 1962.

Reid, Alan: 'All I can manage, more than I could'. *The Guardian.*

Ricks, Christopher: 'The Roots of Samuel Beckett'. *The Listener.*

Robbe-Grillet, Alain: 'Samuel Beckett, or "Presence" in the theatre' in *Towards a New Novel,* Calder.

Schneider, Alan: 'Waiting for Beckett: a personal chronicle'. *Chelsea Review,* No. 2, Autumn 1958.

Scott, Nathan: 'The Recent Journey into the Zone of Zero'. *The Centennial Review,* Vol. VI, No. 2, Spring 1962.
Samuel Beckett. London (Bowes and Bowes) 1965.

Shenker, L.: 'Moody Man of Letters'. *New York Times,* Sunday, 6 May 1956.

Spender, Stephen: 'Lifelong Suffocation'. *New York Times Book Review,* 12 October 1958.

Simpson, Alan: *Beckett and Behan,* London 1962.

Strauss, Walter: 'Dante's Belacqua and Beckett's Bums' in *Comparative Literature,* Vol. XI, No. 3, Summer 1959.

Styan, J. L.: *The Dark Comedy,* London 1962.

Tindall, William York: 'Beckett's Bums'. *Critique,* Vol. 11, No. 1, Spring 1958.
Samuel Beckett in Columbia Essays on Modern Writers, New York 1964.

Walker, Roy: 'Love, Chess and Death'. *Twentieth Century,* Vol. 164, No. 982, December 1958.

Wellershoff, Dieter: 'Failure of an Attempt at de-mythologization: Samuel Beckett's Novels' in *Samuel Beckett: a collection of critical essays,* Prentice Hall 1965.

3. GENERAL

(The following are works which I have found useful while writing this study either because they have a direct bearing on the texts themselves or, because they are concerned with similar areas of experience, help to illuminate Beckett's work in a more oblique way. The list is obviously personal and readers will no doubt make their own deletions and additions but, with the exception of the critical works I have included, continual re-reading of the text has convinced me they are often works Beckett himself has read, probably many times.)

Artaud: a useful anthology of his writing in translation is published by City Light Books, San Francisco.

Barrett, William: *Irrational Man*. Heinemann, London 1961.

Baudelaire: Works.

Bergson, Henri: *Laughter*. Doubleday Anchor Books, New York 1956.

Bunyan: *Pilgrim's Progress*.

Camus: *The Myth of Sisyphus*, translated by Justin O'Brien. Random House, New York 1955.

Dante: *The Divine Comedy*.

Descartes: *Discourse on the Method* and the *Meditations*.

(Also the work of the post-Cartesians or 'Occasionalists', in particular Geulincx—*Ethics*—and Malebranche. A good introduction to Descartes and the problems he left his successors—from Geulincx to Molloy—is S. V. Keeling's *Descartes*. Benn, London 1934.)

Greene, Marjorie: *Heidegger*. Bowes and Bowes, London 1957.

Heidegger: *An Introduction to Metaphysics*, translated by Ralph Manheim. Yale U.P. 1959.

Existence and Being (Four Essays variously translated), Henry Regnery. Chicago 1949.

Ionesco: *Notes and Counternotes*. Calder 1966.

Joyce: *Ulysses*. Bodley Head, London 1960. (Of all Joyce's work this seems to me the most 'present' when reading Beckett.)

Leopardi: the Poems and *Operette Morali*.

Murdoch, Iris: *Sartre*. Bowes and Bowes, Cambridge 1953.

Pascal: *Pensées*.

Proust: *À la Recherche du Temps Perdu*.

Robbe-Grillet: *Towards a New Novel*. Calder, London 1966.

St. Augustine: *Confessions*.

Sarraute, Nathalie: *The Age of Suspicion*. Calder, London.

Sartre: *La Nausée*, translated by Robert Baldick, Penguin Books 1965.

L'Être et le néant, translated by Hazel Barnes as 'Being and Nothingness'. Methuen, London 1957.

Schopenhauer: Works.

Shakespeare: *King Lear* and *The Tempest*.

Sterne: *Tristram Shandy*.

Swift: Works.

Unamuno: *Tragic Sense of Life*. Fontana Library, Collins 1962.

Waldberg, Patrick: *Surrealism*. Thames and Hudson 1965.

Wittgenstein: *Tractatus*.

NOTES

CHAPTER ONE

[1] *The Unnamable*, p. 312.
[2] *Three Dialogues*, p. 125.
[3] *Malone Dies*, p. 206.
[4] *Molloy*, p. 16.
[5] *Ibid.*, p. 19.
[6] *Malone Dies*, p. 195.
[7] *More Pricks Than Kicks*, p. 62.
[8] *The Unnamable*, p. 383.
[9] For Descartes' influence on Beckett, see pp. 86-90.
[10] *Molloy*, p. 10.
[11] *Endgame*, p. 28.
[12] *Proust*, p. 13.
[13] *Waiting for Godot*, p. 43.
[14] *Endgame*, p. 12.
[15] *Endgame*, p. 45.
[16] *The Unnamable*, p. 393.
[17] *Malone Dies*, p. 202.
[18] *The Unnamable*, p. 305.
[19] *The Unnamable*, p. 400.
[20] *Ibid.*, p. 418.
[21] *Waiting for Godot*, p. 9.
[22] *Existence and Being* (trans. Douglas Scott and R. F. C. Hull, New York, 1949), p. 313.
[23] *Endgame*, p. 38.
[24] *Imitation of Christ*, Bk. III, chapter 31.
[25] *Molloy*, p. 17.
[26] *Endgame*, p. 29.
[27] *Ibid.*, p. 9.
[28] *Malone Dies*, p. 239.
[29] *Proust*, p. 67.
[30] *The Unnamable*, p. 416.
[31] *Ibid.*, p. 312.
[32] See the story *A Wet Night* (*More Pricks Than Kicks*, p. 107).
[33] *Endgame*, p. 41.
[34] *The Dying Gladiators of Samuel Beckett* (New York, 1961), p. 167.
[35] *Molloy*, p. 41. Ivan Karamazov, of course, formed an alternative conviction—that 'Everything is permitted'.
[36] *All That Fall*, p. 29.
[37] *More Pricks Than Kicks*, p. 27.
[38] *Watt*, p. 43.
[39] *Molloy*, p. 76.
[40] *Ibid.*, p. 48.
[41] *Ibid.*, p. 88.
[42] *Ibid.*, p. 86.
[43] *Waiting for Godot*, p. 43.
[44] *Endgame*, p. 16.
[45] *Proust*, p. 21.
[46] *Ibid.*, p. 21.

CHAPTER TWO

[1] *All Writing is Pigshit* in *Artaud Anthology*, ed. J. Hirschmann (San Francisco, 1965), p. 38.
[2] *Questioning the Concept of Literature* in *From the N.R.F.*, ed. Justin O'Brien (New York, 1959), p. 41.
[3] *Artaud Anthology*, p. 19.
[4] *Ibid.*, p. 19.
[5] *Ibid.*, p. 18.
[6] *Molloy*, p. 152
[7] Though, characteristically, Beckett dismisses any notion that this supposition is final: 'No truth value attaches to the above' (i.e. Berkeley's dictum), 'regarded as of merely structural and dramatic convenience.' *Eh Joe and other Writings*, p. 31.
[8] *Three Dialogues*, p. 113.
[9] *Ibid.*, p. 102.
[10] *Ibid.*, p. 103.
[11] *Ibid.*, p. 123.
[12] *Ibid.*, p. 110.
[13] *Ibid.*, p. 103.
[14] 'He had two passions beside James Joyce. One was Jack Yeats and the other a Dutch painter, van Velde.' Guggenheim, *Out of this Century* (New York, 1946). Beckett has also written several articles on van Velde: see *Les Cahiers d'Art*, Paris, pp. 349-56, 1945-46; *Bram van Velde* (Grove Press, New York, 1960).
[15] *Three Dialogues*, p. 119.
[16] *Ibid.*, p. 125.
[17] *Ibid.*, p. 123.
[18] *Watt*, p. 74.
[19] *Endgame*, p. 27.
[20] *Malone Dies*, p. 195.
[21] *Samuel Beckett* (Calder, 1962), p. 13.
[22] Quoted, *ibid.*, p. 23.

[23] *Godot*, p. 80.
[24] *Laughter* (Anchor Books, 1956), p. 79.
[25] *Watt*, p. 30.
[26] *Watt*, p. 28.
[27] *Op cit.*, p. 97.
[28] *Watt*, p. 14.
[29] From *The Priest as Clown—Reflections on the Theological Heritage of Modern Thinking*. This passage given in Jan Kott's *Shakespeare Our Contemporary* (Methuen, 1967), p. 131.
[30] *Waiting for Godot*, p. 89.
[31] *Myth of Sisyphus*, trans. Justin O'Brien (Vintage Books, 1955), p. 16.
[32] *Proust*, p. 19.
[33] *Waiting for Godot*, p. 63.
[34] *Concluding Unscientific Postscript*. For Kierkegaard religious man was an absurd figure because of the gulf between man and God. He saw man's condition as comic because man, who is nothing in himself, strives to devote himself to God who is everything, across an infinite divide.
[35] See Ionesco, *Notes and Counternotes* (Calder, 1964), p. 25: 'As far as I am concerned, I have never been able to understand the difference that is made between the comic and the tragic. As the comic is the intuition of the absurd, it seems to me more conducive to despair than tragedy. The comic offers no way out. I say "conducive to despair" but in reality it is beyond both despair and hope.'
[36] *Malone Dies*, p. 185.
[37] *Watt*, p. 47.
[38] *Malone Dies*, p. 282.
[39] *Ibid.*, p. 285.
[40] *Ibid.*, p. 288.
[41] *Ibid.*, p. 289.
[42] *Molloy*, p. 30.
[43] *Endgame*, p. 44.
[44] *Gulliver's Travels*, Part 4, Chapter XI (*Portable Swift*, ed. Carl van Doren), p. 521.
[45] *Molloy*, p. 56.
[46] *Ibid.*, p. 57.
[47] *Ibid.*, p. 57.
[48] *Gulliver's Travels*, Part 3, Chapter X, p. 432.
[49] *Molloy*, p. 76.
[50] *Gulliver's Travels*, p. 433.
[51] *The Unnamable*, p. 304.
[52] *Molloy*, p. 39.
[53] *How it is*, p. 45.
[54] Compare, for example, the Unnamable's re-working of the parable of the wise and foolish virgins, *The Unnamable*, pp. 367-9.
[55] *Molloy*, p. 167.
[56] *Proust*, p. 13.
[57] *Ibid.*, p. 14.
[58] *Ibid.*, p. 15.
[59] *Ibid.*, p. 28.
[60] *Ibid.*, p. 32.
[61] *Ibid.*, p. 31.
[62] *Ibid.*, p. 72.
[63] *Endgame*, p. 21.
[64] *Proust*, p. 45.
[65] *Ibid.*, p. 63.
[66] *Ibid.*, p. 63.
[67] *Waiting for Godot*, p. 91.
[68] *Proust*, p. 78.
[69] *Ibid.*, p. 84. See below, chapter six, p. 60f., and chapter nine, p. 223.
[70] *Ibid.*, p. 87.
[71] *Ibid.*, p. 64.
[72] *Malone Dies*, p. 237.

CHAPTER THREE

[1] *Transition*, The Hague, no. 21, pp. 13-20.
[2] *Purgatorio*, Canto 4, 1.97-139, trans. Dorothy Sayers, Penguin Classics, 1955.
[3] *Molloy*, p. 11.
[4] *Murphy*, p. 56.
[5] *Out of this Century*, Dial Press (New York), 1946, p. 205.
[6] *Watt*, p. 31.
[7] *The Unnamable*, p. 361.
[8] *Proust*, p. 67.
[9] *Paradise Lost*, II, 557-561.
[10] *Proust*, p. 74.
[11] *Endgame*, p. 45.
[12] *Molloy*, p. 36.
[13] *Waiting for Godot*, p. 94.
[14] *Poems in English*, p. 47.
[15] Note also this fragment from the addenda to *Watt:* 'dead calm, then a murmur, a name, a murmured name, in doubt, in fear, in love, in fear, in doubt, wind of winter in the black boughs, cold calm sea whitening, whispering to the shore, stealing, hastening, swelling,

passing, dying, from naught come, to naught gone' (*Watt*, p. 247).

[16] *Molloy*, p. 68.

[17] *Ibid.*, p. 69.

[18] *The Novels of Samuel Beckett* (Chatto and Windus), 1964, p. 15.

CHAPTER FOUR

[1] Mintz: *Beckett's Murphy—a Cartesian Novel* in *Perspective*, XI, no. 3, Autumn, 1959.

[2] The prayers of the 'Godly chandler' refers to the theology of the *Purgatorio*. The ascent of the sinner to Paradise could be brought forward through the intercession of prayers from one already in the higher realm. Ironically, neither Murphy nor, Beckett implies, Belacqua, wishes their idle lifetime's dreaming to be curtailed.

[3] *How it is*, p. 33.

[4] *Samuel Beckett* (Oliver and Boyd, 1964), p. 30.

[5] *Proust*, p. 14.

[6] Compare this passage with a similar scene in *Ulysses* when Bloom leaves the newspaper offices to the imitative antics of the newsboys—'a file of capering newsboys in Mr Bloom's wake ...a mocking kite'. (*Ulysses*, p. 164). The kite also reappears in *Murphy*, to haunt Celia in the park.

[7] *Op cit.*, p. 53.

CHAPTER FIVE

[1] *King Lear*, IV, i, 36.

[2] Quoted in Magarshack, Introduction to *The Idiot* (Penguin Classics), p. 7.

[3] *Ibid.*, p. 251.

[4] *Murphy*, p. 23.

[5] *Molloy*, p. 65.

[6] *Malone Dies*, p. 265.

[7] *Waiting for Godot*, p. 52.

[8] *Murphy*, p. 126.

[9] See John Fletcher: *The Novels of Samuel Beckett*, p. 87. Beckett informed him that the words 'I haf' and 'Ifor', which Jacqueline Hoeffer took to be German in pronunciation and therefore consistent with her interpretation in connection with Wittgenstein, owe their form to the phrase being a transposition of an old Welsh joke. Beckett did not, however, stress which one. The question is complicated still further when, as Ruby Cohn has noted, one realizes that the same expression occurs in *Murphy*. When the hero is in his garret, apparently secure against the world, Beckett writes, 'Do not come down the ladder, they have taken it away'. In the French translation this has become, 'Ne descendez pas par l'echelle, Louis, ils l'ont enlevée'. Louis is of course French for Ludwig, and no character of that name appears in either the English or the French version. Beckett still maintains, however, that he only read Ludwig Wittgenstein within the last few years.

[10] *Introduction to Metaphysics* (trans. Manheim, Yale, 1961), p. 64.

[11] See Ellmann *James Joyce* (Oxford, 1959), p. 661.

[12] *Tractatus*, p. 151.

[13] *La Nausée* (trans. Robert Baldick, Penguin Books, 1965), p. 180.

[14] *Ibid.*, p. 182.

[15] *Ibid.*, p. 179.

[16] *Ibid.*, p. 180.

[17] *Ibid.*, p. 188.

CHAPTER SIX

[1] *Inferno*, Canto III.

[2] *Fragments of a Journal in Hell*, *op. cit.*, p. 45.

[3] *Mercier et Camier* is the most substantial of Beckett's unpublished works. A typescript does exist and has been discussed in both Kenner (*op. cit.*, pp. 68-77) and John Fletcher (*op. cit.*, pp. 110-118). It is probable that certain material in the jettisoned manuscript developed into what is now *Waiting for Godot*. This aspect has been studied by Colin Duckworth in *The Making of Godot*, *Theatre Research*, Vol. VII, no. 3, 1966.

[4] Niklaus Gessner, *Die Unzulänglichkeit der Sprache* (Zurich: Verlag, 1957), p. 32.

[5] Compare with the following remarks of Nathalie Sarraute (*The Age of Reason*, Calder and Boyars, 1963, p. 129): the writer she refers to is her own creation, invested with the traits she wishes to

consider: 'Style...is for this writer merely an instrument, the only value of which is that of serving to extract and embrace as closely as possible the fragment of reality that he is trying to lay bare. All desire to write "beautifully"... is quite inconceivable for him.'

[6] Artaud, *On Suicide, op. cit.*, p. 57.

[7] *Three Dialogues*, p. 123.

[8] Maurice Nadeau, quoted in Fletcher, *op. cit.*, p. 99.

[9] *Op. cit.*, p. 128.

[10] *Molloy*, p. 40.

[11] *The Unnamable*, p. 305.

[12] There is, of course, the additional dimension: that of the critic writing in a room about the writing before him; and then again, of you, the reader, reading and marking these words.

[13] *Bread and Wine.*

[14] Descartes originally intended to call the *Discourse on Method* 'A History of My Life'. Beckett, as I believe Kenner suggests, is probably the first to read it as it should be read—as a novel which, like Beckett's own works, describes the progress of a mind through layers of ignorance.

[15] *Discourse on Method*, trans. Wollaston (Penguin Books, 1960), p. 61. (This translation used throughout.)

[16] *Op. cit.*, p. 60.

[17] See Ellmann, *op. cit.*, p. 594.

[18] *Endgame*, p. 12.

[19] *Our Exagmination round his Factification for Incamination of Work in Progress* (re-issued by Faber and Faber, 1936), p. 14.

[20] *Op. cit.*, p. 84.

[21] *The Artist's Journey into the Interior* (Secker and Warburg, 1960), p. 226.

[22] *Op. cit.*, p. 133.

[23] *Op. cit.*, p. 57.

[24] Unlike the hero of *The End*, see p. 137.

[25] Molloy's name might also contain an allusion to Moly, the magic root which Hermes gave to Ulysses to preserve him from Circe's wiles. Joyce too, was at one time much concerned with the etymology of this name (see Ellmann, *op. cit.*, p. 510). And mention of Hermes, god of signposts and directions can, if one wants, be allowed to introduce still further reverberations in this novel where all roads are now equally right and wrong. Hermes, god of thieves, perhaps encourages Molloy to steal Lousse's silver, and another of his attributes was to predict the future from the position of pebbles. What Molloy learns from his sucking stones, however, is of little assistance.

[26] The experience is by no means unique. Wordsworth too, had felt the presence of 'huge and mighty forms that do not live / Like Living men,' which 'moved slowly through the mind / By day, and were a trouble to my dreams.' Moran's monologue explores the place of these now termed 'archetypal' forms in the creative experience.

[27] *Op. cit.*, p. 107.

[28] Leopardi, 'To Himself': Molloy's disgust and indifference are also anticipated in the same poem. Leopardi writes:

Boredom and bitterness
Is life; and the rest, nothing:
the world is dirt.

[29] The bicycle is a preoccupation he shares with Flann O'Brien, as he does an interest with St Augustine.

[30] Kenner, *op. cit.*, p. 121.

[31] *Op. cit.*, p. 106.

[32] The phrase is Nietzsche's.

[33] *Endgame*, p. 17.

[34] *Op. cit.*, p. 58.

[35] *Hamlet.*, III, i, 156.

CHAPTER SEVEN

[1] *To Himself.*

[2] *Memoirs*, trans. Robert Baldick (Penguin Classics, 1965), p. 21.

[3] *The Waste Land*, l. 215.

[4] *Ibid.*, l. 220.

[5] *Op. cit.*, p. 161.

[6] *Op. cit.*, p. 141.

[7] Compare also with Beckett's definition of the mirthless laugh and the following definition of Bergson: 'Any incident is comic that calls our attention to the physical in a person, when it is the moral side that is concerned'. *Laughter* (*ed. cit.*, p. 93).

CHAPTER EIGHT

[1] *Endgame*, p. 35.

[2] Fletcher (*op. cit.*, pp. 184-5) locates what seem to be the originals, both of the rotunda and Mahood's restaurant. Near where Beckett once lived, in the rue des Favorites, was a dilapidated round wooden building frequented by artists ('La Ruche') which was in turn close to a restaurant, now defunct, named the 'Ali Baba'. The latter had as its sign-board a thief in a jar who supported the menu. In the novel Beckett places the restaurant in the rue Brancion facing the Bust of the horse-meat salesman, Emile Decroix, but the actual 'Ali Baba' was a short distance away in the Rue de Dantzig.

[3] *Failure of an Attempt at De-Mythologization* in *Samuel Beckett: a collection of critical essays*, ed. Martin Esslin (Prentice Hall, New Jersey, 1965), p. 102.

[4] Coe: *op. cit.*, p. 73.

[5] See Driver, *Beckett by the Madelaine*, Columbia University Forum, Vol. IV, no. 3 (Summer, 1961).

[6] *Meditations*, trans. Wollaston (Penguin Books, 1960), p. 106.

[7] In the story *Huntsman Gracchus* Kafka describes a birth into endless dying—a dying into the world—which compares with the time-imprisoned condition of Beckett's later heroes. Years ago Gracchus fell to his death (i.e. birth) but through the negligence of Charon he never reached Hades. His existence, therefore, is to be suspended between being and not-being: he has a place in time but not in the world.

CHAPTER NINE

[1] *Inferno*, Canto VII, 124.

[2] Now six: besides *Imagination Dead Imagine* Beckett's *Risidua* includes *Ping* and *Enough*. In the latter the monologue is, for the first time, spoken by a woman.

[3] Failure, in this instance, refers to the inability to progress beyond the position of *The Unnamable*, not to the actual quality of the *Texts* as writing which, for reasons of space, this summary does not do justice.

[4] Coe, *op. cit.*, p. 83.

[5] *Inferno*, Canto VII, 109-114.

[6] This image reappears among the photographs which the hero of *Film* destroys and the photograph itself, showing Beckett at the age of three kneeling beside a woman in a white dress, is reproduced in the tribute (edited by Calder) by various hands which was presented to him for his sixtieth birthday.

[7] *Proust*, p. 63.

[8] *Discourse on Method, ed. cit.*, p. 80.

[9] *Molloy*, p. 111.

THE PLAYS

[1] To Gessner, quoted in *Die Unzulänglichkeit der Sprache* (Zurich, Verlag, 1957), p. 32.

[2] That is, with the exception of the never printed *Eleuthéria*. The hero of this play in three acts is, incidentally, named Krapp. See Kenner, *op. cit.*, pp. 139-143 for the only existing discussion.

[3] In contrast to *Godot*, *Endgame* is a set script. Where the dialogue of the tramps appears to be provisional (though of course it is not), the actors in *Endgame* know that what they are saying is positive and unalterable.

[4] *Samuel Beckett, or 'Presence' in the Theatre* in 'Samuel Beckett, a collection of critical essays', ed. Martin Esslin, p. 108.

[5] *Ibid.*, p. 108.

[6] *King Lear*, IV. vi. 170.

[7] *Being without Time* in 'Samuel Beckett, a collection of critical essays', p. 151.

[8] Alfonso Sastre, quoted in Pronko, *The Avant-garde Theatre in France* (University of California, 1962), p. 31.

[9] *King Lear*, I. iv. 145.

[10] *Around Theatres* (London: Rupert Hart-Davis, 1953), p. 350.

[11] *King Lear*, IV. vi. 165.

[12] *Prefaces to Shakespeare*, Volume 11 (Illustrated edition, Batsford, London, 1963), p. 38.

[13] Nietzsche, *The Birth of Tragedy*, trans. quoted in Esslin *The Theatre of the Absurd* (Eyre and Spottiswoode, London, 1966), p. 235.

[14] *King Lear*, IV. vi. 192.

[15] *Samuel Beckett and Universal Parody* in 'Samuel Beckett, a collection of critical essays', p. 78.

[16] See Guicharnaud, *Modern French Theatre*, (Yale University Press, 1961), p. 195.
[17] *Dr Faustroll.*
[18] *Molloy*, p. 64.
[19] *Pensées* (trans. Trotter, Everyman's Library, Dent, 1932), p. 38.
[20] *Proust*, p. 28.
[21] 'Samuel Beckett, Dramatist of the Year', *International Theatre Annual*, No. I (London: John Calder, 1961).
[22] *Proust*, p. 65.
[23] *The Rebel* (London: Hamish Hamilton, 1953), pp. 109-110.
[24] 'A Farewell to Something', in the *Tulane Drama Review*, V, no. 1, September, 1960.
[25] *King Lear*, IV. i. 47.
[26] This is made even more explicit by a comparison with Balzac's *Le Faiseur* from which Beckett may have received his original idea. There too the audience spends the evening waiting for a character, named Godeau, who will resolve the situation, and who has still not arrived when he is announced just before the final curtain.
[27] To Duckworth, 'The Making of Godot' in *Theatre Research*, Vol. VII, no. 3, 1966.
[28] *Hamlet*, V. ii. 361.
[29] *Othello*, V. ii. 341.
[30] *Op. cit.*, p. 155.
[31] *Richard II*, III. ii. 162.
[32] *The Tempest*, Epilogue.
[33] *Ibid.*, I. ii. 20.
[34] The phrase is Roy Walker's: see 'Love, Chess and Death', *Twentieth Century*, Vol 164, no 982. December, 1958
[35] *The Tempest*, V. i. 311.
[36] *Ibid.*, I. ii. 39.
[37] *Ibid.*, I. ii. 45.
[38] *Ibid.*, I. ii. 18.
[39] *Ibid.*, I. ii. 33.
[40] *Ibid.*, I. ii. 310.
[41] *Ibid.*, I. ii. 353.
[42] *The Unnamable*, p. 300.
[43] *Ibid.*, p. 300.
[44] *The Tempest*, I. ii. 363.
[45] *King Lear*, IV. vi. 184.
[46] *Les Mamelles de Tirésias*, Prologue.
[47] *More Pricks Than Kicks*, p. 161.
[48] Or the shadows of Plato's cave?
[49] *Whispers of Immortality:* T. S. Eliot, *Collected Poems 1909-1935* (Faber, 1936)
[50] No longer the Fisher of Men.
[51] *Op. cit.*, p. 171.
[52] *Op. cit.*, p. 174.
[53] *Op. cit.*, p. 185.
[54] *Proust*, p. 63.
[55] Roy Walker, *op. cit.*
[56] Coe, *op. cit.*, p. 103.
[57] *Proust*, p. 15.
[58] *Ibid.*, p. 19.
[59] *Ibid.*, p. 92.
[60] *The Unnamable*, p. 309.

AN END

[1] *The Myth of Sisyphus*, trans. Justin O'Brien, *ed. cit.*, p. 85.
[2] *Ibid.*, p. 68.

INDEX